ABUSED WOMEN AND SURVIVOR THERAPY

ABUSED WOMEN

AND

SURVIVOR

THERAPY

A Practical Guide

for the Psychotherapist

by Lenore E. A. Walker

American Psychological Association
Washington, DC

First printing June 1994
Second printing January 1995

Published by
American Psychological Association
750 First Street, NE
Washington, DC 20002

Copies may be ordered from
APA Order Department
P.O. Box 2710
Hyattsville, MD 20784

In the UK and Europe, copies may be ordered from
American Psychological Association
3 Henrietta Street
Covent Garden, London
WC2E 8LU England

Typeset in Minion by Techna Type, Inc., York, PA

Printer: Braun-Brumfield, Inc., Ann Arbor, MI
Cover and Jacket Designer: RCW Communication Design, Inc., Falls Church, VA
Cover Illustrator: Danuta Jarecka, New York, NY
Technical/Production Editor: Paula R. Bronstein

Library of Congress Cataloging-in-Publication Data
Walker, Lenore E.
　　　Abused women and survivor therapy : a practical guide for the psychotherapist / by Lenore E. A. Walker.
　　　　　p.　　cm.
　　　Includes bibliographical references and index.
　　　ISBN 1-55798-229-5
　　　1. Post-traumatic stress disorder.　2. Abused women—Mental health.
　3. Psychotherapy.　I. Title.
　　　[DNLM: 1. Psychotherapy—methods.　2. Women—psychology.　3. Spouse Abuse.　4. Sex Offenses.　5. Stress Disorders, Post Traumatic—therapy.
　WM 420 W1813a 1994]
　RC552.P67W37 1994
　616.85′21′0082—dc20
　DNLM.DLC
　for Library of Congress
93-50591
CIP

British Library Cataloguing-in-Publication Data
A CIP record is available from the British Library.

Printed in the United States of America

Contents

Foreword

Two days before I agreed to write this Foreword, I was engaged in a conversation with a colleague about the denial of health insurance coverage for one of her psychotherapy clients. The client was making her way, slowly and with great pain and courage, out of a relationship in which she had been beaten for many years. For the first time in a life marked by sexual abuse in childhood, racial discrimination on the job, and violence in her marital home, she was reaching out for help. The case manager at the managed mental health care firm that covered dependents for a branch of the military service had flatly denied any coverage for psychotherapy, however. "We don't authorize treatment for social problems," he said. "We only treat mental health problems. Battering's not a mental health problem."

It is because of situations such as this one, and the uncountable others in which women who have survived abuse and victimization have been ill-served by the mental health community, that this volume by Lenore Walker is both invaluable and long overdue. Interpersonal violence and the victimization of women are not simply a social problem; they are also an important risk factor for the development of psychological difficulties, problems that can be addressed and improved with appropriate mental health treatment. The hard data on violence against women, the absence of which might have excused ignorance of the link between interpersonal victimization and persistent emotional distress, are available now. Those data tell a powerful story. One in every three women in the United States will be the target of sexual violence during her life span. More than one quarter will be physically abused in their homes, by their spouse or partner. Unknown numbers are sexually exploited by health care professionals. Even more will experience sexual and gender-based harassment in school and at work. Although naysayers may warn against the creation of a culture of victimization, books such as this make clear that this fear is a shaky straw person. Far from creating victims out of women, the feminist mental health movement from which Lenore Walker's work has emerged is simply allowing the truth to be told about interpersonal violence.

Access to this sort of knowledge about the real and very high base rates of women's victimization experiences constitutes one of the powerful statements made by this book. The reader will come away from this volume informed, aware, and unable to slide into denial. This alone would improve the quality of the care that is available to a vulnerable population. However, what makes this book special is the manner in which it informs clinicians at every level, from the first-year graduate student to the experienced practitioner, about how to concretely approach the sometimes challenging task of working with female victims of violence so that they may be transformed into survivors.

This metamorphic process, and the possibilities for its accomplishment, are detailed by Walker in this book in a manner that alerts clinicians to the common errors that are made in practice with this population. Here, the reader is exposed to the subtleties of diagnosis and case conceptualization with the victim/survivor population. Misdiagnosis is one of the biggest hurdles that the female violence survivor faces when she seeks mental health services, once the veil of denial that surrounds victimization is pulled aside. The tendency to blame victims for their victimization continues to be a problem in the delivery of mental health services to this population; this volume goes a great distance toward the remediation of such errors by exploring and analyzing the theoretical and conceptual underpinnings of misdiagnosis of violence survivors.

Lenore Walker has been one of the pioneers in the mental health field in addressing the needs and realities of battered women. In this book, she takes the next step by presenting an integrated picture of the synergistic effects of interpersonal violence in women's lives. This book is unique in its attempt to encompass a wide range of interpersonal victimization experiences, rather than separating human beings into problem categories. In the real world of the people whom therapists assess, treat, and advocate for, the battered woman is often also the incest survivor who is also the target of sexual harassment. A book that explores the realities and meanings of those intersections and the complexities that can emerge at those convergence points is especially informative. The inclusion of Ken Pope's chapter on exploitation by health care professionals signals an awareness that those who treat female violence survivors must be especially conscious so as to avoid revictimizing the people who seek their help.

All of those who work with violence survivors hope that they will someday be out of business, that the world will cease to create new clients, that no one else will need to seek their services. Until that time, until the process of social transformation and social justice has succeeded in full, this is an essential volume for the practice of every clinician. As Walker's work makes clear, no one can say, "I don't treat violence survivors." This book aids therapists in performing that treatment competently and effectively.

LAURA S. BROWN, PhD, ABPP

Acknowledgments

It is with heartfelt thanks that I express my gratitude to a number of people without whose support this book could not have been written. First, to my good friend and colleague, Ken Pope, whose vision, expertise, persistence, sense of humor, and friendship guided this book from beginning to end, I offer my sincerest thanks. His contributions made this a better book. My children, Michael, Roberta, and Karen, my mom, Pearl Moncher Auerbach, and the rest of my family have always been my best inspiration and my biggest fans. I thank them for sharing me with this book.

Kudos also to the staff of the books department of the American Psychological Association, especially Julia Frank-McNeill and Paula Bronstein, whose gentle and patient guidance shaped the final form. I would also like to express a deep debt of gratitude to Al Gabor for knowing where to cut and edit so that the information here is both readable and palatable. The APA editorial staff's commitment to excellence can be seen throughout this book; any shortcomings are all my own.

Obviously, a project of this scope in a field that is changing as rapidly as is the knowledge about abused women will omit some material inadvertently. I have tried to present a view of the emerging field of study and to help the practitioner integrate the information within an existing set of therapy theories and principles. If I have done my job successfully, millions of women, men, and children who are caught in the tragic web of violence and its consequences will benefit. I offer my hope for and my belief in the possibility of a peaceful and violence-free world.

Introduction

M any, including myself, believe that women's reactions to abuse should not be considered pathological; however, abuse may render some women unable to regain their ability to fully function. Psychotherapy can help these women move from being victims to being survivors. This book is intended to guide both the newly trained therapist and the more experienced practitioner in identifying, assessing, and treating women who have been abused and seek psychotherapy to assist in the healing process.

The use of traditional psychotherapy for trauma victims has not produced the type of treatment that abused women find helpful. In order for clinicians to work effectively with abuse victims, it is necessary for them to consider making modifications in traditional treatment practices. These modifications must take into account the impact of the specific trauma as well as the individual's unique psychological response to the world. I have traveled around the world training clinicians who are struggling to design effective intervention strategies to meet these clients' special needs. This book represents the compilation of strategies that I believe constitute a new form of intervention that I call *survivor therapy*. Survivor therapy can be used in its entirety as a separate therapy system or integrated into a preexisting therapy theory system.

I have treated abused women for more than 20 years as part of my psychotherapy practice. Here I present the major forms of physical, sexual, and psychological abuse experienced by women (and usually inflicted by men) and describe the latest findings regarding these forms of abuse, so that therapists will have a basic understanding of their clients' experiences. Many women who seek psychotherapy as a part of their recovery process have experienced multiple forms of abuse. As a result, existing treatment guides for each specific type of abuse may be less useful in helping to sort out which difficulties have arisen from each traumatic experience and which are products of the interaction of several types of abuse.

I have also attempted to look at the commonalities of intervention approaches for those who experience single traumas committed by an unknown stranger, repeated traumas induced by trusted family and friends during the childhood developmental years, and repeated traumas by family, acquaintances, and those in a special position of trust during adult years. For all forms of physical, sexual, and psychological abuse, the issues of power, control, domination, and humiliation of the woman by the man are addressed from the woman's perspective.

Any instructional book has the potential to be seriously misused, particularly if the therapist does not consider the information supplied in the context of his or her own frame of reference and psychological theoretical approach to treatment. The therapist must also consider the information in the context of the woman's total life experiences, which are much wider than the abuse even when abuse has had a major impact on all aspects of her life.

In preparing this volume, I have attempted to review the relevant research in the field with the understanding that in any rapidly expanding area the knowledge base is continuously growing and changing. The theoretical perspective that I have taken in this book follows the prevailing psychological opinions in the field of woman. If there is controversy, I attempt to present both sides, often explaining my own position, if I have one. I try to blend the studies of trauma victims with the psychology of women so that the psychological effects of the traumatic events can be understood in combination with the effects of social oppression based on gender, race, ethnicity, culture, and sexual orientation. At the same time, I present some information about the interaction of other health and mental health conditions with the psychological impact of the traumas discussed. Thus, suggestions are made regarding the need for medical endocrinological examinations or neuropsychological evaluations, for example, but actual descriptions of such evaluations are not provided.

Epidemiological studies indicate that violence against women does not seem to occur more frequently in one demographic group than in another. Most victims of abuse do not need psychotherapy to recover from their experiences. Rather, crisis intervention and self-help groups consisting of other women who have had similar experiences have been found to be sufficient for many women. Others, however, seek out psychotherapy to help them get on with their lives, although such women are sometimes unaware that the abuse issues are a major factor in their distress. This means that some women who already have other mental health disturbances will be abused and that the psychological effects of these separate factors will interact. Others may be misdiagnosed with more serious mental disorders when the cause of their problems is really the impact of abuse experiences. There are few reliable and valid predictors of who will become an abuser and who will become a victim; perhaps the best indicator is the prior witnessing or experiencing of violence. There are also few reliable and valid indicators to predict the severity of the impact of abuse on an individual or the length of time it will take for recovery.

However, as the information provided here demonstrates, there are certain techniques that are more helpful than others when working with an abused woman. First, it is important to help her regain her own sense of power and control over her life. This is called *reempowerment*. Second, it is helpful to validate her experiences by listening to her story without interruption or interpretation. Third, it is important to help raise her self-esteem. I suggest doing this by supporting her strengths in therapy rather than her difficulties. Finally, it is important to help her end whatever isolation she has endured by reestablishing relationships with family, friends, and others who could be helpful to her in getting on with her life.

A fundamental breach of trust occurs when a woman is abused by someone who also professes to love her; this occurs in most forms of woman abuse discussed in this book. It is important to help the woman reestablish trust in other people by being a good role model as a therapist. Although women treating women helps facilitate this model, it is a fact that many male therapists will treat women victims and need to know how to do so in a responsible manner. This book attempts to look at the issues raised in these situations and provide some answers for the therapist. The section on practical tips for therapists helps explain what underlies the transference and countertransference reactions that often occur when working with these women. Practical information on protection of the therapy relationship as well as risk management in limiting liability are needed by both less experienced and experienced therapists. Ethical complaints from abused women who feel that they were secondarily abused by therapists are common; often these therapists have failed to educate themselves as to the proper treatment approaches in situations of abuse or have actually committed boundary violations. Of all clients, the abused woman might be the most vulnerable to unintentional as well as intentional exploitation.

Some therapists will read this volume all at once, whereas others will undoubtedly read certain applicable sections as they deal with specific cases. This book is designed for either type of use. The reader may be referred to other sections for further information on a specific topic, and some information is repeated throughout the book.

Although each form of woman abuse discussed requires some special treatment techniques, all of the assessment and treatment suggestions are located in one section because of the tremendous overlap between each of the different abuse reactions. For situations in which there are special cautions or findings, these are discussed in the specific abuse chapter. Most of the time, however, the treatment for one type of abuse is not contraindicated for other types. In fact, many women who are seriously damaged by abuse have experienced multiple forms of violence and therefore require the use of a variety of treatment techniques in order to achieve success.

This book grew out of extended conversations with my friend and colleague, Kenneth S. Pope. Our work addressing various types of abuse has overlapped considerably even though he has tended to focus predominantly on therapists' sexual abuse of their clients. Since the 1970s, he has conducted extensive research into therapist–patient sexual involvement, pioneered interventions to assist victims, advanced understanding of the offenders, and testified nationally as an expert witness. In the early 1980s, he cofounded the University of California, Los Angeles (UCLA) Post-Therapy Support Project, which provides services to clients who have been sexually abused by therapists; wrote and cowrote landmark books and articles on this topic; helped focus attention on prevention; and pressed a sometimes resistant profession into confronting woman abuse more openly, realistically, and effectively. Ken and I have learned much from each other and have served each other as sources of mutual support and encouragement through the years. Ken's insightful understanding of social forces that form the context of abuse against women, his empathy for and tireless work on behalf of those who have been abused, and his creative yet rigorous approach to theory and research have made this a better book. He generously agreed to contribute chapter 6 on therapist–client sexual involvement and gave me a great deal of encouragement, extensive feedback, and support while I developed this book. I thank him for all of his assistance throughout the conceptualization, writing, and editing process.

Despite the explosion of knowledge that is evident in the literature dealing with all trauma victims, including at least five new scientific journals devoted to publishing in the areas of child and woman abuse, it often becomes difficult for practitioners to gather data and integrate it into their clinical work. Thus, this book takes one area of traumatic stressors, the group of abuses against women, and reviews the data, examining the implications for victim impact and psychological resolution, in order to assist therapists in better serving their clients as they struggle to become survivors and get on with their lives. As I wrote this book, the elements of a unifying survivor therapy emerged. This treatment approach is more clearly set forth in chapter 10.

Another goal of mine is to inform by identifying fundamental issues in assessment and treatment of the sexual and physical abuse of women. Some clinicians may find this volume to be a useful introduction to the topic and may use it to update their knowledge and skills, adopting all of the survival therapy strategies or taking bits and pieces and integrating them into their own particular type of practice. This volume may also provide a useful resource to review immediately before conducting a comprehensive assessment, consulting with a colleague, or preparing to testify as an expert witness.

HOW THIS BOOK IS ORGANIZED

Part One of this volume includes an introductory chapter, then five chapters reviewing the literature on the five different forms of woman abuse. Although there are numerous forms of abuse, each with unique characteristics as well as similarities to other forms, the focus here is on five of the most commonly reported forms of abuse: rape, battering, child sexual abuse, therapist–client sexual intimacies, and sexual harassment in the workplace and in academia. Each of these chapters follows a similar although not identical format, so that clinicians who are using this book as a desk reference can easily find the information they seek at that moment. Each chapter consists of a description of the abuse and definitions; known empirical and clinical research including incidence and prevalence rates; some discussion of the meaning of the particular abuse for most women and its short and long-term physical harm and psychological and medical impact; associated factors such as alcohol and drug use, neuropsychological complications, and possible associated diagnoses; impact on women's short- and long-term functioning; common transference and countertransference issues; specific assessment and clinical presentation of acute and chronic abuse victims; therapy and other therapeutic interventions; and collaborative approaches with others such as rape crisis centers and battered women shelters. Each chapter approaches the issues from a slightly different perspective.

The next section details the therapist's responsibilities when treating abused women. The chapter that examines the therapists' self-preparation before working with an abuse victim is designed to prevent the exploitation of vulnerable women, whether intended or unintended. It deals directly with the issues that have prevented traditionally trained therapists from being successful in helping most abused women to heal. In many cases the therapist does not even know the extent of secondary damage done because violence victims rarely express their anger outwardly, often assuming responsibility themselves when things do not go right for them. Sometimes victims who can express their anger do so in such inappropriately hostile ways that the therapist never quite understands what he or she has done wrong. It is important to acknowledge and deal with the issues of transference and countertransference by taking active steps to avoid the common pitfalls in which the less experienced clinician may find himself or herself.

Ethical and legal issues are also discussed along with the special difficulties inherent in working with women who may still be in danger of being harmed. This discussion is followed by a more general chapter demonstrating how the experience of abuse itself can create obstacles for the victim, preventing her from seeking help or making the best use of the help she does receive. The breach of trust and sense of betrayal that victims must overcome in order to become survivors are also described.

The final chapter of Part Two explores forensic issues from the clinician's point of view. It is rare that an abused woman does not have some contact with the legal system, and it is important for the therapist to help guide her through it while also preserving her rights and privileges. The chapter is not intended to be a substitute for a thorough understanding of state and local laws governing violence and abuse, nor is it intended to be a guide for the forensic psychologist. It is the individual reader's responsibility to seek knowledge of the specific laws that apply in his or her jurisdiction and seek other materials that are more directly related to forensic applications of psychology.

The five chapters in Part Three focus on strategies of assessment and intervention that are the core of the new survivor therapy system. After a case study and an introductory chapter on survivor therapy, there are two chapters on assessment; one focuses on gathering the data and the other on making sense of the data. There is a chapter on crisis intervention and one that focuses on treatment strategies and that details long-term therapy issues that typically arise while therapists help victims heal and become survivors. Survivor therapy is designed to help both the clinician and the victim become survivors as the growth process of good therapy is explored together.

Although it may not need to be mentioned specifically, it is important that readers be aware of my commitment to eradicating violence against women in all societies. The techniques described herein have arisen mainly from my experiences in American society with the many oppressions and discriminations embedded within the culture, but these techniques can be adapted and used in any society. My travels around the world have taught me that, in any culture, violence is violence. Although there may be special cumulative effects on the individual when there is state-sponsored violence in addition to more private violence in the home, the healing procedure is the same. It is important to understand the cultural context in which women must live in a society, the impact that other forms of oppression can have on the cognitive meaning given to individual violence, the informal and formal resources available to the individual woman, and the impact of particular forms of woman abuse that may be committed against an individual. The more a culture is threatened by annihilation from outside forces, the less likely it is that the individual violence committed against a woman will be exposed for fear of further jeopardizing her subculture, and the worse the woman may feel for needing help and not bearing her burden like others in her group. The international women's movement has provided a context in which it is more permissible for women to speak out against the violence that is committed against them. Using such forums to attempt to change social norms that do not support and even sometimes exploit women can be therapeutic, although this approach is not specific to survivor therapy.

Many therapists engage in numerous preventive activities within their own communities and profession. However, whatever the type of activism in which one may participate, when working as a therapist the first allegiance must be to the client: to help her on her journey to recover from abusive experiences and to prevent them from recurring. Throughout this volume there are many ideas on how this important and rewarding task may be accomplished.

PART ONE

Types of Abuse Against Women

1

Physical, Sexual, and Psychological Abuse Against Women

Close examination of the issues of rape, woman battering, child-hood sexual abuse, therapist–patient sex, and sexual harassment is necessary because of the commonalities found in these abusive actions and their effects. All are perpetuated with higher frequency by men toward women and children, and all are seen as disorders of power and control. All these types of abuse are accompanied by psychological abuse, intimidation, and manipulation of the victim. In most instances of repeated or non-stranger abuse, women become confused because the violence is mixed with kind and sometimes loving treatment.

The effects of the abuse are continuous for most women because of intrusive memories, flashbacks, and feelings of reexperiencing the trauma. These symptoms are often pathologized rather than interpreted as survival mechanisms. Similarly, most women who display coping strategies are blamed for causing their own abuse and held responsible for what are essentially normal reactions to abnormal situations. Many of these victims have lost faith in the future. Some even believe they will not live as long as other people as a result of the trauma. Those who come to a therapist's office may initially be too scared even to speak about the abuse. However, in every abused woman, there is a spark of hope that the recovery process can be completed. The therapist can help her nurture that hope.

This book presents information to help mental health practitioners working with physically, sexually, or psychologically abused women. Clinicians who work with abused women face challenging responsibilities: to learn about emerging research findings, assessment strategies, and intervention possibilities; to synthesize what has been learned in order to use it in the process of therapy with women who have been abused; and to find out what does and does not help a victim heal, become a survivor, and get on with her life.[1]

There are three major reasons why these responsibilities pose such a significant challenge. First, research is only now beginning to show how many women have been sexually and physically abused. Victims can be expected to appear in the average therapist's practice. Virtually any mental health practitioner who works with women needs to have some understanding of the different forms of violence against women and the assessment and treatment of the effects of such violence.

Second, there is a tendency for abuse to remain undetected by poorly trained clinicians in screening, assessment, and even in long-term therapy. An important protective reaction of many clients is to keep the abuse secret so that no one can learn about it. Some therapists may be unwilling to hear about abuse, and in this way may attempt to protect themselves from vicarious traumatization. Even when the abuse is discovered, its relationship to individual symptoms, general syndromes, and formal diagnoses may be misattributed. Obviously, this hinders the healing process. Knowledge of the emerging research and clinical literature can help clinicians to avoid such errors. New developments in the fields of trauma theory and the psychology of women have important implications for work with women who have been abused. Survivor therapy combines these two bodies of literature.

---

[1] In this book, the term *victim* is used when the woman has not received services or has not yet begun to heal after being abused, whereas *survivor* is reserved for those who have made substantial progress on their path to healing.

Third, training programs may not provide adequate education and supervised experience. New graduates, as well as more senior mental health professionals, often lack adequate training in how to develop treatment plans with women who have suffered such forms of abuse as rape, battering, childhood sexual abuse, sexual involvement with a therapist, and sexual harassment. Most continuing education programs offer the clinician the knowledge he or she needs to begin interventions, but lack the specific skill-training that supports the therapist as he or she works with clients who have more complex difficulties.

This introductory chapter provides a brief overview of some of these major themes.

FREQUENCY OF OCCURRENCE

Historically, sexual and physical abuse against girls and women was considered rare (see, e.g., Estrich, 1987; Herman, 1981; Pope, 1991; Russell, 1986). As chapter 4 documents, relatively recent professional texts are still inaccurately asserting that incest, for example, affects only between one and two individuals out of every million United States citizens even though well-respected empirical studies estimate its incidence as closer to one third of all girls and one fourth of all boys. Especially against this historical context, the emerging research-based estimates of abuse have been surprising to many people. A few examples here highlight this trend with additional frequency data presented in subsequent chapters.

A study of 3,187 college women found that one in every six or seven had been raped; a similar study of 2,291 working women found that one in five had been raped (Koss & Harvey, 1991). White and Koss's (1991) latest data from a North Carolina campus found that more than 25% of the women had been battered or sexually assaulted by a date, many in high school. Contrary to prevailing stereotypes in which rape by friends and acquaintances was thought to be extremely rare, relatively few of the rapists were strangers: More than half were dates or previous sexual partners of the victim; in four out of five instances, the victim knew the offender. Although recent legal cases that were highly publicized on "Court TV" have demonstrated that men and women may have different definitions of what constitutes "date rape," even when using fairly conservative definitions provided by the researcher, it is clear that large numbers of women have experienced such events.

Estimates that are based on such statistics may underestimate the occurrence of rape among some groups. Wyatt's (1985) research shows that ethnic minorities are often underrepresented in research, even though African-American women have been described as most at risk for rape at some point in their lives. The U.S. Senate confirmation hearings for U.S. Supreme Court Justice Clarence Thomas are a good example of the complex interaction between race and gender. Thomas accused the senators of racism if they believed Anita Hill's assertions of sexual harassment. One quick walk through this nation's prisons and it becomes clear that African-American, Hispanic, and other minority males are much more likely to be overrepresented in the criminal justice population than White males. Yet, at no time during the hearing was it emphasized by those making the accusation of racism that Anita Hill was an African-American woman accusing an African-American male supervisor of sexual harassment.

Nonprotection of women of color is a symptom of the marginalization of the serious problem of racism in the criminal justice system. Many thought that the senators' inability to take Hill's charges seriously was due to male bonding that crossed racial lines; men did not define the same behavior as sexual harassment as did women. This was further demonstrated after boxer Michael Tyson's conviction of raping a Miss Black America contestant in Indiana in early 1992. Financier Donald Trump suggested that Tyson be permitted to pay reparations to assist rape victims rather than go to prison where his violent behavior against women could be contained. Most women know what it feels like to be the victim of some man's unwanted sexual desires. The spokesmen in the news did not appear to understand the heightened emotional effects experienced by women victims or to recognize the behavior consistently displayed by many abuse victims. Tyson's defense underscored that point when his lawyers presented evidence that Tyson approached all women with verbal and physical violence, implying that, if the victim chose to go out on a date with him, she should have expected to be raped.

Examination of the stories and myths about women throughout the ages provides an important context within which to place some of this information. Gallers (1993) described the moral of the myth of Apollo and Cassandra as one that is just as relevant to abused women today as it was 4,000 years ago when the story was set. In this myth, Cassandra, the daughter of King Priam, accepted the gift of second sight or prophecy from Apollo, the god of light and reason. He demanded that, as repayment for this gift of prophecy, she must become his mistress. She refused to have sex with him but agreed to give him a farewell kiss. Although he seemed to be accepting her "no" gracefully, in the middle of the kiss, he spat into her mouth and issued the curse that she would not be believed whenever she spoke, even though her words would be truthful. Cassandra may not seem like the typical victim because she did agree to the kiss; however, the lesson learned from her punishment for not repaying Apollo's gift is similar to the lesson learned by a woman who is expected to be sexually available to a man who gives her gifts, such as an expensive dinner, then is treated abusively if she spurns his advances.

Even though women and children usually speak the truth about men's physical and sexual abuse, they often are not believed (as evidenced by the current controversy about repressed memories). This and other allegories should remind us that women's reactions to abuse are neither new nor better accepted today than they were thousands of years ago. In fact, women whose behavior is neither liked nor understood have been given many different labels over the years, such as hysterics, witches, and most recently, borderlines, as a way to control and eliminate the behavior that is disagreeable when compared with a community standard that is based on male values. The intervention strategies outlined in this book attempt to define the community standard more broadly to include positive acceptance for all people without regard to gender, color, ethnic or cultural values, sexual orientation, age, or physical or mental ability. Narrow definitions that may have been attributed historically to males, females, or any one particular group are too limiting to help women become survivors of abuse and reach their fullest potential. It is helpful to appreciate people with all of their similarities and differences.

The occurrence of rape, battering, and other forms of abuse among those who seek help from health care providers may be significantly higher than it is for the general population. Carmen, Reiker, and Mills (1984) found that 50% to 80% of the hospitalized psychiatric patients whom they studied had some form of abuse in their history, most of which was discounted by the treating psychiatrists. A. Jacobson (1989) interviewed outpatients at a general psychiatric clinic and found that about two thirds (68%) had suffered major sexual or physical abuse. For women, the most prevalent were physical assault as an adult (42%) and sexual assault as a child (42%), followed by sexual assault as an adult (38%), and physical assault as a child (35%). In a similar interview study of inpatients, A. Jacobson and Richardson (1987) found that the most prevalent form of abuse for hospitalized women was physical assault as an adult (64%), followed by physical assault as a child (44%), sexual assault as an adult (38%), and sexual assault as a child (22%). (See also G.R. Brown & Anderson, 1991.)

Survey findings based on responses from 257 practicing psychologists, social workers, and psychiatrists in North Carolina found that one in every five or six (18.5%) of their current clients had a history of sexual assault (Dye & Roth, 1990). A national survey of 1,320 psychologists found that about half of the respondents reported assessing or treating at least one patient who had been sexually intimate with a prior therapist (Pope & Vetter, 1991). Briere and Runtz (1987) found that almost half (44%) of the women who sought help at an outpatient crisis clinic had a history of sexual molestation.

A national study of adults found that 28% had been physically battered by their partners (Straus, Gelles, & Steinmetz, 1980). Subsequent studies suggest that as many as one out of two women have experienced some form of physical, sexual, or psychological abuse (Barnett & LaViolette, 1993; Dutton, 1992; Pagelow, 1984; Straus & Gelles, 1988; Walker, 1984a).

These research findings strongly suggest that a history of rape, battering, child sexual abuse, sexual involvement with a therapist, and other forms of abuse are not rare among women. It is likely that any clinician who works with women clients is working with at least some victims of sexual and physical abuse. Also interesting is the common belief that there is a difference between clients' and therapists' problems. A recent study (Pope & Feldman-Summers, 1992) of 250 male and 250 female psychologists has found that 33.1% reported having experienced some form of physical or sexual abuse as a child or adolescent. Women were found more likely to have been the victims in all categories except for physical abuse, which was reported by 13.1% of the men and 9.1% of the women. "Slightly over one-third (36.6%) of the participants reported some form of abuse during adulthood. The most frequently reported types of abuse were sexual harassment (20.69%) and nonsexual physical abuse by a spouse (9.66%)" (Pope & Feldman-Summers, 1992, p. 354). Women were significantly more likely than men to report experiencing attempted and acquaintance rape. Further demonstrating that therapists are no strangers to abuse issues personally, about one third of the male psychologists and more than two thirds of the female psychologists reported at least one episode of violence during childhood or adulthood up until the time of the survey. It is important for the treating therapist who has also experienced abuse in her or his life to carefully examine the personal impact of the abuse and how it may affect her or his approach to working with other abuse victims. (This issue is addressed more carefully in chapter 7.)

ABUSE AND TRAUMA

During the past decade, it has become important for therapists to be aware of the issues involved in violence against women, especially because of the large numbers of clients who seek therapy due to the traumatic effects of abuse. Also in the last decade, a great deal of data have been gathered regarding the psychological impact of various types of trauma, and a new field of study has developed in the area of posttraumatic stress reactions and disorders. Figley (1988), one of the primary researchers in the broader area of traumatic stress studies, concluded that all practitioners have the responsibility to identify trauma victims, to learn how they cope with catastrophe by developing strengths as well as difficulties, and then to place the data about an individual client within the context of the larger body of knowledge regarding how trauma victims are affected and expected to cope with the psychological effects, as well as how they integrate the experience into the rest of their lives to become survivors.

Although the impact of trauma has been discussed by mental health service providers for a long time, particularly in relation to the trauma experienced by males who have participated in military combat (Kardiner, 1941), in 1980, with the publication of the third edition of the *Diagnostic and Statistical Manual of Mental Disorders (DSM–III)*, the field of study of traumatic stress disorders became more widely accepted. *DSM–III* listed the category of posttraumatic stress disorder (PTSD) for the first time (American Psychiatric Association, 1980). This category is the only one in the *DSM* nosology system that suggests that any normal person can develop psychological symptoms because of the nature of the trauma experienced. Criteria that defined the disorder were mainly taken from studies of Vietnam War veterans with PTSD and included a combination of heightened arousal or anxiety, generalized avoidance responses including depression, and cognitive and memory changes, particularly the distortions that come from the recurrent reexperiencing of the traumatic events.

The 1987 revision of the criteria in the *DSM–III* (*DSM–III–R*; American Psychiatric Association, 1987) refined the general description further, although there were no additional research studies used to support the modifications recommended by clinicians. Without specifying the actual subcategories that come under the PTSD, such as person-made single or repetitive events leading to rape trauma syndrome, battered woman syndrome, child abuse syndrome, combat stress syndrome, and natural disasters such as earthquakes, fires, and airplane crashes, the *DSM–III–R* nevertheless provides adequate opportunity for the practitioner who specializes in the treatment of these traumas to learn to use its system to make appropriate diagnoses and treatment decisions. However, the situation becomes more complicated for the clinician who sees only a few trauma victims within a private practice. Prepublication drafts of the fourth edition of the *DSM* (*DSM–IV*) indicate that the major change in PTSD criteria in the upcoming edition will be to more clearly define the nature of the traumas that can produce such a psychological reaction. No longer will the trauma be classified as an abnormal experience of the victim nor will it be necessary for the trauma to have ceased in order for the diagnosis to be made. An additional trauma category, posttraumatic stress reactions (PTSR), is proposed that will measure less enduring reactions as opposed to longer lasting disorders caused by exposure to trauma. This book can serve as a guide for both experienced and less experienced mental health providers when making such diagnostic decisions.

ABUSE IN CONTEXT

Blaming the Victim

The forms of abuse that are the focus of this book—rape, battering, childhood sexual abuse, therapist–patient sex, and sexual harassment—share a salient characteristic: For each form of abuse, most perpetrators are male and most victims are female. Among the many results of this gender-based characteristic (see, e.g., Pope, 1990a; Walker, 1988) are the tendencies for the victim's reports to be ignored or discounted and for the victim herself to be criticized and blamed for the abuse. The direct and subtle "blame-the-victim" attitudes that are evidenced by both the public and by mental health professionals were first described by Ryan (1971) in dealing with race relations and were later applied to female abuse victims (Walker, 1979, 1984b) and female victims of racial discrimination and other hate crimes (L.S. Brown, 1992b). Therapists themselves may blame abuse victims (Dye & Roth, 1990; Pope, 1990a) or may fail to take these cultural and gender characteristics into account as they work with victims. It is not uncommon for those who were themselves victimized but have buried the memories to find it too difficult to listen to the similar stories of others. Even those who were not personally touched by abuse can become vicariously traumatized from listening to stories of brutality. Woman abuse is all too common for anyone to be free from its influence on a personal level. Therapists who work with victims to help them become survivors must deal with their own attitudes as part of their skill-building strategy.

Displaying a victim-blaming attitude also serves to protect the person with such an attitude from the awareness of her or his own vulnerability.

This situation is described in greater detail later, but it is most often seen in female therapists who are afraid to acknowledge the sometimes random nature of violence for fear that they could become its next victim as well as in male therapists who cannot acknowledge that they, too, might be capable of inflicting violence against a woman or child in a given situation. Sometimes, therapists who have witnessed violence in their own families are unable to empathize with the current victim because the similarities stir up memories that had been long forgotten. Those who have healed from their own personal experiences with violence may believe that their way of healing is the best and therefore may prevent the client from exploring all of her options. Those therapists who are most successful in helping victims to recover and become survivors do so by helping them learn to feel empowered again through their own mastery of these unsettling feelings. Emphasizing the positive strengths rather than focusing on the person's deficits is the most practical approach toward the goal of empowerment.

Blaming the victim may occur more often when the victimizers are male and the victims are female. This blaming ignores the dynamics of power and victimization. The victims have been harmed by the following misuses of power by those who have some dominance over them: in instances of rape, physical strength, sometimes weapons, and ability to sexually humiliate; in cases of battering, psychological and physical strength as well as financial and social dominance; in instances of child sexual abuse, the physical and intellectual dominance of adults over children; in instances of therapist–patient sex, the power, status, and misuse of trust and special knowledge; and in instances of sexual harassment, economic, social, and career power. In all of these issues (except for the rarest, rape by a stranger), the victim's psychological harm is intensified by the betrayal, violation, and poisoning of a preexisting relationship. The trust and implicit power in the relationship were used by the perpetrator to harm the victim; the relationship was transformed into an opportunity for abuse.

Sex-Role Stereotypes

The new scholarship in the psychology of women has provided alternatives to the psychobiological theories that have dominated the past several decades of psychiatry. These new explanations center around a social learning theory framework that takes into account the differential treatment of men and women in most societies. Historically, men have been socialized into sex-role expected patterns of behavior that include aggressiveness, inability to express many feelings, intellectualization, demands of being a wage earner, and a belief in entitlement to women's caretaking services. Women, on the other hand, have been socialized in sex-role behavior patterns that encourage them to be less aggressive, less intellectual, and better able to express their emotions, and to believe that it is their job to be the nurturers and take care of the needs of men and children before their own. Any deviation from these sex-role-stereotyped behavior patterns can cause a serious diminishing of self-esteem and angry reactions from those whose expectations are affected (cf. Barnett & LaViolette, 1993; Broverman, Broverman, Clarkson, Rosencrantz, & Vogel, 1970; Chesler, 1972; Dutton-Douglas & Walker, 1988; Rosewater & Walker, 1985; Walker, 1984a).

When some men perceive that their needs are not being met by women, they attempt to get what they believe they are entitled to by taking power and control (Groth, 1979; Sonkin, Martin, & Walker, 1985). The means by which men force women to do what they want without regard for the rights or feelings of the women can include physical, sexual, and psychological forms of abuse. Rosewater (1993) advocated the casting off of the old rules that govern relationships in order to decrease the amount of violence between intimate partners. She documented how the cultural mandate for men to be dominant limits their ability to relate as equals with women, sharing power with them, rather than, in a more traditional role, having power over women. Some abuse by men is overtly violent and obvious to observers, and some is more subtly coercive and less readily observable. Often victims cannot accurately describe the abuse because of memory lapses, or because of fears of retribution or of not being believed. Some victims assign different meanings to the abuse, and as a result they do not feel harmed until they experience other traumatic events, perhaps even many years later. Shame in having been exploited or fooled also prevents many victims from verbalizing the harm that has been done to them. Some victims believe they love the man and are grateful for his attention and love, too. The socialized need not to expose a former lover can also be a powerful force preventing the victim from acknowledging the abuse, either to herself or others. In minority women, a fear of annihilation of their race or culture may hinder them from exposing their men, already oppressed by a prejudiced society. There are interview techniques described elsewhere in this volume that can enhance a practitioner's ability to assist women in better describing what they have experienced. The impact on the victim, however, does not appear to be determined only by the form of abuse she has experienced. The relationship with the abuser, the single or repetitive nature of the abuse, its frequency, the conditions under which it occurs, prior history, and seriousness of injuries all seem to play a part in determining the psychological impact and recovery period, as do the support system and resources available to the victim afterward.

In addition to the commonly recognized sex-role stereotypes, which are also subscribed to by mental health practitioners (American Psychological Association, 1974, 1978; Broverman et al., 1970; Pope, 1990b; Rosencrantz, DeLorey, & Broverman, 1985; Walker, 1989b), women are treated as an oppressed group of people in many real-life situations that help shape the coping strategies that they adopt. Such discrimination by gender has been found to result in greater vulnerability to certain mental health problems, such as depression (McGrath, Keita, Strickland, & Russo, 1990) and health problems (Koss & Harvey, 1991). Often this discrimination leaves a woman vulnerable to the flattering attentions of a man or to his neediness. It also helps shape the psychological impact on violence victims.

Integration With Other Forms of Oppression

There are other oppressive contexts that may be important for an adequate understanding of the background against which a woman can experience abuse; the factors that may intensify, expand, and interact with the harm the abuse causes; the meaning the victim gives to the abusive experiences; and the existing barriers to a full recovery.

Economic discrimination against women still exists even though today many women are able to receive an education appropriate for most career opportunities. The American Association of University Women recently issued a report detailing the high levels of math anxiety and low self-esteem that begin to develop in 9th-grade girls and continue throughout their high school years. This report documents the devastating impact of gender discrimination in school on a woman's self-esteem in adulthood. It is sometimes easy to forget that less than 20 years ago, there were still informal or formal quotas that restricted the number of women admitted to most professional schools, including programs in medicine, law, engineering, and clinical psychology. For example, women made up only 18% of the American Psychiatric Association membership in 1986 and approximately 33% of the American Psychological Association membership. Recently, the dean of the Stanford University Medical Center pointed with pride to the fact that in the past 5 years "the fraction of women in the School of Medicine faculty has increased from 9 to 14 per cent" (Korn, 1991, p. A-21). The phenomenon of the "glass ceiling" that is experienced by women in business who reach a certain level of power and then find themselves prevented from advancing further, due to gender bias, has also been documented (Aburdene & Nesbitt, 1992; Faludi, 1991; Hyde, 1994).

Women typically earn less money than men, even in the same jobs with the same education and training. This makes them vulnerable to numerous forms of economic abuse. In the United States in the past two decades, women's salaries have risen only three cents from $0.59 to $0.62 for every $1.00 earned by a man (Aburdene & Nesbitt, 1992). Psychology professionals became concerned about the "feminization" of the profession when it was predicted that, by the year 2000, 50% of those completing graduate school as clinical psychologists would be women. Women are disproportionately underrepresented in leadership and policy-making positions within the psychology field. This is true even for those professions in which the majority of practitioners are women. Historian and futurist Elyse Boulding suggested that groups tend to reach a critical mass of approximately 30% female composition before the status becomes less gender-biased and more integrated. Anything less than 30% can be expected to result in the continued domination over females by males, according to

Boulding. Obviously, this becomes a no-win situation for women and may be the root of some of the greater propensity toward depression and feelings of hopelessness in women.

There are data that demonstrate the negative psychological impact of being oppressed and considered the "other" for a variety of minority groups besides women including ethnic and racial minorities, persons with non-mainstream lifestyles, lesbians and gays, elderly people, and those with physical and mental disabilities (L.S. Brown & Root, 1990; Mays & Comas-Dias, 1988; Midlarsky, 1988). When violence against women is also part of the oppression the impact is heightened (L.S. Brown & Root, 1990; Lobel, 1986; Rozee & Van Boemel, 1989). It is important to consider the cultural context within which meaning is given to woman abuse in order to understand the meaning assigned to the events by victims from different ethnic and cultural groups as well as to understand how that meaning is affected by the types of resources available to each group. For example, Native American women who wish to remain on the reservation have fewer resources to assist in their recovery process than do those who live in the cities. Asian American women are much more likely to experience any event by evaluating and understanding its impact on their family as well as on themselves. Jewish women who are abused by Jewish men are more likely to fear that exposure will contribute to greater levels of anti-Semitism against the entire Jewish population. Refugee women may have already developed PTSD or other responses to the destruction of their countries in addition to the trauma reaction from interpersonal abuse. State-sponsored violence against all people including women may have greater implications for women's mental health in combination with all the other types of abuse they may have experienced. This interaction effect can only be understood through individual women's stories. The interactions described in these stories can then be compared with what is known about all forms of oppression (cf. the special issues of *Women and Therapy* on refugee women, edited by Cole, Rothblum, & Espin, 1992).

Adequate assessment and intervention rely not only on recognition of abuse and its effects but also on the relevant contexts. Feminist criticisms of earlier research that did not place women abuse in the appropriate context have made a clear and convincing case that such inadequate and inaccurate information resulted in the misunderstanding of the abused woman (L.S. Brown & Root, 1990; Dobash & Dobash, 1979; Walker, 1989a).

Social Acceptance of Violence Against Women

It has been suggested that the social acceptance of violence against women facilitates and perpetuates individual men's abusive behavior. There is a debate in the field about whether or not men who commit serious violence, such as familial and nonstranger rape, sexual abuse of children, and life-threatening assault are mentally ill or simply displaying exaggerated and overly socialized male sex-role-stereotyped behavior (Becker, 1990; Dutton, 1992; Ganley, 1981, 1988; Island & Letellier, 1991; Lindsey, McBride, & Platt, 1992; Pence & Paymar, 1993; Saunders, 1982, 1986; Sonkin, et al., 1985). One difficulty with a mental illness hypothesis is that most offenders do not fit into any of the current mental disorder categories. This leads mental health providers unfamiliar with the personality patterns of such males to conclude falsely that many who abuse family members or who do not use major overt abuse tactics and then minimize, deny, "forget," or lie about their behavior could not have done anything wrong because they are as normal and mentally healthy as the next man.

There are those who argue that men's abusive behavior against women falls on a continuum ranging from the less noxious and harmful harassments such as "wolf whistles," advertisements portraying women as sex symbols, and other humiliations and depersonalizations; to "intermediate" abuse such as obscene telephone calls and terrorizing threats of future violence; to serious abusive behavior such as unwanted touching, refusal to accept "no" to unwanted sexual advances, promises of rewards for sexual cooperation (including love, future marriage, job advancement, and protection from other potential abuse); on through the more obvious forms of abuse such as rape with or without physical violence and physical battery whether or not it results in observable physical injuries (Leidig, 1981). Certainly, all of these behaviors have in common the fact that they are used primarily by men to gain more power and control over the behavior of women. This is not to say that abuse does not occur in lesbian and gay relationships. However, the gender analysis of a misuse of power and control within heterosexual relationships can also be used in the context of homosexual relationships, because heterosexual relationships serve as the model families for most gays and lesbians as well.

DISCOUNTING ABUSE

An informed and attentive mental health practitioner can counter the cultural tendencies to deny, discount, or misattribute abuse against women. Making it mandatory for practitioners to ask about abuse at any point in the assessment and therapy process can prevent misdiagnosis and the consequential withholding of appropriate services. Some clients come to therapy without memory of past abuse and may deny its occurrence until later on in treatment when other issues help the memories become unburied. However, many more abusive memories are simply not accessed because the clinician did not ask the right questions. Briere and Zaidi (1989) selected at random 50 charts of nonpsychotic patients who had come to a psychiatric emergency room. These charts were compared with 50 charts in which the clinicians had been asked to inquire about sex abuse. When clinicians were directed to include sex abuse as a topic while taking a history, a large majority (70%) of the patients reported at least one episode of sexual molestation. When clinicians were not prompted to ask specifically about the topic, only 6% of the charts noted episodes of sexual abuse. When conducting an intake examination, obtaining a history, or conducting a psychological assessment, clinicians cannot neglect specific inquiry into the areas of sexual and physical abuse.

Recently, there has been some suggestion that asking women about possible victimization may plant suggestions in their minds that call forth false memories of abuse (Loftus & Ketchum, 1991). This theory is promoted by researchers who have not indicated why sexual abuse questions would bring forth false memories when other clinical questions do not. Briere and Conte (1993) reinterviewed adults who had been sexually abused as children and found that a large number of them had no memory of either the abuse or testifying in court despite the court records that documented what happened to them as children. Such research supports the claims of the numbers of women who legitimately regain memory during assessment or treatment.

Even when clinicians become aware of abuse, the effects may be minimized or misattributed. The emerging research suggests that the effects of abuse may be deep, pervasive, and lasting. For example, a series of studies that are now in progress are providing evidence that childhood abuse may not only increase the risk for suicide, depression, and drug abuse, but may also cause sharp drops in measures of intelligence ("Childhood Abuse," 1991). Such effects may not be confined to a brief period immediately after the abuse. Sexual victimization in childhood may have long-term effects lasting into the women's adulthood. Research has shown that such abuse in childhood may be associated with the adult woman's depression, increased distress, lowered self-esteem, and sexual problems (Gold, 1986; McGrath et al., 1990).

The variety, intensity, and duration of some of these symptoms may obscure the original abuse and lead to misdiagnosis. For example, research has supported the hypothesis that a general history of sex abuse is linked to increased suicidal risk, substance abuse, sexual problems, multiple diagnoses, and personality disorder diagnosis, particularly with borderline features (Briere & Zaidi, 1989). Self-mutilation, difficulties in concentration, self-hatred, dissociative and multiple personality disorders, and sleep and eating disorders have all been linked to childhood abuse (Courtois, 1988). Koss, Woodruff, and Koss (1991) have found that the medical consequences of rape result in a disproportionate amount of chronic illnesses and that victims increase the frequency of their visits to physicians by 56% between the second and fifth postrape years. Kilpatrick (1990) found that the single most predictive factor in alcohol and drug abuse for women is a history of physical and sexual abuse. In my own work with battered women, I have found the development over time of neurological symptoms similar to those developed by boxers from too much head-shaking and head-banging.

Tendencies to ignore or discount reports of abuse can occur, sometimes in blatant forms, even among those charged with investigating such reports.

The police, for example, may refuse even to investigate reports of rape. One investigation found that a major metropolitan police department had failed to adequately investigate 203 rape cases; in 37 instances, the victim was never even interviewed (Gross, 1990). The police chief subsequently admitted that the cases were mishandled. Sexual harassment of female students and nontenured faculty on university campuses has typically not been addressed. Even in cases in which other former employees have come forward to support a sexual harassment victim who has filed legal charges, on the academic campus, most employees are too afraid of derailing careers to speak out.

Even when the police do investigate, women sometimes fear that filing a rape report will simply add to their own suffering. Some women believe that filing a report means unintentionally waiving all effective rights to privacy and leaving oneself open to punishing examination. In one prominent case, involving a woman who alleged that she was raped, the *New York Times* not only released the name of the woman in the days immediately after her report to the police, but also subjected her to a critical examination in which the paper revealed the woman's high school grades, the price of her home, her traffic tickets, information about the father of her illegitimate child, her mother's salary, and an alleged affair into which her mother had entered, and quoted an anonymous source saying that the woman alleging rape had a "wild streak." Indeed, the unwritten rule of the media not to reveal the name of the victim while documenting charges and countercharges may be in jeopardy after several high-publicity trials in which the press did expose the alleged victims.

INADEQUATE INFORMATION AND EDUCATION

Perhaps it is partly due to the general tendency to ignore and discount abuse for which women are the most frequent victims and men are the most frequent victimizers that training programs tend to neglect the topic of woman abuse. Graduate programs, medical schools, and internships that provide adequate education, training, and supervised experience are exceptionally rare. A national survey of psychologists found that only 15%

reported that their training in the area of assessing and treating victims of therapist–client sexual intimacies was adequate (Pope & Vetter, 1991). Similarly, courses on child sex abuse are rare (Alpert & Paulson, 1990), despite Alpert's pioneering development of such a course at New York University. Although social work students receive more information about child abuse, they rarely receive training in theoretical context or in providing effective treatment strategies. Often the only available training takes place in state agencies whose responsibilities are to identify and stop abuse and neglect rather than to reverse the psychological effects. In many of these agencies, mental health professionals find that the role of being a quasi-state enforcer is inimical to providing good treatment. In fact, many psychologists feel that the mandatory state child abuse report laws actually produce a chilling effect on access to treatment. In any case, failure to provide adequate education and training about abuse makes it more likely that clinicians will fail to recognize it, understand its effects on the client, and be able to respond most helpfully. Ignoring the impact of abuse on mental disorder symptoms during training sends the indirect message that the experiencing of such trauma has little to do with subsequent emotional difficulties. One goal of this book is to provide information about abuse that may not be available in many formal training programs.

SUMMARY

As far back as there are historical records, women have been abused by men. Definitions of and issues surrounding abuse appear to be different for each gender. The tendency to blame the victim, her class, color, or other aspects of her status has interfered with the ability of practitioners to provide assistance to women who have been abused.

Women often seek therapy to assist them in dealing with psychological reactions that are the result of having been abuse victims even though they may not connect the symptoms they are experiencing with the victimization. Mental health practitioners are often unprepared for dealing with abused women, sometimes because of their own abuse experiences and sometimes because they have not familiarized themselves with the new knowledge base that combines the study of women with the study of reactions to trauma. The new therapy program described in this book consists of a combination of these two fields and is called *survivor therapy*.

One of the major criticisms of the current approaches taken in treating abused women is that woman abuse is not seen within the context in which it occurs. Thus, after looking at sex-role socialization patterns, it is possible to see how the resulting stereotypes and expectations, gender issues, and perceived vulnerabilities of individuals all can lead to further victimization. Economic realities for women have made them more dependent on men. Oppression due to race, color, ethnic and cultural background, class, sexual orientation, disability, and other factors contributing to diversity also interact with the abuse causing further harm to the woman. Although cultural relativity is often cited euphemistically to prevent action when someone from another culture is being abused (e.g., in the case of clitoridectomies for women in some African societies), culture still must be understood in order to understand the meanings women assign to their abusive experiences.

Some of the reasons that societies accept violence against women are currently being discussed from a feminist perspective. There is a continuum of behavior, ranging from nasty remarks and "catcalls" to obscene telephone calls, stalking, harassing, and eventually physical and sexual abuse, that degrades and devalues women. Often mental health practitioners discount a woman's recounting of abuse, either because the woman is unable to articulate clearly what has happened to her or because the practitioner is unable to be sensitive to how the woman felt when she experienced the abuse. The questions asked by clinicians have been described by female clients as discounting the feelings of the women, not taking the women seriously, or appearing to blame the women for what happened. Mental health professionals are urged to examine the results of the research, much of which is summarized in the next five chapters, in order to improve their ability to meet the responsibilities of working with abuse victims.

2

Rape and Sexual Assault

A s with many of the other types of abuse discussed in this book, clinicians are likely to underestimate the incidence and prevalence of rape and sexual assault in women's lives, thereby underestimating the likelihood that sexual assault victims will be encountered in clinical practice. However, given the large number of women who are sexually abused at some time in their lives, and the devastating effects that such abuse can cause, it is probable that every clinician will treat some women whose mental health issues are related in some way to having been sexually abused.

In this chapter, after defining what constitutes rape and showing how prevalent sexual assault is, I discuss the impact of rape by strangers and by acquaintances. Finally, I examine assessment and therapeutic intervention issues. Marital rape is discussed both here and in the next chapter on battered women because the data show it rarely occurs unaccompanied by threats or actual physical abuse. It is appropriate to apply the information in this chapter to the other forms of sexual abuse covered in this book.

OVERVIEW AND DEFINITIONS

Until the emergence of the women's movement in the late 1960s, rape was defined legally, as well as socially, as the forcible penetration of the vagina by the man's penis (see, e.g., Estrich, 1987). As women began to speak out to one another about their forced sexual experiences, the legal definition of rape was modified to include a variety of sexual assaults, and as a result more accurately reflected the violence and abuse of power that were the driving forces of these unwanted sexual intrusions. Many states adopted sexual assault laws of varying degrees of severity. The highest level of sexual assault included forced oral, anal, or vaginal penetration by a man's penis. Lower level sexual assaults included unwanted touching of sexual areas, digital and manual penetration, sexual harassment, and threats. Rape definitions also eliminated the utmost resistance standard. Courts began to look at the totality of circumstances and to allow express verbal resistance as sufficient to prove resistance (where still required) and lack of consent. This change reflected the fact that many women were so fearful of further violence or death that they gave in to the man's demands without physical resistance. In some situations any attempt to fight off the attacker placed the girl or woman in much greater danger. In other situations, intimidation was sufficient to force acquiescence (Bart & O'Brien, 1985).

The psychological effects of a rape or sexual assault occur when the woman says "no" and another person continues unwanted sexual behavior. In some states, the law holds that a rape or a sexual assault occurs when the woman says "no" and another person continues unwanted sexual behavior. In most states, however, lack of consent is only one element of rape. Some force or threat of force extrinsic to penetration itself is generally also required. The burden is on the presecution to prove that force was used. Most of the current relevant theories about human sexual aggression acknowledge that desire for power and control, rather than sexual desire, motivate the typical rapist (Becker & Abel, 1981; A.W. Burgess, 1985, 1988; Finkelhor & Yllo, 1985; Groth, 1979; Prentky & Quinsey, 1988). Rape and various levels of sexual assault are considered crimes of violence and not crimes of passion. This definition clarifies the lack of responsibility borne by the victim and thus avoids blaming the victim.

Reflecting the gender-neutral legislation of the 1970s and 1980s, the laws acknowledge that men also can be raped, although the numbers of reported sexual assaults on men, which are usually committed by other men, are significantly lower than those for women. Although the legal definitions of rape do vary slightly from state to state, they are sufficiently consistent to be used as definitions by clinicians (see, e.g., Chappel, Geis, & Geis., 1977; Estrich, 1987; Koss & Harvey, 1991). The levels of severity that the law assigns to the various types of sexual assault correspond adequately with the psychological impact on the victims. Clinicians who treat victims of rape and sexual assault will likely find it useful, if not essential, to become familiar with the relevant laws in their state.

In the past 10 years, two additional categories of rape have been studied and added to the legal definition: marital rape and date or acquaintance rape (Estrich, 1987; Koss, 1988; Koss & Harvey, 1991; Koss, Woodruff, & Koss, 1991). In the case of marital rape, although the nature of the assault is the same, the nature of the relationship between the offender and his victim, and the probability of the assault being repeated if the relationship remains intact, places it in a special category. The very idea that a husband can rape his wife is one that surprises many who hold traditional beliefs; marriage often implies sexual consent. In some instances, couples may live separately yet remain legally married. Forced sex that occurs either when living apart but still married, when married and living together, or even when living together but not married, is still considered to be marital rape.

Acquaintance or date rape turns out to be far more prevalent than stranger rape, yet it is less likely to be reported to the police or prosecuted if it is reported. It is also not likely to be considered rape by mental health professionals (Koss & Harvey, 1991), although women who have reported the experience are harmed psychologically in a manner consistent with others types of rape. Many women are forced into sex when all they seek is friendship; others are forced into going further than they intended. Perhaps kissing and hugging was the woman's goal, but her date refused to stop until sexual intercourse was completed. Just because a woman has previously consented to sex with a man does not mean that he is entitled to sex each time they see each other. Consent must be given each time a sexual encounter takes place.

Including these separate classifications of sexual abuse in the legal definition will assist therapists who are helping a client to understand that if the client has experienced a forced sexual encounter, then she has indeed been raped. Sometimes the therapist is the first person who helps the victim to restructure the experience cognitively, to understand that a forced sexual encounter is a crime of violence using sex as a weapon, and to make sense of the emotional difficulties resulting from the event or events.

INCIDENCE AND PREVALENCE

A landmark study of 930 women found that more than one in five (22%) reported that they had been subjected to rape or attempted rape at some time during the course of their lives (Russell, 1984). Yet even such striking statistics may severely underestimate the occurrence of rape and attempted rape because victims may discount the fact that certain events in their lives constitute rape or attempted rape. For example, in the study cited above, subsequent questions did not mention the word *rape*, but asked whether the individual had experienced intercourse obtained by threat or actual force. When rape was defined as unwanted or coerced sex, the percentage of women who had experienced rape or attempted rape rose to 56%. Almost one out of four (24%) had actually been raped.

Kilpatrick and Veronen's (1983) study of 2,000 rape victims suggests that the behavior women define as rape is likely to be at the most serious end of the sexual assault level, often excluding date and acquaintance rapes and marital rapes. The data on marital rape suggest that it occurs in one half to three quarters of those relationships in which physical battering also takes place and an indeterminate number in which the abuse is primarily psychological (Kilpatrick et al., 1989). In another study, one out of four teenage girls was found to have been physically or sexually abused by a boyfriend (Levy, 1991). A study by Koss and Burkhart (1989) found that 25% of all college women had been sexually assaulted, usually when on a date.

Mental health professionals who work in outpatient or inpatient settings can expect to work with a number of female patients who have experienced rape. A. Jacobson's (1989) research reported that about 38% of female outpatients and 38% of female inpatients have experienced sexual assault as an adult. Carmen, Reiker, and Mills (1984) found that over 60% of all patients whose charts they reviewed were victims of an assault at some point in their lives; many of the women were sexual abuse victims. It is not uncommon for private psychiatric hospitals to set up posttraumatic stress disorder (PTSD) units that treat large numbers of women who have been raped, many of them victims of multiple assaults. Sexual assault is a major cause of psychological distress for women who eventually seek psychotherapy.

Those who work in drug treatment programs have often noted the high frequency of reports of rape (Finkelstein, 1990). Kilpatrick (1990) found that sexual abuse is a primary factor in alcohol and drug abuse among women. When drug treatment programs ignore the sexual abuse and its impact, women are more likely to continue their chemical dependence as a way of self-medicating. Others in drug treatment programs report addiction as a predisposing factor for women to be sexually assaulted because female addicts may not take the precautions other women take when faced with dangerous situations.

Many police forces, prosecutors, and emergency room staff have been trained to change the ways in which they handle encounters with rape victims. Women reporting rape are now less likely to be treated insensitively, viewed as possible fabricators of fictitious attacks, or blamed for inciting a rape. As a result, women may be much more likely to report a rape and to seek treatment. In addition, since the definition of rape was broadened to include a variety of unwanted sexual behavior, more women have been found to have been raped (Bart & O'Brien, 1985).

EMPIRICAL AND CLINICAL RESEARCH

Medical Care Issues

A recent study by Koss et al. (1991) found that only 17% of all rape victims receive a rape examination following the assault and only about one half of all rape victims who are injured actually receive medical care. Even if the client does not appear to be severely injured, if at all possible, administering a prompt medical screening at a facility offering comprehensive services to rape victims can be important. Medical injuries and complications that may not be immediately apparent need to be ruled out. Furthermore, the results of a prompt medical examination, performed by physicians who are trained in assessing and treating rape victims, can be an important component of any prosecution of the rapist.

Koss et al. (1991) found that almost one third of the women who receive treatment in trauma centers report oral and anal penetration as well as vaginal contact:

> Rape-related injuries include minor and major abrasions or contusions to the head, neck, and face (50%), or involve the extremities (33%) or the trunk region (15%). Half of rape victims seen in trauma centers have some degree of vaginal and perineal trauma. The incidence of significant vaginal tears is 15% with 1% requiring surgical repair. (p. 1)

Genital injuries, as may be expected, are more common in older women victims than in younger ones.

Long-term medical complications include gastrointestinal complaints, as found by A.W. Burgess and Holmstrom (1974) and Koss et al. (1991). In the latter study, among a sample of women seen at a university-based gastroenterology clinic, almost one half (44%) reported some type of sexual or physical victimization as a child or adult. Frequent nausea, gagging, vomiting, diarrhea, and constipation are common responses when a woman's body has been violated. These symptoms often last long beyond the direct connection with the assault. Women who had the worst histories of victimization had the most pain symptoms. A large number of women (40%) who seek medical treatment for premenstrual syndrome and chronic pelvic pain also report childhood or adult victimization experiences. Many reproductive tract complications are not reported to doctors because women find them more annoying than medically significant. Such reactions might include spotting between monthly menses and involuntary uterine contractions.

Koss et al. (1991) also suggested that sexual victimization may be considered an etiologic agent for psychogenic seizure patients. Multidisciplinary pain clinics reported that more than 50% of their patients who were referred for chronic pain (e.g., headache, back pain, facial pain, temporal mandibular joint disorder, and bruxism) had sexual and physical abuse in their histories and that more than 66% of those referred to a pain clinic for chronic headaches reported such a history. Finally, all kinds of stress-related chronic illnesses that involve the immune system seem to be associated with high frequencies of sexual and physical abuse histories among women. Koss et al. suggested that the interrelation with other negative behavioral adaptations to abuse such as increased alcohol consumption, increased cigarette smoking, poor dietary habits, and frequent sleep interruptions may also account for the poorer physical health of rape victims.

Koss et al. (1991) found that sexually transmitted diseases (STDs) are estimated to occur in up to 30% of rape victims. These STDs can come from 15 different organisms. Gonorrhea, chlamydia, neisseria, trichomonal infections, and syphilis are the most commonly seen; hepatitis B and human immunodeficiency virus (HIV) are life threatening consequences. Herpes, candida, and other STDs that are also passed by intercourse and other sexual conduct should also be of concern. Koss et al. found that fear of contracting acquired immunodeficiency syndrome (AIDS) was spontaneously mentioned by 26% of rape victims interviewed soon after the sexual assault. She found that rape resulted in pregnancy in 5% of the cases reported.

The fear of STDs is a major concern for women who are sexually assaulted. Yet a recent national study, as reported by Koss et al. (1991), indicates that 73% of those who sought medical intervention (which is a significantly lower number than those who are raped) did not receive any information or testing for exposure to HIV, and 39% received no information about or testing for other STDs (e.g., herpes and candida). The fear of infection from the HIV or AIDS is a relatively new one, but, given the spread of this deadly disease through the heterosexual community, not an unwarranted one. Appropriate medical testing and follow-up treatment should be encouraged by the therapist. Equally important, however, is the therapist's willingness to help women sort through their fears so that they can learn how to take steps to deal with them in a rational and appropriate way without succumbing to the overwhelming feeling of helplessness that can follow such a traumatic event.

Psychological Impact

Sexual assault can produce a psychological reaction that was first labeled *rape trauma syndrome* (RTS) by A.W. Burgess and Holmstrom (1974) and that is now considered a subcategory of the PTSD. Burgess and Holmstrom examined thousands of women seen postrape in a busy Boston city hospital and found consistent psychological reactions. Over the years, these symptoms were noted in empirical research that included women who did not report their assaults to anyone besides the researchers and those who had experiences that met the legal definitions of rape but did not identify themselves as rape survivors. These data have helped shape both rape crisis interventions and longer-term therapeutic strategies (Ellis, 1983; Foa, Steketee, & Olasov, 1989; Kilpatrick & Veronen, 1983; Koss, 1985; Koss & Harvey, 1991; Rothblum, Foa, & Hoge, 1988). (Later in this chapter, the section titled PTSD Diagnostic Criteria covers the symptoms suffered by rape victims.)

The factors most commonly associated with rape victims, in addition to the short- and long-term medical complications detailed earlier, include the use of alcohol and drugs in attempts to eradicate the pain and intrusive memories, eating disorders including bulimia and anorexia, and a vulnerability that prevents adequate defense against other subsequent violence. Serious anxiety disorders, including panic attacks and phobias, are sometimes associated with the aftermath of rape, especially when conditioned stimuli are not addressed. Sometimes the client who experiences an acute anxiety attack becomes so fearful of a repeat experience that, unconsciously, she literally scares herself into an anxiety disorder by becoming anxious about the fear of uncontrollable anxiety. A separate diagnosis for anxiety or panic disorder may be warranted with specific treatment strategies incorporated within the survivor therapy program. Foa et al. (1989) and Rothblum et al. (1988) have designed some of the most effective interventions in this area for rape victims.

Self-Blame

The attributions that the victim makes regarding the rape—particularly concerning her own responsibility or blameworthiness—can be a crucial determinant of recovery. There are significant factors that support the victim's tendency to blame herself for the rape. A major factor is the cultural tendency to "blame the victim" (Ryan, 1971). Another is the tendency to blame women (who are significantly more likely than men to be victims of rape) more than the male perpetrators (Howard, 1984; Walker, 1989a). Another major factor involves the view held by some professionals that assuming responsibility may be adaptive for the victim, enabling her to regain a sense of control over events. Janoff-Bulman (1979; see also Janoff-Bulman & Lang-Gunn, 1988), for example, hypothesized, on the basis of her research, that behavioral (as opposed to characterological) self-blame was adaptive and positively associated with recovery. She found that almost three out of every four (74%) rape victims engage in self-blame. Behavioral self-blame (69%) tended to be much more typical than characterological (19%) self-blame.

Meyer and Taylor (1986; see also Taylor, 1990), however, found that both behavioral and characterological self-blame were associated with poorer outcome. Similarly, in a carefully designed study, Frazier (1990) found that most victims do not blame their behavior, their character, or themselves in general and that victims rate the causes of the rape as generally external. Thus, although many victims blame themselves to some degree, they appear to blame other factors more than they blame themselves. Frazier further found that all types of self-blame were associated with greater depression after a rape. Rose (1986) examined the ways in which self-blame as an adaptive strategy has profound and pervasive effects.

Burt and Katz (1987, 1988) studied 113 rape victims to determine their attributions, coping strategies, and the effects on their recovery. They identified five major types of coping strategies: (a) *avoidance*, in which the women used strategies to make the rape go away in their minds; (b) *expressive*, in which feelings were encouraged; (c) *nervous/anxious*, in which high anxiety symptoms predominated the response; (d) *cognitive*, in which women tried to get back to business by intellectually processing the trauma; and (e) *self-destructive*, in which high risk-taking, self-inflicted cuts, and substance abuse predominated. Those who used the expressive and cognitive styles, learning to express their feelings and get on with their lives, tended to make the best recoveries from rape.

In their empirical research evaluating rape victims' cognitive attitudes toward rape, Burt and Katz (1987, 1988) found that victims used self-blame as a defense, perhaps as a way to attempt to regain feelings of control, omnipotence, competence, and predictability in themselves and others. The data in their study indicated that only by directly dealing with self-blame and resolving it could recovery be achieved.

Taylor's (1990) research also provided examples of simple types of self-blame that can seriously interfere with the healing process. Note the negative consequences of self-blame explicit in the following statement by a rape victim: "I am very careful about where I park my car now; if I were ever raped again while in a parking lot, I could never stop blaming myself for it" (Taylor, 1990, p. 820).

Additional types of self-blame can center around the woman's involuntary responses to the actual assault itself. Some women experience involuntary sexual arousal during the rape. The normal physiological response of sexual arousal, of course, is not always under conscious control, and may occur even when the woman is in fear for her life. Arousal under these circumstances can cause great confusion, anger at her body for betraying her, and self-blame for experiencing any physical relief. This aspect is difficult for a victim to discuss, especially with a male therapist. Therapists must use great sensitivity in choosing whether and when to introduce this topic; addressing it in an awkward, ill-timed, or sudden manner may strike the victim as voyeurism or victim-blaming.

Powerlessness

Research on reactions to rape, illness, and other tragic or near-tragic events reveals that one of the most common reactions experienced by victims is a feeling of loss of control. Rape violates the victim's sense of control over her entire life, not just her body. Taking her sexually without her consent affects extremely personal and private aspects of her body, mind, and spirit. The victim's ability to avoid, escape, or resist is overpowered. The trauma of this event can be profound and can permeate her entire sense of efficacy or control.

Feeling out of control can produce emotional problems such as depression and an inability to take action in other areas of life that remain controllable. The assault on personal control is all the more threatening because research on reactions to stressful events so clearly indicates that beliefs in control promote successful adjustment. The loss of control engendered in victimization, then, can have far-reaching consequences. (Koss, 1990a; Koss & Harvey, 1991; Taylor, 1990). It is not uncommon for rape victims to feel so disempowered that they fail to take normal precautions to prevent other attacks. Interviewed rapists (Groth, 1979) remarked that they often could pick out a former rape victim as their target by the way she walked and failed to protect herself, making her an easier victim than someone who might be more likely to put up a struggle. Rape victims often feel caught between their natural inclination to try to resist and police cautions that to do so could cause them to be more seriously injured. The results of Bart and O'Brien's (1985) study, showing the more frequent success of resistance than police might acknowledge, may also be due to the difference between those who have already been assaulted and those who have not. However, a woman should never be held responsible for her victimization; rape victims do not "ask for it" if they have lost the ability to protect themselves because of prior attacks. Instead, victims must be encouraged to use common precautions again as they move into survivor roles while not blaming themselves for being harmed should they not be ready to do so. Organized programs such as street fighting, self-defense, and model-mugging types of classes are examples of such reeducation. Effective therapy must address rebuilding an abused woman's strengths, including the feeling of reempowerment.

Feminist Analysis of Rape

Burt and Katz's(1988) research suggests that a victim's belief in her culture's rape myths influences her recovery. Therefore, it would be useful for therapists to be familiar with such myths and to introduce them into treatment when needed. Many of these myths, such as victim responsibility, self-blame, and stigmatization, have been challenged by the feminist movement as being part of the social milieu that facilitates rape. Brownmiller (1975), in one of the earliest feminist historical treatises on rape, claims that rapists are tolerated by other males because they serve as "shock troops" to keep all women in line, obedient and monogamous to one man in order to avoid sexual abuse by others. Jones (1981), another feminist historian, views men who beat and rape their wives as the "home guards." One main conclusion of the feminist analysis of rape is particularly worth noting: Men must become more active in preventing rape. Feminists need to work directly with men to help them understand the terrible humiliation and psychological damage that sexually assaulted women experience, damage that may prevent them from ever being healthy sexual partners for men who love them and whom they love in return.

Reviewing the impact of rape from the feminist political perspective can help practitioners to understand the depth of pain and anger felt by women that can be directed for a time toward all men. Like many oppressed groups who must make accommodations to live with those who may also be viewed as their oppressors, some women mask this rage and others express it quite openly. As Fodor (1985), among others, pointed out, women are punished for expressing anger and rage at men. Effective therapy both validates this anger and eventually assists women in focusing it more narrowly on the specific target while also mobilizing that anger to change the larger society. Many male therapists seem to fear this generalized anger and try to shut it down before the client is finished processing it. As discussed in chapter 1, focusing a woman's anger can be seen as successful only when the woman perceives a sense of reempowerment and control over her life.

SPECIFIC ASSESSMENT ISSUES

PTSD Diagnostic Criteria

The PTSD diagnosis, of which RTS is considered a subcategory, is not truly adequate for the entire set of symptoms often seen in rape victims who seek therapy to heal from a sexual assault. This section applies the symptoms for PTSD as listed in the *Diagnostic and Statistical Manual of Mental Disorders,* third edition, revised (*DSM–III–R;* American Psychiatric Association, 1987; see Appendix C) to rape victims. Previews of the fourth edition of the *DSM* criteria suggest that there will be few substantive changes.

Recurrent and Intrusive Memories

The criteria in this category of responses are so typical of rape victims that most victims report experiencing all four of the following criteria at some point in the healing process.

Intrusive memories. Crisis stage victims are often overwhelmed by intrusive memories of the assault and associated images of fear and anger. They report ruminating about the event, often seeing what happened in their mind's eye when they are at rest or engaged in unrelated activities. Long-term survivors may unknowingly perpetuate the psychological effects of the rape because of the constant rumination and reexperiencing of the trauma. This tendency to have recurrent, intrusive memories of the sexual assault may occur as a conditioned response or without any identified stimulus. In these cases, cognitive therapy techniques are the most appropriate forms of survivor therapy strategies to initiate during the assessment period and at the beginning of treatment.

Absence of dreams. Rape victims often do not dream during the acute phase, frequently waking themselves up when rapid eye movement sleep begins to occur. As they begin to move from the acute to long-term resolution phase, their dreams begin to return. Often there are indirect dreams of the attack, usually of other forms of danger rather than the assault incident itself. Many report symbols and metaphors in their dreams that may require interpretation.

Reexperiencing the trauma as though the assault is recurring. This is reported quite commonly among rape victims. For those who have been multiple victims, particularly incest survivors, dissociative responses are common, although flashbacks occur too. In women with previously established relationships, the act of sex may precipitate the feeling of the rape recurring. Treatment strategies include helping the client gain control over the reexperiencing of the trauma so that healing is not continuously interrupted. Many clients must alter previously enjoyed sexual activities or even move from their homes in order to reduce this symptom.

Anniversary reactions and other conditioned responses. Adverse responses to stimuli associated with the rape are fairly common in rape victims. For example, driving by the parking lot where the rape occurred, entering a crowded elevator that is similar to the one from which a woman was abducted, or seeing a man wearing a pair of gloves similar to those of the man who attacked her may all bring about extreme psychological distress, sometimes without the woman understanding its direct association with the rape. A woman who decided to bear and raise a child that resulted from a rape had to find ways of separating her memories of the rape from the experience of loving the child.

High Avoidance Symptoms

It is not uncommon for rape victims to demonstrate symptoms similar to situational depression following the traumatic event or events. Repeat victims may be more prone to such depression, although the research data are not clear about specific etiology (McGrath, Keith, Strickland, & Russo, 1990). In any case, if depression symptoms persist, it is appropriate to make an additional diagnosis of the type of affective disorder that best describes the symptoms in addition to the PTSD diagnosis.

Forgetting the trauma. Many rape victims make great efforts to avoid thinking or experiencing feelings about the rape, although "forgetting" may also take place through the unconscious use of defense mechanisms such as denial, minimization, repression, and psychogenic amnesia. Some victims go to the extreme of actually forgetting that the assault occurred at all until something else brings back the memories. For example, one client "forgot" the date rape that she experienced while in college until her sister was sexually abused and the client was called on to help her.

Avoiding situations that remind the victim of the trauma. Many rape victims avoid activities or situations that arouse recollections of the trauma. One woman dropped out of school after she was assaulted on the campus because she could not tolerate the extreme anxiety attached to simply attending classes.

Psychogenic amnesia. Some type of memory loss is often experienced by rape victims, particularly those who experience repeated assaults. Some victims initially remember many details as a way to keep themselves hypervigilant and protect themselves from another such incident, but then "forget" once they begin to feel safer.

Apathy and loss of interest. Many rape victims become less interested in previously significant activities, particularly if they are associated with exposure to potential danger. When shame and self-blame have not yet been worked through, victims are more likely to avoid social activities.

Estrangement from others. Rape victims, as the myths discussed earlier imply, feel like they are "damaged" or "soiled" goods; this feeling causes them to become detached and estranged from others. They may become more sensitive to slights in friends, hostile to those who do not want to treat them as though they are special for long periods after the assault, or even less trusting simply because their perception of the world has been shattered.

Restricted range of affect. Many rape victims demonstrate a restricted range of affect. Some are quite masterful at covering up their real feelings and continuing to put on a good outer face, and as a result their affect is not easily ascertained, even by experienced counselors. For many rape victims, particularly those who continue to function well in day-to-day life, it is important to look good and continue their lives in as normal a way as is possible. These women may eventually break down because of the excessive stress that such coping methods can cause.

Sense of doom. Rape victims may become terrified that the offender will return and repeat their abuse, especially when the offender remains at large and may or may not continue to harass them. Many victims truly believe that they will be killed or that they will have a shorter life span than others. Sometimes this leads to more accidents or illnesses. In addition, they often dread exposure to STDs, including AIDS.

High Arousal Symptoms

High anxiety, including specific panic attacks and anxiety disorders, are commonly experienced by rape victims. High anxiety—such as extreme phobic reactions to people, settings, events, items, or activities that are associated in any way with the rape—can be almost entirely debilitating. In any form they are acutely painful, distressing, and disruptive. Often these symptoms increase during the first few weeks after the sexual assault, causing the victim even more anxiety about the anticipated emotional response. This "fear of anxiety" can become a full-blown panic attack without supportive treatment and is more typical of RTS than other PTSD subcategories that include repeated abuse. If these high anxiety symptoms persist over time, then a separate additional diagnosis should be considered.

According to the *DSM–III–R*, sufferers of PTSD will exhibit at least two of the following symptoms of increased arousal:

Difficulty in falling or staying asleep. Both are typical of the sleep disturbance reported by rape victims. If the woman was raped in her own bed, it becomes even more difficult to relax sufficiently to get a good night's rest. The debilitating effects of poor sleep patterns make coping with other symptoms even more difficult.

Irritability or outbursts of anger. Most rape victims do not understand why they are so irritable or why they cannot stop themselves from taking out their anger on their loved ones. Some enter therapy as a way to preserve relationships that often are under strain from repeated yet unexpected attacks. For example, one woman who was raped while out jogging by herself during a vacation with her husband found herself snapping at him each time he tried to be helpful. With therapy she began to understand that she had underlying, though perhaps unrealistic, feelings of anger and blamed him because he had not gone running with her and did not find her sooner. Her anger at her supportive parents also frightened her until she realized that she blamed them for the reactions of other family members. She attributed these reactions to her parents' inability to explain the situation to them properly. It is often the strength of their own anger and the persistence of their irritability that causes rape victims the most difficulty. Obviously, it is easier and safer to be angry with supportive family and friends than at the frightening offender.

Difficulty in concentrating. Rape victims report difficulty in concentration and attention, and other forms of cognitive confusion that often affect their ability to complete tasks that call for intellectual abilities that were not impaired prior to the assault.

Hypervigilance. Rape victims, particularly during the acute phase, see images of the rapist in many other men. Often, they recognize something about a man's hair, the way he holds an umbrella, the color of his shirt, a car that is the same model as their attacker's, or some other small detail and conjure a frightening image of the rapist from that information. During this period, most rape victims cannot tolerate being in the company of any man who is not a familiar part of their lives. After time, more information is required before the danger cues become activated.

Exaggerated startle response. This response lasts a long time in women who are raped and usually occurs in combination with other responses of hypervigilance. It sometimes can interfere with spontaneity and playfulness in intimate relationships.

Physiological reactions to events that symbolize or resemble an aspect of the rape. These reactions are commonly experienced by most rape victims, as noted earlier in the sections describing medical and health issues.

Other Common Sequelae or Symptoms

Certain aspects of the consequences of rape and of the therapeutic issues they present may be relatively common, even though each victim's situation is unique. Perhaps more than victims of any other type of abuse, those who have been sexually assaulted demonstrate an overlay of chronic physical symptoms as well as psychological distress. Often those who have buried the memories of a rape find themselves with psychological symptoms that have no conscious cognitive determinant. Sometimes their bodies remember what happened to them better than their minds do. As discussed earlier, gastrointestinal and reproductive tract complaints are common among sexual assault victims. The pain is a constant reminder that their bodies do not work as well as before.

Sexual dysfunction complaints are also common in rape victims. These include difficulties in enjoying sex even with loving partners. It is common to see all kinds of physical difficulties with sexual intercourse as well as high anxiety and specific fears of pain.[2]

Suicide

The suicidal risk of the rape victim must be carefully assessed and monitored. For some rape victims, suicidal thoughts are related to depression. For others, ending their lives may seem the only way to escape the acute anxiety

---

[2]Detailed examinations of various sequelae and therapeutic issues or approaches have been presented by Atkeson, Calhoun, Resick, and Ellis, 1982; Bowie, Silverman, Kalick, and Edbril, 1990; A.W. Burgess and Holmstrom, 1974; Burt and Katz, 1987, 1988; Forman and Wadsworth, 1983; Frazier, 1990; B. Gilbert and Cunningham, 1986; Koss and Burkhart, 1989; McGregor, 1985; Moscarello, 1990; Roehl and Gray, 1984; Rose, 1986; Sutherland and Schuerl, 1970; Taylor, 1990; and Whiston, 1981. The reader is referred to those sources for more extensive discussion than is provided in this chapter.

and panic or the terrorizing cognitions (e.g., flashbacks, nightmares, intrusive thoughts) associated with the rape. For still others, suicide may seem an expiation for the guilt and shame they are experiencing; they feel that they are so worthless, culpable, or disgusting that they deserve to die. Victims of multiple sexual assaults may be particularly vulnerable to suicide. Ellis, Atkeson, and Calhoun's (1982) study of women who were victims of multiple sexual assaults found that more than half (52%) had made a serious attempt to take their lives. Especially in light of the possibility that distress and dysfunction may become worse during the acute phase, it is important to reassure the assault victim that these effects worsen because of the need to reexperience the rape and work through the terrorizing feelings and that this is part of the healing process.

CLINICAL PRESENTATION

This section discusses the long-term reactions to rape that are more analogous to the PTSD that comes with the presentation of at least 1 month or more of the symptoms. However, in most long-term RTS reactions, the chronic phase does not begin for 2 months or longer. In fact, Kilpatrick and Veronen (1983) found that rape victims took an average of 18 months to heal from psychological symptoms usually caused by the sexual assault itself. The maximum amount of heal-ing was expected within that period, unless there was outside assistance beyond immediate crisis intervention during the recovery period. (For information about helping acute rape victims, see chapter 13.)

Therapy, Interventions, and Collaborative Approaches

Once the acute postrape crisis and emergency needs of the patient have been addressed, the therapist and client can attend to the more enduring and the delayed-onset effects of rape. Although certain general trends have been reported in the literature, it is crucial to remember that each rape victim is a unique individual who experienced a unique assault (whatever similarities it may share with other rapes) and that she will suffer consequences and attempt recovery within the unique context of her own life. Nevertheless, the general trends reported in the literature may be reassuring to some women. For example, during the acute postrape phase (see, e.g., A.W. Burgess & Holmstrom, 1974), which may take about 4 to 6 weeks, some immediate symptoms may become more intense and other symptoms may begin to emerge.

Some women report virtually no memories or images of the rape immediately after the attack. Cognitively, such women may be experiencing a form of shock in which traumatic images are protectively blocked from consciousness because they would be too painful and overwhelming (in a manner similar to the physical numbness that shock can impose immediately after a car wreck: A person who has sustained numerous serious injuries can be conscious and yet unaware of pain). With the passage of time, however, the protective cognitive blockage begins to yield so that healing can occur. As a result, the victim may begin to experience terrifying nightmares, intrusive images, unbidden thoughts, and flashbacks about the rape. This acute phase, when distress and dysfunction may grow worse and new symptoms may appear, can be both frightening and demoralizing to a rape victim. It can be reassuring to the victim if she is told that this phase is one that often occurs in the weeks and sometimes months after a rape has happened or is acknowledged.

In some instances, the client who has sought emergency services from a rape trauma center may have begun counseling or therapy at the center and may desire to continue therapeutic work there. Some centers, however, are not equipped to provide longer term contact with and services to victims. King and Webb (1981), for example, found that rape crisis centers tend to provide exceptional services during the initial response to the rape. Their study of 6,596 victims from 17 centers, however, identified potential problems in the areas of ongoing counseling and follow-up services. Only 62% of the victims received one follow-up contact by the center; 33% received 2–5 follow-up contacts; and 8% received more than 5 contacts.

In some cases, it is possible for the client to continue working with her therapist and also receive rape crisis counseling from a special center. It is the therapist's responsibility to make contact with the rape counselor and to be alert for signs of confusion, triangulation, or other potential problem areas that can occur when a client is working with two different therapists. This may take some sensitivity on the part of the therapist, especially if there are differences in theoretical orientation or if the therapist is embarrassed that she or he does not know as much about rape trauma as does the rape counselor.

"Hidden" Rape Victims

There are many women who have survived a rape that occurred many years earlier, did not report it, and did not seek therapy at the time of the trauma. They are often called the "hidden" rape victims or survivors. Later, sometimes 20 or 30 years later, they seek therapy for the reduction of high levels of anxiety and depression that are vaguely described as slowly increasing over the years without any specific incident to which they seem to be related. In these cases, the anxiety and depression must be considered to arise directly from the breaking through of emotions connected with the rape that occurred long ago. Treatment in these cases must first address the psychological issues the woman faces as a rape victim, rather than assuming that other diagnoses are primary.

Occasionally, a hidden victim deals successfully with the sexual assault at the time that it occurs, but finds that some recent event has brought it back into her consciousness, necessitating a new round of therapy with some focus on the residuals from the rape. Each successive trauma brings parts of previous traumas into the mind, causing an interaction effect that must be worked through in the new treatment intervention. It is easy for the clinician to miss the influence of old abuses on current issues and often the client does not want to dredge up old, painful memories. In this situation, it is important for the therapist not to negate the work the victim performed in the past to survive the sexual abuse. Instead, the therapist must help the client understand that she is a different person today, simply by virtue of her additional life experiences, and therefore the old trauma must be revisited and resolved in the context of her new growth.

Most rape victims seek therapy at the time the sexual assault is experienced or later on when there are other, seemingly unrelated problems. Survivor therapy deals with the client's issues in the cognitive, affective, and behavioral domains, attempting to reach some congruence between these three essential areas of experience. One of the first and most important tasks of therapy with rape victims who either have not yet begun to heal or have only been able to partially integrate the traumatic experience into their lives is to assess the cognitive meanings assigned to the abuse and attempt to restructure those meanings to reflect a new approach. Although this task may begin as an intellectual exercise, it helps establish that the client is not "crazy," that she is able to think for herself, and that she does have some control over how the uncontrollable abuse has affected her.

Recognition and Acknowledgment of the Rape

As noted in other sections of this chapter, rape victims (as well as large portions of society) may fail to recognize that certain behaviors constitute rape. In such cases, the fact that a rape has occurred is discounted, dismissed, or denied. Survivor therapy strategies deal directly with the abuse experienced by the victim, validate those experiences, and offer sympathetic understanding, but do not attempt to do anything that might be misinterpreted as victim-blaming or even slightly negative toward the woman's behavior. It must be stressed that she did not deserve to be raped and that it is the perpetrator's responsibility not to engage in nonconsensual sex. Furthermore, no matter when the rape occurred, it is the responsibility of the therapist who is using survivor therapy techniques to discover the meaning that the victim assigns to the assault, how she has integrated it into her everyday functioning, and how she views its impact. Knowing the victim's strengths helps the therapist to convince her that she will survive the painful emotional reexperiencing of the trauma and that, in the end, she will become a survivor.

It is crucial that therapists understand clearly and specifically the range of conditions under which rape can occur and the range of behaviors that constitute the sexual abuse of a woman. Adequate understanding enables therapists to help clients explore, understand, and make informed decisions about what has been done to them. Simply validating the fact that the client was indeed raped may be the most important therapeutic action that a practitioner can take. The changes in cognitive beliefs that help women become survivors include the following:

Rape is rape regardless of any characteristics (age, occupation, family background, etc.) of the victim, regardless of what she may have been wearing, regardless of the setting, and regardless of her prior behavior (e.g., kissing the man who would eventually force her to engage in sexual acts against her will or even engaging in sexual intercourse at a prior time but refusing this time). No prior set of circumstances or conditions legitimizes forcing a woman to engage in sex against her will.

Rape is rape even when the woman does not struggle or attempt to resist. Research suggests that men may be more likely than women to consider that a rape is less serious (or perhaps is not in fact rape) if the woman does not struggle. Scroggs (1976) found that male subjects, asked to evaluate a rape scenario, believed that the rape was less serious when the victim offered little or no resistance. Female subjects believed the reverse. The female subjects, according to the investigator, believed that the more terrifying the aggressor, the more paralyzed the victim would be and the less she would dare to resist. Failing to recognize the seriousness of forced sex in which the victim does not resist may also result from a failure to understand how resistance might affect the perpetrator. "Physical resistance will discourage one type of rapist but excite another type. If his victim screams, one assailant will flee, but another will cut her throat" (Groth, 1979, p. 8).

Rape is rape even when the perpetrator is a close friend, acquaintance, or lover. "The majority of victims are raped by acquaintances and most are unable to define the event as a rape" (Koss & Burkhart, 1989, p. 28; see also Estrich, 1987; Frieze, 1986). Bart and O'Brien (1985) found that those victims who fought back were less likely to suffer serious psychological (and often physical) injury, despite police data that suggest that in some cases fighting back may be even more dangerous (Bart & O'Brien, 1985).

Rape may also be rape even when penetration, intercourse, or ejaculation does not occur or it cannot be proved in a court of law. Each state has its own set of laws defining unwanted sexual acts as different degrees of sexual assault or rape, as mentioned earlier. Although unwanted touching of a woman's genitals or breasts may be legally prosecuted at a lower crime level than forced oral, anal, or vaginal intercourse, the psychological effects may be equally serious if the victim believed that more was to come and something stopped the assailant from going further. There are some data to suggest that those women who additionally experience the rape as life-threatening have more difficulty recovering. A national study, as reported by Koss et al. (1991), found that half of all rape victims feared being seriously injured or killed during the assault. Thus, the psychotherapist needs to know some details about what happened in order to assess potential psychological impact. Care must be taken not to appear to be perversely interested, particularly if the psychologist is male or is sexually aroused by the recounting of details. Compassion, interest, validation, and sincere comments about the woman's courage for surviving and retelling the story are often most helpful.

Rape is rape even when the perpetrator is a spouse, although some states still exempt spousal rape from the laws criminalizing rape (Estrich, 1987; Finkelhor & Yllo, 1985). The form in which the marital rape occurs may be relevant to the treatment needs of the victim. Finkelhor and Yllo (1985) identified three basic types of marital rape: (a) *battering rapes,* in which beatings are combined with or prior to nonconsensual sex; (b) *force-only rapes,* in which the man uses only the force required to make his wife engage in sex with him; and (c) *obsessive rapes,* in which the man's sexual interests are bizarre or perverse (in a way unwanted by his spouse), and he forces his wife to engage in them.[3] The therapist should be sensitive to the fact that it is extremely difficult for some women to discuss sexual assaults by their husbands. Such assaults can occur in an extremely confusing context. The sexual activity may seem to reflect warm and loving feelings as well as hostility, anger, or sadism.

---

[3]Because therapy needs are similar to those suggested for battered women, the therapist working with a victim of marital rape should also be familiar with the material in chapter 3.

Treatment for Anxiety and Avoidance Responses

Avoidance responses associated with RTS include a refusal to leave the home or go anywhere near the scene of the rape (if it occurred outside of the home). Many victims feel better, and experience reduced symptomatology, if they can leave town for awhile, perhaps to visit family or go on a business trip. If the rape occurred in their home or place of work, they may desire to move or change jobs in order to avoid thinking, feeling, or being exposed to memories of the trauma. When these changes are impossible, some women develop depression to numb their extreme feelings. They often restrict their interpersonal relationships, fearing that they are stigmatized by those who know them or even fearful of being hurt by them in some other specific or nonspecific way.

Survivor therapy uses a combination of techniques from other therapies. For some clients, cognitive–behavioral approaches to these avoidance responses have been effective. These approaches include systematic desensitization, cognitive therapy, stress inoculation procedures, and flooding (Forman, 1980; Holmes & St. Lawrence, 1983; Pearson, Poquette, & Wasden, 1983; Steketee & Foa, 1987). Psychodynamic therapy issues, particularly in the recapitulation of interpersonal relationships through the therapy relationship, may also be useful. For many clients, feminist therapy is also important because it encourages reempowerment of the woman (L.S. Brown & Ballou, 1992; Dutton-Douglas & Walker, 1988; Rosewater & Walker, 1985). The attention that feminist therapy pays to the power differential between therapist and client helps to avoid intentional or unintentional victim-blaming that arises from inappropriate questioning about victim protection and safety measures, poor timing of certain therapeutic strategies, and attempts to do too much or too little to assist the victim in her healing. Survivor therapy also recognizes the importance of the ethical issues that affect a victim of violence (Lerman & Porter, 1990) as well as how a woman's race, ethnic and cultural background, sexual orientation, and able-bodiedness shape her experience of rape and the recovery process (L.S. Brown & Root, 1990).

Physiological Reactions

A.W. Burgess and Holmstrom (1974) were the first to detail some of the accompanying physical reactions in the gastrointestinal and reproductive systems that occur during the therapy process. Some women have a constant nausea, gagging, and vomiting response, especially if the man forced his penis into the victim's mouth. Diarrhea and constipation are also common, as is rectal bleeding if there was forced anal penetration. Often fissures are opened that cause great pain even if they are not medically serious. Stomachaches accompany many of these symptoms or are experienced in isolation. Vaginal pain, bleeding, and infections also frequently follow a rape, sometimes with increased menstrual pain and bleeding that is similar to endometriosis. These responses may occur even if there was no physical trauma, indicating a close relationship between psychophysiological reactions and rape.

The Koss et al. (1991) research further underscores this point. They found that rape victims use medical services more frequently for at least 5 years after a rape than they did prior to it. They have more serious medical illnesses, which suggests a link with a depressed immunological system. Kilpatrick's (1990) findings that prior abuse is most likely to predict alcohol or drug abuse in women further suggests that women may be using these substances as a way to self-medicate themselves, particularly if their difficulties are not taken seriously by physicians. A psychologist may be of assistance here by calling the physician so that they can consult each other to treat the woman's physical and mental symptoms in a holistic manner.

Sexual Identity and Behavior

Rape may make a woman fearful and unable to enjoy (or even participate in) sexual activity (cf. Gilbert & Cunningham, 1986). Sexual activity—or anything usually associated with sexual activity—may trigger flashbacks or other reactions to the rape.

The woman's sexual identity and sense of sexuality may be profoundly distorted. If she is heterosexual, she may experience some form of the fear or belief that "all men are rapists." If she is a lesbian, she may not only experience continuing sexual trauma but may also encounter discrimination if she attempts to report the rape or to begin counseling or psychotherapy (Orzek, 1988). Some women use increased sexual activity to avoid any long-term intimacy with someone who might cause pain from overcontrol and humiliation similar to the rape experience. Other women who have never had multiple sex partners use this experience as an excuse to experiment in ways about which they had previously fantasized but never dared to try. The reactions may be different but the meaning is the same; rape victims are terrified that their capacity to respond sexually has been damaged, and they find different ways to find out if this is so. This process can be especially difficult for single women, although at some point during the healing process the woman may become attracted sexually to a particular man and spontaneously move beyond the social anxiety that was caused by the rape.

Survivor therapy attempts to deal with these issues cognitively and with the affect that they produce. It is important for the therapist to dispel misinformation, such as the belief that a rape victim is "spoiled goods," although certainly some people whom the victim encounters will probably hold this ignorant view. The therapist should respect the grief that these attitudes bring to the rape victim, but point out that they are the products of a sexist society.

A second contribution of survivor therapy is to provide optimism that the woman will not always feel the way she does at this particular time. When she feels safer and has regained power and control over her life and her body, she will be surprised by her own natural reactions to a particular man. Many women need to hear repeatedly that sexual assault interferes with the normal psychological arousal response. The recovery process will usually spontaneously restore that internal trust, a trust that will then encourage new, positive relationships with significant men in the woman's life.

Interpersonal Relations

Like other forms of abuse discussed in this book, rape may destroy the most basic trust that a woman has in all the people, men and women, around her and in her ability to be with others without risk of harm. The rape may so disrupt her life that she feels unable to resume her customary friendships, conversations, and social interactions. She may feel so guilty and ashamed that she believes that she is not acceptable company for anyone else. She may feel such acute self-blame that she cannot imagine that other people do not also blame her. In some cultures, young women who are raped on a date often feel they are unworthy for anyone else to marry. Some marry the rapist only to condemn themselves to a lifetime of continued abuse. Women who are raised in homes with a fundamentalist religious view are more prone to this reaction.

As is repeatedly emphasized in this book, there is no single, uniform way to address the problems of all victims. Some who are alienated from others may need a period of relative isolation, even before beginning to work with a therapist. Others may work best with an individual therapist, someone with whom they can build up trust gradually. Still others may benefit most from group treatment, particularly in groups with others who have been similarly victimized. Those who have experienced disruptions in their interpersonal relationships may need a corrective group experience to regain their social competence. This is particularly important for women who do not have a social network of friends who continue to support them through the long recovery period.

Various models of open-ended group therapy, either in conjunction with or instead of individual treatment, have been helpful in the recovery of rape victims (Cryer & Beutler, 1980; Sharma & Cheatham, 1986; Sprei & Goodwin, 1983; Turner & Colao, 1985). Time-limited models may better meet the needs of some victims (Perl, Westin, & Peterson, 1985; Xenarios, 1988). Often, women need individual as well as group therapy in order to continue to work on the unique issues that the crisis of a rape precipitates.

Conjoint Therapy With Spouses

When the rape's consequences include disruption of an intimate relationship with a spouse or other partner, couples therapy may be useful (Earl, 1985). Spouses need to be encouraged to give the woman time to heal. Nonsexual holding, caressing, and support is important to this process. Too much pressure to get back to "normal," including regular sexual relations, has the consequence of invalidating the woman's experience and may cause a fundamental breach in the relationship. Some women may comply, feeling that they are unable to resist, and then may not properly heal from the rape. Many then reexperience the psychological effects of the rape while under other stresses. As with any crisis, recovery from rape gives a woman the opportunity to reevaluate her life and make some changes that may have been unanticipated or even briefly considered prior to the assault. This can cause gulfs in marital relations that may need attention before they widen beyond repair.

Both the rape itself and its consequences may profoundly affect not only the life partner of the victim but also her other loved ones such as family members. In some cases, family therapy may be useful (Figley, 1987, 1990; Lundberg-Love & Geffner, 1989). In others, the affected loved ones may work through their reactions more effectively in individual or group sessions (Bateman, 1989; Finn & Nile, 1984; Gurley, 1986). Rodkin, Hunt, and Cowan (1982), for example, described a support group for men, including husbands, boyfriends, and fathers of victims. These loved ones used the group setting to work through their own feelings of guilt, revenge, jealousy, and anger, and the need to protect the victim. Such groups can help ensure that the rape victim is not made to feel that she must somehow take care of or carry the burden of the reactions of her loved ones.

Rape Crisis Centers

As described in chapter 13, rape crisis centers provide critical support for the victim who has just experienced a sexual assault. Often staffed by trained community volunteers, many of whom are survivors themselves, the center is usually well-respected by police, medical personnel, and other community groups. Psychologists and other trained mental health professionals sometimes provide pro bono services as supervisors, trainers, consultants, or counselors for special needs clients. Private therapists sometimes view these centers as competitive, especially in communities where there are more therapists than therapy clients or dollars for treatment available. Usually working on a sliding scale, these centers provide badly needed self-help and facilitated groups that make it possible for those who do not specifically need psychotherapy to get therapeutic interventions. Often, private therapists can refer their individual therapy clients to one of these groups that then provides adjunct therapeutic intervention. Rape crisis counselors can assist clients in legal situations, medical crises, and location of other resources. Collaboration is frequently positive for both the client and the therapist, although in some cases deficits in training and philosophy make interventions less than successful. Gaining the trust of the rape crisis groups, particularly when there is divisiveness among them, can put the therapist in a position to offer valuable consultation or even training in exchange for the opportunity to receive client referrals when a woman needs further treatment.

Pregnancy Counseling

If a woman becomes pregnant as a result of a rape, counseling needs to address her decision as to whether to terminate the pregnancy. Referral to those who have expertise in helping a rape victim make such a decision may be most effective, especially if the therapist has no special training in this area. Local branches of National Abortion Rights Action League and Planned Parenthood, or private abortion clinics, usually provide such services at a sliding scale fee. In some cases it is appropriate for the therapist to help the woman make such arrangements; in others it may be best to let the woman follow through after making sure she understands her options. Many states have passed or are considering legislation that will limit a woman's choice of abortion unless she promptly reports the rape (see Pennsylvania, Louisiana, and Utah legislation in particular). In some of these cases, a therapist to whom the rape is reported may testify as to the woman's emotional inability to make such a prompt police report. These issues, controversial to begin with, have become quite complicated in the past several years and can make it much more difficult for many practitioners to be helpful to victims.

SUMMARY

Rape is considered a crime of violence using sex as a weapon. Most agree that the goal of the rapist is power and control over his victim through humiliation, coercion, and infliction of pain. Definitions of what constitutes rape have broadened over the past 20 years. Acquaintance or date rape is considered the most common form of sexual abuse, although many women do not recognize or report it. Marital rape is also considered sexual assault, and in many states it is considered a criminal act.

The incidence and prevalence of rape is higher than reported statistics indicate because many women do not report being sexually abused. Research suggests that one out of four women will be raped or sexually abused during their lifetime, most by someone who knows them. Approximately 20% of reported rapes are perpetrated by strangers.

The psychological impact of rape can result in anxiety and depression symptoms, such as sleep disturbances, eating problems, frequent and uncontrollable crying, lack of interest in activities, and high levels of shame and humiliation. Behavioral changes in rape victims include a diminished interest in previously enjoyed activities, changes in interpersonal relationships, and changes in typical routines. Sexually assaulted women often show the symptoms of PTSD, including hypervigilance, recurrent and intrusive memories, and psychogenic amnesia.

Alcohol and drug abuse, neuropsychological complications, and medical problems are all associated with rape victims. A significant increase in visits to physicians and incidence of surgeries occurs in the 5 years following a rape. There are some data to suggest the breakdown of the immunological system in assault victims, causing a greater incidence of stress-related diseases.

Survivor therapy techniques are geared toward helping victims regain a feeling of control after their experiences. The first step is often helping the victim get over blaming herself for the assault. The therapist can then work to restore the woman's independence, trust, and enjoyment of her sexuality. Interpersonal relationships, suicide potential and risk factors, and other factors in client management must also be considered. Important shifts in the mental state of the victim can be achieved by reducing her belief in erroneous rape myths and reducing self-blame. Educational materials, self-help groups with other rape victims, and cognitive restructuring as part of therapy all help to provide such cognitive changes.

Community agencies, volunteer groups, medical and other professionals, rape crisis centers, women's centers, and shelters are all helpful in providing support for the assault victims. The victim's recovery is facilitated when the therapist can work closely with these groups.

Battering

The most frequently asked question about battered women is, Why don't they leave? Until the past 15 years, there were no adequate answers to this question. Even today, many therapists still believe that the abuse will stop if they can only get their client to leave the abusive man. Research demonstrates, however, that leaving does not stop the violence. Instead, it continues, often escalating at the time of separation to life-threatening proportions. Some women have also become so dependent on the batterer that they believe they cannot survive without him. An important point regarding battered women, moreover, is that they may actually be physically safer staying with the abuser, over whom they still have some influence, rather than being alone and unprotected without the ability to calm him down. Many men who batter women stalk and harass them. They do not let the women go. Battered women with young children are often forced to maintain contact with their abuser so that he can spend time with the children. Sometimes, if these women refuse to allow the men to have contact with their children, they are threatened with loss of custody, even though the men have not developed the parenting skills needed to take proper care of children. Women sometimes maintain a relationship with an abusive husband as a way to keep their children.

It is important for the therapist not to make leaving the battering relationship a treatment goal. Rather, the goal must be to live in a violence-free environment. This may be difficult or impossible while living with the abuser, but it may be equally difficult or impossible when living apart.

After delineating the types of abuse to which a battered woman may be subjected, the first section of this chapter looks at typical behaviors of batterers. The following section examines how prevalent these abuses are and who they affect. The section on research details, among other things, a three-part cycle common to battering relationships. Finally, after a discussion of clinical presentation and assessment issues, I close with a look at how clinicians working with battered women are likely to find it necessary to collaborate with other professionals.

OVERVIEW AND DEFINITIONS

Types of Abuse

A battered woman is one who has been physically, sexually, or psychologically abused by a man (or, in a proportionally small number of instances, by a woman) with whom she is in an intimate relationship. An intimate relationship is one in which there is a close, loving, romantic, emotional bond, usually including sex. Women are battered by partners to whom they are married as well as those with whom they live or whom they date. Although most of the reported abuse is inflicted by the man on the woman, there are also reports of women abusing their partners. The goal of woman abuse is usually to exert power and control over the victim. Most physical and sexual abuse is accompanied by psychological intimidation and bullying behavior used to maintain power and control over the woman. The pattern of abuse usually has an obsessional quality to it rather than a lack of control by the batterer.

Physical Abuse

Physical abuse occurs in as many different forms as can be imagined. It frequently ranges from slapping, pushing, shoving, grabbing, punching, hair pulling, shaking, biting, head banging, kicking, throwing bodily, and choking, to using knives, guns, hot objects, cars, and other objects as lethal weapons. The threat of physical abuse is often sufficient to keep control of the woman as long as she is convinced that the man will beat her to get what he wants or punish her for disobeying him and making him angry. Some battered women have been chained to bedposts, locked in houses with the windows and doors nailed shut, kept inside of coffinlike boxes, and held under surveillance at gunpoint. Others have been held hostage with no means of communication or transportation. Still others have access to the telephone and to a car, but their calls are monitored and the mileage is recorded daily. Whether the imprisonment is enforced by physical means or not, most women know that the batterer is willing to use physical force to get what he wants. These women soon learn to obey rather than face the escalating violence that inevitably follows if they fight back. Other battered women do fight back, even though they know that they will be abused even more, perhaps as a way to defend psychologically their sense of self.

Sexual Abuse

Sexual abuse within the context of a battering relationship includes a variety of coerced sexual activities, with or without accompanying physical abuse. The abuser may demand forced oral, anal, or genital sex, insert objects into the woman's vagina or anus, or tie her up and demand sex involving ropes, handcuffs, and so forth. Most battered women report that abusive partners initiate sexual contacts to which the women must respond positively or face a heightened risk of further physical, sexual, or psychological abuse.

Sexual abuse in battering relationships most often occurs along with physical and psychological abuse, although the physical abuse may not occur simultaneously with the forced sex. Sometimes battered women give in to the batterer's unwanted sexual demands as a way to calm him down and protect themselves from further abuse. It is not unusual for battered women to describe some positive sexual experiences as well as other coercive ones with the same man, rarely being able to predict which will occur at a particular time. The coercion and violence that accompanies sex may include forced shaving of pubic hair, mutilating the genitals, stabbing the breasts, brutal anal rapes, holding the woman's head down on the man's erect penis to force oral sex, inserting objects in her vagina and anus, punching her pregnant abdomen, and kicking at the vagina and other vulnerable areas. In some cases women are coerced into sex with other people and sex with children. It is not unusual for the batterer to watch and to film as well as to participate in these sexual activities. Videotapes and pictures, sometimes depicting the woman looking pleased as if she were a totally willing participant, may be used as threats for further coercion. Many battered women suffer recurrent vaginal infections and gynecological problems, even when no overt sexual abuse is reported.

Psychological Abuse

The psychological terror created by the abuse itself does not always correspond clearly with the particular abuse inflicted at any given time. Once serious violence has been used on a woman, she may respond with similar terror to less serious abuse or even the threat of abuse. Violence in the home is similar to other forms of interpersonal violence; it has both carry-over and cumulative effects (Surgeon General's Workshop on Violence and Public Health, 1986). Each successive instance of violence from a loved and trusted partner is magnified by the memory of previous incidents. Thus, many battered women may spend the rest of their lives both fearing additional abuse and seeking to prevent a recurrence. Violence that seems irrational and unprovoked by any clear cause can make women's attempts to avoid future attacks much more desperate.

The woman's attempts to recover from battering and to avoid future victimization, and in some instances to escape from the relationship with the batterer, can be thwarted by the batterer's constant harassment. The batterer may attempt to control virtually every aspect of the woman's life. He may bombard her with questions, tell her exactly how she is to spend her time, and subject her to constant surveillance. It is not unusual for battered women to report being kept awake at night by long harangues designed to tell them what to do or being suddenly awakened to receive trivial, aversive, or frightening demands. Such harassment has obvious debilitating psychological effects, but it can also be physically debilitating (e.g., sleep deprivation). Some forms of harassment such as surveillance (which deprives the woman of privacy), sleep deprivation, and repeated periods of intense, prolonged questioning are similar to those used by torturers and can constitute a form of torture (see, e.g., Pope & Garcia-Peltoniemi, 1991).

Batterers control, intimidate, and terrorize women not only through violence directed specifically at them, but also by creating an atmosphere or environment of expected violence. A battered woman may find that her abusive partner physically abuses family members, tortures or kills the family or neighborhood pets, picks fights with strangers, drives aggressively and dangerously, destroys valued possessions (such as the woman's family heirlooms) in the house as well as anything (such as a garden) in which the woman may take pride and which might make her environment seem more pleasant, familiar, and nurturing. There is a point in most abusive relationships at which the woman recognizes the possibility that she will be killed by the batterer. After that point is reached, the women are much more likely to react to threats or actual violence with a greater sense of terror and understanding of its dangerous consequences. It is not unusual for battered women to contemplate suicide as a way to escape the physical and psychological pain, while exercising what they perceive to be the only aspect of their lives that they can still control: whether they live or die.

Traits of the Batterer

Possessiveness

The batterer often shows no respect for (or, in some cases, no recognition of) the autonomy of the battered woman or, if the abuse occurs in the context of a family setting, for other members of the family. He treats the woman and the family members as if they were his personal property. This sense of possession may place any children present at increased risk for child abuse. Indeed, according to informal estimates from some child protective service groups, approximately 60% of the children in these homes are likely to be physically and sexually abused. If maltreatment is included, then all of them are exposed to abuse.

Sexual Jealousy

Possessiveness also makes many batterers prone to extreme sexual jealousy. Battered women are often falsely accused of wanting sex with others, flirting, dressing provocatively, and engaging in extramarital affairs. Whether or not accompanied by physical abuse, this barrage of unexpected false accusations of intended or actual infidelity is psychologically abusive in itself. In many instances, batterers conduct terrifying inquisitions that create prolonged psychological paralysis and trauma. They may ask questions for which there is no "right" (or acceptable) answer, thus placing the woman in a double bind. If the woman says that the accusations are false, the batterer can claim that she is lying to him. If the woman says that the false accusations are true, the batterer has "proof" that the woman has betrayed him. In either case, the woman is likely to suffer punishment for her answer. If the woman remains silent, the harassment may escalate, and the abuser may begin to batter her until she gives him an answer.

The batterer's jealousy and obsession with the woman's sexuality may cause the woman to go to great lengths to avoid being subjected to false accusations and inquisitions. Such attempts often have a desperate quality to them because the accusations are usually groundless or based on kernels of distorted truth. Virtually any social contact can serve as an occasion for the abuser to become pathologically jealous. Any time the woman is away from home, the abuser may obsessively imagine that she is having an affair. Thus, jealousy, overpossessiveness, and intrusiveness tend to lead to the isolation of the battered woman. She may cease normal social activities, stop seeing her friends and family, and become a prisoner in her own home, sometimes without ever needing to actually lock the door, although it is not unusual for the batterer to lock her in the house without easy access to a telephone. She may even feel that it is too dangerous for her to meet with her therapist on a regular basis, if she is permitted to have one. The abuser attempts to cut her off from "the world at large," from social supports and resources, and from people or organizations to whom she might turn for help, understanding, or solace. If she is permitted social contacts, the abuser controls who they are and monitors all aspects of the contacts. Increasingly isolated, the woman becomes more vulnerable to the abuser.

Batterers may feel jealousy not only about their partner, but also about adolescent daughters. They may punish a daughter's age-appropriate desire to make friends, to date, or to become more independent. Punishment may range from withholding attention and affection to verbal and physical battering. Batterers may impose such isolation in part to ensure that the daughter does not develop friendships with those in whom she might confide about the abuse that she, her mother, or other family members may have experienced. They are also demanding of their son's time and attention. Preferring the "he" man for a son, male children who are less than what their fathers expect can expect the same scorn and ridicule otherwise saved for girls and women. Above all, the batterer demands total loyalty from his family.

INCIDENCE AND PREVALENCE

As with the many forms of woman abuse discussed in this book, epidemiological research can provide only a rough estimate of the occurrence of battering. Victims and perpetrators alike may be reluctant to reveal their experiences in this area, even in the context of an anonymous survey. The phrasing of the questions may be crucial, and any individual study may fail to inquire about relevant (e.g., contextual or situational) factors. More detailed discussion of the research problems and the qualification of findings is provided by Walker (1984a, 1989a). Nevertheless, the available studies suggest that the battering of women in society is not a rare event. Straus, Gelles, and Steinmetz (1980), for example, found that in more than one quarter of all American homes there has been at least one incident of physical abuse during the past year. In a replication study to update incidence and prevalence data, Straus and Gelles (1988) found that 161 out of every 1,000 American families had been experiencing violence during the general period immediately preceding the study. Drawing from her own research and a review of the available studies, Walker (1979, 1984a, 1989a, 1989b, 1989c) estimated that one out of two women will be abused at some point in her life.

Clinical studies suggest a higher incidence and prevalence rate of domestic violence among women who seek psychotherapy services. Carmen, Reiker, and Mills (1984) reviewed psychiatric hospital records and found that more than 60% of the women had a history of physical abuse, although they were not diagnosed or treated specifically for the battering. Often there is a history of multiple forms of abuse that are not carefully documented in intake interviews (Herman, 1992). A battered woman seeking therapy may be reluctant to disclose the battering to the therapist. She may fear that the therapist will not believe her or will blame her, or that the therapist will not maintain confidentiality and that the abuser will ultimately find out that the woman has told a third party about the abuse and will punish or even kill her for breaking the silence. The woman may be concerned about having the abuse made a part of her permanent clinical or medical record. She may fear that the therapist will issue an ultimatum or attempt to force her to take steps to address the problem. The battered woman fears being caught in the middle: endangering herself further and subjecting herself to retribution by the abuser if she follows the therapist's advice. She also may be concerned about encountering disapproval from and perhaps abandonment by the therapist if she fails to act.

The battering of women occurs across all demographic groups. Some research studies have found a greater frequency of battering in homes with multiple problems, in which poverty and other social problems interact (Straus et al., 1980). Other studies have found that there are significant numbers of affluent battered women who do not come to the attention of the usual community resources but may use services specifically for battered women or private psychotherapy (Hansen & Harway, 1993; Hansen, Harway, & Cervantes, 1991; Herman, 1992; Pagelow, 1984; Walker, 1984a, 1984b, 1989a, 1989b).

Battering cuts across educational levels, religious affiliations, and racial and ethnic groups. Battered women who live in rural areas and within minority group enclaves may have less access to services and protection should they choose to terminate a relationship with an abusive man (L. S. Brown & Root, 1990). Lesbian women who report battering in their relationships also must deal with the lack of services when attempting to seek protection (Lobel, 1986).

Professional career women or those with independent financial sources may not have access to the money because of the constant surveillance and control by the batterer. Guilt, desire not to damage the batterer's earning capacity, and fear that they will not be believed because the professional man is less likely to be identified as a batterer, all of these factors can convince middle-class and affluent women not to disclose abuse or seek assistance.

EMPIRICAL AND CLINICAL RESEARCH

The Cycle of Escalating Violence

Clinicians working with battered woman often find two major patterns of violence. First, the violence and psychological manipulation tend to grow more intense, vicious, and frequent. Second, the violence tends to occur in a predictable (although perhaps not to the woman) three-stage cycle rather than as randomly distributed incidents (Walker, 1979, 1984a, 1989b). This cycle begins with a period of *tension building* that does not start until after a long courtship period, with the abuser showing unusually loving behavior. Some time after the woman makes a commitment to the man, the tension begins. The woman often senses that something is wrong, and she may try a number of strategies to calm her partner and defuse the situation. These strategies have some impact on the escalation of the abuse, reinforcing her behavior and belief that she is capable of controlling his violence for him.

The *acute battering incident* occurs during the second stage. The tension is discharged through a violent attack on the woman. This is the shortest period of the cycle, often lasting a few minutes, hours, or at most, days. The woman often recognizes that she has no control over the batterer during this second stage; only he decides when to stop the attack.

The third stage is a period of *loving-contrition* and *absence of tension.* During this third stage, the batterer may offer profuse apologies (as well as indirect apologies and self-serving explanations and excuses), solemn assurances that the attacks will never happen again, and declarations of love and caring for the woman he has just attacked.

The violence occurs in a repetitive cycle. The third stage is followed (sometimes days, weeks, or months later) by another period of increasing tension. This three-stage cycle tends to occur in at least two thirds of battering incidents (not relationships) reported (Walker, 1984a). Often the violence increases as each cycle is repeated. Most of the rewards of the relationship occur during the third stage, which reminds the woman of the earlier courtship period when there was no abuse. The relationship tends to remain fairly stable when the balance between the costs of the abuse and the benefits are similar. As the violence escalates, the cost–benefit ratio begins to shift, and the relationship becomes more unstable. If the woman begins to pull away emotionally or physically, the man may escalate either his charming or his abusive behavior in an attempt to return to stability.

Certain situational and life events may increase the severity and frequency of abuse: pregnancy, presence of infants, presence of teenagers, and other events associated with high levels of unpleasant emotions, stress, and frustration for the abuser. This may include holidays and televised sports, especially football games. Unemployment is frequently associated with battering. It does not appear to cause abuse but may increase its frequency and severity once the violent behavior pattern is present.

It may be useful to obtain detailed information about four specific battering incidents in order to gain a clear understanding of possible patterns to the violent attacks on the woman. The clinician may ask the woman to describe the following: the first incident she can remember, a typical incident (more than one if it appears that there may be several patterns over time), the worst or one of the worst incidents, and the most recent attack. Details about what led up to the abusive incidents (the tension-building period, if present and identifiable)—the specific violence used during the acute battering incident, how the abuse ended, and any apologies or loving-contrition behavior—are helpful in teaching the woman to understand how the dynamics keep her hooked into the relationship.

For women who are still with the abuser, understanding the details of the cycle of violence in which they are caught, as well as recognizing their own reinforcing behaviors, will help in their attempts to stay violence-free. It is interesting that, when most battered women are asked to tell about the worst incident, they usually pick one that has more psychologically humiliating elements than physical abuse. Rarely do battered women discuss sexually abusive incidents unless specifically asked about them. The sexual abuse, however, may indeed be the worst in terms of both humiliation and physical pain.

Battered Women and Violence

Some battered women learn that the only way to defend themselves is by using aggressive behavior against others including the batterer. Although these relationships have been termed *mutual violence* by some (Steinmetz, 1978), such terms may be somewhat misleading or at least incomplete in that they may connote roughly equal degrees of violence inflicted on each other by two people who are fairly matched in terms of their ability to defend themselves. However, a battered woman tends to be less physically strong than her male batterer. Most of the women who do fight back almost always suffer more violence than they inflict. Even those women who fight back verbally are in greater danger of more serious abuse. If the woman threatens or attempts to leave the relationship, she and her children may be more likely to be killed or seriously hurt. Some of these women grew up in violent families and learned to use violence to resolve conflicts. They may need special treatment to help them stop their own violence and deal with their own victimization. Others adopt a tough, streetwise attitude that may hide their vulnerability and victimization. It is important not to form judgments about treatment and diagnosis before these defensive strategies are well understood.

In some instances, a battered woman may inflict violence on other vulnerable members of her family such as young children or aged parents. Sometimes it is defensive behavior, designed to protect herself from further abuse. Sometimes it is intentional violence, designed to gain power or some other advantage. Many of these women were also victims of child abuse.

The more common pattern, however, is for the battered woman to assume the blame for her partner's violent behavior in an attempt to protect herself and others from future episodes of abuse. Often a woman may erroneously take responsibility for starting a battering incident because she said something that she should have known would provoke or anger the man. Most battered women believe that if only they could close their mouth when the man is tense, they would not be battered. Actually, studies suggest that they do not control the man's use of violence; he makes those decisions only on the basis of his mood and needs (Lindsey, McBride, & Platt, 1992; Sonkin et al., 1985).

Clinicians and the lay public alike may hold the stereotypical view that a battered woman will tend to have a history of multiple battering relationships. According to this view, the abused woman seeks out, perhaps unconsciously, a succession of violent partners. Battered women shelters also report that many people hold the same stereotypical view of women who use shelters. The research, however, has not tended to support this stereotype. Pagelow (1984) and Walker (1984a), for example, found that less than 10% of the battered women whom they studied reported more than one adult battering relationship. Researchers have found that batterers who were studied while in treatment programs tended to repeat their behaviors no matter who their female partners were.

Walker (1984a) found that almost two thirds of the battered women whom she studied had either witnessed their fathers batter their mothers or experienced battering as a child. Almost 50% of her sample had been sexually molested or abused as a child. This is somewhat higher than the data for the general population, which suggest that 38% of all women have been sexually abused as children (Russell, 1988). The data support a gender difference in the impact of experiencing early violence on experiencing or inflicting future violence; women tend to be more likely to become victims, whereas men tend to become abusers. The question, Who is the batterer? is often asked if the woman hits back. This becomes even more controversial when the battering couple is composed of two women in a lesbian relationship. Some have suggested that the existence of situations in which women batter women negates the patriarchal model that is used to explain the power and control issues. After all, here is a woman who is abusing another woman—a man cannot be blamed for the abuse. Although that is true, it is important to remember that the single most important marker when analyzing battering relationships is the witnessing or experiencing of abuse in the childhood family home. Most lesbian women were raised in heterosexual homes, some in homes where abuse took place. Female abusers may perceive themselves as vulnerable and have therefore come to identify with and become one with the aggressor as a means of self-protection and defensiveness. Graham and Rawlings (1991) discussed the *Stockholm syndrome* in battered women, which describes this identification with the aggressor as a survival strategy. (See chapter 10 for a more complete discussion of the Stockholm syndrome.) Lobel (1986) provided a more thorough discussion of these issues as they apply to battered lesbian women.

Substance Abuse

Alcohol and drug abuse are commonly associated with battering, particularly the more serious forms of violence. To my knowledge, no data exist to demonstrate causation, although some studies suggest that more than one half of known batterers drink alcohol to excess. Walker (1984a) found that 60% of the battered women reported that their batterers drank to excess frequently; these batterers were intoxicated during at least one of the abusive incidents reported. In a further analysis of these data, Eberle (1982) found that those who reportedly engaged in battering incidents only while under the influence of alcohol made up approximately 20% of the sample, which was consistent with the alcoholism rate in the region in which the study was conducted. However, excessive use of alcohol was found in more than 80% of cases in which a homicide resulted, leading researchers to conclude that assessment of alcohol abuse needs to be part of a lethality assessment (Browne, 1987).

Other chemical dependencies are also reported for men who batter women. The substances that are most frequently associated with violence are cocaine and crack, methamphetamines, and heroin. Sexual abuse is frequently associated with cocaine use, as is sleep deprivation. Again, the data suggest that the violence increases in severity when the batterer is under the influence of these substances.

Less is known about the battered woman's dependence on alcohol and drugs, although the research suggests that it tends to be significantly less than the abuser's. Walker (1984a) found that less than 25% of her sample of women used alcohol to excess, compared with 60% of the men (see Eberle, 1982, for further analysis). A large number of these women reportedly reduced the frequency of their drinking once they were out of the battering relationships. Many of the battered women also reported that they had not been dependent on alcohol prior to the abuse in the relationship. Interestingly, most of these women had alcoholic partners and said that they drank to keep their partners company and reduce the threat of abuse. Others said that they drank to numb their feelings, so that they could better tolerate the battering. Kilpatrick (1990) found that the single most important variable in predicting whether a woman would abuse alcohol or other drugs was if she was sexually abused or physically battered as a child or adult. Taken as a whole, such research strongly suggests that issues of alcohol and drug use should be explored by clinicians working with battered women.

Drug abuse is also not well-documented in research with battered women, although more is known about abuse of prescription drugs than abuse of illegal drugs. Stark and Flitcraft (1988) and Warshaw (1989) found that emergency room physicians were more likely to overprescribe antianxiety and antidepressant medication for battered women than for other patients who came into the emergency room. Reports from battered women shelters indicate that battered women arrive at shelters with numerous psychotropic prescription drugs from family physicians and psychiatrists. This finding has obvious significance when considered in light of Walker's (1984a) findings that battered women tended to be unable to terminate the abusive relationship and protect themselves until they were free of drugs, including prescription drugs. The women said that their ability to think clearly about what they wanted to do was impaired by the various medications.

There is a subgroup of battered women who are known to be substance abusers during pregnancy (Amaro, Fried, Cabral, & Zuckerman, 1990). Most of these women tend to be young, poor, and undereducated. They live in chaotic, dysfunctional, and abusive homes (if they are not homeless), often in the inner city. Information is gathered about these women when they seek treatment either voluntarily or under court order and as the result of drug testing that occurs in inner-city hospitals (Chasnoff, 1990). It is unusual for suburban hospitals or therapists serving more affluent patients to question women about alcohol and drug use or about physical abuse. Thus, it is difficult to estimate the numbers of drug-exposed infants whose mothers have been unable to protect them because of their own battering issues (Gomby & Shiono, 1991). It is also hard to separate the complex effects of violence, substance abuse, poverty, and other environmental conditions on infants (Kronstadt, 1991; Sonderegger, 1991a, 1991b; Zuckerman, 1991).

When women are suffering from both battering and drug addiction or dependence, the treatment plan obviously needs to address both issues as well as their possible interaction (Finkelstein, 1990; Kumpfer, 1991; Turner & Colao, 1985). For example, withdrawal from some chemical substances frequently elicits increased flashbacks, intrusive images, and related memories of the abuse. These painful cognitive phenomena may place the woman at greater immediate risk for relapse. The courts have become quite punitive with abused women who are pregnant and using alcohol or drugs, frequently arresting the woman and ordering her into jail to await the birth of the baby, who is then immediately taken away from the mother (McCollough, 1991; McNulty, 1987/1988; Paltrow, 1990, 1991; Paltrow & Shende, 1990; Pollitt, 1990). Considering the difficulties many drug-exposed babies are known to have in bonding with people, it seems like a non-treatment-oriented public policy such as this one will only create more dysfunction rather than improve the relationship between the baby and mother.

CLINICAL PRESENTATION AND ASSESSMENT ISSUES

Many battered women have no significant psychopathology prior to the abuse and may need a minimum of psychological assistance to return to their previous level of functioning. However, most battered women who seek therapy appear to be suffering from a set of psychological symptoms, called *battered woman syndrome* (BWS), that is commonly seen as a result of the abuse. This syndrome meets the diagnostic criteria for posttraumatic stress disorder (PTSD) as listed in the American Psychiatric Association's (1987) *Diagnostic and Statistical Manual of Mental Disorders,* third edition, revised *(DSM–III–R).* The syndrome includes cognitive disturbances, high avoidance or depression behaviors, and high arousal or anxiety disturbances.

Cognitive and Memory Disturbances

The cognitive disturbances occurring in BWS are much like those seen in other PTSDs. The woman reexperiences the traumatic event or fragments of traumatic events spontaneously or in association with a familiar stimulus. Time sequences may be distorted. Abusive events may merge, telescope, or become confused. Fear or anticipation of battering may prompt flashbacks of past abuse. Nightmares may contain elements of the trauma, often reflective of the woman's fear that she will do something to set off the man's anger and precipitate a violent reaction.

Other cognitive disturbances include mental confusion that may resemble a thought disorder. The disordered thinking may serve a protective function, helping to shield the woman from a constant, pervasive, and intense awareness of the likelihood or inevitability of the next violent attack. One of the most valuable interventions a therapist can provide is to offer reassurance that what the woman is experiencing—however strange it may be—is a common and understandable reaction to the events she has experienced and to the situation in which she has been living.

Battered woman syndrome can also include cognitive disturbances in the area of attention. A battered woman may find it difficult to attend to various aspects of her physical and social environment or to her inner self. Sometimes her attention may involuntarily focus on either external (e.g., some aspect of the room she is in) or internal (e.g., a memory, a waking dream) fragments. This intense selective cognitive focus may bring about a dissociative state, and the woman may appear to enter a mild trance. Again, this cognitive function may serve a protective function, enabling the woman to reduce (at least temporarily) the degree of psychological and, when she is being battered, physical pain that she is experiencing. This dissociative trance is similar to a mild hypnotic state induced by recognition of the impending danger. Those battered women who have previously experienced abuse as a child tend to be more likely to enter dissociative states. In more moderate to severe dissociative states, there may be associated memory loss and an "out-of-body" type experience in which the woman describes watching herself being beaten by the abuser.

Trauma theorists such as van der Kolk (1985, 1987, 1988) suggest that biochemical changes occur in the brain during these incidents. He made the case for the hyperarousal symptoms of a PTSD being congruent with symptoms of opiate withdrawal and postulated that there is a disturbance in the normal balance between the central andrenergic and opioid systems (van der Kolk, 1985). Walker (1989b) found that repeated intrusive memories and flashbacks could also stimulate dissociative experiences. Waites (1993) has found that dissociative states may be the underpinning of PTSD in women who have abuse histories. Gallers (1993) also tied together dissociation and PTSD in women who have experienced sexual and physical assault. Many battered women understand that most people who have not been battered would probably not consider such trances as common or normal. They may be afraid or ashamed to report such experiences. Therapists must work carefully to ensure that the therapeutic relationship creates authentic, reliable feelings of safety, trust, and support. Only in such a relationship is the battered woman likely to report trance states and other aspects of her experience.

Some research suggests that chronic, repeated abuse brings about a pessimistic cognitive style that is often associated with depression. Seligman (1990) called this "learned helplessness." Those who have developed learned helplessness are not "helpless" as the name might suggest, but they may be unable to anticipate that their behavior will affect events in any reasonable, reliable, or systematic way (Walker, 1978, 1979, 1984a, 1989b). Both

Seligman (1990) and Beck (1976, 1988; Beck & Emery, 1985) suggested cognitive therapy to reverse these effects. Seligman (1990) suggested child development techniques to stimulate the development of an optimistic cognitive style to prevent learned helplessness and presented evidence that adopting optimism can reverse the learned helplessness effects.

Avoidance Symptoms

In addition to the cognitive disturbances, avoidance behaviors associated with depression are common among victims of battering. Battered women adopt coping strategies to avoid further abuse or to minimize the pain and harm when the abuse seems inescapable. Denial, minimization, and repression, all used extensively by those who experience other forms of abuse, are part of this constellation of symptoms.

The isolation that many battered women experience has many sources. Batterers tend to impose isolation on their partners in order to keep power and control, to calm their own fears of abandonment and feelings of intense, irrational jealousy, and to make it less likely that the victim will be able to report the "secret" or find help. A battered woman may believe that the less she and her abusive partner go out into the world of other people, the less likely some social event will trigger another violent outburst. Even when she has a career in which she appears to function well, a battered woman may feel estranged from other people.

It is sometimes hard for even seasoned clinicians to appreciate the degree to which some battered women feel completely vulnerable to a violent partner whose actions are perceived as unpredictable. Even if the woman understands intellectually the unreasonableness of her fears, her emotional vulnerability may govern her actions. Many battered women believe that they could be killed by the batterer if he so chooses. The risk is heightened during preparations to temporarily or permanently leave the relationship, even if the man appears to initiate or want the separation. In light of the number of women who have been killed by a partner, it is crucial that the therapist not reflexively, defensively, or carelessly discount such beliefs as fantasies, exaggerations, or cognitive distortions. The extent to which the woman is at genuine risk must be carefully and realistically explored and constantly reassessed. Because minimization and denial are more common ways to deal with the abuse, when a woman reports her fear of being killed, the report should always be taken seriously.

Some battered women give up hope that things will ever change, become less interested in activities that they used to enjoy, and withdraw from life. It is not unusual for a battered woman to report that she hides her happy feelings from the batterer as a way to prevent him from taking away whatever might cause her joy. At the same time, she may have no choice but to hide her feelings of anger for fear that the anger will provoke another attack. The woman's self-imposed restriction on the range of her feelings may become chronic.

High Arousal Symptoms

The third group of mental health symptoms demonstrated by battered women includes high arousal behaviors such as anxiety, phobias, sleep and eating disorders, sexual dysfunctions (especially when marital rape is present), and a hypervigilance to cues of further danger, including a more pronounced startle response. Although the battered woman often reacts to cues that are imperceptible to the nonabused person, most of the time her perceptions are accurate. This sensitivity to potential danger often lasts long after the abusive relationship is terminated, and the woman is involved in another nonviolent relationship. It is often important to explain to the new partner that the strength of the woman's reaction may be fueled by the results of prior battering. The behavior is similar to that of animals who have been in a forest fire; they have learned that their survival depends on their ability to detect smoke early and, as a result, they are more likely to react to something as minor as cigarette smoke. Psychophysiological symptoms usually associated with high stress and anxiety—such as heart palpitations, difficulty in breathing, panic attacks, extreme nervousness, stomach pains, and physical illnesses—are all associated with the overstimulation of the autonomic nervous system. In chronic abuse, many of these symptoms are present at different times, depending on the particular situation. Although research has not yet established a clear link between chronic abuse and a breakdown of the immunological system, accounts of an increase in use of the medical system by abused women strongly suggest such links (Koss, Woodruff, & Koss, 1991).

Malingering and Fabricated Claims

One of the most difficult dilemmas faced by clinicians is deciding when to believe the accounts of abuse that are described by a woman, especially if she has something to gain from being labeled as a battered woman. This becomes even more problematic if the alleged abuser is denying everything. Research data suggest that women seeking treatment rarely make up stories of abuse. They are more likely to minimize and hide the abuse until trust is established. However, some are angry, scared, and eager to vent their complaints. This becomes problematic when there are legal proceedings that could be affected by allegations of abuse, such as property, custody, and visitation decisions. A litany of "he said–she said" arguments may cause the therapist to unnecessarily doubt the woman's descriptions of violence. Stereotypes and myths that women who report battering tend to be hysterical, vindictive, or "man-hating," and have consequently fabricated the abuse, also have led to the invalidation or minimization of countless valid reports.

No claim of abuse should be routinely dismissed or discounted, no matter how much secondary gain is involved. Each claim must be fully acknowledged and carefully, sensitively explored, even if the accused is a well-known, upstanding community figure or the woman appears to be disagreeable, confused, or vengefully angry. Clinicians often must conduct assessments and engage in treatment when there is inadequate access to external verification. During such periods, clinicians must avoid neglecting the risks of harm or death that may be faced by the woman but that cannot be immediately verified. This includes taking precautions to prevent disclosure of confidential information in the attempt to verify information. This is especially important when the woman is another professional in the community and is known to others in the therapist's social or professional circle. The temptation to request information from mutual acquaintances may be great, but the danger in which these requests may place the woman makes it too risky to ask.

It may take considerable time to create an adequate therapeutic or working alliance, to explore the woman's situation fully, and to make a more informed assessment of the degree to which the woman's account is complete and accurate. During this period, it is important that clinicians seriously consider the question, If this woman's claims are partially, substantially, or completely accurate, are there risks for further harm, and, if so, how can these risks be addressed in a way that helps ensure her safety and welfare? As noted earlier, clinicians must not only consider whether what the woman describes actually happened, but also whether the woman may be providing an incomplete account of the abuse (i.e., that she is failing to disclose the extent of the violence she has experienced because of fear or other psychological defenses). Even in situations in which the woman may appear to be exaggerating the danger, sometimes out of fear or hypervigilance to danger cues, careful attention to her need for a sense of adequate safety (e.g., helping her to find a shelter) may be therapeutic.

Common Misdiagnoses

Battered women are frequently misdiagnosed as suffering from a personality disorder. Clinicians may tend to disregard the abuse itself and focus almost exclusively on the sequelae. When such symptoms as dependency, disruptions in interpersonal relationships, dissociation, intense anger, and "hysterical" features are viewed without the context of the battering relationship, the syndrome may seem to be inherent in the woman's personality organization. Herman, Perry, and van der Kolk (1989) compared the records of those diagnosed with borderline personality disorder with those of women diagnosed with PTSD and found that only the knowledge of previous abuse made the difference for those patients who received the PTSD diagnosis. Similarly, Rosewater (1985a, 1985b, 1987a, 1987b) found that Minnesota Multiphasic Personality Inventory (MMPI–1) results were more likely to be misinterpreted and clients misdiagnosed with schizophrenia or borderline personality disorder if the history of battering were not present. Other psychological tests such as the Millon Clinical Multiaxial Inventory also can contribute to misdiagnosis by emphasizing personality disorders rather than situational problems such as abuse. Such research underscores the necessity of adequately exploring a woman's claims of abuse and of arriving at a diagnosis on the basis of the full array of clinical information.

Diagnosis of BWS becomes more complex when there is a history of other abuse. The current PTSD criteria emphasize single incidents of trauma even though the stressors explicitly include repeated abuse. The PTSD criteria do not fit as well when the abuse has ceased but the symptoms are still present, or, as is more common, when the physical abuse has ceased but the psychological abuse remains. However, the reexperiencing of the traumatic battering incidents keeps the abuse alive in the woman's mind and serves as a powerful reinforcer. The *DSM–IV* corrects this problem by accounting for many of the effects of repeated abuse. According to Primo Levi (1988), "the memory of a trauma suffered or inflicted is itself traumatic because recalling it is painful or at least disturbing" (p. 24). For battered women, each new acute battering incident also stimulates the recollection of partial or complete memories of prior abuse, magnifying the psychological impact.

Confusion with the adjustment disorders diagnoses sometimes occurs because many of the symptoms can be similar. However, an adjustment disorder occurs when there is an abnormal emotional response (usually judged by length of time or severity of reaction) to normal life cycle situational events. A PTSD occurs when there is a normal (albeit demonstrated by severe emotional symptoms) reaction to an abnormal or unexpected situation. In making a differential diagnosis, questions about physical, sexual, or psychological abuse must be fully explored.[4]

Organic Brain Syndromes

Some battered women develop organic brain damage because of frequent blows to the head. Some have experienced repeated head shaking that results in syndromes similar to those that boxers develop. A thorough neuropsychological evaluation may be necessary to determine the impact of frequent

---

[4]Further discussion of standardized tests can be found in chapter 11 on assessment. Dutton (1992) offered a fairly complete discussion about using other assessment instruments.

head injuries and any resulting diagnoses. Often, serious problems resulting from the subtle damage do not show up until many years after the abuse has ceased. Thus, formerly battered women may begin to experience progressive deterioration including general feelings of disorientation, sensorimotor difficulties, language difficulties, coordination problems, and the like. The new Reitan norms are better at measuring this subtle damage (A. Appel, personal communication, December 1991).

Because battered women come from a heterogeneous group, some may also have had other mental health symptoms or diagnoses prior or subsequent to experiencing the abuse. More serious depressions and bipolar disorders should be properly assessed and listed on Axis I, if the *DSM* system is used. Panic attacks or phobias should also be listed separately. Substance abuse disorders require a separate diagnosis. If more serious dissociative states are present, they too require a separate diagnosis. Long-term personality disorders should not be conclusively diagnosed until the woman is safe and in treatment for at least 6 months in order to give the symptoms a chance to dissipate.

It is not unusual for a formerly battered woman to enter therapy without presenting the abuse as the primary reason for treatment. These women are usually out of the abusive relationship and, for the most part, have worked through the immediate crisis issues, constant fearfulness, and the effects of being under surveillance. However, many of the same symptoms of BWS are present but are not diagnosed as such. Instead the woman's depression, anxiety, or another symptom constellation becomes the focus, often because either she or the therapist does not understand the remaining impact of the abuse on her mental health.

There may be residual symptoms that last for years, especially the hypervigilance to cues of danger and jumpiness. Those women who have never dealt with the emotional aftermath of abuse find that they are more anxious, sometimes more angry, and less optimistic about life in general. Some are still being harassed by the same men with whom they no longer live. Some have children who have behavior and other problems directly traceable to the abuse that they witnessed or experienced. Some of these children have mimicked the abuser's behavior and are now abusive toward their mothers.

COLLABORATIVE APPROACHES

It is frequently important to refer a battered woman to another professional during the course of therapy. Such referrals might be made to a neuropsychologist, as described above; a medical doctor; a dentist, for temporal mandibular joint disorder or grinding of teeth; an attorney; or another psychologist for other family members. It is particularly important to set appropriate boundaries with battered women as with other abuse victims. Avoidance of dual relationships is an important consideration when making such referrals. For example, a referral to the therapist's own wife or husband would not be appropriate.

Clinicians should always consider whether referral to a battered women's shelter, if available, would help ensure the woman's safety and recovery. Shelter staff are usually trained to facilitate self-help groups. Some shelters or task forces that provide services have trained therapists available at little or no cost to the client. Participation in a group can also be a valuable adjunct to individual therapy. Well-coordinated provision of services by an array of professionals, especially if "turf issues" are minimized, may increase the woman's sense of connectedness to the outside world. She may feel rapport with and support from a variety of people and may have less cause to feel that her therapist is her only lifeline. (See chapters 13 and 14, on treatment, for further discussion of group therapy.)

As with the other forms of abuse addressed in this volume, it is important for therapists to be aware of the range of services in the community that are specifically designed for battered women. Sharing this information with the client and, when appropriate, helping her to gather and evaluate additional information about sources of help, can be an important part of recovery and reempowerment. As she learns what steps she can take independently to contact a shelter, to contact police teams specially trained to address domestic violence, and so forth, her ability to find the help she needs may improve (especially if she is in crisis or in immediate danger and her therapist is temporarily unavailable). Mastery of this information may reverse some of the process of learned helplessness and restore self-esteem, and it may enable the woman to become a more knowledgeable, active, self-confident participant in her own treatment and recovery.

SUMMARY

Battered women are those who suffer from physical, sexual, or psychological abuse that is inflicted by someone with whom they are in an intimate relationship. The abuse by the batterer is generally part of a pattern of obsessional behavior rather than an expression of sudden loss of control. Clinicians note two major patterns of battering: First, the abuse becomes more violent and frequent. Second, a three-step cycle repeats itself, consisting of periods of tension-building, violence, and contrition in which the tension is gone. The batterer is often prone to extreme sexual jealousy and shows little sense of the autonomy of other people in the household. Research indicates that one of every two women will be abused at some point in her life.

In response to the abuse, women sometimes fight back or become abusive toward their children or aged parents. More often the woman tends to blame herself for her partner's violence, believing that if she could only find a way to appease him, the house would be peaceful. Alcohol and substance abuse often play a role for the batterer and the abused woman. The batterer's outbreaks can become more violent when he is under the influence; many abused women use alcohol or other drugs to numb their pain.

Most battered women who seek therapy suffer from BWS, which consists of cognitive disturbances, high avoidance or depression, and high arousal or anxiety disturbances. Battered women are frequently misdiagnosed as suffering from personality disorders or adjustment disorders. Some have organic brain damage caused by repeated blows to the head. While treating a battered woman, it is often important to refer her to other professionals, for example, a neuropsychologist, an attorney, or the staff from a battered woman's shelter.

4

Adult Survivors of Child Sexual Abuse

Only recently has there been recognition of the large numbers of female clients who have been sexually abused as children and of the extent of the effects of that abuse. Although Freud originally traced the etiology of neurosis and hysteria among his female patients to incest experiences, he later renounced his findings, stating instead that these apparent memories of incest were actually wish-fulfilling fantasies (Freud, 1896/1959a, 1898/1959b). The issue of reliability and validity of children's memories is still being debated by some researchers and clinicians today (Doris, 1991), even though the serious psychological effects of child sexual abuse are visible in many adult women who seek therapy. Arguments about the origins of repressed memories of child sexual abuse that surface during clinical treatment, sometimes labeled *false memories* by some nonclinical researchers discussed later, have made treating clinicians more cautious in helping clients to understand their memories. This chapter is designed to assist clinicians in avoiding pitfalls and in being comfortable while working with their clients.

Before the therapist begins to work with a woman who has been sexually abused as a child, information about the current controversy about whether memories of the abuse that surface during treatment are just suggestions planted by the therapist or actual delayed or repressed memories must be understood. Groups that have members who claim to have been unfairly accused of committing such abuse, such as a Philadelphia-based group called the False Memory Foundation, insist that therapists "create" these memories when questioning and treating clients about the possibility that sexual abuse occurred when they were children. Although these groups may be discredited when their members are more closely scrutinized for self-interest in denying that children are sexually abused (Quina, 1994), the fact remains that they have been partially responsible for the profession's reexamination of the issue of child sexual abuse and methods of assessment and treatment.

Perhaps influenced by Freud's later views, which were consistent with those of the times and society in which he lived, professionals and the lay public alike, until the early 1980s, discounted reports of child sexual abuse and concluded that it rarely, if ever, occurred (cf. Herman, 1981; Lerman, 1986; Masson, 1984; Rush, 1980, for more complete discussion). This tendency to deny or to minimize the scope of the phenomenon has persisted to relatively recent times and may still be fueling the arguments of the doubters. In the past half century, for example, a few widely read professional volumes still have erroneously placed the incident rate for incest at between one and two instances for every million U.S. citizens (e.g., Henderson, 1975; Weinberg, 1955). The research described in this chapter presents a different picture.

Although there is some debate about the exact incidence rates among different age groups of various forms of child sexual abuse (e.g., incest, sex with a nonrelated adult), there is general agreement that the sexual abuse of children is not a rare event (cf. Daro & Mitchell, 1990, for statistics on reported cases in the United States). More girls than boys are known to have been sexually abused as children, and more males than females are known to have been the perpetrators, even when males are their victims. Thus the gender issues are somewhat consistent with other forms of woman abuse, except that a larger number of males are victims of this type of abuse than of other types of abuse discussed in this book, even though most of the perpetrators also are male. Because the focus of this book is on the assessment of and intervention with women who were abused as children, only sexual abuse of girls is dealt with here, although the harm done to young boys by abuse often leads them, too, to seek therapy when they are older. Much of the treatment outlined here can be appropriately adapted for nonperpetrating sexually abused males.

MEMORIES OF ABUSE

Acknowledgment of childhood sexual abuse and its effects has been enhanced by research supporting the notion that children do have memories of the abusive trauma, that these memories can be trusted at least as well as an adult's memories (Goodman & Helgeson, 1988), and that such early abuse can result in psychological traumatization that often pervades virtually every area of a child's development (Alpert & Paulson, 1990; Briere, 1989; Courtois & Sprei, 1988; Finkelhor & Browne, 1988; Herman, 1992; Walker, 1990). This research has countered the claims of authoritative-sounding professionals that a child's expression of sexual desires can be positive for both the child and the pedophile (cf. Pope, 1990a, for a further review and discussion of these claims).

Most people believe that if they were sexually abused as children, they would not be able to forget such traumatic events. Common sense dictates that children could not forget such terrible acts and, therefore, it could not be possible to repress memories that surface years later in therapy. However, incest experiences and the memories of such experiences do not necessarily follow logic or common sense. Loftus (1992, 1993), an experimental and forensic psychologist who researches adult memories, uses this argument to support her defense, in forensic cases, of men who have been accused of child molestation. Loftus uses theoretical constructs and methods that were developed from research on adults, whose memories and other cognitive functions do not follow the same developmental patterns as those of children, to demonstrate that children's memories can be altered by new information to which they are exposed after an event is over. She then concludes that children are so confused by their suggestible or malleable memories that their accusations of sexual abuse cannot be trusted. Often presenting single forensic cases, Loftus designs small-sized analogues to fit her own personal experiences and theories. None of her research has addressed the issues that are raised by trauma memory research suggesting subcortical mediation and storage of trauma memories (van der Kolk, undated; van der Kolk & Kadish, 1987). Katch (1993) analyzed the language that Loftus used in her writings to describe her research results and found that much personal bias is cloaked within the rhetoric of science.

Others who have specifically researched children's memories for the impact of traumatic events argue that children's memories are variable according to the stage of development, conditions of the event, amount of trauma inflicted, and means used to assist them in remembering the trauma (Briere, 1992; Briere & Conte, 1993; Goodman & Bottoms, 1993; Herman & Schatzow, 1987; N. W. Perry, 1992; Steward, 1992; Summit, 1992; van der Kolk, undated; van der Kolk & Kadish, 1987; Williams, 1992). The reports of therapists who specialize in the treatment of sexually abused women have shown that women who were sexually abused often experience periods of time during which they cannot remember the abuse. Briere and Conte (1993) found that more than one half (59%) of their clinical sample had failed to remember childhood sexual abuse at some time during their lives. Herman and Schatzow (1987), also using a clinical sample of women in treatment, reported that 28% did not remember the childhood abuse at some point in their lives.

Williams's (1992) study is particularly interesting because of its focus on researching adult memories of childhood through a longitudinal study. Williams followed a group of 200 women who reported sexual abuse as children in the early 1970s. The details of their sexual abuse were recorded during a National Institute of Mental Health study 17 years before the research follow-up in 1990–1991. These subjects varied in age from infancy to 12 years at the time that they and their family members were interviewed at a large city hospital for treatment and collection of forensic evidence. The abuse consisted of a range of sexual touching and fondling through sexual intercourse, and was perpetrated by males who were usually 10 or more years older than the child. In 32% of the cases the perpetrator was a member of the girl's family, 29% were friends of the child or family, 30% were casual acquaintances of the family, and 22% were strangers. These data are similar to the relationships found in Conte and Berliner's (1988) data. Detailed follow-up interviews that were designed to examine the health and lives of women who used the hospital during the 1970s also asked questions about any sexual abuse that might have occurred during their childhood. Those women who denied that any sexual abuse had occurred were asked if anyone else might have made such a report about them. The results indicated that more than one third of the women interviewed (38%) did not report that any sexual abuse had occurred during their childhood despite knowledge by the interviewers that such abuse had been documented. Most of these women appeared to be amnestic for such abuse. Many of these women provided details of other painful and equally embarrassing events, and therefore shame was not seen by the researchers as a major factor in their failure to report. As these women did report the abuse as children when it happened, it may well be that one third is a conservative estimate of the number of women who do not remember such a traumatic event.

Why would adult memory researchers contradict the clinical findings and some research findings that adult women who were sexually abused as children may have memory problems and often remember the abuse during therapy? Certainly personal biases, such as distrust of therapists, desire to support male perpetrators, denial that "nice" men can molest children, enjoyment of the recognition provided by groups that rally around men who are allegedly falsely accused, prior experience with one or more unfounded (not untrue but unprovable legally) cases, and need to stand by a previously expressed position, may figure into such motivation. It is also important to understand why other professionals, the media, and other people would be so willing to believe the stories of false accusations of abuse that are presented either by poorly trained therapists or, for whatever reason, by female abuse victims. The lessons learned by a profession that chose denial over accuracy during its earliest days, when Freud turned away from the truth as related to him by his clients, are important to remember.

Most clinicians who work with women who are survivors of childhood sexual abuse understand the need to go slowly in helping clients to retrieve lost memories. If a client tries to replace no memories or incomplete ones with memories that could have been suggested by a therapist, the "new" memories are often rejected after a short time. Thus, it is important not to encourage the client to take any steps that would treat newly emerging memories as the final product until other factors in the client's life authenticate such memories. Pharmacology and biochemical research suggest that memories for trauma are experienced and stored in subcortical centers of the nervous system, often as visual images or kinesthetic or physical sensations (cf. van der Kolk, undated). Thus, what may seem like verbal or congitive amnesia occurs; the memories may not be repressed at all but stored instead on a somatosensory level. Psychotherapy may simply help translate these subcortical memories into the cognitive areas of the brain so that they can be more easily communicated to others. In any event, it is important for therapists to treat client's emerging memories appropriately, without making undue suggestions that might tamper with the memories and jeopardize the client's use of the legal system for redress later.

Many women have been sexually abused as children, and it is important to be particularly sensitive to their needs and requests. One of the issues raised is the preference to use the term *survivor* instead of *victim* (Bass & Davis, 1988). In order to be consistent with the other categories of abuse discussed in this book, the term *victim* will continue to be used when the woman has not received services or has not yet begun to heal after being abused, whereas the term *survivor* is reserved for those who have made substantial progress on their path to healing. However, any such term may have special meanings to an individual woman who has experienced child sexual abuse. If such terms come up in the course of assessment and treatment, it is always sound practice to discuss with the client her understanding of and preference for terminology and to respect her wishes as part of the empowerment process.

OVERVIEW

In the first section of this chapter, I define child sexual abuse and explore the role of the mother in an abusive relationship. Next, I examine the research regarding the prevalence of this abuse, the ages at which a child is most vul-

nerable, and the effects on a child's development. In the section on associated factors, I describe the drug use and dissociative disorders that can
plague child abuse victims. The sections on clinical presentation and assessment stress matters of credibility: How trustworthy are a child's memories?
How accurate are the accusations of parental alienation? Why does a child
recant? Other topics covered are theoretical models and the misdiagnosis of
child abuse victims. Finally, this chapter deals with the transference problems that these clients might have and examines the types of therapy available to help them.

Definitions

The legal definition of child sexual abuse varies from state to state. The definition used in a particular state's legislation may differ from the definitions
that clinicians find useful and appropriate in identifying such abuse. It is
important to understand the child abuse laws even when working with
adults, because some clients may want to take some legal action, particularly
in those states in which the civil laws permit more flexible time delays in
reporting abuse either because of recent knowledge of the harm such abuse
has caused or because of extended or eliminated statutes of limitations.
(This subject is discussed further in chapter 9 on forensic issues.) Other
clients may be comforted by the understanding that what happened to hurt
them is against the law. In a few states, there are legal mandates for reporting allegations of past child sexual abuse as well as current suspicions of
child abuse (for information on mandated reporting, see Kalichman, 1993).

Although there is not one universally accepted definition, child sexual
abuse is often defined as any touching of a child's genital or other body areas
that has a sexual or seductive connotation or any coerced touching by the
child of an adult's genital areas. Showing children pornographic movies and
pictures, coercing a child to pose for such pictures, or telling sexual stories is
also considered sexual abuse. Unlike the adult sexual assault and rape laws,
there is no need to deal with the issue of consent as the laws of all states
define any sexual contact with a child as child abuse. In some legislation, the
definition may be dependent on the age discrepancy between the child and
the offender; such cases are commonly considered offenses when there is at

least a 5-year age difference between victim and offender. This requirement is meant to differentiate between the common sexual exploration of peers and exploitive relationships in which one child is much older than the other.

Incest is usually defined as sexual contact by a family member. The most frequent incest perpetrator is a girl's father or stepfather, with brothers, grandfathers, and uncles next in frequency (Conte & Berliner, 1988; Russell, 1988). It is unusual but not impossible for the mother to be the incest perpetrator of her daughter or her son. In rare cases, abusive men may force women into sexual acts with children using threats of further violence should they not comply. There is a growing trend to include certain others—religious leaders, family doctors, teachers and administrators, babysitters, and coaches—in the list of those whose sexual abuse is considered incest. These individuals are, like older family members, in a position of power, responsibility, and authority in relation to the relatively vulnerable and dependent child. In these cases, promises of love and gifts may be sufficient to coerce the vulnerable child into compliance and secrecy.

Definitions of child sexual abuse, when they enumerate specific acts, generally include vaginal–penile penetration, anal–penile penetration, oral sex, and digital and other fondling. Stroking the inside of a child's thigh may or may not be considered sexual abuse depending on the situation, the age of the child, and prior behavior. Although some laws restrict incest to sexual behavior that involves some physical contact between the child and the offender, in some cases an offender may refrain from touching the child and yet clearly be understood to be engaging in sexual abuse of a child. For example, a father may direct his daughter to take off her clothes, to masturbate, or to engage in other sexual behavior while he watches or films the events.

Some fathers or stepfathers engage in what has come to be termed *psychological incest*. In these situations, the father will refrain from engaging in or encouraging overt sexual acts but will use his relationship with his daughter as an emotional substitute for a healthy romantic relationship with a woman. Clinical assessment and intervention become much more complex in such situations. The state's child abuse reporting laws may not be relevant to such psychological abuse, and county or municipal child protective services may be reluctant to respond unless there is some form of physically inappropriate (i.e., overtly sexual) behavior. Nevertheless, the consequences for the victim may be quite similar to those for women exposed to more traditionally defined incest, often interfering with the adult woman's interpersonal relationships and other facets of her life.

Role of the Child's Mother

As the nature and scope of child sex abuse has been realized, the issue of the mother's direct and indirect involvement has become prominent. Although the data indicate that mothers rarely engage in the sexual abuse of their children unless psychotic or abusive men force such behavior, mothers have traditionally been blamed for the abuse and were believed to be facilitators, if not actually collusive co-offenders. The assumption has been that the mother must have known what was going on but failed to take protective action, probably seeing it as a way to avoid her "sexual duties" to her husband by permitting her daughter to substitute for her (cf. Cammaert, 1988, for a more complete discussion). Many daughters express rage at their mothers for not doing more to protect them, further fueling this woman-blaming misconception. However, it is important to remember that, in most abusive families, the dynamics prevent easy communication between all members; instead there are secrets shared between different groups. Thus, mothers may suspect but are often excluded from sharing in the father–daughter relationship. Abusers often prevent their wives and children from forming any intimate relationships with other family members.

By the early 1980s, the accumulating research tended to discredit this theory of mothers who know of abuse but do nothing, at least in most cases (cf. Cammaert, 1988). The research suggested that most mothers did not intervene because they did not know about the abuse or, if they did discover the abuse, were terrified that any attempted intervention would only lead to increased danger or harm for the daughter (Herman, 1981; Rush, 1980). Many of the mothers were themselves victims of early sexual abuse (Walker, 1989b); sometimes the perpetrator was the mother's own father, who then molested his granddaughters or grandsons.

Whether or not a mother knew, at times she was powerless to protect her daughter because she herself was a victim of the same man's physical and sexual abuse (Herman, 1992; Walker, 1984a). Some mothers were forced to settle for an extremely difficult but much more limited goal than preventing the child sex abuse: keeping everyone alive in an extremely dangerous home (Walker, 1989b) and attempting to keep some contact with their children in the face of disbelieving courts. As discussed in the previous chapter on battered women, attempts to end the relationship or even to achieve a temporary separation and protection often precipitate even greater violence.

Unfortunately, many daughters, regardless of whether they themselves were abused or were witnesses to the battering of their mothers, blame their mothers for not promptly and effectively stopping the abuse. They say their mothers should not have provoked so many arguments, should have loved their husbands more, or should have been more emotionally available to the entire family (Briere, 1989; Butler, 1978; Courtois, 1988). It is important for clinicians to understand this perspective while also realizing that it is incomplete. Understanding the child's perspective may form the basis for making sense of a fairly common phenomenon: A daughter who has been sexually abused by her father may be more willing to forgive her father for the abuse than to forgive her mother for "allowing" the abuse to occur. Obviously, this is an important treatment issue, especially considering Conte and Berliner's (1988) study that indicated that the most important factor influencing an incest daughter's recovery is the relationship with her mother.

In some cases, however, the mother herself is the perpetrator. There have been increased reports of mothers using enemas and other forms of health care or discipline methods that have sexual overtones. It is important to keep in mind the context of the times in which these events occurred. Obviously, there were periods in the history of medicine when enemas were considered a normal part of health care and not sexual abuse. Research on women who were in prison for sexually abusing children found that there were two groups. The larger group was made up of those women who were coerced into sexually abusing their children by abusive men; the smaller but nonetheless important group committed the abuse independently. Most of these women were sexually abused themselves, at an early age, and had serious mental health problems including psychosis, as well as poor social skills.

These women had difficulty seeing their daughters as separate from themselves. Although most female victims do not become aggressive, some do, and they must receive adequate treatment for their violent behavior in addition to the other damage that has resulted from the abuse.

INCIDENCE AND PREVALENCE

As with virtually all the types of abuse discussed in this volume, research on adult survivors of child sexual abuse is difficult and plagued by methodological dilemmas (see Pope, 1990a, for a discussion of these issues). Nevertheless, a wealth of sufficiently rigorous research has been conducted that enables practitioners who have adequate qualifications to draw with confidence a number of inferences about frequency and psychological impact. It is important to be familiar with the information on the abuse of children so that a victim's retrospective memories can be compared with the common patterns that are suggested by the research.

The accumulated research suggests that the sexual abuse of girls is far more common than was previously thought. In one study (Russell, 1988), for example, 38% of a random sample of women reported that they had been sexually abused before the age of 18; 28% had experienced sexual abuse before the age of 12. In addition, most (as high as 80%) of these sexual episodes were perpetrated by family members or close family acquaintances, with the majority committed by fathers and father-substitutes against their daughters (Conte & Berliner, 1988). Pope and Feldman-Summers (1992) found that 21% of the female therapists that they studied were sexually abused by a relative, 1.96% by a teacher, 1.96% by a physician, and 16.34% by a nonrelative. Female therapists report that a higher rate of their female clients were sexually abused as children than do male therapists, although male therapists with training in this area report greater numbers of survivors of child sexual abuse. It is difficult to know whether this is due to a tendency of female survivors to select female therapists or due to a lesser awareness in male therapists of their client's sexual abuse experiences.

Child sexual abuse perpetrators are more often (although not exclusively) male, whereas the victims are more often (although not as frequently as in other forms of abuse) female. It is important to note, however, that the understanding of the relative rates at which boys are sexually abused (usually by other males) is still in its initial phases, even though the psychological consequences are documented. As a result of his survey of college students, Finkelhor (1984) suggested that 10% of all boys are sexually abused, most by father figures or close male acquaintances. Pope and Feldman-Summers (1992) found that 5.4% of the male therapists that they surveyed had been sexually abused by a relative, 0.73% were sexually abused by a teacher, and 9.49% were sexually abused by a nonrelative. Some clinicians suggest that close to one quarter of all men who seek therapy were sexually abused in childhood (Bolton, Morris, & MacEachron, 1989; Finkelhor, 1990). The physical and sexual abuse rate is extremely high in convicted rapists, child molesters, murderers, and serial killers. Thus, although at present the known rate of abuse of boys tends to be less than that of girls, the damage to their lives seems to have monumental significance. Gallers (1993) suggested that an important difference is that boys react by dissociating and doing harm to others, whereas girls are more likely to dissociate as they become the recipients of further victimization.

Offender Behavior

Some information about women who were sexually abused as children is gained through the study of offenders. A brief review is provided here to assist the practitioner in better understanding clients' reports about offender behavior.

Some abusers are considered to be predatory sex offenders who have abused many children in addition to the one who reports the offense (Becker, 1990; Groth, 1979). Often current offenders were abused themselves as children, began their sex offenses by early adolescence, and continued to abuse numerous children, boys and girls, as they moved through life (Becker, 1990; Bolton, et al., 1989). Early intervention obviously provides prevention for the next generation. Untreated child molesters may stop their incest behavior temporarily after their victim reaches adolescence and starts to date peers, but they are at high risk to resume sexual abuse with the next available child. In some cases, the abuser may molest not only his children but also his grandchildren, nieces and nephews, and others who are conveniently available (Conte & Berliner, 1988).

Ages When Children Are at Risk

Although sexual abuse can occur throughout childhood, there are three major developmental times when children appear to be at highest risk for abuse. First, the preschool years provide an opportunity for fondling and related abuse. The offender may take advantage of an infant's sucking needs, curiosity, and tendency to touch everything she sees. Such young children may be unaware of the concept of abuse, let alone be able to understand that a trusted adult, on whom they are dependent, may be violating them. It is easy to keep such children relatively isolated, and their limited verbal skills may make it difficult for them to communicate. When memories of abuse that occurred during this age group appear, they are often trace memories of fear and other scary feelings with few specific incidents able to be remembered. There are reports that, historically, nannies in some countries used to sexually stimulate the babies to soothe their cries.

Often these memories become more accessible when similar emotionally fearful situations occur. If participating in cultlike activities (e.g., ritual abuse) with groups of children and adults, the victim's conditioned fear stimuli may also precipitate trace memories of the terrifying activities. A general progression of sexual activities usually occurs over time. An offender may begin with a series of sexually stimulating activities, often presented as games with rewards for the victim's cooperation, and postpone initiating actual intercourse until the child is 8 or 9 years old, although sometimes it occurs earlier. Childrens' behavior may suggest that they have been subjected to such abuse even if they cannot talk about it. Such behavior—including early sexually seductive behavior (learned as a way to obtain love and affection), inappropriate boundaries between themselves and others, and sexual touching of themselves and other children—warrants careful clinical assessment, particularly if there is accompanying vaginal irritation, infection, or both.

A second period of high risk for abuse to begin occurs when the child is about 7 or 8 years old. Rewarding the child's search for love and affection with seductive behaviors that are sometimes called *presexualizing experiences*, abusers teach the activities inappropriate to her age. Sex-role socialization experiences play an important role here with little girls learning to make their "Daddy" happy. Part of the presexualizing process includes keeping little secrets that only the child and father figure are permitted to share; obviously, these lead to the big one that will come shortly.

Usually by age 9 sexual touching begins, although it may have started earlier in showers or during "bedtime stories." Some men come into the child's room at night and fondle her while she is or pretends to be asleep. Some children learn not to "awaken" when the sexual behavior begins, aided by their confusion and use of dissociation and the denial process. Pedophiles who sexually abuse while children are in a sleeplike state frequently deny their behavior, further confusing adult women if the women attempt to confront them. Should the child awaken, she is often told that she is having a bad dream and is soothed in a more conventional manner, further confusing her.

Other men begin sexually abusing the child by spanking the child's bare bottom and then progress into digital, oral, and penile sexual penetration. In many cases, men develop unique rituals that are regularly repeated and that become a special secret that the child is made to understand must never, under any circumstances, be disclosed to anyone else. When buried memories of this period of abuse surface, they are more likely to include details of sexual incidents along with details of nonsexual accompanying events. Children of this age often learn to dissociate by focusing on something else to distract themselves from feeling the pain and uncontrollability of the sexual experience. Even those children who like the immediate attention and pleasure of the gentle stimulation often have negative aftereffects.

The third period of high risk begins when the child is a teenager. In many cases, the father may have initiated a psychologically seductive relationship with his daughter during her childhood, but he does not force her into an overtly sexual relationship until she is sexually mature. Often, alcohol and drug abuse is involved. Many offenders who initiate sexual relations with their daughters during this third period of risk use no birth control or protection from sexually transmitted diseases. The positive correlation between teenage pregnancy and other forms of family abuse, such as incest, is well-documented in the clinical intervention programs for pregnant teens (D. Boyer & Fine, 1992; Finkelhor, 1990). Memories of the sexual abuse at this stage are usually more complete than at the earlier periods. However, some girls are able to dissociate, minimize, deny, repress, and forget such behavior until some time later in their lives when the memories return along with the stored-up emotions, particularly anxiety, fear, and depression. Complications occur when these women become confused by their own inability to stop the abuse and sometimes by abusers who accuse them of their own desire and complicity. Obviously, the adolescent's own awakening of sexual feelings and desires become confused with the perpetrator's manipulation and coercion.

Development of Memories

The issue of how children remember, why they forget, and whether their memories can be manipulated by suggestion has been raised by those who do not believe that children are sexually abused at the rates that the research suggests. It is important for therapists who work with adult women who were sexually abused as children to be familiar with the literature on child development. Memory research suggests that children's memories develop in the same way as do those of adults (Goodman & Bottoms, 1993; Goodman & Helgeson, 1988; N. W. Perry, 1992; Steward, 1992). The process consists of acquiring memories by perceiving and paying attention to an event, storage of the memory, and retrieval with ability to report the memory. Although even infants are capable of perceiving and paying attention to events, while experiencing trauma children may dissociate, and this will interfere with perception of and attention paid to the ongoing abuse. It is suggested that memories that arise from a dissociative state are perceived subcortically through visual and kinesthetic somatization rather than through cognitive attention. Thus, experiencing a similar affect state could bring about the recall of some memories of emotions in very young children, even those who are preverbal.

Developmental research suggests that storage of the memory does not vary much with development. Once information is stored, children of any developmental age can be expected to remember it as well as adults (N. W. Perry, 1992). The ability to recall the information, however, is affected by a child's level of development. The usual ways to remember information is through *recognition, reconstruction,* and *free recall. Recognition* is the simplest form of remembering and, developmentally, even infants are capable of it, although recognition for complexity and accuracy improve with age. Some research suggests that there are certain times during the developmental years in which recognition memory is even better than at other times, but by the time children enter school such memories are pretty accurate.

Reconstruction involves remembering and accurately re-creating a scene mentally. Again, although even very young preschool children are capable of reconstruction, they often need context clues in order to increase their accuracy, and as children get older their accuracy on complex tasks improves. Asking questions as prompts can assist in reconstruction of the surroundings, sights, sounds, temperature, smells, and other details. *Free recall* is considered the most complex form of memory because it requires information to be retrieved with little or no clues (Goodman & Helgeson, 1988; N. W. Perry, 1992). Younger children are less able to perform free recall than older ones, although they can still answer some direct questions without prompts. Again, the older the child, the better the recall memory.

There has also been some research that attempts to measure the effectiveness of different techniques that are used to retrieve the memory. Steward (1992) found that 3- to 6-year-old children's memories were not as malleable as was suggested by adult analogue studies, particularly when the memory was of some painful event. She used the example of trying to take a recalcitrant child back to the doctor's office after a painful procedure. Steward found that the children in the study actually underreported what they remembered. She found that accuracy and consistency rates improved over time with appropriate cues, particularly with use of anatomically detailed dolls.

The issue of therapist contamination of a child's memory, or of an adult's memory of what happened to her as a child, is important, particularly when assessing for accuracy in legal issues. Because so many abuse victims eventually have some contact with the court, as is discussed in chapter

9, it is important to pay attention to the possibility that suggestions can be made by a therapist that cause the client to recover false memories. Most clinical data suggest that it is rare for memories that have been altered through therapist suggestion to be held convincingly or to remain without some other corroborating situation that reinforces them (Faller, 1992). The goal of therapy is to reduce any aftereffects that may have resulted from sexual abuse experiences. To this end, the issue of false memories is less important in achieving treatment goals. It is only when accusations are made outside of the therapy office that the issue of accuracy of memory becomes salient. Thus, therapists need to use special caution when a client discusses the need to pursue confrontation with the perpetrator or contact with the legal system.

Dynamics of Abuse

Although the child's age at the time the sexual abuse begins may be important in understanding the psychological meaning of the incest and any developmental disruption that might have occurred, the control and choice of when the abuse begins is made by the sex offender and not the child. "Provocative" or "seductive" behavior on the part of the child should be understood as either part of gender-role socialization for girls, which emphasizes sexualized behaviors, or a survival technique in a home in which there was no protection from the incest. The behavior of the child should not be seen as an excuse for the man's inability to control his own behavior. It is not unusual for the sexualized behavior to continue into adulthood with women using seduction to keep men calm and avoid additional abuse.

One of the major goals of healing is to help the girl or woman understand that she is not to blame for the abuse: The abuse was not her fault, no matter what her behavior. Some women blame themselves because they liked the attention and did not stop the man. Some even learn to like the sexual stimulation some of the time. It is not unusual for incest fathers to provide the major source of affection for the child, especially if the mothers have become emotionally numb from their own abuse. Some survivors learn to hate the man who betrayed their love and trust, whereas others still have strong feelings for the father but feel little for their emotionally unavailable mothers. None of the victims liked the repeated, unwanted sexual demands that they could not control. As discussed later in this volume, blaming oneself is one way to feel more powerful; if a girl or woman stops doing whatever she thinks that she did to "encourage" the abuser then she can fool herself into thinking that the abuse will not happen to her again.

Impact of Abuse During the Teenage Years

Female adolescents often try to stop the abuse themselves through use of resistant behavior, sometimes leading to outright rebelliousness. Some lose motivation to complete school, dropping out early. These girls may run away from home only to find further abuse and exploitation on the streets. They may become sexually active with a number of men, sometimes selling their bodies as a way to afford drugs that keep them from feeling the pain and experiencing flashbacks of the abuse. Edwall and Hoffman (1988) and James (1978), among others, found that large numbers of girls who run away and end up in drug treatment centers are incest survivors. Not surprisingly, many of these girls become involved in abusive dating relationships (Levy, 1991).

Recent research on sexual abuse as a factor in teenage pregnancy has found that two thirds of the adolescent mothers surveyed had been sexually molested or abused (D. Boyer & Fine, 1992). On average, the first sexual molestation occurred by age 9, with one quarter of the women reporting abuse prior to age 5. More than three quarters of the women had experienced repeated sexual abuse, with 54% of the abusers being family members, usually the father, stepfather, mother's boyfriend, uncle, brother, or grandfather. Also interesting is the high degree of physical force used to discipline teenage sexual abuse victims, as well as the threats and force that are used to gain their compliance with sexual demands. D. Boyer and Fine suggested that the high rate of maltreatment inflicted by these adolescent mothers on their own children is more likely to be associated with the stress of their histories as abuse victims rather than the immaturity associated with their young age. There are obvious implications for teenage sexual abuse victims who become pregnant: The pregnancy and the infant perpetuate the mother's view of herself as powerless in an unpredictable world.

Development of the "Nasty Kid"

Some children who are raised in sexually abusive homes attempt to protect themselves by developing a nasty or aggressive side to their personalities. In most children this side of their persona is integrated but often hidden and only allowed to emerge when there is some kind of actual or perceived danger. Sometimes, it comes out during a dissociative state, which is also a learned way to protect themselves from the impact of further abuse. Thus, the angry, hostile side tries to fend off the attack while the dissociative state prevents the child from experiencing the pain of it. In those who dissociate at a very young age, the different sides of their personality, particularly the negative sides, may split and fail to become integrated. Many believe that this is the genesis of some dissociative disorders in adults (Courtois, 1988; Gallers, 1993; Herman, 1992).

The angry, hostile, nasty side is one that is often repressed as the child grows up. However, once grown, the adult woman knows that, within her, there exists the potential for being very mean, and she fears unleashing it. Often the "mean side" comes out at seemingly uncontrollable, inappropriate, and embarrassing times. Sometimes, the buried anger is suspected or actually seen by friends and associates. The woman may enter into a serious depression or even a psychotic state rather than face this enemy within her. The abused women expends an enormous amount of energy in denying her dark side. However, until that rage is faced and tamed, some women will not heal from their abusive experiences. They must learn to accept what has happened to them, that it was not their fault, and that there are many ways to protect themselves from what appeared to them as children to be unpredictable, violent attacks.

ASSOCIATED FACTORS

Alcohol and Drugs

The use of alcohol and drugs to numb the pain from the abuse is common among child sexual abuse victims. Kilpatrick (1990) found that the single best predictor for a woman's abuse of alcohol or drugs is whether she has been sexually abused or battered. Edwall and Hoffman (1988), Conte and Berliner (1988), and Briere (1989) all found an incidence of substance abuse in their studies of women who were child sexual abuse victims. Most of the data suggest that the substance abuse begins as early as age 9 for some and may become part of a self-destructive coping style that is sometimes seen in incest victims. It is not unusual for the abuser to facilitate the child's initiation into alcohol and drugs, particularly when these substances are used as a way to prepare the child for compliance with the sexual experience. Obviously, some memories of the details of the abuse will be affected by the use of alcohol and drugs. For some women, the use of the chemicals is designed to erase the painful memories, and total recall may never occur. Nevertheless, healing can take place using the memories of the feelings as well as those details that are retrievable.

Early Abuse and Dissociative and Multiple Personality Disorders

Children who are severely physically, sexually, and psychologically abused in early childhood (often by the age of 4) are at high risk to develop a multiple personality disorder (MPD) or other related dissociative disorders. Unable to integrate the pain and both "good" and "bad" images of themselves, they develop fragmented personalities. Their feelings are separated from the reality of what is happening to them. Dissociation is a psychological technique used as a defense mechanism, unconsciously protecting the mind from the impact of severe abuse. Those with MPD are not likely to initially reveal their other personalities to a therapist; it takes time and the development of trust before they feel safe enough to reveal their alter egos. Therapists who have worked with those with MPD describe their surprise at the distinct differences between the various personalities. Physical changes such as eye color, degree of alcohol or drug intoxication, and cessation of menstruation all can occur within a short time. In milder dissociative states, changes in voice tone and maturity, facial features, and eye movements may also be observed (see Courtois, 1988; Kluft, 1985; and Putnam, 1989b, for a discussion of MPD).

One of the most difficult aspects in working with MPD clients is their demand on the therapist's time. Frequently, these women must be hospitalized because of their dangerous behavior and threats of suicide and self-mutilation. Sometimes psychotic transferences develop. There is a recent trend toward forming MPD or dissociative disorder units in private psychiatric hospitals in order to begin the treatment and to provide a back-up during long-term, outpatient treatment. Often women are misdiagnosed with personality disorders when they are placed in a standard psychiatric hospital with staff who have little or no training in working with dissociation in abused women. Even the new specialized inpatient units may create more difficulties for the abused woman. If the unit has neither a trained staff nor a special program to work with child abuse survivors and multiple abuse victims, then hospitalization should be used only as a brief and last resort when it is not possible to keep the client safe any other way.

Many women who have been hospitalized report ritual abuse in addition to multiple forms of severe physical, sexual, and psychological abuse. There is some controversy about the increasing numbers of MPD cases being uncovered, particularly as these new hospital units have opened. Some of the controversy is fueled by the fact that it is still rare to see children in whom the MPD is observed at various developmental stages, although it is not unusual to watch clients develop new alter personalities once MPD becomes diagnosed. As might be expected, if clients keep developing more and more alters, the therapist's treatment techniques must also be carefully reviewed. Secrecy about the severe abuse, temporary coping skills adapted by the developing child, or even potentiation of the symptomatology in adult women are speculative keys to this puzzle. (Further discussion on treatment issues raised can be found in chapter 14).

Concurrent Physical Abuse

Many sexually abused children are also physically abused, although the two forms of abuse may not occur simultaneously. Some girls may view the sexual abuse as less painful than the physical abuse, whereas some say they would rather be beaten than be forced to engage in sex. Some girls may not rate which form of abuse, if any, is worse. Reports of those women who suffered multiple forms of abuse as children indicate that the psychological impact is likely to be greater than in those who suffered a single form of abuse. In young children, learning disabilities and attentional deficits frequently accompany multiple abuse. In adult women, such side effects appear in different forms. Women who have experienced both physical and sexual abuse are at a higher risk for relational difficulties.

CLINICAL PRESENTATION

The Conspiracy of Silence and Parental Alienation Syndrome

Therapists can sometimes find themselves in unintentional collusion with the child abuser. Most people do not want to believe that children are being hurt in such a painful way and often do not want to believe that a "nice" man who is their friend, colleague, or neighbor could do such a terrible thing. Some therapists, for a variety of personal reasons, have such difficulty in dealing with sexual issues that they cannot listen to their patients tell stories of incest and other forms of sexual abuse. Clients receive both subtle and direct messages not to discuss these events. If such a reaction occurs, it is best to be honest and refer the client to another trained practitioner. It is important to avoid any ambiguities that would permit the client to blame herself for causing the therapist discomfort. Instead, clearly state the need for specialized training to deal with the issues raised.

It is common for abuse to be revealed during child custody or visitation disputes, often because the child and the mother may feel safe from the abuser's anger. Mothers who were themselves abused at the same age that their child has reached during the custody dispute may feel freer to make a report of suspicions that they were unable to recognize while they were still living with the abusive man. Unfortunately, this is also the time at which a therapist may be the most likely to disbelieve the mother or the child's disclosure. Child protective services are so overloaded that they are rarely able to sort out the issues when reports are made at this juncture. Fathers who are abusive know how difficult it will be for a professional to believe a child and may take advantage of the situation, frequently accusing the mother of poisoning the child's mind as some kind of revenge. This process has been labeled *parental alienation syndrome*, and, although there is no research to support that such a syndrome even exists, its existence is readily believed by psychologists and judges. Some of the same people who are involved in the False Memory Foundation, mentioned earlier in this chapter, are also involved with promoting the existence of parental alienation syndrome.

Most children in divorcing families want to retain close relationships with both parents. When this does not occur, it is important to understand what is actually causing the child's difficulty in trusting the other parent. Too often, claims of parental alienation—usually the custodial parent alienating the child from the noncustodial parent—are made. Typically, the child who is residing with the mother becomes fearful of visitation with the father and refuses to go. Although a parent certainly can influence a child's opinion of the other parent, not unless that parent's behavior warrants the child's fear or dislike will such an attitude remain over time. Parental alienation syndrome seems to be defined as the cause of this long-standing attitude (cf. Gardner, 1987). Many divorce court judges seem to readily accept the idea that mothers are responsible for children's dislike for visitation with their fathers. A gender analysis of cases in which this label has been applied reveals the cultural bias against women: Mothers are almost always the parents who are accused of attempting to alienate fathers, not vice versa. Often these mothers do express their anger at feeling powerless against the man's manipulative and aggressive behavior. They may be frightened that they cannot better protect their children or stop the man's abusive behavior toward either their children or themselves. The developmental psychology theories suggest that children rarely become alienated from a parent unless they believe they are unprotected from either abuse or psychological abandonment. Although it may be difficult to sort out the facts in these cases, common sense dictates that giving the woman or child the power to regulate custody will increase their safety and reduce their anger and hostility, ultimately resulting in a better relationship with the man if he changes the behavior that frightened the child in the first place.

Reluctance to Believe the Child

There is a natural reluctance to believe children when they speak about sexual abuse, particularly if there is no physical evidence, which is common.

Preschool children may need props and leading questions in order to relate their memories. Goodman & Helgeson (1988) have empirically tested the reliability and validity of the child's memory and have found it to be as good as an adult's in most instances. Walker (1991b) described the dilemma of having to decide when to go beyond the nonleading question-and-answer interview, scrap the possibility of legal intervention, and get the information needed for therapeutic planning. Sometimes it is possible to tell whether a child has been sexually abused from the psychological symptoms observed while still not being sure who is the offender. Adult women survivors relate that the disbelief that they experienced as a child when they told someone about the abuse has had an impact on their ability to heal from the abuse. Most report that they gave up trying to get someone to help them and instead adopted coping strategies to protect themselves.

Achieving an appropriate therapeutic resolution, while protecting the rights of everyone involved, can be accomplished by taking a slow, deliberate approach to the investigation and keeping the woman and child safe. Sometimes, in cases in which there is a history of familial child sexual abuse, the addition of an outsider in the home is a better alternative than having the child removed. Or, in some cases, the father's voluntary removal from the home for a specified period is the best approach. Use of the legal system, particularly the new domestic violence protection laws that evict the suspected abuser temporarily while an investigation takes place, may need to be invoked. It can be difficult to try to balance the needs of each family member, as they often conflict with one another. Although some practitioners find no conflict with using family therapy when incest is discovered, most agree that the victim, at minimum, should have a separate therapist. This is also true when memories of sexual abuse surface for an adult woman in family treatment. A period of individual treatment is appropriate for helping her to deal with these memories. Partners or families need to understand what is happening to the woman and why she is so angry, and to learn how to provide assistance, especially during the crisis points. Davis (1991) presented materials that may be helpful to the survivor's family.

Recanting

It is not unusual for a child to report sexual abuse, then become so frightened that she recants her story and denies it ever happened. Many adult women continue to do the same. Sometimes recanting occurs after the child has been removed from the home and placed in a shelter, detention center, foster home, or group home. Despite being told that she did not do anything wrong, her observation tells her she must have done so. Why else would she be the one who is punished? Recanting is common in children who become frightened when the family starts to disintegrate or turns against the reporting child. Pressure is brought on the child by one or both parents, who are hurt by the allegations, and the child cannot cope with the guilt she feels as a result. When these children become women, they may recant either to themselves or to others, as a way of trying to feel better about the breakthrough memories.

In still other cases, a child who reports abuse is encouraged to retell the story with "enhanced memories" so that legal remedies can be more readily pursued. This may place the child under so much pressure that she recants everything, wanting to make it all go away. Unfortunately, many adults are more willing to believe a recantation than the original story of sexual abuse. It is not unusual for those who believe in the false memory syndrome to use stories of recantation by both children and adult women to demonstrate that either the work of the therapist or the reading materials given to the women cause the emergence of false stories of sexual abuse. Given the emotional difficulties of both children and adult survivors, it is often difficult to obtain reliability and validity data from the individuals involved. However, the clinical data on large numbers of children and women who have sought therapy services from a wide variety of therapists suggest that recantations are far more common than false accusations (see, e.g., various journal articles in *Journal of Child Sexual Abuse, Journal of Interpersonal Violence,* and *Violence and Victims* for further discussion).

It is important for the therapist to remember that an unfounded report does not mean that the sexual abuse did not happen; it does mean there is not enough legal evidence to go forward with a case. Most cases are filed in criminal courts, in which the standard is proof beyond a reasonable doubt, but many cases cannot meet that high burden of proof. Civil court, in which the standard of proof is lower—that the act was more likely than not to have happened—may be a more viable option. Many states are beginning to change their statute of limitations for filing civil lawsuits for personal injury so that adult women who remember incest and are strong enough to be able to file such a lawsuit have an extended period of time during which they can do so. Usually the time limitations are 1 to 2 years beyond the date of the injury or the date at which the injury became known to the plaintiff. The legal definitions of the word *know* also have been adapted for the typical child sexual abuse claim by an adult survivor, so that it legally means when the harm became known, not simply knowledge that the abusive incident occurred. It is important for clinicians to understand the criminal penalties, possible juvenile court action, and lawsuits for civil damages that may entangle some clients.

Ritual Abuse

Some child sexual abuse may involve ritual abuse such as the (sometimes fatal) mutilation of animals and people. Such ritual abuse may be performed in cults or may be associated with a preschool program (Finkelhor, Williams, & Burns, 1988; Kluft, 1985). Although the rituals are often associated with some genuine beliefs (e.g., devil-worship or various cults and sects) of the abusers, they may be more cynically designed to achieve two goals: (a) to frighten the children sufficiently to ensure that they will never tell others and (b) to create a sufficiently bizarre experience so that if children do tell adults about the abuse, the stories will seem so outlandish and confused that the adults (perhaps including the police or a jury) will dismiss the reports as a child's disturbed but imaginative fantasy. Reports of ritual abuse have been on the increase, particularly among those clients who are hospitalized for dissociative disorders. Although it may be difficult to document the actual existence of such ritualized behavior, it is important to help the client deal with the frightening images without making a judgment about their veracity.

COMMON SEQUELAE

The first documented psychological symptoms of child sexual abuse were Freud's observations of the hysterical and conversion reactions in his patients, made after visiting French psychiatrists Charcot and Janet (cf. Lerman, 1986, for a complete discussion, and Masson, 1984, for a historical account). Recent clinical studies of sexually abused children report a large number of other effects as well, including depression; guilt; learning difficulties; sexual promiscuity; running away and truancy; somatic complaints; phobias; nightmares; compulsive rituals; self-destructive behaviors such as cutting, head-banging, and other mutilation; sexual dysfunction; relationship problems; poor self-image; dissociative disorders; isolation; depersonalization; and suicidal ideation and behavior. Not all children are affected in the same way by the experience of sexual abuse. Of course, this also means that not all adult survivors will experience the same impact from the same type of abuse.

Conte and Berliner (1988) empirically measured psychological symptoms from a study of 369 children who had been referred to a large Seattle treatment facility after reporting sexual abuse. The symptoms measured were then subjected to factor analysis, and eight factors resulted. The factors included items that measured self-esteem, aggression, fearfulness, conscientiousness, concentration problems, withdrawal, acting-out behavior, and anxious-to-please and tries-too-hard type of compliance. Conte and Berliner further developed 12 clinical dimensions on the basis of conceptual and statistical analysis that included concentration problems, aggression, withdrawal, depression, somatic complaints, character and personality style difficulties, antisocial behavior, nervous and emotional problems, behavioral regression, body image and self-esteem problems, fear, and posttraumatic stress.

Differences between abused and nonabused children were statistically significant on these 12 clinical dimensions. Of course, it is important to remember that these clinical findings are also indicative of emotional disorders other than sexual trauma. However, most of them are reported by female survivors of child sexual abuse. Certain patterns of symptoms may be clues to early abuse such as types of dissociation, serious difficulties with boundaries and limitations on interpersonal behavior, spontaneous and explosive rage, self-mutilation, and developmental gaps around the ages of high risk.

Conte and Berliner (1988) also found that the degree of psychological impact seemed to be directly related to the amount of force used, the frequency of sexual abuse, the closeness of the relationship between the offender and the child, the type of forced or coerced sexual activities, and the type of coping during abuse including cognitive attributions. A mitigating factor in the impact and healing process was the amount of support that the child received. The single most important support person is the nonoffending parent, usually the mother. Siblings proved to be an important additional source of support for the victim.

Family intervention with the child, mother, and siblings (not necessarily all in the same room at the same time) that focuses on supporting the child may be an important adjunct to treatment of the child, according to Conte and Berliner's (1988) research. These data are especially important to remember when the adult client is deciding what type of relationship to have with her family. Most clients heal faster when they can figure out how to establish a relationship with family, including learning how to set appropriate boundaries. Only in unusual cases would a separation from parents be an appropriate therapist recommendation. Sometimes, a temporary separation is necessary to help the client decide what boundaries are important for her to establish. However, advice from a therapist to discontinue contact with family members, even those who are clearly taking advantage of the woman, may take away the woman's own power to make such decisions or to learn how to set limits with which she can live.

SPECIFIC ASSESSMENT ISSUES

Theoretical Models

Traumatization Model

Finkelhor (1990) has developed a theoretical model that explains the traumatization that occurs in child sexual abuse victims and survivors and that is based on empirical and clinical reports in the literature rather than clinical work. He suggested that one important benefit of using such a model is the avoidance of the tendency to pathologize the impact of child sexual abuse. In this model, four areas of development are affected that he called *traumagenic dynamics*: (a) traumatic sexualization, (b) stigmatization, (c) betrayal and trust, and (d) powerlessness (Finkelhor & Browne, 1988).

Traumatic sexualization is the process that shapes a child's sexuality in developmentally inappropriate and interpersonally dysfunctional ways. Certain parts of the child's body may be overstimulated and given distorted importance, resulting in later obsessive avoidance or fetishlike behavior. Use of force increases the amount of fear that the child attaches to sexual activities. If the child is rewarded for her compliance with inappropriate sexual behavior, she may develop seductive patterns to demand attention. Confusion around arousal and sexual control issues also emerge in adulthood. Aggressive responses to other children may also be adopted.

Stigmatization refers to the negative connotations that are communicated to the child about the sexual experience. The need to keep the "secret" contributes to the sense of powerlessness and shame. The reciting of the story contributes to a new sense of empowerment. Adult victims may feel "spoiled" or "different," or have other feelings connected with low self-esteem, much like those from which rape victims suffer. It is suggested that adult survivor guilt, criminal behavior, and suicidal ideation and attempts come from the stigmatization dynamic.

As a result of the abuse, the child develops a lack of trust and a fear of betrayal. Often there is a slow awareness that a person in a position of trust is not treating them well. Then there is guilt at remembering the exploitation and abuse rather than the loving behavior. The sense of betrayal and lack of trust extend to adult relationships in which victims do not expect constancy in noncontingent love and affection. Depression, dependency, and anger are common manifestations of the betrayal and lack of trust dynamic.

Powerlessness or disempowerment of the child occurs when the child's will, desires, and sense of efficacy are continually contravened. Lack of boundaries and invasion of the child's own body contribute to the power-lessness. It is suggested that fear, anxiety, and phobic responses, as well as lowered self-esteem, may stem from this sense of powerlessness. Reempowerment of victims is seen as an important therapeutic tool for overcoming the impact of powerlessness.

Posttraumatic Stress Disorder (PTSD) Model

The PTSD model is most helpful in developing a treatment plan and under-standing the psychological damage experienced by the child. A useful expansion of the model would be a more detailed evaluation of the impact on the developing cognitive and social skills of the child, particularly in rela-tionships with peers.

Blume (1989) suggested a *postincest syndrome* in women with incest experiences, whereas Courtois and Sprei (1988) used the term *retrospective incest*. Each of their lists of symptoms fits the three major groups of PTSD symptoms (described in more detail in earlier chapters and later in chapter 13). These symptom groups include (a) cognitive disturbances, including intrusive and amnesiac memory disturbances; (b) high avoidance or depres-sive symptoms, including minimization and denial of the inappropriate sexual experiences; and (c) high arousal, anxiety, panic, and phobic symp-toms. Even though some of the early memories seem to be sealed over when the child is still young, the symptoms develop over time. Eventually the symptoms break through without the woman regaining direct memories of the incest experiences, causing emotional disequilibrium. Some of the last-ing emotional impact seems more severe than that resulting from other traumas experienced as an adult, probably because of the developmental status of the child.

Aside from the PTSD symptoms, incest survivors often have two addi-tional categories of disturbances. The first is sexual dysfunction and includes such behavior as an aversion to being touched; aversion or attraction to cer-tain sexual acts; feeling betrayed by one's body; trouble integrating sexual and emotional intimacy; power and control issues in sexual relationships; excessive seductiveness or sexual aggression; separating sex from emotion through becoming a prostitute, stripper, or sex symbol; perceiving sex as "dirty"; or an erotic response to abuse and dominance. Frequent physical problems in the reproductive tract and gastrointestinal systems are also reported.

The second area of disturbance that goes beyond the PTSD criteria is in the development of emotional intimacy that usually takes place during the early teen years. It has been theorized that girls need to develop strong same-gender peer relationships at around ages 12 to 13, a step that is developmentally essential in the formation of emotional intimacy. But this developmental stage is often not experienced by incest victims because they feel different from other girls their age and fear the exposure of their secret. It is common for early teenage girls to sit on the telephone for hours talking about their latest discovery, boys. Incest victims are less able to engage in this type of discussion because of their early sexual experiences. Those incest victims who are sexually attracted to women feel double victimization, especially because there is usually no one to talk to about their "different" and frightening feelings.

PTSD or Personality Disorders: Diagnostic Issues

Although most victims and survivors report symptoms consistent with a PTSD, the diagnosis they more typically are assigned is a personality disorder, not PTSD (see chapter 12, for further discussion, and Herman, 1992, for a review of the literature). Even with the *Diagnostic and Statistical Manual of Mental Disorders* diagnostic system that requires therapists to make a differential diagnosis concentrating on the less serious diagnostic categories first, the confusion with borderline, dependent, and self-defeating personality disorders continues to be a problem. Practitioners may base the personality disorder diagnosis on the presence of boundary and other relationship issues between the victim or survivor and others, or they may simply infer its existence from a few behavioral incidents without understanding the relationship of such incidents to the survival and coping strategies developed during the abuse experience.

The impact of prior incest experience on adult women's interpersonal relationships really does need a separate conceptual paradigm for diagnosis. Fundamental lack of trust and difficulty in having needs met, particularly intimacy needs, are fairly common symptoms of survivors. Many survivors have lost the capacity to know when they have achieved approval from people who are important to them, and therefore they never feel satisfied or content with their relationships. There are some similarities with other types of survivors, such as children who have grown up amid war, torture, or political oppression. For all these types of survivors, the uncertainty of knowing what will be expected of them in order to survive the next day is an important factor in disrupting the expected and actual continuity of relationships.

Millon (1981/1991) suggested that a personality disorder is a pervasive and enduring disruption in the ability of a person to function normally. Of course, what is normal is also the subject of much debate in the mental health field. Millon stated that less than 10% of the population has a personality disorder. His taxonomy of types of personality disorders parallels the *DSM* nosology system. However, when looking at the reliability and validity of diagnoses of personality disorders, the field trials of the *DSM–III* categories indicated statistically low ratings for the various categories and each had a great deal of overlap with the others (Kirk & Einbinder, 1994; Kirk & Kutchins, 1992; Kutchins & Kirk, 1986). The debate over the *DSM–III* revision in 1987 focused on the sexist assumptions that underlie each of the personality disorder criteria (Caplan, 1991; Pantony & Caplan, 1991; Walker, 1994). Although there was a great deal of focus on the proposed *masochistic personality disorder* that eventually was renamed *self-defeating personality disorder*, in fact, the criteria chosen to make such a diagnosis were predominantly culturally normative sex-role socialized behavior for women (Caplan, 1985; Rosewater, 1987b; Walker, 1987a, 1994).

The issue of whether sexually abused girls have developed a pervasive and enduring limitation to their emotional functioning that can be labeled a personality disorder is not yet settled. Those who wish to avoid sex-role stereotyping will probably find the personality disorder criteria too unreliable and limiting to the treatment focus. They probably will be more comfortable using the PTSD diagnosis with sensitivity to the additional areas of sexual and interpersonal relationships. During the preparation of the *DSM–IV*, there was discussion of a *complex PTSD* category, which ultimately was not included, that measured the more enduring characteristics demonstrated by repeated trauma victims, many of whom are incest survivors (see Herman, 1992, for discussion). Although Kilpatrick (personal communication, July 1992) found that only 4% of PTSD survivors need the additional criteria that the proposed complex PTSD category would have provided, many of that 4% are incest survivors. Many therapists who treat incest survivors believe that such a diagnostic category would permit greater access to appropriate treatment focusing on the situational trauma and its subsequent sequelae (Herman, 1992). Other therapists find the personality disorder diagnosis more to their liking. The important result of this debate is the need to begin treatment with the methods used in treating PTSD rather than a personality disorder, whatever the diagnostic category.

Other Common Symptoms

The importance of sorting out the most accurate diagnosis lies both in acceptance of treatment by victims and survivors and in appropriate treatment planning. Blume (1989) listed more than 30 common symptoms of what she called "postincest survivor syndrome" in her checklist. Many of the symptoms represent both extremes of particular behaviors. These symptoms include fears of being alone, particularly at night; swallowing and gagging reflex sensitivity and problems with feelings of suffocation, especially when water gets on one's face; poor body image; covering one's body with lots of loose clothing; extreme privacy needs in the bathroom or bedroom; eating or substance abuse disorders; cutting one's skin and other self-destructive behaviors; phobias; need for invisibility or exhibitionism; suicide ideation and attempts; obsessive rumination; anger and rage issues; depersonalization and other forms of numbness; no sense of humor or constant wisecracking; intense anxiety and fears as a child; high risk taking or inability to take risks; inability to trust or indiscriminate trust; fear of losing control and need for intense control; multiple victimization experiences; abandonment issues; relationships demanding unconditional love; extreme need to please others; ambivalent or conflict ridden relationships; blocking out early childhood years; limited tolerance for happiness and other limited range of emotions; quiet-voiced; great appreciation of small favors by others; and frequency of certain behaviors such as stealing, firesetting, and avoidance of mirrors.

Of course, not all of these symptoms would appear in any one person, and they are all symptoms commonly seen in other emotional disorders. However, the frequency with which the particular pattern of symptoms is seen in child sexual abuse survivors who seek treatment makes this a useful checklist guide for the therapist. It is important not to let the presence of some or even most of these symptoms be the sole determinant of a diagnosis when there is no other evidence of child sexual abuse in the woman's history. However, selecting survivor therapy treatment techniques may still be an appropriate option, even though it must be clear that there is no confirmation that sexual abuse did occur. Knowledge that others have had similar experiences with some of these symptoms may help a particular woman feel less stigmatized or different from other women and facilitate her healing, whether or not child sexual abuse is ever discovered.

Breakthrough Memories

Recent estimates suggest that at least one third of women who were sexually abused as children may, as adults, lack conscious awareness of the abuse. Such women typically seek therapy for a seemingly unrelated problem, such as depression (McGrath et al., 1990). The buried incest memories may begin to surface sometime during the course of therapy. Those women who are aware of their childhood sexual abuse may be more likely to seek out therapists specializing in what is sometimes called "retrospective incest therapy" (Courtois, 1988; Courtois & Sprei, 1988). More often, women come into therapy with symptomatology (as described earlier in this chapter) that interferes with their ability to function and live in the way in which they would like. They may have some very vague but negative memories of abuse in their childhood, or they may have no memory of anything that happened to them before a certain age as a child. Obviously, these symptoms are also indicative of disorders other than those caused by incest situations. Sometimes the only "proof" that the memories are accurate is the enormous relief that is experienced by clients once the possibility of childhood abuse is discussed, often akin to having a heavy burden lifted from their shoulders.

Initially, breakthrough memories are traces, accompanied by the uncomfortable feeling that something awful happened but without clues as to what it was. With some support from friends, family, books, and a therapist, the victim slowly begins to become aware of more specific memories. This may occur during dreams, in a therapy session, or when the woman experiences or views a similar event on television. In other instances, spontaneous recollections simply intrude on the woman's thoughts. Many women struggle to recall more details and experience great emotional agony as the memories unfold. In some cases, the pain is so great that they need to be hospitalized briefly for their own safety. These women are often terrified to find out what actually happened, even though they have enough clues to recognize that they were sexually abused. Courtois (1991) described techniques useful in helping women as they regain these memories. In some cases victims have trace memories going all the way back to their infancy. Although it is difficult to verify such early sexual abuse, these women have dreams, symptoms, and other trace memories that seem to support its occurrence. Although legal issues concerning such memories have been raised by researchers, making this area a difficult one when court cases are involved (cf. Doris, 1991; Goodman & Helgeson, 1988; Loftus & Ketchum, 1991; Loftus & Loftus, 1980), the therapist should be most concerned about the impact of the client's perception of the abuse.

THERAPY, INTERVENTIONS, AND COLLABORATIVE APPROACHES

Incest victims often need the same type of treatment intervention that other types of abuse victims need to become survivors and to heal from their trauma. Because the abuse occurred so much earlier in their lives, the treatment must deal with memories of the trauma rather than with ongoing abuse. A combination of feminist therapy principles, including empowerment and validation of the victim's experiences and memories of experiences (that may or may not be accurate because of history and contamination), are important. Memory researchers believe that the current meaning assigned to past experiences may have a greater impact on the current functioning of the victim than what actually happened to her. In order for treatment to be effective, it is less important to determine the accuracy of the memories than it is to help the woman deal with the meaning that she assigns to what she remembers about her experiences. Often these memories are not verbally descriptive but are, instead, based on memories of feelings. The therapist using survivor therapy is encouraged to respect these feelings and to help the woman deal with them effectively.

Dissociative States

Most victims of early childhood abuse, either physical or sexual, learn to go into dissociative states as a way of coping with their terror and physical pain. Survivor therapy helps the woman become aware of this dissociation and learn how to control it. Mild dissociative states are often described by children as "making their mind go somewhere else" and by adults as "out of body experiences." Here the separation of the mind from the body permits the victim to keep control over what she thinks while being unable to protect her body from being overpowered by the offender. Often she focuses intensely on something else, sometimes on the bedspread, a painting, or a segment of wallpaper in the room in which the abuse frequently takes place. Some women talk about floating above themselves, watching what is taking place and trying to shout out ineffectively because there is no one there to listen.

When victims report abuse incidents, they may go into a dissociative state in the practitioner's office. Their eyes may move back and forth as if they are reporting what they are seeing in their mind's eye. Or they might change the tone or tense of their language from past to present tense, a shift that reflects the fear and intense emotions occurring at the time of the incident. They generally come right out of the dissociative state after the report of abuse is completed. Sometimes they interrupt their story and talk about seemingly unrelated topics in order to stop the dissociation or even block the pain. It is the ability to intensely concentrate on a small detail rather than on the abuse itself that seems to protect the abuse victim from feeling the pain of the violence. However, that same person might be capable of making serious complaints about the intensity of what appear to be minor pains that occur in between the abusive incidents.

Memory loss that can be termed *psychogenic amnesia* also occurs in child sexual abuse victims. Frequently children seal off the memories of abuse so that they remember the emotional anxiety and fear but are unable to recall later to what these feelings were attached. Often partial memories surface during dreams. Subsequent abuse in a relationship may also cause the buried memories to surface. The memories may return with therapy or chemical withdrawal; in other instances, there is no apparent reason why they do or do not return. Adults who were sexually abused prior to the development of language often have a free-floating anxiety that may have sexual abuse as its origin. There are few empirical studies of this group, because such experiences are difficult to document and most records are poorly kept. There is always skepticism when these reports surface, although adult women who have nothing to gain from telling lies continue to make major therapeutic gains when treated as though the undocumented abuse did occur. Courtois (1991) provided a detailed discussion of dealing with emerging memories during the treatment of the adult retrospective incest victim. The belief that there may even be memories on a cellular level suggest that body therapy techniques may be as important as verbal therapies in order for some women to heal. Nonverbal techniques for working with preverbal memories have been developed. *Eye movement desensitization* (D. L. Shapiro, 1990) is one of the newer techniques that helps erase these painful trace memories in some women.

Other ways in which dissociative states are manifested in incest survivors include sleepwalking and altered states of consciousness. Partial psychogenic amnesia is more common. Sometimes total amnesia occurs, although this is rare. In severe cases, several complete personalities form, although the person is aware of behaving differently and thus is more integrated than those who develop multiple personality disorder. Cases have been reported in which each part of the personality has its own structure and engages in behavior that the main personality could not or would not perform.

For example, a woman who was in an incestuous relationship from ages 7 through 12 systematically embezzled money from several business firms for which she worked for many years. After being apprehended, she made up stories of having a serious medical illness. All of this behavior, including the court proceedings, was carefully hidden from her husband and children with whom she lived as a typical wife with the responsibilities of child care and work outside the home. Interestingly, most of the stolen money was given to her incestuous stepfather. In another case, a woman kept a separate apartment in which she stored sexy clothes that she would never wear in her regular life. She used this apartment as a safe hideaway, occasionally picking up men and bringing them there. Neither her husband nor her family and friends knew anything about this secret life. Although there were many instances of dissociative behavior in these women, their different personalities were complete and not fragmented out of their awareness.

Transference and Countertransference Issues

Some women who seek treatment who were abused as children, particularly incest victims, have developed difficult patterns of relating to others that transfer to their therapist. Afraid that even someone who cares about them will cause them intense pain, these women keep testing the therapist as a way to protect themselves from unanticipated harm. Therapists need to set strict boundaries with such clients and refrain from raising the clients' expectations that they can get more from the therapist by their manipulative behavior. This is often difficult to assess, especially because most abuse victims need to know that the therapist is on their side. One of the damages caused by the abuse is the inability to perceive neutrality: Everyone is seen as either being with them or against them. At the same time, restrictions on dual relationships are particularly difficult for incest victims who have had to live with boundary violations that they could not control. They may demand special favors, attempt to get the therapist to pay more attention to them, and try to break the rules concerning dual relationships involving time, money, activities outside of therapy, and sexual boundaries. It is important for the therapist not to become seduced by the belief that he or she can handle the "extras" requested by such clients.

In some cases the client develops a psychotic transference toward the therapist. Often, these clients believe that they have fallen in love with the therapist and interpret certain signals to support their wish that the therapist also loves them. A therapist's attempts to terminate therapy when the client's behavior starts to get out of control may only escalate anger and violence. In one case, a client shot arrows at the therapist's lawn and car tires when she refused the client's constant telephone calls and terminated the relationship. In another case, a client sent death threats to a therapist's wife and was observed stalking his home and office after he terminated therapy because of a job change. He went to court to obtain a restraining order to stop her harassment. She retaliated by filing a lawsuit accusing him of sexual misconduct. Fortunately, he had numerous notes that documented the content and process of their sessions and the escalation of her psychotic transference and violent behavior. He also had sought consultation as her behavior escalated.

In a third case, a client attempted to obtain a copy of the therapist's travel schedule so that she could meet her in another city. When she admitted this plan to the therapist, she reasoned that she could get the therapist to violate the boundaries against a sexual relationship if they accidentally met in another city. This therapist suggested both she and the client participate in a consultation with another therapist in order to help the client feel less pain about the limitations that must occur in a therapeutic relationship. In a fourth case, a client filed a grievance against the therapist, accusing her of sexually abusing her, after the client angrily terminated therapy when the therapist tried to set limits to telephone calls and outside behavior. In yet another case, a therapist who felt sorry for a client who was thrown out of her home permitted her to stay at the therapist's home for several days until she was able to find another living situation. Seemingly grateful, the client cooked dinner, helped with housework, and generally made herself a welcome guest. However, the client became enraged at the therapist's confrontation when she did not seem to be trying to find another living situation as originally agreed. This client could not tolerate the time that the therapist spent attending to her own family's needs and eventually filed a grievance alleging that the dual relationship seriously affected her mental health. Good intentions, which appeared to be the motivation for the actions of each of the therapists described above, were not sufficient to prevent further harm to the client.

Therapists working with women who have been sexually abused as children, and who may have been abused in other contexts as well, must anticipate that transference and countertransference issues will arise. These women have survived because they have been able to please their abusers, often at the expense of their own emotional stability. They have been exploited by their abusers, some of whom have also given them love and nurturing. Victims' confusion about what they must do in order to continue to be cared for by a consistently caring person, such as a therapist, is to be expected. Their ability to manipulate people must be seen as a survival skill, and their attempt to manipulate the therapist should not come as a surprise. On the other hand, it is also appropriate for a therapist to expect the client to follow the rules agreed on earlier. It is important to make sure that boundaries are clearly established, perhaps using a disclosure statement (required by law in Colorado and other states and discussed further in chapter 10). Consultation and careful record keeping will also help defend the therapist against any potential charges. Most clients respond well to firm limits within a caring relationship. Discuss the client's wishes openly, and explain patiently and consistently why, for the benefit of the client, certain wishes cannot be met. As troublesome as it is, it is far easier to deal with complaints to the state licensing boards and association ethics committees, especially if liability risks are minimized, than to have to cope with the violence that a number of abuse victims are capable of inflicting on their therapists if they develop a psychotic transference.

Intervention Modalities

Individual Therapy

Women who have experienced incest need to feel empowered so that they can regain control of their lives. A combination of feminist and trauma therapy appears to be the most successful approach to healing, although many psychoanalysts claim that feminist-oriented analytic therapy is also effective (Alpert & Paulson, 1990). Whatever the title, the victim or survivor needs to deal directly with the abuse issues and to stop any self-destructive behaviors that may have developed, including eating and substance disorders, self-mutilation, and threatened or actual suicide attempts.

Courtois and Sprei (1988) and Courtois (1990) have developed a feminist-oriented treatment program that systematically deals with the issues that incest survivors face. Courtois viewed the incest experience as having a profound effect on the developing child's core personality. Helping the adult go back and fill in the developmental holes is an important part of the treatment plan. Briere (1989) also has developed a treatment model that has been found to be effective. (More discussion on treatment can be found in chapter 14.)

Group Therapy

Therapy groups for incest survivors have become popular in many communities. Some such groups are led by trained therapists or facilitators, whereas others are patterned after the self-help models. Therapy groups may follow an Alcoholics Anonymous 12-step model, or use some of the self-help books such as the Bass and Davis (1988) model. Although most of these groups are therapeutic, not all provide therapy. They may be used as an adjunct to individual therapy or even as preparation for therapy to deal with individual issues after group participation. It is important for many incest survivors to know that they are not the only victims and to learn about the commonalities, especially shame and self-blame, that many victims experience.

Recent information put out by the False Memory Syndrome Foundation suggests that these self-help groups plant false memories about incest into the minds of women who attend the sessions. If they also use self-help books, the foundation literature suggests that women can be coerced into believing they were sexually abused when nothing ever happened to them. There are no data to support the accusations of the False Memory Syndrome Foundation (FMSF), although there are a few testimonial stories from women who might be recanting their stories for other reasons. One of the FMSF leaders' daughters has presented evidence of abuse conflicting with that provided by her mother, raising questions about the motivation for the participation of the mother, and of other parents, in the group. In addition, a founding FMSF board member considered resigning after an interview of him, printed in a Dutch journal, suggested that he supported sex between adults and young boys.

However, the accusations against therapists that are made by those who believe that memories can be inserted into people's minds must make all therapists more introspective about their work. There are some therapists, who are either deliberately unscrupulous or unintentionally harmful, who use inappropriate treatment that leads vulnerable women to think that they were sexually abused when there is no evidence to support these claims. It is important for the therapist to carefully evaluate and document each case in order to avoid any bias or appearance of bias.

Family Therapy

There are numerous issues involving victims' families of origin that may need to be addressed in therapy, particularly when incest issues are a focal point of the therapy. Although a child's recovery is enhanced by the perpetrator's acceptance of responsibility and apologies to the victim, there are no data to suggest that direct confrontation with the perpetrator facilitates healing as an adult. Nevertheless, many women decide that they must confront their abuser as a part of the healing process. Sometimes this confrontation can be performed effectively with the therapist present. In other instances, the client can handle the confrontation herself. Families deal with this disclosure in a variety of ways, some supporting the client, others supporting the accused perpetrator, and others refusing to take sides.

Women may also talk to members of their family separately. Disclosure to sisters often brings the abuse out into the open, with each of the victims able to share their old secrets with each other. In some cases, though, a sister is unwilling or not yet ready to acknowledge what happened to her. If the client is the only one who has been victimized, her siblings may refuse to believe her disclosure. Mothers also have reactions that run the gamut, with some staunchly supporting the incest perpetrator and some clearly taking the victim's part. The family is often skeptical and emotionally unexpressive, but willing to think about it. When alcohol abuse is present in the family, the dysfunction may be so profound that effective family intervention for the sexual abuse issue is not possible.

Couples Therapy

Child sexual abuse brings with it difficulties in interpersonal relationships and sexual dysfunctions that seriously affect an intimate relationship. Sometimes couples therapy is indicated, either simultaneously with, or as an adjunct to, individual treatment. If the woman's partner is supportive during the intense periods of treatment, the relationship may survive with greater strength and mutual commitment. However, sometimes it is impossible for the partner to forgo having his or her needs met for the length of time that it takes for the victim to begin to recover. The woman's self-absorption and pain is so great that she may not be able to relate to her partner or her children for long periods of time.

Self-Help Books

There are several self-help books that are popular and that offer assistance to clients and professionals. The most popular is the Bass and Davis (1988) book, *Courage to Heal*, and the workbook that accompanies it, *Survivor's Handbook*. A new book in the series for partners of survivors is also now available (Davis, 1991). Blume's (1989) book also provides self-help type of information. Most bookstores are filled with other titles. Many women find reading these books helpful if they do it slowly, when they are ready, and with the opportunity to ask questions of their therapist in order to personalize what they read. It is important that, if these books are used, they be used only as adjuncts to treatment rather than in place of the therapy itself. Because survivors with partial memory can be suggestible as regards information that implies what should have happened to them, it is important that the survivor books are not used as a substitute for the woman's own experience. Therapists must assist clients in their own journey toward recovery.

Collaborative Approaches

Specialized Hospital Units

It has become popular for private hospitals, particularly those looking for a way to fill beds, to offer a special unit for treatment of multiple personalities and other dissociative disorders, as discussed earlier. Many women who have entered these brief (usually less than 1 month) programs have experienced early, severe physical and sexual abuse in their homes. Different treatment philosophies are followed at different inpatient programs. In some treatment programs it is considered better to permit patients to regress so that rebuilding of an integrated core personality can occur. Other programs hold that too much regression hampers any progress toward integration, which is a primary goal in order to help the woman live a more normal life. Survivor therapy is more consistent with the latter, more positive, approach. It is best to approach these hospital units with a healthy skepticism. Careful evaluation of a unit may include paying attention to the presence of an integrated trauma theory treatment philosophy, of staff trained in abuse issues, and of an understanding of the social context in which abuse occurs in order to help women avoid future victimization. The availability of an all-woman group on the unit is important. Most women are unable to deal effectively with sexual abuse issues unless they are in a women's group. The presence of men inhibits their recovery.

Liaisons With Community Groups

Most large communities have self-help groups for incest survivors to provide support for one another. Organized groups such as Parents United may provide some support to parents and survivors of incest. In some communities these groups are used by child protective services as a means of helping children overcome the effects of more current abuse. Recovery may be more difficult in groups in which disclosure of certain information could result in the filing of criminal charges. Parents who may also be survivors themselves sometimes find assistance in self-help groups. Other groups are designed for women who begin to deal with their sexual abuse when they are adults. Sometimes these women tried to deal with the abuse as children; in other cases, they did not tell anyone about the abuse until they joined the group. Some survivors find that their boundaries have been violated too often for them to be comfortable in these groups initially, but others find the support of women in the same situation invaluable in their healing process. Again, a women's group is necessary in order for many women to make strides toward recovery.

It is important to be aware of the community resources and to provide clients with the option to attend self-help groups as an adjunct to therapy if they so choose. (See chapters 7, 13, and 14 for further discussion about self-help groups.)

SUMMARY

In recent years the idea that incest and child sexual abuse are rare crimes has been disproved. Child sexual abuse is generally defined as any touching of the genital area, or any other area of the child's body, that has a sexual connotation. Coercing a child to touch an adult's genital areas, showing sexually explicit material to a child, or coercing a child to pose for such pictures also constitutes child sexual abuse.

Children are most vulnerable to child sexual abuse during the preschool years, at ages 7 or 8, and during the teenage years. Most girls who have been sexually abused, particularly those who have experienced incest, put blame (unfairly, in most cases) on the mother for not preventing the abuse. The ability to accept, understand, and perhaps even forgive their mother is an important issue in treatment. Data also suggest that children who can depend on support from their nonoffending mothers or siblings make faster recoveries than those who cannot.

Alcohol and drug use, teenage pregnancies, prostitution, difficulty with intimacy, fears of betrayal, and a deep-seated rage that can interfere with the ability to maintain interpersonal relationships are all traits that may be found in women who have been sexually abused as children. Many clinicians have traced the origins of dissociative disorders to the use of dissociation as a coping strategy during child sexual abuse.

One of the most controversial areas of child sexual abuse is the legitimacy of the adult woman's memories of abuse when she was a child. Some researchers insist that these are planted or false memories. The clinical data are presented here with guidelines for therapeutic practice in order to minimize risk of liability. Similarly, mothers who try to protect their children from abuse are often accused of trying to take revenge on the children's fathers by instilling in the children negative feelings toward their fathers. This is sometimes called parental alienation syndrome.

Common sequelae from research on children include items that measured self-esteem, aggression, fearfulness, conscientiousness, concentration problems, withdrawal, acting-out behavior, and anxious-to-please and tries-too-hard types of compliance. These factors continue to be seen in adult survivors.

The two major theoretical models discussed include Finkelhor's (1990) traumagenic model and the PTSD model (Walker, 1990). A major controversy in treatment involves the issue of whether to treat the symptoms or the entire personality of the woman. Survivor therapy takes the position that the construct of personality disorders, as currently defined by the *DSM–III–R* (and planned for the *DSM–IV*), is not relevant to women who have been sexually abused as children (Walker & Browne, 1985). Many of their symptoms disappear after supportive therapy that takes a feminist and trauma survivor focus, suggesting that these disorders were actually learned coping strategies and not integrated within victims' personalities.

The therapist must prepare for potential transference and countertransference problems that arise when treating women who were sexually abused as children. There are many different forms of therapy from which the woman can choose: individual, group, family, and couples therapy. Local self-help groups and the reading of certain self-help texts can be a useful adjunct to direct, individual therapy. Clinicians who work with adult survivors of child sexual abuse should be knowledgeable about what therapies and services the community has to offer.

5

Sexual Harassment and Discrimination at Work and in Academia

The sexual harassment of women in the course of their jobs or in educational settings is an often overlooked type of abuse. The abuser is most often a powerful male and the victim is most often a less powerful female. Like other repeat abuse victims, the woman who is sexually harassed in academia or on the job faces repeated, unwanted, often unpredictable sexual advances from men who hold some power over her life, in this case, the ability to influence her career. Interestingly, the public awareness of sexual harassment on the job radically changed after the media coverage of the October, 1991, Senate hearings to confirm U.S. Supreme Court Justice Clarence Thomas, who was accused by University of Oklahoma School of Law Professor Anita Hill of sexually harassing her when he was her supervisor, first at the Department of Education and then at the Equal Employment Opportunity Commission. The latter, ironically, is the U.S. government agency that has the enforcement of the laws prohibiting sexual harassment as one of its mandates. As the all-male senatorial committee both elicited and listened to testimony from Hill and Thomas, it became clear that men and women do not agree on what constitutes sexual harassment. Empirical research supports this observation. For example, Fitzgerald, Gold, Ormerod, and Weitzman (1988) found that, whereas 26% of the male faculty members whom they studied admitted to engaging in sexual intimacies with their students, only 1% defined it as sexually harassing behavior.

During the Thomas confirmation hearings, most women who were questioned were able to identify with having experienced unwanted sexual attention during their careers, but were inconsistent in specifying which behavior they would describe as sexual harassment. Many believe that those widely televised hearings were a watershed event for better defining, understanding, and dealing with sexual harassment. Recent polls have found that more than 80% of women now consistently define similar behaviors, to which they have been subjected, as harassment. Only a small percentage of men have been able to identify these same behaviors as sexual harassment of women. Again, Fitzgerald, Shullman, et al. (1988) empirical research support these differences in men's and women's definitions of harassing behavior (Fitzgerald & Ormerod, 1991; Fitzgerald & Shullman, 1985; Fitzgerald, Shullman, et al., 1988).

Indications that public attitudes toward the seriousness of sexual harassment are changing could be seen in the fall session of 1992 when members of Congress were themselves called to account for their behavior toward female staffers. Senator Brock from the state of Washington chose not to run for reelection. Senator Packwood from Oregon won his reelection bid, although he was then publicly held accountable for the accusations of at least 9 women, in addition to 20 former female staffers who had come forward as of the end of 1993. Most of these women reported that they were intimidated and threatened with retaliation should they disclose information during his reelection campaign. Although the Senate Ethics Committee is investigating these accusations, these women recently told their attorneys that they are still too frightened of reprisals to come forward and testify about the intimidation and threats against their character. Obviously, other women watch these public displays, and they have a chilling effect on women's willingness to report both harassment and subsequent bullying tactics.

OVERVIEW

As a result of these and other highly public cases, it appears that the victim's definition of harassment may become the ruling one in the future. For victims and their subsequent therapists this is good news: Survivor therapy goals of validation of the experience and reempowerment of the victim become easier to meet when society stands behind the woman. In most other forms of abuse that have criminal as well as civil liabilities, the definition often comes from what the abuser intended to do (criminal codes insist that the level of criminal responsibility come from the actor's intentions) as well as from the impact on the abuse victim. But, because sexual harassment is considered a form of a civil rights violation against all women, the intent of the man is not considered relevant. If it can be proven that the man has engaged in such behavior and that any woman might be harmed by it, it is a violation of her civil rights. Although it is now possible for the individual woman to collect actual economic and punitive damages under the new civil rights legislation passed by the U.S. Congress in 1991, the legislative goal of exposing sexual harassment is to remedy the situation and prevent its recurrence so that women's rights do not continue to be violated.

The impact of the experience of sexual harassment on the victim, unlike most other forms of abuse, seems to have wide variance, with the most overt and egregious misconduct having the most negative effects. Often the victim does not tell anyone, although sometimes she is able to talk about what has happened many years later, especially if others have come forward and accused the man. It is not clear why some women appear to have less psychological distress on exposure to behavior that seriously traumatizes other women. Some women and most men still do not take most forms of sexual harassment seriously, often blaming the victim for seductive behavior. When harassment produces major psychological stress in a woman, she is often seen as oversensitive. However, there is more understanding when the most egregious forms of sexual touching occur. In fact, the difficulties in defining what behaviors constitute sexual harassment make it hard for clinicians to conduct empirically based research and to recognize the negative effects in patients.

After defining sexual harassment, this chapter summarizes research that shows how prevalent the problem is both in the United States and in other countries. The psychological damage of harassment is then examined, along with its effect on marriages and friendships. The final section looks at therapy and intervention issues that could arise while treating a victim of sexual harassment.

Definitions

The most commonly accepted definition of sexual harassment is cited in the United States Equal Employment Opportunity Commission (EEOC) Guidelines on Discrimination Because of Sex and states the following:

> Unwelcome sexual advances, requests for sexual favors, and other verbal or physical conduct of a sexual nature constitute sexual harassment when (1) submission to such conduct is made either explicitly or implicitly a term or condition of an individual's employment, (2) submission to or rejection of such conduct by an individual is used as the basis for employment decisions affecting such individual, or (3) such conduct has the purpose or effect of unreasonably interfering with an individual's work performance or creating an intimidating, hostile or offensive working environment. (EEOC, 1991, p. 1604.11)

Furthermore, such actions must be considered in the context of the complete working conditions:

> In determining whether alleged conduct constitutes sexual harassment, the Commission will look at the record as a whole and at the totality of the circumstances, such as the nature of the sexual advances and the context in which the alleged incidents occurred. The determination of the legality of a particular action will be made from the facts, on a case by case basis. (EEOC, 1991, p. 1604.11)

And, to make sure that other civil rights violations that might simultaneously occur are not overlooked, the rules further state,

> Harassment on the basis of sex is a violation of Sec. 703 of Title VII (The principles involved here continue to apply to race, color, religion or national origin). (EEOC, 1991, p. 1604.11)

The connection between other forms of discrimination in the workplace and sexual harassment is clear. In my experience, it is often the woman of color, the woman who has a physical disability, or the lesbian who is more likely to be picked on and sexually harassed, especially if she appears to be vulnerable for some other reason. As might be expected, the workplace atmosphere has much to do with individual workers' behaviors. Those sites in which diversity is accepted are less likely to have reported sexual harassment complaints. The 1990 Americans with Disabilities Act (ADA) is now being used in conjunction with other civil rights protections including the new Civil Rights Act's provisions, which were enacted by Congress in 1991 and signed by former President Bush after the uproar over the confirmation of Justice Thomas, to enforce equitable treatment of women at work sites.

Psychologists and other mental health professionals are being called on by the courts to help determine the extent of damage that arises from oppression because of gender, racial or ethnic group, sexual orientation, or disability. Both presentation of the social psychology research on the negative psychological effects of discrimination in general (see, e.g., *Price-Waterhouse v. Hopkins*, 1989, in which the American Psychological Association submitted an amicus brief to support social psychologist Susan Fiske's research on identification and impact of discrimination) as well as the clinician's assessment of specific damages to a particular individual have provided important information in these federal lawsuits.

Subtle Harassment

Obviously, there is a line drawn between behavior that is clearly considered sexual harassment and that which is considered normal bantering between men and women. Women often define the line as the point at which they become uncomfortable enough for the behavior to bother them. Sometimes they hide their true feelings of discomfort by pretending to ignore this behavior or even talking back to the men. Often, it is the cumulative effects of much subtle harassment that finally causes the harm. Sometimes, the same behaviors can be classified differently by different women. Gutek, Morasch, and Cohen (1983) found that some behaviors might be tolerated from a peer but viewed as harassing from a supervisor. Sexual harassment differs from flirting in that the behaviors are often uninvited, invasive, and embarrassing and persist despite the woman's obvious displeasure or lack of interest. Other terms used to describe this behavior include *seductive behavior*, *sexual bribery*, *sexual coercion*, and *sexual assault*. Sometimes, sexual harassment is contained under the legal term *sexual discrimination*.

Most victim advocates would put the theoretical understanding of sexual harassment at a place similar to the understanding of rape in this culture 20 years ago (cf. Russell, 1984). Herman (1992) found that "what constitutes rape is set not at the level of women's experience of violation, but just above the level of coercion acceptable to men. That turns out to be quite high indeed" (p. 73). MacKinnon (1983) agreed, claiming that "rape, from women's point of view, is not prohibited, it is regulated" (p. 651). Because most women who have experienced sexual harassment are aware that their interpretation of what happened to them is different from the interpretation of the men who committed the acts, and that other people are more likely to view the behavior from the male cultural standard and not from the victim's viewpoint resulting from her own personal experience, women are less likely to report such harassment or even pay much attention to it until it becomes emotionally impossible not to deal with the effects. Bart and O'Brien (1985) attempted to debunk the myth that women cannot effectively persuade some men to stop rape or sexual harassment. They described many different types of attempts made by women, some of which may be successful in limiting the harm they experience. Their data also support the validity of the individual woman's perceptions of danger while in the middle of the attack. It is important to understand the differences in male and female views of sexual harassment when designing a treatment plan to assist a woman in recovery.

Types of Sexual Harassment Behaviors

The American Psychological Association's brochure on sexual harassment (American Psychological Association Office of Public Affairs, 1993) suggests that, although there are many different types of behavior that constitute sexual harassment, the defining characteristic is that it is unwanted. The brochure lists broad categories with the first two considered the most common types of behavior. The categories listed are as follows:

- Generalized sexist statements and behavior that convey insulting or degrading attitudes about women. Examples include insulting remarks, offensive graffiti, obscene jokes or humor about sex or women in general, and the display of graphic materials of a sexual nature.

- Unwanted, inappropriate or offensive social invitations, sexual overtures or advances. Examples include unwanted letters or phone calls of a personal nature, insistent requests for social contacts (drinks, dinners, dates), repeated unwanted requests for sexual contact.
- The subtle or overt solicitation of a personal relationship or sexual activity by promising benefits, for example, a promotion or a pay raise.
- Coercion of social contact or sexual activity by threat of negative consequences. For example a negative performance evaluation, withholding of promotions, or threat of termination.
- Unwanted physical contact, including touching, feeling, pinching, grabbing, or kissing.
- Threats of coerced sexual activity.
- Sexual assault. (American Psychological Association Office of Public Affairs, 1993, p. 2)

The most commonly reported modes of harassment are verbal comments about the woman's body, jokes about sex, sexual innuendos, and sexual invitations that persist for a long period of time regardless of the woman's response. In my experience, more than one half of the women report also being subjected to repeated physical advances including touching and kissing. Definitions of sexual harassment have been used in training companies to prevent such behavior and to limit their liability in potentially expensive litigation. Webb (1991) suggested to employers that there are three parts to a commonsense definition of *sexual harassment*. First, the behavior must be "sexual in nature or sex-based" (p. 26). She further suggested that the behavior does not necessarily have to mean that the perpetrator intends to have sex with the victim. Rather, the entire continuum of sexual behavior is included "ranging from the least severe end—sexual jokes, innuendoes, flirting, asking someone for a date—to the most serious end—forced fondling, attempted or actual rape, sexual assault" (Webb, 1991, p. 26). She further defined sex-based behavior as "negative behavior that is directed at, or has an impact on, only one gender. Negative gender-related behavior can include men putting down the women or women making negative remarks about the men—in other words, a serious battle of the sexes at the job" (Webb, 1991, p. 26). Webb suggested that, where this sex-based behavior occurs, the more serious forms of sexual harassment are not too far behind.

The second part of Webb's (1991) definition of sexual harassment is that "the behavior has to be deliberate and/or repeated" (p. 26). This stresses that some forms of the behavior are so offensive that the first time they occur they are considered deliberate, hurtful, wrong, and maybe even illegal. For example, forcing a woman to have intercourse or oral sex, pushing one's clothed genital area against the woman while making writhing movements and suggestive sounds, or grabbing a woman's breasts and fondling them would be considered deliberate behavior by most people. Definitions become less clear in cases in which the behavior is more common, such as patting the woman on the behind, running one's hand seductively up and down the woman's back under her sweater while she is pinned against the wall, breathing heavily at her desk or whispering in her ear about how sexually aroused she makes him. Whereas some of these behaviors may be sexually offensive to some women immediately, others may find them amusing at first. Even if the individual behavior is not considered illegal, exposure to it day after day can grow oppressive and create a hostile work environment.

Companies with a history of discrimination against women in their employment practices often have such negative attitudes toward the first few women hired that less repetition is necessary before the behavior causes the same problems as more serious harassment and abuse. Webb (1991) suggested that "the more severe the behavior is, the fewer times it needs to be repeated before reasonable people define it as harassment; the less severe it is, the more times it needs to be repeated" (p. 27). I would add that the greater the negative attitudes are toward women in general in the workplace, the less repetition is needed to produce severe psychological effects.

The third part of Webb's (1991) definition of sexual harassment behavior is that "sexual harassment is not welcome, not asked for, and not returned" (p. 27). This does not mean women should be considered as accepting of the harassing behavior when they do not take strong action to try to stop it because of fear of reprisals. Some women may try to make a joke about it while also sending the message that such attention is unwanted. Behavior that might not be defined as harassment when it is mutually acceptable outside of the work environment is often unwanted in a work situation. Even mutually desired behavior may be considered unacceptable if it promotes a hostile work environment that appears to facilitate or even just tolerate other men's sexual behavior toward other women in the same environment. On the university campus and in small offices with civil service career workers this is a particularly difficult problem (see, e.g., Bravo & Cassedy, 1992; Herman, 1992; MacKinnon, 1983; Webb, 1991). Obviously, if one woman is perceived as gaining advancement through sexual behavior, this creates an environment in which women who refuse to submit sexually feel that their work will not be considered with equal weight.

Perhaps the most critical factor in defining sexual harassment in the workplace or in academia is that the issue of mutuality of consent cannot exist when there is an unequal power difference between the man and woman involved. Thus, although the woman may believe that she willingly engaged in a sexually intimate relationship with a male in a supervisory or power role, in fact, the power differential between them makes equality and therefore, mutual consent, impossible; the exchange, consequently, involves more than sexual affection. Legal definitions often call this quid pro quo, an exchange of this for that. In such cases, an exchange of sexual favors for better work conditions or job advancement of some kind may be offered. In typical quid pro quo cases the woman is approached by a more senior-level male with direct or indirect ability to affect her career and is asked to provide sexual favors (sometimes presented in more affectionate terms) in return for job benefits (sometimes using a less direct promise). In many cases in which the woman believes that she consented to the sexual relationship, whether or not an explicit bargain existed, she will not demonstrate psychological harm even if the behavior reaches the legal standard of sexual harassment. Sometimes, it is a long time after the sexual behavior has stopped before the actual damage becomes visible.

Identifying the Offender

Most frequently the reported offender or harasser is older than the victim and has a supervisory responsibility of some kind for her. Often he has the direct ability to fire or promote her, or he can influence her official job performance ratings. In a university setting, the influence the man has over the woman's training or promotion may be indirect, such as the ability to make comments about her competence (or lack of it) in a faculty meeting or informally to other faculty, or it may be more direct, such as clinical or research supervision or professional mentoring. Sexual behavior between faculty and students persists despite its classification as a dual relationship that is forbidden according to most professions' ethical codes. Promises of future success as well as embarrassment and threats of retaliation may coerce the woman into submission and silence. Sometimes the man's behavior is so subtle, initially, that the woman is not sure that the man has sexual intentions. Many women ignore any initial misgivings, hoping the behavior will stop without having to take some embarrassing action themselves. Initial reports suggest that some harassers do not stop even when confronted with direct messages from the woman, whereas others will not continue to pursue a victim who they sense is not vulnerable.

Like other perpetrators of repeated abuse against women, the harasser's goal is power and conquest of the woman as well as simple sexual gratification. He is often able to keep his promises because of his professional prominence or job position. Although women develop a variety of coping strategies to deal with unwanted sexual harassment, once it begins, regardless of their efforts, the outcome is usually detrimental to their future careers. This is often because the person in authority may be the harasser or does not take the complaint or the potential injury to the woman seriously. Almost all of the victims of sexual harassment on the job who were studied reported suffering some type of emotional stress that interfered with their subsequent job performance (Bravo & Cassedy, 1992; Crull, 1982). However, many victims believed that they would be less likely to suffer job or career consequences if they just went along with the supervisors' requests.

As with other offenders, sexual harassers (a) do not believe they are doing anything wrong; (b) if they do understand it is wrong, they do not believe they will be caught; (c) if they are caught, they believe they can talk their way out of it; and (d) if they cannot talk their way out of it, they believe that the consequences will be light. Unfortunately, they are usually correct.

Feminist Analysis

As is the case with the other forms of violence against women discussed in this volume, feminists have provided the most compelling analysis of sexual harassment at the workplace, describing both its theoretical underpinnings and individual motivation. A feminist analysis of the problem of sexual harassment suggests that it often appears in conjunction with other discriminatory conditions such as unequal pay, inadequate job training, and sexual segregation of jobs that are major forces in maintaining the low status of all women in the workforce. Women who are fired or pressured to leave their jobs have special difficulty getting back on their feet economically. Employers whose advances are rejected or exposed are reluctant to assist these women in obtaining another job, and prospective employers are skeptical of hiring them, perhaps not believing their explanations. MacKinnon (1983) suggested that the feminist perspective on sexual harassment is consistent with the unequal power relationship between men and women in society, not just the workplace. She believed that, until equality between women and men is achieved, men will not stop their sexual advances toward women. However, feminist theory holds that sexual harassment is used as a way to keep women from striving toward that equality.

Feminist analysis also suggests that sexual humiliation is an important tool that men use against women, especially when men fear the loss of their own power. Sexual harassment has been an acceptable way of keeping women in their "proper place," although the new laws have helped establish the inappropriateness of such behavior.

Several factors influence whether a particular act is perceived as sexual harassment: the gender of the perceiver, the severity or explicitness of the incident, and the behavior of the woman (Fitzgerald & Ormerod, 1991; Gutek et al., 1983). MacKinnon (1979) made a now commonly held distinction between two main forms of behavior constituting sexual harassment, which has been used in the courts. She called them (a) quid pro quo "in which sexual compliance is exchanged or proposed to be exchanged, for an employment opportunity" (p. 32), and (b) when sexual harassment is a "persistent condition of work" (p. 32):

> In the quid pro quo, the coercion behind the advances is clarified by the reprisals that follow a refusal to comply. Less clear, and undoubtedly more pervasive, is the situation in which sexual harassment simply makes the work environment unbearable. Unwanted sexual advances can be a daily part of a woman's life [even though] she is never promised or denied anything explicitly connected with her job. (MacKinnon, 1979, p. 40)

Obviously, in attempting to determine the difference between behaviors that seem to be reciprocal between men and women on the job and in the academy and those that may or may not be labeled sexual harassment, there is a point at which subjective perception becomes an important part of the definition. The major argument against the sexual harassment laws, suggesting that government stay out of sexual behavior between "consenting" adults, is that regulating such adult conduct implies a lack of control and infantilization of women. The problem here is that a woman who may blame herself or think she has engaged in flirtatious behavior of her own volition may well be acting out behavioral patterns that are conditioned within sex-role socialization norms. Indeed, it may well be a combination of the behaviors themselves and the misuse of the power dynamic that causes the ultimate psychological harm to the woman. As in other forms of woman abuse, it is important for the therapist to help the woman get beyond self-blame and understand the contributions of the individual harasser as well as societal norms in placing her in the victim role.

Because many women, including feminists, do not want to have their sexual behavior regulated by outside prohibitions, the legal and ethical implications of sexual relations between faculty and students have been major points of tension. The last draft of the revised ethics code for psychologists includes a prohibition on sex as well as other dual relationships between faculty and students. This prohibition generated a great deal of controversy during the commentary period.

The prevalence of sexual harassment by psychology professors toward their students may be an important reason why women hesitate to participate later in professional activities that enhance their psychology careers (Dziech & Weiner, 1984; Fitzgerald & Ormerod, 1991; Fitzgerald, Gold, et al., 1988; Fitzgerald, Shullman, et al., 1988; Paludi, 1990). Furthermore, such behavior may also serve as a model for male students to sexually exploit their own therapy clients or students later (Walker, 1989a).

INCIDENCE AND PREVALENCE

Harassment in the Workplace and in Academia

Sexual harassment of women appears to be prevalent throughout the world. In 1992, *USA Today* reported a study by the International Labor Organization, which showed that 30.5% of Austrian working women reported serious incidents of harassment. In addition, 21% of French women, 58% of Dutch women, 74% of British women, 24% of Spanish women, and 17.5% of Czechoslovakian women all report experiencing some form of sexual harassment (Webb, 1991). Webb also reported that a 3-year study of 650 women by a University of Michigan professor, James Gruber, in Estonia, Finland, Sweden, the Soviet Union, and Michigan found that nearly 50% of the women reported sexual harassment, with the most common form of harassment being repeated requests for dates and sexually suggestive remarks. A 1991 report issued by the Santama Group to Consider Sexual Harassment at Work in Japan found that 70% of Japanese women said that they had experienced some type of sexual harassment on the job. About 60% of the 6,500 women surveyed said that they had been fondled or forced to listen to unwanted sexual jokes or descriptions of sexual experiences. Interestingly, 90% said that they were sexually harassed during their commute to or from work (Webb, 1991). Many countries are taking actions similar to those taken by the United States in trying to stop sexual harassment on the job. The Council on Europe, led by the Greek commissioner, a woman, set down guidelines in 1993 for its member nations.

In the United States, a 1980 study of 20,000 federal employees by the

United States Merit Systems Protection Board found that 42% of all female employees reported having been sexually harassed on the job during the preceding 24-month period (Crull, 1982). Although many federal workers are protected from being fired by civil service laws, they can be reassigned to other areas that may dead-end their careers.

These studies were completed prior to the publicity received from the Clarence Thomas hearings, which were broadcast on Cable News Network around the world. A poll taken by the *New York Times* during the Thomas hearings found that approximately 40% of working women said they had experienced sexual harassment (Webb, 1991). Since the hearings, the percentages that have appeared in the popular press are higher, often as high as 80% to 90% of all women. If this change holds true in other industrialized countries, it is fair to say that most women experience some form of sexual harassment on the job. Possibly, the discussion of what constitutes sexual harassment has enabled women to recognize experiences that they previously had failed to define as harassment, because they felt comfortable in how they had handled the situations, they did not experience lasting psychological harm, or the occurrences were so common that they had not paid much attention to them before.

In 1991 the National Association for Female Executives reported that 53% of its 1,300 members had been sexually harassed by people who had power over their jobs and careers. Interestingly, 64% of them said that they had never reported the harassment, and more than half of those who did report it said it was not resolved to their satisfaction (Webb, 1991).

The incidence and prevalence of sexual harassment in academic settings mirrors that of other occupations. Paludi (1990) reported that 41% of female graduate students and 34% of female undergraduate students reported unwanted sexual advances. Paludi (1990) also reported that 32% of tenured female faculty and 49% of untenured female faculty have reported sexual harassment. A study by Bond (1988) found that 75% of female faculty surveyed had experienced jokes with sexual themes during their graduate training, 69% were subjected to sexist comments, 58% reported remarks made about their clothing, body, and sexual attraction, and 12% reported unwanted sexual intercourse or breast or genital stimulation. It is interesting to compare statistics for mental health professionals with those in other career paths. Here, too, the recognition of what constitutes sexual harassment has increased. For example, in a survey of 287 randomly selected American Psychological Association members, reported in 1985, 9% of the women said they had been subjected to sexual harassment as employees (Robinson & Reid, 1985). Pope and Feldman-Summers (1992) found that 38% of the female and 1.5% of the male psychologists whom they surveyed had experienced sexual harassment. In their sample of 296 randomly selected members of the association, sexual harassment was the form of abuse most frequently experienced, although 57% of the women and 14% of the men had experienced some form of abuse in childhood or as an adult, almost all by a perpetrator who was known to them. Interestingly, most of the responding psychologists felt only moderately competent to treat clients who had had abuse experiences. Perhaps as expected, most of the respondents found that their training programs had been inadequate in preparing them to work with this population, with training in the area of sexual harassment issues given the lowest rating.

Women Working in the Sex Industry

A brief discussion of sexual harassment and abuse in the contexts of prostitution, nude dancing, and the pornography industry in general is necessary here. One view of the sex industry holds that it constitutes sexual exploitation of women and teaches the objectification of women's bodies and, therefore, should not be tolerated. Another view is that most women in the sex industry work there for economic reasons; the jobs pay well and can be brought under the control of the working women, not those who purchase their services. The debate within the feminist community centers around whether prostitution, for example, can be stripped from the analysis of the damage its very existence causes for all women because of the philosophy surrounding it, which is promoted by a patriarchal society. Although the work could be considered more dangerous than working in an office, certainly considering the exploitation by pimps and unavailability of health care, Pheterson (1986) argued that, if prostitution and the rest of the sex industry were cleaned up, it would probably be no more dangerous than some other high-risk jobs such as serving as a police officer or being in the military. On the other hand, Barry (1992) posited the argument that, by definition, the sex industry cannot be cleaned up. There is no such concept as free prostitution; the women's labor is exploited by men in much the same way that power and control is usurped from other physically and sexually abused women who are discussed here. Many would agree that the stigma associated with pornography, prostitution, and even exotic dancing often takes its toll on women's self-esteem.

Perhaps because of the stigma associated with a woman selling her body, if such a woman is sexually harassed, assaulted, or beaten, it is rarely considered rape, and she is rarely offered protection. If it is determined that women enter into the sex industry without consent and through coercion, then would the actual use of force constitute an expected job risk? Indeed, many of the prostitutes who are assaulted are raped by prominent citizens who are their customers (cf. Barry, 1992). Exposing the abusive behavior of individual men also exposes their consumption of the sex industry, and many in power react with great fervor in keeping such information secret.

A 1991 case in Fort Lauderdale, Florida, illustrates this point. This case exposed the vice mayor of Fort Lauderdale and other prominent citizens who were listed in the customer book of a local prostitute and appeared in home videos taken by her voyeuristic husband who was a deputy sheriff. The case received national publicity when the press learned the identities of the prominent citizens who were involved and the preposterous defense that the couple offered. The conflict with the vice mayor's previous hardline stance on pornography and topless bars in his community was an ironic feature of the case. When the accused prostitute's prominent defense attorney, Rubin Ellis, allegedly made an attempt to sell the videotape to the television show, A Current Affair (which has become a commonplace practice among certain high profile legal cases), the court reacted quite harshly toward both the defense attorney and the clients, but not toward the community standard represented by the vice mayor who had already resigned. If new proposed legislation in Europe concerning prostitution were in effect here, the community would have had to show more concern about the violation of all women's civil rights, as demonstrated by the public officials involved in this behavior, than in only prosecuting the woman for her behavior. Such cases seem to support the arguments by Barry (1992), the Coalition Against Trafficking in Women, and UNESCO, that the "object of the sale or the purchase of women's, children's, and men's sex is always for man's profit and the exercise of masculine sexuality. Prostitution of the Other is the special expression of man's power" (Tamzali, 1992, p. ii).

Many prostitutes are bound to their pimps by violence in ways similar to battered women. Linda Lovelace, the movie star of several popular pornographic movies, including *Deep Throat*, detailed the brutality of her marriage to her pimp and movie director and was written after she was able to escape from him (Lovelace & McGrady, 1980). Barry (1979, 1991) described the bondage of many women who become sex slaves after lives of abuse as children and adults. Their continued participation in the sex industry as dancers, whores, prostitutes, and other types of call girls can be seen as analogous to the actions of battered women who are psychologically unable to leave their abusive partners. Pheterson (1986) and others in what is called the "pro-prostitution lobby," which argues for better protection of women so that they can be free to engage economically in the sex industry, also demand better protection for these women. There is a good possibility that women who work in the sex industry will seek individual therapy at some point when their psychological trauma becomes too difficult to manage on their own. Whatever the political analysis of pornography, prostitution, exotic dancing, or other sex industry work, or whatever personal feelings a therapist may have regarding these activities, psychologists must recognize that these women who are raped, beaten, and sexually harassed have similar traumatic reactions as might any woman in any occupation and must treat them accordingly and without judgment.

Empirical and Clinical Research

Most of the research in the area of sexual harassment has concentrated on defining the behavior and assessing its incidence and prevalence in the workplace and in educational settings. The research on the impact of the behavior on the victim has been primarily in the social psychology field with an emphasis on the negative effects of sex-role stereotyping and discrimination. The few clinical studies that have been done support the social science research (Hamilton, Alagna, King, & Lloyd, 1987).

Studies have not separated those who have experienced sexual harassment without any negative impact from those who have experienced harmful results. If the research in other abuse areas can be used as a guide, exposure to sexual harassment has cumulative effects resulting in greater damage as the rate of exposure increases. For example, several studies indicated that 17% of psychologists had had sexual contact with an educator (cf. Glaser & Thorpe, 1986; Pope, Levenson, & Schover, 1979). In the Glaser and Thorpe study, most of the female psychologists believed that such contact was negative for them. In a discussion of Glaser and Thorpe's (1986) study, Pope and Feldman-Summers (1992) stated that whether or not the respondents had experienced student–faculty sex, "most participants believed that such student–educator contact was unethical whether it occurred during (96.2%) or outside (72.8%) of the working relationship" (p. 353).

A Working Women's Institute study (Crull, 1982) of 92 respondents who had written for assistance in fighting sexual harassment provides some information on the incidence and prevalence of different behaviors. Although the average age of respondents was 30, as a group their ages ranged from 16 to 65 years. Most of the women who reported sexual harassment on the job depended on their jobs for economic sustenance. More than 75% were unmarried, and 50% were the sole supporter of their families. The profile of the harasser that emerged showed a man who, 79% of the time, was married and was, on average, 14 years older than the woman. The women generally held the lower salaried jobs with more than half working as clerks or secretaries, 15% as service workers, 15% as professional and technical workers, and 4% as salespeople.

CLINICAL PRESENTATION AND ASSESSMENT ISSUES

Diagnostic Issues

It is not unusual for sexual harassers to choose as their victims women who have been previously abused. Thus, sexual harassment victims who seek evaluation and therapy may be multiple abuse victims, complicating diagnosis and treatment issues. As with other abuse victims, women who have been sexually harassed may use alcohol and drugs to numb their pain. They may also somaticize their feelings and develop a multitude of physical ailments that become exacerbated under stress.

The most common diagnosis for victims of sexual harassment is posttraumatic stress disorder (PTSD). Like other repeated sexual abuse victims, those who have been sexually harassed often demonstrate most of the PTSD symptoms. The two symptoms that are most likely to be prominent are the effects on cognitive skills and the disruption of interpersonal relationships. By the time they get to the mental health professional's office, victims of sexual harassment have experienced the harassment for so long that it has become unbearable. They may no longer be able to perform their jobs or, in fact, any job tasks assigned to them at that time. A victim may describe herself as fearing that she has lost her mind; she may recognize her incompetence at work and compare it with earlier times when she felt in control of her job performance and of the management of her work career. Most of these women need to work in order to survive, both economically and emotionally.

Use of psychological tests to measure disruptions in concentration, cognition, and personality functioning may be important if a legal case is pending. The Weschler Adult Intelligence Scale–Revised (WAIS–R) often illustrates the impact of high anxiety and depression on the woman's level of achievement, although in cases in which the woman has had developmental interference (such as with some child sexual abuse victims), the results need careful interpretation. The Minnesota Multiphasic Personality Inventory (MMPI-1) profiles of harassment victims often look like a combination of those of sexual and physical abuse victims, with elevations on scales 1, 3, and 7 as found in sexual abuse victims and scales 2, 4, 6, and 8 as found in battered women. It is not uncommon to find neuropsychological dysfunction signs from standardized testing, although the damage may be too subtle to be detected on more extensive testing. Because exposure to sexual harassment may be long-standing, it is not clear what the long-term effects are on both organic and emotional functioning. If previous abuse also occurred, some of the dysfunction may be a result of that as well. It is important in legal cases as well as in treatment planning to remember that the last abuse act may have potentiated the current symptoms even if prior abuse helped them begin to form. In some cases, even after some healing has occurred the effects of previous abuse, those effects may reappear when the new trauma occurs.

Associated Illnesses and Stress Reactions

Sexual dysfunction, gastrointestinal, and gynecological problems often seen in other sexual assault victims (described in chapter 2) may be present. Headaches, lethargy, dermatological reactions, weight fluctuations, and sleep disturbances and nightmares are also frequently reported.

Psychological distress reactions include depression, shock, anxiety, denial, anger, fear, irritability, frustration, insecurity, embarrassment, feelings of betrayal, confusion, feelings of being powerless, shame, self-consciousness, low self-esteem, guilt, self-blame, isolation, phobias, panic reactions, and sexual problems.

False Accusations

It can be predicted that the newer penalties against individuals and companies will bring demands for a high standard of proof that the woman really was sexually harassed by the man. Unlike abuse that occurs in the home and the therapist's office, in many cases the behavior has been witnessed by others in the workplace. However, most witnesses are reluctant to get involved, especially if they perceive that their own jobs and careers are on the line. Legally, most companies can be found liable if they displayed a pattern of discrimination that is consistent with the type of environment that is known to promote or to facilitate sexual harassment. However, the fact that the accused men now face such serious career derailment of their own can be predicted to have its own repercussions, including accused men filing more lawsuits to force the company to prove that they were not wrongfully terminated.

Proving that sexual harassment occurred may be almost as difficult as proving other forms of sexual assault. The psychological damage caused by sexual harassment will become an important part of the evidence, calling on mental health professionals to be more precise in their diagnoses. Although some women may make false accusations, it is important to understand that their perception of the situation probably was quite different from that of the accused. Many women who make unfounded (unprovable) or false charges have been previously abused and may perceive danger more readily than those who have not had such experiences. Some of the women who have made unfounded charges have experienced so much betrayal in their lives that they have become unable to distinguish between compassionate or noninvolved behavior and seductive or rejecting behavior. The psychological treatment for these women would not be different, but there are serious implications in such instances for legal cases.

Often the defenses against charges of sexual harassment include the attempt to prove that whatever problems the woman has were caused by preexisting conditions. Defense psychologists often use information gained in the history or psychological test data to claim that there was a long-standing preexisting personality disorder. This defense rarely is useful in that psychological injuries from sexual harassment do not have to be proven in order for the victim to receive compensatory or punitive damages. Instead, the best defense is to demonstrate that the sexual harassment was not known to the company, that it violated existing company policies, or, if something did occur, that the individual who may have committed the harassment was appropriately punished. Indeed, companies that take prompt action against offenders usually mitigate the damages that individual women suffer.

THERAPY AND INTERVENTIONS

Those women who report the harassment, particularly in federal civil service jobs, may be treated similarly to other whistle-blowers, causing a worsening of interpersonal relationships on the job or at school that may extend to other relationships, too. Although students who have been sexually harassed often know others who have had similar experiences, those others may fear that exposure will cost them their reputations, degrees, and careers and so fail to come forward. This may leave the victim who does report vulnerable to attacks on her personality, making it even more difficult for similar victims who observe this character assassination to come forward. This reaction can make the victim hesitant to trust anyone as a friend. As was discussed earlier, a common way to defend against the charges of sexual harassment is to attack the credibility and personality of the victim. Once the individual is labeled a troublemaker, other interpersonal dynamics set in, complicating diagnosis even more.

A downhill spiral begins, with the sexually harassed woman forced, because of economic and emotional reasons, to stay in the environment in which the abuse occurred. Such women perform their duties less competently because of the stress and the inappropriate or unsympathetic reactions of colleagues. As with battered women who develop learned helplessness, these women are unable to predict which actions will bring about success and which actions will cause further erosion of their position. This inability to predict the consequences of their behavior appears to result from the exposure to the abuse, not from preexisting conditions or vulnerabilities.

The typical sexual harassment victim who comes to a therapist's office usually presents herself as justifiably angry and afraid. The woman may express more anger initially than other abuse victims. Although a sexual harassment victim may give clear descriptions of what has happened, she is often unsure that she will be believed or that her early perceptions were valid. In other instances, the victim may not be able to give a systematic description of events, often leaving out incidents because of the typical minimization, denial, and memory distortions that occur in victims of repeated abuse. Instead, the woman may focus on a few egregious incidents that had a major impact on her. It takes time to understand how the incidents slowly built up, eventually culminating in the major emotional upset that the woman remembers more clearly.

In many of what have been called the quid pro quo cases, the woman liked the supervisor, who kept many of his promises, and she now blames herself because she was ambitious and supposedly voluntarily agreed to the bargain. She is not sure how to define her own behavior and may be less angry if the harasser was not the one to break the bargain. In short, she may be dealing with guilt feelings regarding her part in the quid pro quo. However, by definition one can always see the power difference between the parties as making it impossible for the woman to act voluntarily when responding to the man's seduction. This is particularly difficult for those who perceived themselves as lucky to have someone of higher status interested in them. In the situations in which the man breaks the bargain, demands sexual favors long after he can provide any further advancement for the woman, or betrays her with another woman, the client's anger is more readily apparent. In other quid pro quo cases, the woman does not give in to the offender's advances but still experiences psychological harm because of the man's constant demands and the resulting lack of advancement. This punishment can be devastating to the woman's ability to function in her job or in school.

In cases in which the woman considers the harasser's behavior inappropriate or even disgusting, the woman is likely to present with more anger and hostility toward him and toward those co-workers who protect him. If she has other areas in which she may also be vulnerable to different forms of discrimination, such as ethnic or racial minority status, a disability, or lesbian sexual orientation, she is less likely to talk about what happened. The psychological damage for these women is usually more serious.

Like other victims of rape, sexual assault, and exploitation, the harassment is likely to bring about feelings of powerlessness and anxiety. Some of their perceptions of powerlessness are accurate. Studies (Crull, 1982) report that although 76% of the women who reported harassment took direct steps to stop the unwanted behavior, including telling the harasser or some other authority figure that they wanted the behavior to stop, in less than 9% of the cases did the harassment stop completely, and in 17% of the cases the complaint caused only a small reduction in the unwanted behavior. In one half of the cases, the women were not taken seriously and nothing changed, whereas in one quarter of them, there were more serious repercussions. One third took their complaints to lawyers, unions, or local civil rights departments but experienced little change. Although these data were obtained before Anita Hill's testimony at Clarence Thomas's Senate confirmation hearing, it is important for therapists to know the grim realities of their clients' abilities to receive satisfactory resolutions in such cases.

In some cases, women become suicidal, perhaps seeing killing themselves as the one way that they still have control over their lives. Others doubt that they will ever feel happy again. This feeling is particularly true in women who have survived other forms of abuse, but it also occurs in women who have never previously felt the pressures of sexism. Perhaps this situation illustrates the profound disillusionment these women experience as they lose their feelings of invulnerability.

Dynamics and Common Sequelae

Many victims of sexual harassment develop PTSD symptoms of high arousal and anxiety, high avoidance behaviors and depression, and cognitive changes including recurrent intrusive memories. They often show signs of learned helplessness. One key difference between sexual harassment victims and other abuse victims who develop PTSD symptoms is their intense anger toward and lack of trust in people who they thought were their friends. This sense of betrayal is profound and may disrupt the ability to form a therapeutic alliance until the therapist in some way proves himself or herself. Sometimes the woman's partner and family relationships are so disrupted that she cannot rely on them for emotional support. Like the partners of rape victims, if the sexually harassed woman's partner permits her to keep control in their relationship, including not putting pressure on her for a resumption of their sexual intimacies until the woman is ready, she is less likely to become hostile at home. She may, however, remain irritable and take out her anger on close friends and family.

Termination of the Job

In the Working Women's Institute study (Crull, 1982) the women reported nervousness, fear, anger, and sleeplessness among their symptoms. About one quarter of the women who were subjected to sexual harassment were fired whether or not they complained, and another 42% eventually resigned from their jobs. Prior to their termination, employers began to find fault with their job performance where none had been found earlier. Women reported being denied the opportunity to do even routine work, being passed over for raises and big opportunities, and being blocked from even routine advancements. They reported spending emotional energy in fending off their attackers rather than in concentrating on their jobs. Some quit because of the stress, preferring to take a risk on being able to find comparable work elsewhere. Others felt that the experience eroded their ambition and motivation to continue to perform, particularly in companies in which their loyalty had never before been questioned.

In these cases the harassment spoiled what had been considered a wonderful work experience up until that point. The possibility of a long future career in that particular company no longer seemed appealing even if it was still possible. Moreover, for many women, being hired by another company might also be difficult, especially if they have acquired the reputation of being "trouble" and "difficult." In one case, the harasser was fired but not before the vice president asked the woman to prove the harasser's misbehavior by luring him to her hotel room during a company meeting at which the supervisors would plan to arrive and rescue her before the sexual behavior went too far! For this woman, the plan was such an insult to her credibility and a compromise to her safety that, even after the supervisors abandoned the plan and fired the man, this woman was unable to trust them to keep her well-being in mind.

Women who work for the government in various civil service capacities are often led to believe that their agency is taking action in response to complaints of harassment, when in fact it turns out to be simply job-shuffling with the offender and the victim shifted to other work sites. However, the gossip mill assures the woman that her experience will follow her wherever she is transferred. Often, she meets another sexual harasser at the new job site, perhaps even someone who was transferred there after a different incident with another woman at his former job site (Bravo & Cassedy, 1992). As legal penalties become more likely, transfers elsewhere within the system will become less frequent and terminations of offenders will become more standard. However, protracted litigation, involving wrongful termination of employment, instituted by men who feel unfairly treated, will cause the problems for these women to continue.

Friendships

Sexual harassment victims often experience tensions in their friendships with other men and women. They are less likely to trust anyone, particularly those on the job. The invalidation of their own perceptions often causes them to have continuous obsessions about ways to "prove" that they are good, believable, and competent workers, sometimes resulting in overperformance. Often, they become angry that they are not able to effect change and this anger turns into hostility that spoils future relationships. They fear that the harasser will continue his abuse covertly so that other co-workers remain unaware of his actions. The victims' built-up anger and rage, at the offender, at co-workers who failed to support the victim or actually colluded with the offender, and at themselves for having been so stupid to have trusted others (including the offender if they actually believed his seduction for a time), may taint any relationship that they try to maintain.

Suspiciousness

Most prominent in the constellation of PTSD symptoms for victims of sexual harassment are the heightened suspiciousness and paranoia that color their relationships with other people. The victims are so hypersensitive to being betrayed, even by those who behave in trusted ways, that they push away those who want to be their friends. Walker (1990) has called this the "porcupine" syndrome because victims of sexual harassment seem to purposely throw out obstacles preventing anyone from even trying to get close to them. Victims no longer trust their ability to tell who can be trusted and who cannot. Actually, a certain amount of this skepticism is healthy when a legal battle is going on, and these last for years in most cases.

The Issue of "Consent"

Treatment interventions for women who have been sexually harassed are similar to those for other abuse victims (see chapters 13 and 14). However, some of the special issues that arise concern consent, particularly with students in a university. Although sex between students and professors (or employees and supervisors) is considered unethical by many professional association ethical codes, others argue that two consenting adults should be permitted to engage in sexual intimacies if they so choose. Of course, this argument skews the real issue of the dominant power and control the man as professor has over the woman as student. There is no equal basis on which the woman may knowingly give consent. The damage occurs because of the man's misuse of his power, but women must understand the risk they take by responding to his sexual advances.

Although most students who engage in sexual intimacies with a professor believe it had a negative effect on them, this insight usually comes in hindsight, often after the relationship is over, sometimes even many years later. This leaves the woman open to attack on the grounds that it is her anger at being rejected (even if she was the rejector) and not the relationship itself that causes the negative attributions. This argument was made against Anita Hill, who was accused of being angry with Clarence Thomas for marrying another woman, in this case, a White woman who supposedly had higher status than did Hill, who like Thomas was African-American. The myth that every woman wants to marry the man she is dating has been debunked by new research on relationships between men and women (Rosewater, 1993), but it still persists in the minds of many men.

Another argument points to the supposedly large number of happily married couples who met and dated while in student–teacher or employer–employee roles. Here again, the issue is not that every person will be harmed by the relationship but that the potential for harm is so great that it should not be ethically permitted. Furthermore, the potential for harm lasts long after the start of the relationship. Similar to incest and other abuse, such victimization takes a toll on the woman's resiliency, making her more vulnerable to future victimization. Treatment involves helping to set up a safety net for the woman who may not have as many overt and identifiable symptoms initially, but who continues to develop them in more easily identifiable patterns over the years. Those women who resist being in treatment because they feel that they were complicit in the initiation of the relationship need to understand the power and role issues before they can deal with their guilt.

Women who have been led to believe that they consented to the relationship often feel tricked, lied to, and manipulated by the man when the relationship ends. If they have been economically harmed by the damage done to their careers, their sense of betrayal and anger at their exploitation becomes a major issue in treatment, particularly if they gave their time, love, and sometimes property unselfishly, as women have been socialized to do for the men they love. Victims have difficulty reconciling their "good girl" behavior with the pain of rejection and humiliation that follows the termination of such a relationship. Once women have some distance from the relationship, they are better able to assess the man's lack of sincerity. Often they ignored telling signs early in the relationship and thus, suspended their good judgment in order to justify their behavior. These issues need to be resolved and integrated so that the women can go on to have successful relationships in their lives with restored trust in their own judgment.

On the other hand, there are those who argue that women should not be expected to conform their behavior to outside standards and who disagree with prohibitions on sexual relationships with other adults, whatever their professional position. This argument seems to have two proponents: those who believe that restrictions on sexual behavior between consenting adults is an abridgement of civil rights and those who believe "all is fair in love and war." Keeping the balance between ethical and legal considerations in order to protect those who can be harmed by certain types of relationships while still permitting the greatest amount of freedom possible is a difficult task.

Working With the Isolated Woman

Some women become isolated and mark time in unessential job positions (because all meaningful work has been taken away from them), retire, resign, or leave on disability. This is particularly common among women who work in nontraditional careers or for the federal, state, or local government. For these women a career switch is often necessary in order to get them back on track. Yet, they may become so obsessed with vindication, justice, or revenge that they cannot let go. Interestingly, many of these women have learned how to mask their distress externally, but are unable to function very well because of major internal distress. If they are involved in litigation, they become consumed with the legal case and see the outcome as the only way to regain self-esteem. If this is the only issue the therapist concentrates on in treatment, then the therapy will probably terminate when the legal battles are resolved. However, supporting the woman's pursuit of legal remedies may be one of the most important therapeutic goals. At times intervention on a victim's behalf with lawyers or other mental health professionals is appropriate and useful in creating the therapeutic relationship. This intervention could include assistance in breaking the bonds at work and in obtaining some kind of compensation, such as sick leave or disability.

Encouraging friendships with other women is another important adjunct to therapy. Victims of sexual harassment are often too anxious to work in a therapy group, at least initially. Their rage, anxiety, and tendency to strike out defensively can make them isolated and more dependent on the therapist. It becomes important for the therapist to pay attention to transference and countertransference issues in these cases.

The therapist should deal with these issues by attempting to support and validate the woman's feelings, but should also help her resist making a defensive response until she has fully analyzed the situation. Encouraging this delay and analysis may sometimes provoke a defensive reaction against the therapist. Like many other PTSD clients, these women need reassurance that a verbal expression of anger against the therapist will not result in termination of the therapy. Disagreements can be misperceived as major threats to the woman's personal or professional integrity. Therefore, timing, a good sense of humor, and supportive gentleness are essential therapy tools when using either interpretation or confrontation. It may be helpful to the process of therapy if the therapist attends a court hearing with the client in order to lend support and then uses the observational data in the therapy sessions to discuss reactions to sensitive points that arose. It is often an eye-opening experience to observe some of the outrageous things that can occur in the courtroom.

Resistance Issues

Clients may be afraid of becoming too dependent on the therapist too quickly and may begin to cancel or not show up for scheduled appointments. It is appropriate to allow some latitude on regularity at first, but any pattern of cancelled or missed appointments needs to be carefully examined and openly discussed. This fear of dependency is understandable in light of the way in which a previous professional relationship (either in academia or a work setting) led to abuse.

Some clients may also fear dependence because they are afraid that the relationship will suddenly terminate and that they will lose their supportive relationship with the therapist. It may be helpful to provide the woman with explicit reassurance that under ordinary circumstances the therapist will continue to provide therapy sessions until both agree that the woman is ready to be on her own.

Some clients, particularly other professional women, raise the issue of the relationship after therapy terminates. Because those with a PTSD can be expected to have a lower resiliency to other stresses in their environment, it is expected that they will need to return for some additional therapy at different crisis points in their lives. Thus, the admonition against dual relationships should be followed even after termination, although in small communities it will be difficult if not impossible to avoid any out-of-the-office contact. It is important to discuss these ground rules adequately at the beginning of therapy, partly out of respect for the client's right to informed consent but also for clinical reasons. It is not atypical for clients to become angry when a therapist fails to meet their expectations. Therapists can avoid needlessly (and sometimes harmfully) eliciting such anger by distinguishing between realistic and unrealistic expectations.

Career Issues

For some women, helping them get out of a career position in which the actual or recalled sexual harassment is still present is an appropriate form of treatment. This is particularly true when disability will assist in providing rehabilitation services for their retraining. Unless they are out of the offensive and trauma-producing situation, victims of sexual harassment will continue to suffer PTSD symptoms. However, even if they cannot leave the situation yet, a retraining plan, which can be revised if the initial goals are not met, should be negotiated at this time.

University women who are still students need to be able to complete their chosen programs. If the offender is no longer a threat, and others treat the victim without hostility or resentment, she may be able to finish up at the original school. It is sometimes appropriate, however, for her to transfer to another university. Often these decisions are made with reference to practical considerations, such as the amount of time the woman might lose or the costs that will be incurred if she has to transfer. Sometimes the student needs extra time to complete the program requirements, especially if the harasser was also her major advisor or research supervisor.

Therapists sometimes attempt to protect the woman from too much stress by suggesting that she stop work or her studies, even temporarily. Although this is sometimes necessary, it must be weighed against the benefits of the woman performing meaningful activities. Depression may become more serious and obsessive thinking may shift from a particular work situation and generalize to any activity, causing more serious mental health problems. Thus, it is usually a good idea to find ways to reduce the stress without totally avoiding the activity unless there is no other alternative. For example, in one situation the client was unable to stabilize her diabetic condition while working at her job. The life-threatening nature of the disability along with the harassment made it more important that she take a temporary leave of absence than stay there.

In another case, the client was an older television news anchor; if she had left her job, she would have immediately been replaced by a younger woman. In her business, being off the air for even a short time could mean the end of her career. Still another woman, an engineer in an all-male environment, quit her job after spending a short time on sick leave. A well-trained, competent, woman, she quickly found another job, so leaving the company did not hurt her career. Yet another engineer felt so much better while on temporary sick leave that she made the decision to terminate her work on disability. The difference in her mental health and outlook on life improved dramatically, even though she did not have future goals in mind at the time that she exercised what is legally called a *constructive discharge.* Thus, these decisions need to be made carefully with the client, evaluating all options before final action is taken.

Helping the Client to Care for Her Responsibilities

It may be appropriate for the therapist to help the client get her affairs in order when psychological stress causes her to become sporadically non-functional. Sometimes setting up a system to monitor her finances, keep track of her appointments, complete her doctoral research data collection, or other peripheral issues can be therapeutically indicated for a temporary period. Clients may begin to regain trust in people if the therapist acts as an advocate in certain situations early in treatment. For example, it may be important to talk to an attorney or other party in order to support the reliability of the client's statements. Of course, the therapist must be very careful not to engage in dual relationships or conflicts of interest in which the client's welfare is sacrificed for the professional or financial gain of the therapist.

SUMMARY

The recognition of sexual harassment at the workplace or on college campuses has increased because of the dramatic testimony by Anita Hill before the Senate Judiciary Committee during the confirmation hearings of U.S. Supreme Court Justice Clarence Thomas. Studies suggest that men and women differ regarding which behaviors they believe constitute sexual harassment. However, the legal definitions prohibit any unwanted direct or indirect sexual behavior or the creation of a hostile work environment.

Offenders are often male colleagues at work and on the university campus. Although it is difficult to accurately assess the incidence and prevalence of sexual harassment, newspaper surveys show that upward of 90% of women respondents reported having been sexually harassed. Data show that most who complain of sexual harassment see little or no improvement in their working conditions.

The psychological dynamics and sequelae of sexual harassment are similar to those of other abuse victims. Many develop PTSD symptoms and lose trust in authority figures and, sometimes, in friends. In some cases the woman's disillusionment is profound because of other prior abuse.

There are arguments that the power differential and its potential misuse make it impossible for a woman to actually "consent" knowingly to a sexual relationship with a supervisor. Those who disagree point to the ability of adults to make decisions and suggest that it is an abridgement of civil rights to prohibit relationships between consenting adults. Others point to couples who appear unharmed and happy even though a power differential existed when their relationship began. Still others believe that "all is fair in love and war." The large numbers of women who report harm long after such relationships ended should help put this argument to rest (Bravo & Cassedy, 1992; Hamilton et al., 1987).

Therapy strategies are similar to those used in other traumatic situations. These clients often feel isolated and are resistant to friendships. In addition, they may face several different courses of legal remedy that often do not support the woman. While avoiding a dual relationship or a conflict of interest, the therapist might find it helpful to take an active role in exploring the patient's options.

6

Therapist–Patient Sexual Involvement

Kenneth S. Pope

Therapist–patient sexual involvement at least partially reflects the dynamics and consequences of many of the other forms of abuse addressed in this book. Numerous works have noted the ways in which therapist–patient sex is similar to battering, rape, and incest.[5] Chapters 10 through 14 discuss the general assessment and treatment issues that seem to emerge across these various forms of abuse. This chapter focuses on (a) the cultural and other contexts and the emerging research that are vital to an adequate understanding of therapist–patient sexual involvement and its consequences and (b) special clinical issues affecting assessment and intervention. Drawing heavily on prior books and articles that address assess-

I would like to thank Oxford University Press for granting permission to reprint Table 6-1; the Division of Psychotherapy (Division 29) of the American Psychological Association (APA) and Donald Freedheim, editor of *Psychotherapy*, for permission to reproduce Table 6-3 and other copyrighted material from articles published in that journal; and Paula Bronstein of APA Books and Karen Thomas of the APA Permissions Office for helping to secure permission to reprint Tables 6-2 and 6-4 and Exhibit 6-2.

[5]See, for example, Bailey (1978); Barnhouse (1978); Bates and Brodsky (1989); Benowitz (1991); Borys (1988); L. S. Brown (1984); A. W. Burgess (1981); Chesler (1972); Connel and Wilson (1974); Dahlberg (1970); Finkelhor (1984); Freud (1915/1958); Gabbard (1989); L. A. Gilbert and Scher (1989); Herman (1992); Herman, Gartrell, Olarte, Feldstein, and Localio (1987); Kardener (1974); Kavoussi and Becker (1987); Maltz and Holman (1984); Marmor (1972); Masters and Johnson (1976); Redlich (1977); Russell (1986); Saul (1962); H. F. Searles (1959); Siassi and Thomas (1973); A. A. Stone (1990); L. G. Stone (1980); M. Stone (1976); Walker (1989a).

ment and treatment issues in this area, this chapter refers readers who seek more detailed information to those works.[6]

Although alertness to similarities among forms of abuse and trends within a particular category of abuse, such as therapist–patient sexual involvement, can be exceptionally useful in providing clinical services to victims, it is important to note that just as each client is unique so are the consequences of an abusive act. Clinicians need to be careful to avoid making reflexive or stereotypic assumptions about a client who has been sexually involved with a prior therapist. Similarly, reflexive assumptions must be avoided when considering allegations of sexually abusive behavior. In no case should the conclusion that a patient's allegations are true or false be based solely on the presence or absence of individual sequelae that are often associated with therapist–patient sex.

CONTEXT AND RESEARCH

Sexual exploitation of therapy patients never occurs in a vacuum. Similarly, attempts to understand the abuse and its consequences, to help women who have been exploited in this way, and to avoid placing patients at unnecessary risk for such involvements occur in a complex matrix of historical, cultural, professional, and other contexts. Part of the preparation for providing assessment and intervention services for abused women is to take into account these contexts.

Gender Patterns, Contexts, and Influences

Therapist–patient sexual involvement is similar to the forms of abuse discussed in previous chapters—rape, battering, and child abuse—in that men are far more likely than women to be perpetrators (see Table 6-1) and

---

[6]See, for example, Bates and Brodsky (1989); Bouhoutsos and Brodsky (1985); Gabbard (1989); Pope and Bouhoutsos (1986); Pope and Gabbard (1989); Sonne, (1987, 1989); Sonne, Meyer, Borys, and Marshall (1985); Sonne and Pope (1991). For reviews of the research, readers are referred to Gabbard (1989), Pope (1990a, 1990b), Pope and Vasquez (1991), and Pope, Sonne, and Holroyd (1993). This chapter addresses sexual involvement between therapists and patients; readers interested in the topic of sexual involvement between physicians who are not therapists and their patients are referred to Feldman-Summers (1989); Feldman-Summers and Jones (1984); Gartrell, Milliken, Goodson, Thiemann, and Lo (1992); Kardener, Fuller, and Mensch (1973); and J. A. Perry (1976).

Table 6-1

Self-Report Studies of Sex With Clients Using National Samples of Therapists[a]

Ref. no.	Publication date	Sample size	Return rate	Male	Female
1[b]	1977	1,000	70%	12.1%	2.6%
2	1979	1,000	48%	12.0%	3.0%
3	1986	1,000	58.5%	9.4%	2.5%
4[c]	1986	5,574	26%	7.1%	3.1%
5[d]	1987	1,000	46%	3.6%	0.4%
6[e]	1988	1,000	39.5%	3.5%	2.3%
7[f]	1989	4,800	56.5%	0.9%	0.2%
8	in press	1,000	43%	3.6%	0.5%

Reference Key: 1) Holroyd & Brodsky; 2) Pope, Levenson, & Schover; 3) Pope, Keith-Spiegel, & Tabachnick; 4) Gartrell, Herman, Olarte, Feldstein, & Localio; 5) Pope, Tabachnick, & Keith-Spiegel; 6) Akamatsu; 7) Borys & Pope; 8) Bernsen, Tabachnick, & Pope.
[a]This table presents only national surveys that have been published in peer-reviewed scientific and professional journals. Exceptional caution is warranted in comparing the data from these various surveys. For example, the frequently cited percentages of 12.1 and 2.6, reported by Holroyd and Brodsky (1977), exclude same-sex involvement. Moreover, when surveys included separate items to assess posttermination sexual involvement, these data are reported in footnotes to this table. Finally, some published articles did not provide sufficiently detailed data for this table (e.g., aggregate percentages); the investigators supplied the data needed for the table. [b]Although the gender percentages presented in the table for Studies 2 through 8 represent responses to one basic survey item in each survey, the percentages presented for Study 1 span several items. The study's senior author confirmed through personal communication that the study's findings were that 12.1% of the male and 2.6% of the female participants reported having engaged in erotic contact (whether or not it included intercourse) with at least one opposite-sex patient; that about 4% of the male and 1% of the female participants reported engaging in erotic contact with at least one same-sex patient; and that, in response to a separate survey item, 7.2% of the male and 0.6% of the female psychologists reported that they had "had intercourse with a patient within three months after terminating therapy" (p. 846). [c]Respondents were asked to specify the number of male and female patients with whom they had been sexually involved" (p. 1127); they were also asked "to restrict their answers to adult patients" (p. 1127). [d]The survey also included a question about "becoming sexually involved with a former client" (p. 996). Gender percentages about sex with current or former clients did not appear in the article but were provided by an author. Fourteen percent of the male and 8% of the female respondents reported sex with a former client. [e]The original article also noted that 14.2% of male and 4.7% of female psychologists reported that they had "been involved in an intimate relationship with a former client" (p. 454). [f]The original article also asked if respondents had "engaged in sexual activity with a client after termination" (p. 288). Six percent of the male and 2% of the female therapists reported engaging in this activity. Adapted from Pope, in press-a. Used with permission.

Table 6-2

Percentages of Therapists Reporting Male and Female Patients Who Were Sexually Involved With a Previous Therapist

Ref. no.	Profession surveyed	Geographic area	Return rate[a]	% Reporting such patients[b]	Male patients[c]	Female patients[d]
1	psychology	California	16	45	6	94
2	psychiatry	national	26	65	9	91
3	psychology	national	50	50	13	87
4[e]	psychology	Missouri	31	44	—	—

Reference Key: 1) Bouhoutsos, Holroyd, Lerman, Forer, & Greenberg, 1983; 2) Gartrell, Herman, Olarte, Feldstein, & Localio, 1987 [see also 1986; Gartrell, Milliken, Goodson, Thiemann, & Lo, 1992]; 3) Pope & Vetter, 1991; 4) Stake & Oliver, 1991.
[a]Percentage of psychologists or psychiatrists who returned survey forms. [b]Percentage of respondents who reported encountering at least one patient who had been sexually involved with a previous therapist. [c]Of all patients reported as having been sexually involved with a previous therapist, the percentage who were male. [d]Of all patients reported as having been sexually involved with a previous therapist, the percentage who were female. [e]This survey did not ask the gender of the patients who were reported as sexually involved with a previous therapist. Adapted from Pope, 1993, p. 376. Used with permission.

women are far more likely than men to be victims (see Table 6-2). For example, the survey reported by Bouhoutsos, Holroyd, Lerman, Forer, and Greenberg (1983) found that 92% of the instances in which a therapist reported that a client had been sexually involved with a prior therapist involved sexual acts between male therapists and female clients. Similarly, the survey reported by Gartrell, Herman, Olarte, Feldstein, and Localio (1986), which was based on therapists' anonymous self-reports about their own sexual involvement with patients, found that 88% of the "contacts for which both the psychiatrist's and the patient's gender were specified occurred between male psychiatrists and female patients" (p. 1128). Studies in which therapists report data about whether their own patients have been sexually involved with a prior therapist and self-report surveys in which therapists report anonymously on their own sexual involvements with patients provide two sources of data about gender patterns in therapist–patient sex. Data from licensing disciplinary actions for therapists who have been sexually involved with patients provide a third. Information from this third source suggests that about 86% of the instances in which licensing boards impose discipline in therapist–patient sex cases involve male therapists and female patients (Pope, 1993).

If, as the research suggests, perhaps as many as 86% to 92% of the instances of therapist–client sex involve male therapists and female patients, the gender imbalance is far greater than might be accounted for by figures showing that most therapists are male and most patients are female. Any understanding of therapists' sexual involvement with their patients must take into account this sharp gender imbalance.[7] The sexual involvement itself, for example, may reflect issues of sex-role stereotyping and bias that are found in the culture at large. Jean Holroyd, principal author of the first national study of therapist–patient sex and professor of psychology at the University of California, Los Angeles (UCLA), for example, concluded that, "sexual contact between therapists and patients is perhaps the quintessence of sex-biased therapeutic practice" (Holroyd, 1983, p. 285).[8] Holroyd and Brodsky's (1977) landmark research prompted a second national study that examined not only therapist–patient, but also professor–student, sexual involvement. The findings suggested that the gender issues discussed by Holroyd (1983) were frequently manifested in terms of role-power and role-vulnerability:

> When sexual contact occurs in the context of psychology training or psychotherapy, the predominant pattern is quite clear and simple: An older, higher status man becomes sexually active with a younger, subordinate woman. In each of the higher status professional roles (teacher, supervisor, administrator, therapist), a much higher percentage of men than women engage in sex with those students or

---

[7]"To acknowledge and attempt to address the significant gender differences that have consistently emerged from the diverse national studies of dual relationships does not, of course, imply that men are the only perpetrators, that women are the only victims/survivors, or that victimization of male clients is somehow less damaging or important" (Borys & Pope, 1989, p. 290). This book focuses on abused women, and it is important to be aware that a small minority of the abusers are female therapists. Yet even this form of female–female abuse occurs in a social context in which the overwhelming majority of abusers are male. Readers seeking works focusing on therapist–patient sex that involves female perpetrators are referred to L. S. Brown (1988) and Benowitz (1991).

[8]See also L. A. Gilbert and Scher's (1989) discussion of therapist–patient sex as an expression of a male sense of entitlement.

clients for whom they have assumed professional responsibility. In the lower status role of student, a far greater proportion of women than men are sexually active with their teachers, administrators, and clinical supervisors. (Pope, Levenson, & Schover, 1979, p. 687)[9]

Similarly, clinical attempts to assess the condition of patients who have been sexually involved with a therapist, and professional attempts to address this issue, may reflect historical trends in how the larger culture addresses forms of harm whose perpetrators are generally (though not always) male and whose victims are generally (though not always) female (L. S. Brown, in press; Chesler, 1972; Herman, 1992; Walker, 1989a).

Professional Patterns, Contexts, and Influences

Psychologists Carolyn Bates and Annette Brodsky (1989) gave their case study, *Sex in the Therapy Hour*, the subtitle *A Case of Professional Incest.* Their analysis explores the ways in which a therapist who chooses to enter a sexual relationship with a patient engages in an act that is similar (e.g., in dynamics and consequences) to incest. This pattern creates obvious difficulties for a woman who has been sexually abused by her therapist. If she is to seek therapy for the issues that originally prompted her to enter therapy or for the consequences of the sexualized therapy, she must risk entering therapy with yet another therapist. Yet on the basis of her own experience, therapy may not offer a safe environment in which she can trust. Her own experience may tell her that a therapist is one who may knowingly and deceptively place her at risk for deep and lasting harm rather than attempt to help her.

The fear and confusion that many women experience when faced with this dilemma is understandable. It is part of the context essential to understanding the phenomenon of therapist–patient sex and providing helpful services to patients who have been sexually involved with a therapist. But it is also part of the context for understanding the profession's response to the problem of therapist–patient sex. Typically, the profession views itself as

---

[9]See also Glaser and Thorpe (1986), Pope (1989b), and Robinson and Reid (1985).

attempting to help people whose difficulties are caused by a variety of social–environmental, personal, or biological factors. In the case of therapist–patient sex, however, the problem is caused by a member of the profession itself (i.e., a colleague). Thus, the profession must confront the fact and the implications of the fact that the perpetrators are among its own members.

Bates and Brodsky's (1989) use of the incest analogy suggests a little-discussed professional dynamic: Part of the context for the professional response to issues of therapist–patient sex is professional awareness that perpetrators are fellow members of the profession. Consequently, nonoffending therapists are in a position that is similar, in some respects, to that of nonoffending family members who are aware that other family members are engaging in incest. Consequently, the profession, in order to address the phenomenon of therapist–patient sex, may need to acknowledge and understand any tendencies to collude with perpetrators, to deny or minimize their offenses, or to enable them to continue or resume a practice that puts unknowing patients at risk (see Pope, 1994).

As used in this chapter, *the profession* refers to those mental health workers who provide assessment, therapy, and other clinical services. But the profession, in that sense, is really several professions: psychology, psychiatry, social work, marriage and family counseling, and so on. It is important to acknowledge not only the similarities among these professions, but also the significant differences between them that may be relevant for an adequate understanding of therapist–patient sex and its implications. A study designed to compare the rates at which psychiatrists, psychologists, and social workers engaged in sex with their patients found that the "professions did not differ among themselves in terms of . . . sexual intimacies with clients before or after termination" (Borys & Pope, 1989, p. 283). Yet, when professionals are expelled from an association on the basis of such unethical behavior as sexual involvement with patients, the steps each association takes may be viewed from the perspective of how likely it is that the decision will become known to the perpetrator's current patients and potential patients (who may be at considerable risk for abuse), colleagues in other disciplines (who may employ or refer patients to the perpetrator), and the general public. Currently, for example, the American Psychological Association notifies its members through a confidential mailing when someone's membership is discontinued on the basis of a serious ethics violation. The American Psychiatric Association, on the other hand, reports "all expulsions by means of a press release to the media in the area in which the member lives and [publishes this]. . . information in *Psychiatric News*" (Sharfstein, 1993, p. 1580).

The Problem Without Name or Real Coverage

The patterns, context, and influences of gender and profession—to name two examples—may be among the factors that help account for the phenomenon of therapist–patient sex transforming so quickly from the "problem with no name," in the words of psychiatrist Virginia Davidson (1977), to the problem with no insurance coverage. Viewing this phenomenon in its historical context may help illustrate the power of some of the factors that have made it difficult for the general profession as well as for individual practitioners to respond effectively to this form of abuse.

It was only in the 1970s that the major mental health professions explicitly addressed therapist–patient sex in their formal ethics codes, but the prohibition against this form of exploitation has a long history. The explicit prohibition against sexual involvement between doctor and patient is found in the Hippocratic Oath and at least one earlier code (Brodsky, 1989). Freud, as he and his colleagues pioneered the "talking cure," set forth the injunction against sex with a therapy patient. Although explicit mention of therapist–patient sex was absent from the ethics code until the 1970s, the act was contrary to various code sections and offenders could be held in violation of those ethical principles. Rachel Hare-Mustin (1974), a former chair of the American Psychological Association's Ethics Committee, for example, published an article 3 years before her association's code addressed therapist–patient sex explicitly. She noted that the 1963 *Ethical Standards of Psychologists* of the American Psychological Association set forth standards that would prohibit engaging in sex with a patient. She wrote that "a review of principles relating to competency, community standards and the client relationship [show] that genital contact with patients is ethically unacceptable" (Hare-Mustin, 1974, p. 310).

Similarly, UCLA Professor Jean Holroyd, senior author of the first national study of therapist–patient sex, emphasized in her testimony that the 1977 APA ethics code did not change the standards regarding sexual activities with patients.

Administrative law judge: Was it [the 1977 ethics code] a codification of what was already the standard of practice?

Holroyd: Yes, it was making it very explicit in the ethics code. . . .

Administrative law judge: What I am asking is whether or not the standard of practice prior to the inclusion of that specific section in the [1977] ethics code, whether or not that changed the standard of practice.

Holroyd: No, it did not change the standard of practice. The standard of practice always precluded a sexual relationship between therapist and patient.

Administrative law judge: Even though it was not expressed in the ethics codes?

Holroyd: From the beginning of the term psychotherapy with Sigmund Freud, he was very clear to prohibit it in his early publications. (*In re Howland*, 1980, pp. 49–50)

As early as the mid-1970s, there was judicial recognition of the professional consensus that therapist sex was clinically contraindicated, a consensus that stretched back toward the beginning of the century. For example, Justice Markowitz of the New York Supreme Court noted that, from Freud's time to the present, therapist–patient sex had been viewed as harmful: "Thus from [Freud] to the modern practitioner we have common agreement of the harmful effects of sensual intimacies between patient and therapist" (*Roy v. Hartogs*, 1976, p. 590).

The delay in including an explicit reference to therapist–patient sex in the formal codes seems due in part to difficulty believing that this form of exploitation occurred on any but an extremely sporadic basis. In the absence of research suggesting that a number of professionals were engaging in this behavior, there was a tendency to dismiss allegations as fabrications. For example, a report based on malpractice suits filed against psychologists over a 10–year period failed to mention any valid allegation of therapist–patient sex. Rejected and spurned women were, according to this report, the cause of the (false) allegations regarding sexual intimacies. According to this report, the insurance data reveal

> that the greatest number of [all malpractice] actions are brought by women who lead lives of very quiet desperation, who form close attachments to their therapists, who feel rejected or spurned when they discover that relations are maintained on a formal and professional level, and who then react with allegations of sexual improprieties. (Brownfain, 1971, p. 651)

In the absence of evidence that therapist–patient sex actually occurred in anything more than extremely rare and isolated cases, the profession seemed to hold the belief that it almost never occurred and thus did not warrant mention in the codes.

> The definitive proscriptions by Hippocrates and Freud appeared to be sufficient. It was simply assumed that therapist–patient sexual intimacy was such an egregious act on the part of the therapist that to include mention of it in, for instance, a textbook or ethical code would be entirely unnecessary. It would be like writing a manual for pilots on how to fly a plane and including the prohibition: "Do not crash the plane into the side of a mountain." The principle seemed so obvious as to not need explicit mention. (Pope & Bouhoutsos, 1986, p. 26)

Two factors seemed particularly powerful in overcoming professional resistance to acknowledging that therapist–patient sex occurred in substantial numbers. First, there was the research. Holroyd and Brodsky (1977) modeled their national study on a county study of male physicians conducted by a an interdisciplinary team at UCLA (Kardener, Fuller, & Mensch, 1973; see also J. A. Perry, 1976). One hundred male psychiatrists responded to the question, "Do you engage in erotic practices [with your patients]?" (p. 1079). Ninety-five reported that they "never" did, four reported that they did so "rarely," and one reported that he did so "occasionally." Thus, 5% of the male psychiatrists reported engaging in erotic involvement with their patients; the same percentage reported that the erotic involvement included intercourse. This and subsequent studies (see Tables 6-1 and 6-2) provided evidence suggesting that a substantial number of therapists engaged in therapist–patient sexual activities.

The second factor that seemed to awaken the profession to the scope of this problem was the growing number of patients who refused to keep secret what a therapist had done, who filed malpractice suits, and who prevailed in the legal action. Although the research evidence suggests that only a relatively small percentage of patients who have been sexually involved with a therapist file any type (e.g., malpractice, licensing, ethics, criminal) of formal complaint (see, e.g., Bouhoutsos et al., 1983; Pope & Vetter, 1991; Pope, Sonne, & Holroyd, 1993), the frequency of such claims is not insignificant. According to the president of the insurance company that provided liability insurance to members of the American Psychological Association in the 1980s, therapist–patient sex claims accounted for about half of the costs related to malpractice suits filed against psychologists (Pope, Sonne, & Holroyd, 1993). Perr (1989), a psychiatrist and attorney, wrote, "Complaints concerning psychologists' sexual involvement with clients are the leading cause of lawsuits. Sexual involvement by psychiatrists with patients now constitutes the second leading cause of all professional practice litigation" (p. 212).

One of the most prompt, decisive, and visible responses to the increasing number of malpractice suits alleging sexual offenses by therapists was a change in malpractice policies making it much less likely that patients who had suffered harm from therapist–patient sex would be able to secure legal representation or to obtain adequate jury awards. The policy offered to members of the American Psychological Association, for example, first eliminated coverage of judgments due to therapist sexual misconduct. As noted earlier, the problem of therapist–patient sex had passed quickly from one with no name to one with no coverage. In subsequent years, the APA policy restored some coverage but limited it with a cap of $25,000 for awards. However much the elimination or capping of therapist–patient sex coverage may have saved therapists generally in terms of malpractice premiums, it made it much more difficult for patients who had been abused to find attorneys to represent them. Therapist–patient sex cases tend to be extraordinarily complex, and attorneys generally take them on a contingency basis (i.e., most patients do not have sufficient financial resources to hire an attorney and to pay the costs of preparing and trying a case). Therapists who are reading this chapter would—at best— smile at the assertion that therapists tend to possess great wealth. If other funds aside from insurance coverage (which now tends to exclude coverage for sex claims or to cap them) are unavailable, few plaintiff attorneys have both sufficient financial resources and inclination to pay the costs of preparing and trying a case if the most that they can realistically hope to recover is a percentage (e.g., 0%–33%) of a nonexistent or severely capped insurance coverage.

The contexts of gender and professional relationships noted in the previous sections of this chapter may be relevant to an adequate understanding of a shift in professional liability coverage that (a) affected a tort in which the overwhelming majority of perpetrators are male and the overwhelming majority of victims are female and (b) served to make it less likely that offending therapists would be sued. A. A. Stone (1990), a former president of the American Psychiatric Association and currently professor of psychiatry and law at Harvard, focused on the contexts of gender and profession in his observation that "we should all realize that there is a serious conflict of interest between APA's [American Psychiatric Association] professional concerns for the victims of sexual exploitation in therapy and its financial concerns when the association's economic interests are at stake" (p. 26). He emphasized that the elimination or capping of coverage not only seemed to connote unfair gender discrimination, but also appeared to violate the professional commitment to patient welfare:

> Each of us contributes by paying liability insurance to a fund that has two functions: to protect us and to compensate those who are unfortunate victims of our negligence. With this in mind, the policy decision to exclude victims of sexual exploitation, who are typically women, from participation in our victim compensation fund is difficult to defend. If we are concerned about them, why should they be "victimized" by the exclusion? (A. A. Stone, 1990, p. 25)

The patterns, context, and influences of gender and profession may also be among the factors that might help clinicians, patients, and the general public to understand the tendency that has enabled therapists who have sexually abused their patients to be allowed to resume practice (if their practice is interrupted by formal action that is based on a valid complaint). Perpetrators of therapist–patient sexual involvement seem remarkably adept, even once a licensing board or other agency has become aware of their exploitation, at finding ways to continue or resume practicing. Often they are able to find colleagues who are quite helpful, through specific acts or failures to act, in this process.

Questions regarding whether there is any evidence, based on independently conducted and replicated studies, that any form of rehabilitation actually works (see, e.g., Pope, Butcher, & Seelen, 1993, pp. 177–186; Pope, Sonne, & Holroyd, 1993, pp. 255–258) seem to have received inadequate attention in light of the potential consequences: allowing those who previously have consciously chosen to place a patient at risk for severe and lasting harm (perhaps including suicide) to have access to new patients who are unlikely to know that they are being placed at risk. The lack of adequate attention to these questions seems particularly puzzling in light of such assertions as that from the American Psychological Association Insurance Trust, "the recidivism rate for sexual misconduct is substantial" (1990, p. 3), and the conclusions of the executive directors of California licensing boards for psychology, social work, and marriage and family counseling, that "prospects for rehabilitation are minimal and it is doubtful that [therapists who have been sexually involved with a patient] should be given the opportunity to ever practice psychotherapy again" (Callanan & O'Connor, 1988, p. 11).

Beyond the questions of whether rehabilitation is possible and whether there is adequate research evidence that any of the proposed methods are effective, however, is a more fundamental policy question: Is providing perpetrators with renewed access to vulnerable patients a policy that is consistent with patient welfare and professional integrity?

> A judge might take a bribe to decide a major case, lose the judgeship, subsequently pay the debt to society through a prison term, and undergo extensive rehabilitation; yet the judge would obviously not

resume the bench. A teacher running a preschool might sexually abuse the children, subsequently undergo extensive treatment and rehabilitation and satisfy the legal requirements (i.e., jail or probation), and seem to present no threat of further abuse; yet the teacher would not subsequently be granted a license to operate a preschool.

. . . If people found to have used their positions of trust to accept bribes for rendering certain legal decisions or to victimize students were allowed to resume the positions of trust that they had betrayed, the nature of these positions—what they mean to the society and to those whose lives they influence—would be profoundly changed. Violation of a clearly understood prohibition against such a grave abuse of power and trust precludes further opportunity to hold these special positions in the legal or educational professions, although numerous other opportunities in law or education (e.g., research, writing, and consultation) remain available to the rehabilitated perpetrator. (Pope, 1990a, p. 234)

Decades ago, an occasional perpetrator, facing a formal complaint, would allege that the sexual intimacies were part of a legitimate treatment approach. One perspective used to evaluate such claims focused on gender (and age): If this treatment approach was generally legitimate, why did the overwhelming percentage of such "treatments" seem to occur between older male therapists and younger female patients (Hare-Mustin, 1974)? The ways in which the profession now addresses the policy issue of rehabilitation (see, e.g., Pope, 1989a) might benefit from the same sort of inquiry that takes into account gender contexts: If the offenders were predominantly female and the victims were predominantly male, would the profession be conducting a much more rigorous examination of rehabilitation policy? Is the professional response to this issue at all affected by issues related to gender and sex roles (Pope, 1990a, 1994)?

Readers seeking a more detailed examination of these contextual issues and the professional resistance to this topic are referred to the chapters "The Topic That Isn't There" and "Awareness of Context" in *Sexual Feelings in*

Psychotherapy (Pope, Sonne, & Holroyd, 1993, pp. 23–35 and 57–77) and to the article "Therapist–Patient Sex as Sex Abuse: Six Scientific, Professional, and Practical Dilemmas in Addressing Victimization and Rehabilitation" (Pope, 1990a).

SPECIAL ASSESSMENT AND INTERVENTION ISSUES

The research summarized in Table 6-2 suggests that around 50% (i.e., 44% to 65%) of therapists report that they have seen at least one patient who has been sexually involved with a previous therapist. This research supports the notion that therapists generally should be well-trained to work with this population. As previously mentioned, chapters 10–14 discuss some of the more general assessment and treatment issues in working with abused women. The sections below note a few assessment and intervention issues of special relevance in helping women who have been sexually involved with a therapist.

General Information

In offering assessment and intervention services to women who have been sexually involved with a therapist, it is important for the mental health care provider to be familiar with the research and theory in this area. The works cited in this chapter (particularly those in Footnote 6) review much of this information and provide reference lists for additional reading. The following four exhibits and tables summarize information about common scenarios in which therapist–patient sex occurs, common dynamics of perpetrators, common consequences for patients, and other information about patients who report sexual involvement with a therapist.

The clinician who is familiar with the topic of therapist–patient sex and is well-prepared and competent to consider the prospect that a patient may have been sexually involved with a prior therapist is knowledgeable about the most common scenarios of therapist–patient sexual involvement. Pope and Bouhoutsos (1986, p. 4) presented 10 of the most common scenarios as follows:

1. *Role Trading*: Therapist becomes the "patient" and the wants and needs of the therapist become the focus
2. *Sex Therapy*: Therapist fraudulently presents therapist–patient sex as valid treatment for sexual or related difficulties
3. *As If. . .*: Therapist treats positive transference as if it were not the result of the therapeutic situation
4. *Svengali*: Therapist creates and exploits an exaggerated dependence on the part of the patient
5. *Drugs*: Therapist uses cocaine, alcohol, or other drugs as part of the seduction
6. *Rape*: Therapist uses physical force, threats, and/or intimidation
7. *True Love*: Therapist uses rationalizations that attempt to discount the clinical/professional nature of the professional relationship and its duties (see also Twemlow & Gabbard, 1989)
8. *It Just Got Out of Hand*: Therapist fails to treat the emotional closeness that develops in therapy with sufficient attention, care, and respect
9. *Time Out*: Therapist fails to acknowledge and take into account the fact that the therapeutic relationship does not cease to exist between scheduled sessions or outside the therapist's office
10. *Hold Me*: Therapist exploits patient's desire for nonerotic physical contact and possible confusion between erotic and nonerotic contact.

Despite the frequency with which these 10 seem to occur, it is crucial to acknowledge the almost limitless ability of perpetrators to improvise, take advantage of situations, create opportunities, and present the abuse as if it were some innocuous, innovative, or altruistic pursuit.

As emphasized explicitly in a subsequent section in this chapter, reflexive judgments about the validity of allegations must be avoided. It is important to avoid assuming that an allegation is valid simply because it presents one of these common scenarios. It is equally important to avoid assuming that an allegation is invalid simply because it presents an atypical scenario.

Topics such as the dynamics of therapists who become sexually involved with their patients are beyond the scope of this chapter. A typology using 10 categories for understanding perpetrators is presented on pages 256–257 of Pope, Sonne, and Holroyd (1993). It is important to note that many abusive therapists are at least partially aware of these dynamics and have become quite adept at masking them from others. The personal, interpersonal, and professional skills that the therapist has developed as a therapist, as well as the knowledge of psychological processes, are put in the service of not only perpetrating the abuse but also avoiding detection or, if detected, avoiding or minimizing negative consequences from the abusive behavior.

Exhibit 6-1 presents 10 of the most common consequences that tend to afflict patients who have been sexually involved with a therapist. These sequelae of therapist–client sex often seem to cluster into a distinct syndrome, with both acute and chronic phases that are similar to forms of post-traumatic stress disorder (PTSD) brought on by interpersonal violence (Hare-Mustin, 1992; Mann & Winer, 1991; Pope, 1985, 1986, 1988, 1989c, 1994, in press-a, in press-b; Pope, Sonne, & Holroyd, 1993; Sonne, 1989). The victim may experience, for example, profound and extensive cognitive dysfunction with impairment of attention and memory processes. Flashbacks, nightmares, memory fragments, intrusive thoughts, and unbidden images may assault the awareness of the victim and often assume a quality of intense immediacy as if they constituted her current experience. Some of these consequences are discussed in more detail in subsequent sections of this chapter. Issues in the assessment of sequelae commonly termed *post-traumatic stress disorder* are discussed in chapter 12.

In considering the usefulness of this conceptualization with a specific patient, two cautions are crucial. First, this syndrome emerged as a way of describing the most frequently observed sequelae of therapist–patient sex. From the earliest discussions (e.g., Pope, 1985), it has been emphasized that some patients may not experience all or even any of these consequences. A woman who has been sexually abused by her therapist is no more certain to develop any or all of these sequelae than a woman who is raped will inevitably suffer rape trauma syndrome or a woman who is battered by a partner will inevitably develop battered woman syndrome.

The usefulness of the conceptualization is in helping clinicians to be aware of and understand the most common consequences. In this sense, it

Exhibit 6-1

Therapist–Patient Sex Syndrome

Reaction	Comments
1. Ambivalence	Just as victims of incest abuse may experience contradictory impulses to cling to and flee from the abuser, victims of therapist–patient sex may experience contradictory impulses to cling to (and protect) and to flee from the offending therapist
2. Guilt	The irrational guilt is similar to that experienced by many rape and incest victims (who blame themselves and their own behavior); the guilt is irrational because it is always the therapist's responsibility to refrain from sexually exploiting a patient
3. Emptiness and Isolation	Patients often feel empty and as if they can only be "filled up" by the offending therapist; even if they cognitively "know" that other patients have been exploited by therapists, they may feel as if they are the only one and as if the experience has separated them forever from the human race and from a normal life
4. Sexual Confusion	Patients may come to feel as if their only worth or only way of relating to significant others is sexual
5. Impaired Ability to Trust	The therapist having violated and exploited a relationship that is founded on deep trust, the patient may find it difficult to trust anyone again
6. Boundary/Role Disturbance	The therapist having violated one of the most basic and important boundaries and roles, the

	patient may have difficulty recognizing and maintaining interpersonal boundaries and roles
7. Emotional Lability	The patient's emotions may seem out of control; there may be large or frequent mood swings
8. Suppressed Rage	Offending therapists are often skillful at directing patients to turn rage back on themselves; patients may become terrified of acknowledging or expressing their anger
9. Increased Suicidal Risk	An extremely careful assessment of suicidal risk should be a part of the assessment of any patient who has been sexually exploited by a therapist
10. Cognitive Dysfunction	Dysfunctions may affect particularly the areas of attention and concentration, and may involve intrusive thoughts, unbidden images, flashbacks, and nightmares

From Pope, 1985. Used with permission.

is similar to PTSD. PTSD outlines common sequelae of psychologically traumatic experiences. Not all people who experience a traumatic event develop PTSD, nor do those who develop PTSD inevitably experience all sequelae. However, clinicians familiar with the concept of PTSD may be more alert to—and therefore less likely to overlook, minimize, or misinterpret—the common sequelae that constitute the syndrome. Each person is unique and experiences "this destructive event in his or her own way in the context of his or her unique life" (Pope & Bouhoutsos, 1986, p. 21).

Second, the common sequelae should not be used as an infallible indicator of whether allegations of therapist–patient sex are valid. A patient who reports all aspects of therapist–patient sex syndrome (TPSS) may not have been sexually involved with a therapist; a patient who fails to report any of the TPSS aspects may nevertheless have been sexually involved with a therapist. (For a review of forensic applications and implications of TPSS, see Pope, 1994.)

Table 6-3 summarizes the results of a study of 958 patients who were judged to have been sexually involved with a therapist. Subsequent sections discuss some of these findings.

Personal Reactions

Patient accounts of sexual victimization by a therapist can evoke powerful feelings in the subsequent treating therapist. The experiences of the patient can interact with the feelings of the new therapist, and with the forces of context that were described in the opening sections of this chapter, in a way that threatens the process of healing, understanding, and empowerment. It is important that therapists who work with sexually abused patients be aware not only of research and theory but also of their personal patterns of feeling.

Clinicians may themselves have a history of abuse. As the research summarized in Table 6-4 shows, for example, about 14% of the male therapists and about 57% of the female therapists reported having experienced some form of abuse during adulthood, and about 2% of the male therapists and 5% of the female therapists specifically reported having engaged in sexual involvement with their own psychotherapists during adulthood. This research also found that about 26% of the male therapists and about 39% of the female therapists reported experiencing child abuse. About one third (33%) of the male therapists and more than two thirds (70%) of the female therapists reported having experienced at least one form of abuse at some time during their childhood, adolescence, or adulthood (Pope & Feldman-Summers, 1992).

Whether therapists have suffered some form of abuse may influence how they respond to patients who report abuse. Knowing a particular kind of experience firsthand—that is, having "been there"—may in some instances constitute a valuable therapeutic resource, helping a clinician to respond sensitively and empathetically. On the other hand, it is also possible

Table 6-3

Characteristics of 958 Patients Who Had Been Sexually Involved With a Therapist

	n	%
Patient was a minor at the time of the involvement	47	5
Patient married the therapist	37	3
Patient had experienced incest or other child sex abuse	309	32
Patient had experienced rape prior to sexual involvement with therapist	92	10
Patient required hospitalization considered to be at least partially a result of the sexual involvement	105	11
Patient attempted suicide	134	14
Patient committed suicide	7	1
Patient achieved complete recovery from any harmful effects of sexual involvement	143	17[a]
Patient seen pro bono or for reduced fee	187	20
Patient filed formal (e.g., licensing, malpractice) complaint	112	12

[a]17% of the 866 patients who experienced harm.
Adapted from Pope and Vetter, 1991, p. 431. Used with permission.

Table 6-4

Percentage of Male and Female Therapists Reporting Abuse Experienced During Adulthood

Type of abuse	Men	Women
Sexual harassment	1.46	37.91
Attempted rape	0.73	13.07
Acquaintance rape	0.0	6.54
Stranger rape	0.73	1.31
Nonsexual physical abuse by a spouse or partner	6.57	12.42
Nonsexual physical abuse by an acquaintance	0.0	2.61
Nonsexual physical abuse by a stranger	4.38	7.19
Sexual involvement with a therapist	2.19	4.58
Sexual involvement with a physician	0.0	1.96
At least one of the above	13.87	56.86

From Pope and Feldman-Summers, 1992, p. 335. Reprinted with permission.

that a "history of abuse, if insufficiently acknowledged, examined, and resolved, [can] render practitioners less able to help a client suffering from a similar form of abuse" (Pope & Feldman-Summers, 1992, p. 357). An honest evaluation of how their own history of abuse or lack of such personal experiences influences responses to patients who describe abusive experiences can be a vital developmental step for therapists working in this area.

The research suggests that some emotional reactions to patients (e.g., sexual arousal, fear, hate) may be relatively common and yet difficult for therapists to acknowledge, accept, and respond to in a therapeutic manner (Pope & Tabachnick, 1993). For example, it is not uncommon for therapists to report engaging in sexual fantasies about a patient either during sex with another individual who is not the patient (Pope, Keith-Spiegel, & Tabachnick, 1986) or at other times (Pope, Tabachnick, & Keith-Spiegel, 1987). Yet just as experiencing a sexual fantasy about a patient who is an incest victim may represent a clinically significant countertransferential response (Ganzarain & Buchele, 1986, 1988), experiencing a sexual fantasy about a patient who has been sexually abused by a prior therapist may represent countertransference that warrants careful acknowledgment and exploration so that it does not disrupt the therapeutic work with the patient.

In summary, the therapist's personal reactions that are evoked when working with a patient who has been sexually involved with a previous therapist can, depending on the degree to which they are acknowledged and understood, serve as a rich clinical resource or an unfortunate source of therapeutic mistakes and possible revictimization of the patient. Exhibit 6-2 summarizes a 1991 article that set forth 10 sources of errors in working with sexually involved patients, with each source representing a common personal response. These 10 potential causes of treatment mistakes can be reviewed periodically by therapists to ensure that errors in all areas are avoided and that the clinical services provided are as helpful as possible.

Information Regarding the Prohibition

A client who has been sexually abused by a prior therapist may not be aware that such abuse is prohibited. The perpetrator may have provided forceful and detailed assurances that the abuse was a legitimate (and perhaps the

Exhibit 6-2

Common Clinician Reactions to Victims of Therapist–Patient Sexual Intimacies

1. Disbelief and Denial	The tendency to reject reflexively—without adequate data-gathering—allegations about therapist–patient sex (because, e.g., the activities described seem outlandish and improbable)
2. Minimization of Harm	The tendency to assume reflexively—without adequate data-gathering—that harm did not occur, or that, if it did, the consequences were minimally, if at all, harmful
3. Making the Patient Fit the Textbook	The tendency to assume reflexively—without adequate data gathering and examination—that the patient must inevitably fit a particular schema
4. Blaming the Victim	The tendency to attempt to make the patient responsible for enforcing the therapist's professional responsibility to refrain from engaging in sex with a patient and holding the patient responsible for the therapist's offense
5. Sexual Reaction to the Victim	The clinician's sexual attraction to or feelings about the patient; such feelings are normal but must not become a source of distortion in the assessment process
6. Discomfort at the Lack of Privacy	The clinician's (and sometimes patient's) emotional response to the possibility that under certain conditions (e.g., malpractice, licensing, or similar formal actions against the offending therapist; a formal review of assessment and

Exhibit 6-2 continues

Exhibit 6-2 continued

	other services by the insurance company providing coverage for the services) the raw data and the results of the assessment may not remain private
7. Difficulty "Keeping the Secret"	The clinician's possible discomfort (and other emotional reactions) when he or she has knowledge that an offender continues to practice and to victimize other patients but can not, due to confidentiality or other constraints, take steps to intervene
8. Intrusive Advocacy	The tendency to want to guide, direct, or determine a patient's decisions about what steps to take or what steps not to take in regard to a perpetrator
9. Vicarious Helplessness	The clinician's discomfort when a patient who has filed a formal complaint seems to encounter unjustifiable obstacles, indifference, lack of fair hearing, and other responses that seem to ignore or trivialize the complaint and fail to protect the public from offenders
10. Discomfort with Strong Feelings	The clincian's discomfort when experiencing strong feelings (e.g., rage, neediness, or ambivalence) expressed by the patient and focused on the clinician

Adapted from Pope, Sonne, and Holroyd, 1993, pp. 241–261. Used with permission.

only effective) treatment for the client's difficulties; that the abuse was entirely unrelated to the therapy (an assertion that is often withdrawn when a malpractice suit is filed and the therapist wants the abuse to be covered under the professional liability insurance policy); that there was no harm because the client either invited or failed to resist the sexual activity; or that the sexual activity represented an experimental, "cutting edge" treatment beyond the scope of the "dated" ethical codes (although such therapists generally fail to obtain the client's written informed consent to serve as a research subject for such bogus "investigations").

It is crucial that information be provided to the client only at a pace that fits the client's needs and wishes. The information may come as a great shock. The client may only be ready and willing to learn about the prohibition and the nature of therapist–patient sexual intimacies in stages, and in each stage may require a period of assimilation, reflection, and decision-making.

While learning about the prohibition, a client who has been sexually involved with a previous therapist may need extensive support as she seeks to understand the possible implications of the information for her life. One victim of therapist–patient sex had abruptly terminated her relationship with the abusing therapist but was unaware that he had done anything "wrong." She knew something was not right in her life, that she was extremely confused, upset, and panicky. She signed up for an adult education class in psychology. One day the professor lectured on the ethics of therapy and spent considerable time discussing the ways in which therapist–patient sexual involvement can be destructive for the patient. There was no way for the professor to know that this was the first time that this woman had heard anything about the topic. In crisis, the woman asked the professor for an immediate appointment right after the class. The professor then referred her to a therapist experienced in helping clients who were abused by therapists. However, it was a matter of months before the client was able to make the phone call to the new therapist. She immediately withdrew from her adult education course and spent the intervening months in relative seclusion.

This woman's experience illustrates one of the diverse ways in which those who have been abused may suddenly, accidentally learn that therapist–patient sexual involvement is unethical and may be extremely harmful. The abused woman may be in a state of shock, confusion, panic, or despair when she seeks consultation with a new therapist. It is crucial that subsequent therapists be aware of the needs that such patients may have for extensive information, validation, support, and reassurance, as well as time to make their own decisions about what to do.

To learn that a therapist's "loving" sexual behavior was in fact abusive can be an important step toward recovery. The abused woman becomes better able to understand the source of her distress and dysfunction. Distorted attributions (e.g., "My wonderful, caring therapist did everything for me and now I feel even worse than before; there is no hope for me.") may be identified and reexamined. The woman then has the ability to decide, on an informed basis, what steps to take to address the damage that she has suffered. This is a crucial initial step in her reempowerment. An adequate assessment of the abuse to which the woman was subjected can enable both patient and subsequent therapist to create an appropriate treatment plan.

Many women find it useful and therapeutic if, in addition to discussions with the subsequent therapist, they can read about the topic. First, seeing clear printed statements in a variety of publications explaining that therapist–client sex is unethical can help them to transcend any doubts or denial and to rethink beliefs, nurtured by the abusive therapist, that sexual involvement is an accepted or acceptable component of treatment. Second, reading and perhaps repeatedly rereading such materials in privacy can be helpful to those who are experiencing cognitive dysfunction that interferes with the processing of information. Third, reading first-person accounts of other women who have been through such experiences can help the victim to feel less isolated and alone. Among the accounts that many women have found useful are those by Bates and Brodsky (1989), Freeman and Roy (1976), Noel and Watterson (1992), Plaisil (1985), and Walker and Young (1986). Hare-Mustin's (1992) discussion of poet Anne Sexton's experiences has also been valuable; its shorter form (an article rather than a book) may make it more accessible, at least as a first account, to women who have been so devastated that attempting to read a book seems to be too daunting a task.

To help ensure that sexually abused therapy clients are adequately informed about the unethical nature of therapist–client sex, the California Department of Consumer Affairs, which is the umbrella agency for the state's licensing boards, prepared a 16-page pamphlet, *Professional Therapy Never Includes Sex* (1990). The pamphlet was sent to every licensed therapist in the state. Therapists are legally required to provide a copy of this pamphlet to any client who indicates that she or he has been sexually involved with a prior therapist. The American Psychological Association Office on Women's Programs has also prepared a helpful pamphlet, *If Sex Enters Into the Therapy Relationship* (Committee on Women in Psychology, 1989). Therapists may find it useful to obtain copies of these and similar pamphlets as they consider sources of information that many exploited patients find helpful. Such pamphlets may provide clinicians with an overview or summary of the relevant law in this area, but it is important that therapists working with women who have been sexually involved with a previous therapist maintain an adequate knowledge of the current relevant laws and regulations. These laws and regulations, which vary according to jurisdiction, address not only the clients' rights but also therapists' responsibilities (in regard to confidentiality and privilege, discretionary or mandatory reporting, etc.).

Reflections and Evocations of the Previous Therapy

Clinical interventions addressing therapist–patient sex abuse tend to differ from clinical interventions addressing the other forms of abuse described in this book in at least one significant way. Except in rare instances, the perpetrators of battering, incest, rape, and so forth, were not the abused woman's therapist. The abuse did not occur within the therapeutic relationship itself. The new therapeutic relationship has the potential to reflect or evoke memories of the former one, causing other issues to interfere with the treatment process.

Abuse by therapists can destroy trust in therapy and therapists. Some abused patients are never able to seek subsequent help from a mental health professional. The harm can reach far beyond withholding prompt and appropriate help for the patient's presenting problem, professional help for which the therapist has been contracted and, in many instances, paid. The betrayal of trust can effectively cut abused patients off, sometimes permanently, from help for those original presenting problems, for the harm they suffered as a result of the abuse, and for other mental health needs they may discover or develop at subsequent stages in their lives. Any woman who has been sexually exploited by a therapist and who consults a subsequent therapist is taking a difficult and courageous step. Because therapy involves trust and vulnerability, she is putting herself at risk for betrayal once again.

It is important that subsequent therapists understand, respect, and empathize with fear and the other feelings that a victim may experience when consulting a new therapist. General aspects of the therapeutic process (e.g., regular meetings in a closed room to discuss private and sensitive material) may trigger flashbacks or similar cognitions as well as intense emotional reactions. Actions of the subsequent therapist may remind the victim of the abusing therapist. Material that was a subject of the work with the prior therapist may, as it emerges, elicit terrifying responses from the patient. In diverse ways, the subsequent therapeutic situation may tend to re-create, reenact, or represent, at least symbolically, the abusive situation.

It is not uncommon for therapy to re-create situations that will trigger memories of prior events, situations, or people. This is a part of what many psychodynamic theories term *transference*. For patients who have been abused by a prior therapist, the transference may be exceptionally intense. The new therapeutic relationship may seem to reflect or re-create the previous abusive situation in horrifying ways.

This potential for a subsequent therapeutic situation to evoke traumatic memories of a previous abusive therapy is similar in some ways to the potential for a subsequent therapeutic situation to evoke traumatic memories in a victim of torture.

> The dyadic therapeutic situation itself may be evocative of certain aspects of the torture experience: for example, two people, one of whom is licensed by or a representative of the state or larger society and the other of whom is vulnerable and in need, meeting privately in a room; the questioning of extremely personal matters, a process often experienced as intrusive; the character of the regular sessions being explicitly subject to privacy; the discrepancy in power; and the intensity of emotion usually evoked by the process. It is crucial that the therapist monitor and maintain safe, appropriate, and therapeutic boundaries so that the therapeutic relationship does not unconsciously recreate [*sic*] or act out the destructive relationship between torturer and victim. . . . Moreover, the setting itself as well as certain

procedures (e.g., an institutionalized bureaucracy, even spending time in the waiting room) may evoke traumatic memories. An awareness of these potential similarities can enable clinicians to minimize the extraneous points of similarity and the likelihood that the treatment situation itself will elicit flashbacks and other traumatic recreations [*sic*]. As Primo Levi . . . wrote, "the memory of a trauma suffered or inflicted is itself traumatic because recalling it is painful or at least disturbing." (Pope & Garcia-Peltoniemi, 1991, pp. 271 –272)

The subsequent therapist must be adequately alert to any emergence of such reactions and to provide the patient with sufficient support to help enable her to handle these feelings safely, realistically, and therapeutically.

Suicidal Risk

Both the clinical and the research literature indicate that when a therapist engages in sex with a client, he or she is choosing to act in a way that may ultimately be fatal for the client (Gabbard, 1989; Pope, 1994; Pope & Bouhoutsos, 1986). The evidence suggests that about 1 out of every 100 patients who are sexually abused by a therapist takes his or her own life and that somewhere between 10% and 15% of those who are sexually abused require subsequent hospitalization (Bouhoutsos et al., 1983; Pope & Vetter, 1991). Subsequent treating therapists must constantly assess and monitor the risk of suicide and must attend carefully to ideation, affect, verbal warnings, behavioral signs, situational changes, and changes in the therapeutic or working alliance that might influence or reflect a client's likelihood of ending her life.

There are certain situations that may increase suicidal risk. A patient may, for example, find it extremely difficult to confront—perhaps at a legal proceeding—a former therapist whose behavior and demeanor make her feel sorry for her abuser and guilty that she is causing her abuser all this pain. She may block her own pain from the abuse in order to be empathetic to the perpetrator's needs, creating a conflict that appears unsolvable. In order to meet her own needs, she must take actions that will hurt someone she trusted. Her desire to withdraw and run away from the conflict can prompt or aggravate a serious depression or even result in an attempt to end her life.

Ambivalence

As has been noted in prior chapters, victims of child abuse and battering may experience feelings of ambivalence about the perpetrator. Like victims of these other forms of abuse, the woman who has been sexually intimate with a therapist may at times experience intensely negative feelings about the abuser. She may want to escape the perpetrator at all costs. She may want to report the perpetrator so that he or she can be brought to justice or be prevented from abusing other women. But at other times, the victim may seek to cling to, meet the needs of, and protect the abuser. She may find it impossible to believe that the perpetrator was not doing everything solely, selflessly, and altruistically for her welfare.

This ambivalence can be one of the most confusing and difficult aspects of rendering adequate help to sexually abused patients. Unprepared therapists may find the phenomenon confusing. Clients likewise may be baffled by their own conflicting feelings. The woman may realize that an abusive therapist has made a conscious choice to place her at risk for severe and lasting harm, but she may still want to ensure that the offender's feelings are not hurt in any way. Confronted with such a situation, the unprepared subsequent therapist may experience confusion similar to that which many therapists may have experienced when first working with victims of woman battering or child abuse: It may be shocking to see a physically or sexually abused child or adult run to, cling to, and try to protect the perpetrator at all costs.

As in other instances of victimization, this ambivalence is a consequence of the abusive behavior of the therapist, and it is a phenomenon that many abusers, including abusive therapists, have learned to exploit skillfully. It is important to realize that such ambivalence may be deep, pervasive, and chronic. Sexually abused clients may still be struggling with intense ambivalence years into their subsequent therapy.

The ambivalence has obvious potential to disrupt the subsequent therapy. Simply going to a subsequent therapist and talking about the abuse may seem, to some sexually abused therapy clients, like a betrayal of the perpetrator, just as some incest victims may feel that they are betraying their parent if they seek therapy and talk about the "secret." If the abusive therapist and client are both from a minority group, the need to protect the therapist may become entangled with the need to protect the entire minority class. As with all aspects of the subsequent therapy, it is crucial to allow clients to consider and work through this dilemma at their own pace, without intrusive pressure by their therapist, which will likely be counterproductive and may reenact coercive elements of the prior therapy.

Guilt

Many victims of therapist–client sexual intimacy feel chronic and irrational guilt. There is no exception to the long-standing rule: It is always the therapist's responsibility to refrain from engaging in sexual intimacies with a patient. Nevertheless, like women who have been battered, harassed, or raped, patients who have been sexually exploited often feel as if they were responsible. Many have experienced the positive, perhaps romantic or sexual, transference that therapists are taught in introductory courses in graduate or medical school to anticipate, recognize, and respond to respectfully, sensitively, and therapeutically (Pope, Sonne, & Holroyd, 1993). Some patients may have originally sought therapy because of concerns relating to sexuality, romance, or intimacy. Some may have a general tendency toward self-criticism or toward accepting blame or responsibility. Whether or not these factors play a role in the individual patient's situation, a sense of irrational guilt tends to be a consequence that is either caused or elicited by the abuse.

One woman vividly described her experience of guilt:

> Always I felt a sense of collusion. And for months I chose to feel more than my share of guilt. It was one of the most difficult things for me to relinquish because I often thought, "But I agreed; I didn't run from that office." As with incest, as with any situation wherein one individual is dependent upon another, it is difficult for the victim to come to the position of clearly laying the blame where it belongs. (Bates & Brodsky, 1989, p. 99)

The same woman illustrated her subsequent therapist's support for her by repeating a story that the therapist told her. The therapist told her the story of another patient who had been sexually involved with a therapist and who had later attempted to get help from a subsequent therapist. Rather than addressing the patient's needs, the subsequent therapist became a defender of and advocate for the abusive therapist, telling the patient:

> "Well, he's been having a bad time, going through some tough times in his career; he's trying to rehabilitate himself." In making excuses, the second therapist had only confused the patient. Instead of saying, "What happened to you should not have happened to you; you were violated, and there is no excuse for it," he attempted to displace the abusive therapist's responsibility for his sexual misconduct. (Bates & Brodsky, 1989, pp. 99–100)

Any factors that seem to elicit, encourage, amplify, or validate a patient's irrational guilt work against the recovery of the patient and can cause additional harm. In some instances, the abusing therapist may attempt to blame the patient. In others, the subsequent treating therapist may attempt to hold the abused patient accountable for being abused. In still other situations, the abused patient's friends or family may place the responsibility on her. Charges may be leveled that her clinical condition (e.g., borderline disorder, hysterical character disorder, schizophrenia) elicited, prompted, or caused the therapist to behave unethically; that her dress, manner, or words produced the abuse; and so on. All such charges can deepen the harm that she has already suffered and block or delay recovery.

Assessment Instruments and Procedures

Taking a careful history is essential. In many instances, sexually exploited patients have experienced prior abuse, trauma, or difficulties. Of the 958 patients reviewed in Table 6-3, for example, almost one third (32%) were reported to have experienced incest or other child sex abuse and one tenth (10%) to have experienced rape prior to the sexual involvement with the therapist. In assessing the harm caused by the therapist's abuse, the subsequent treating therapist must use care to ensure that such prior conditions do not mask the harm and dynamics associated with the therapist–client sexual abuse. Such prior conditions may in fact intensify the negative consequences of sexual involvement with a therapist. Feldman-Summers and Jones (1984; see also Feldman-Summers, 1989), for example, studied women who had been sexually involved with a prior therapist (as well as women who had been sexually involved with a physician who was not a therapist and women who had not been sexually involved with a health care professional) and found that greater harm resulting from therapist–client sexual involvement was associated with greater distress and dysfunction from prior conditions.

Herman, Perry, and van der Kolk (1989) found that what are commonly (and sometimes mistakenly) termed borderline features or symptomatology can, in the absence of an extremely careful and accurate history, mask the original trauma and cause a diagnosis of PTSD to be prematurely (and sometimes inaccurately) ruled out.

> It appeared that memories of the abuse had become essentially ego syntonic. The subjects generally did not perceive a direct connection between their current symptoms and abusive experiences in childhood. This finding is compatible with observations from follow-up studies of trauma victims . . . which indicate that fragments of the trauma may be transformed over time and relived in a variety of disguised forms, e.g., as somatic sensations, affect states, visual images, behavioral reenactments, or even dissociated personality fragments. (Herman et al., 1989, p. 494)

Although Herman and her colleagues' research focuses on how people who have been abused may be misdiagnosed if the clinician fails to take an adequate history, the intense feelings that may arise when working with a patient who has been sexually abused by a therapist (see the previous section on personal reactions) may also foster the misuse of the borderline or other diagnostic labels (Reiser & Levenson, 1984).

The evaluating clinician should never reflexively discount the possibility that a patient may have been sexually abused, as a child, by a therapist. The public discussion, systematic research, and professional literature about therapist–client sexual involvement tends to focus on adult victims. It is understandable that there would be a tendency to overlook the possibility that clients may have been subjected to child sexual abuse by a psychotherapist. Unfortunately, there are therapists who use their position vis-à-vis young clients to engage in child sexual abuse. Bajt and Pope (1989), for example, found, on the basis of an anonymous national survey, a total of 81 instances of reported sexual involvement between a therapist and a minor patient. Most (56%) involved female patients, whose average age was 13 years 9 months. The ages of these abused, minor, female patients ranged from 17 to as young as 3 years old. Another study of 958 cases of therapist–patient sexual involvement found that 5% of the patients were minors at the time of the sexual involvement (see Table 6-3).

Clinicians must be prepared to assess a possible history of abuse in a careful and sensitive manner. Some patients may not volunteer information about profoundly abusive or traumatic events. They may find it difficult to put such experiences into words. Some may render their accounts out of sequence or in puzzling descriptions. Others may say only a sentence or two, indicating that they have suffered some atrocity, but then feel too threatened to continue.

> The ordinary response to atrocities is to banish them from consciousness. Certain violations of the social compact are too terrible to utter aloud: [T]his is the meaning of the word unspeakable. Atrocities, however, refuse to be buried. Equally as powerful as the desire to deny atrocities is the conviction that denial does not work.... The conflict between the will to deny horrible events and the will to proclaim them aloud is the central dialectic of psychological trauma. People who have survived atrocities often tell their stories in a highly emotional, contradictory, and fragmented manner which undermines their credibility and thereby serves the twin imperatives of truth-telling and secrecy. When the truth is finally recognized, survivors can begin their recovery. But far too often secrecy prevails, and the story of the traumatic event surfaces not as a verbal narrative but as a symptom. (Herman, 1992, p. 1)[10]

---

[10]See also Briere and Zaidi (1989), Feldman-Summers and Pope (in press), Freyd (1993), and Pruitt and Kappius (1992).

When standardized psychological tests are used as part of an assessment, it is important that the tests be adequately validated for this population and for the task to which the test is put. Test results may be invalid and misleading if these two criteria are not met. In the early 1980s, the UCLA Post-Therapy Support Group assessed the usefulness of the Minnesota Multiphasic Personality Inventory (MMPI) as a screening device for people who had been sexually involved with a therapist and who were seeking admission to group treatment (in which all group members would have a history of sexual involvement with a previous therapist). However, the traditional MMPI indicators for ability to participate in and benefit from group therapy appeared to lack predictive validity for this population (Pope & Bouhoutsos, 1986).

Adequate interpretation of test results also requires an adequate history. Research conducted by psychologist Lynne Rosewater (1985b, 1987a), for example, found that if actual abuse histories are either unknown or not taken into account in the attempted interpretation of MMPI profiles, misinterpretation is likely, particularly with a diagnosis of borderline personality disorder or schizophrenia.

Pope, Butcher, and Seelen (1993) provided chapters addressing forensic assessments, with a special section (pp. 165–186) focusing on assessment, testimony, and cross-examination in hearings at which therapist–patient sexual involvement is an issue (see also Pope, 1994).

Delayed Onset of Sequelae

Aspects of harm caused by sexual involvement with a therapist may appear after a substantial delay. The process may follow diverse courses similar to those traditionally reported for PTSD. Delayed onset describes the appearance of sequelae after a period of at least 6 months following the trauma; sequelae may be reexperienced after months or years of latency (American Psychiatric Association, 1987). This delayed onset (i.e., with the injury that is caused by the abusive act only manifesting itself after a period of delay following the abusive act) has been judicially recognized at the appellate level:

> Indeed what evidence there is in the record suggests [plaintiff's] injury *did not occur* at the time of the alleged sexual relations. . . .

[Plaintiff's] description of delayed symptoms is consistent with the view of clinicians who have described the injury caused by the patient–therapist sexual relations as "post-traumatic stress." (*Mason v. Marriage and Family Center*, 1991, pp. 543–544)

Awareness that harmful consequences of sexual involvement with the therapist may not affect some patients until after a substantial latency period is crucial for clinicians who are providing assessment and intervention services.

Formal Complaints or Legal Actions

Research (Bouhoutsos et al., 1983; Vinson, 1987) suggests that only a small percentage of patients who have been sexually involved with a therapist will file a formal complaint. However, it is useful for clinicians to be aware of some of the major complaint processes. There are at least four major avenues for taking formal action against a perpetrator of therapist–patient sexual involvement. (Note: More general forensic issues are discussed in chapter 9.)

Criminal

Masters and Johnson (1975) were among the first to state that criminal penalties were appropriate for all therapists who become sexually involved with their patients.

We feel that when sexual seduction of patients can be firmly established by due legal process, regardless of whether the seduction was initiated by the patient or the therapist, the therapist should initially be sued for rape rather than malpractice, i.e., the legal process should be criminal rather than civil. (Masters & Johnson, 1975, p. 1)

In an increasing number of states therapist–client sex is a felony. An attorney may be useful in helping a client to consider filing criminal charges. Such charges are generally filed with the police or with the local district attorney. In some areas, there may be a victim/witness assistance program that can provide information, guidance, support, and sometimes funding for subsequent therapy. As with each of these four areas, the pamphlet prepared by the California Department of Consumer Affairs (1990) provides useful information, although it is keyed to the specifics of California law.

Civil

Sexually abused patients may seek to recover damages by filing a civil suit against the perpetrator and perhaps also against the perpetrator's supervisor, employer, facility, and so on. Patients considering this option can gain important information by consulting with attorneys who are skilled in this area. Abused patients should be aware of how many cases of this type (i.e., malpractice in psychotherapy) the attorney has handled and what his or her track record is. The first-person accounts mentioned previously (i.e., Bates & Brodsky, 1989; Freeman & Roy, 1976; Noel & Watterson, 1992; Plaisil, 1985; Walker & Young, 1986) all describe in detail the woman's experience in bringing suit against a prior therapist.

In many instances, the civil process tends to be stressful. The perpetrator, through his or her defense attorney, may attempt to shift responsibility to the client and may try a variety of tactics to besmirch the reputation of the client. One attorney who had previously handled rape defenses emphasized that the primary "defense [in the therapist–client sex cases] includes trying to prove that the victims are promiscuous, trying to prove the clients were asking for it" (Terwilliger, 1989, p. D1). Bates and Brodsky (1989) described various types of questions that were put to the plaintiff by the defense attorney:

> Could [you] mentally control vaginal lubrication? At what angle were [your] legs spread? Did [you] have orgasms? . . . Have you ever had occasion to swap sexual partners with anybody? . . . Have you ever had sex in front of anybody else? . . . And when you engaged in sex, did you just have intercourse with these people or would you have oral sex with them, too? (Bates & Brodsky, 1989 p. 66)

The sexually abused patient herself is put on trial, and the most intensely personal and private aspects of her life (e.g., her sexual fantasies, her prior sexual experiences) may be made part of a public record.

Licensing

In licensing actions, the defendant who is found to have violated state laws or regulations may have his or her license revoked or suspended. The licensing action affects the perpetrator's ability (or authorization) to practice in that state. (In criminal actions, a defendant who is found guilty may be fined or given a term in jail; in civil actions, a defendant who loses the case may be required to pay money to the plaintiff.)

Procedures differ according to the state, but often the complaint is filed with the appropriate licensing board (e.g., psychology, psychiatry, social work), and in any resulting administrative hearing, the attorney general's office represents the board and tries the case. Sometimes there are different results from criminal, civil, or administrative hearings due to different ways the charges are posed, different rules of evidence, and different standards of proof.

Professional Ethics Committee

An ethics complaint can be filed against a perpetrator only if he or she is a member of an appropriate professional association such as the American Psychiatric Association, American Psychological Association, or National Association for Social Work. These are voluntary associations; membership is not mandatory. These associations do not have the authority to impose jail sentences, to revoke or suspend the professional's license to practice, or to require the perpetrator to pay damages to the abused patient. They can impose censures or reprimands, require remedial actions (such as supervision), and suspend or revoke the perpetrator's membership in the association.

In all instances, it must be the client's decision whether to take action in any or all of these four legal arenas. Subsequent therapists must be careful not to steer a client either toward or away from taking such actions (Sonne & Pope, 1991). For many victims, taking such action tends to be therapeutic and to constitute an important step in coming to terms with the abuse and its effects (see, e.g., Pope & Bouhoutsos, 1986; Vinson, 1984, 1987). For each victim, however, the meaning and potential effects of this decision are unique.

SUMMARY

Sexual abuse of women by therapists never occurs in a vacuum; understanding the context is essential for the mental health professional who wants to be of help to women who have been exploited in this way. One important aspect of the context is that therapist–patient sex is a phenomenon in which the overwhelming majority (though not all) of the perpetrators are male and the overwhelming majority (though not all) of abused patients are female.

That offenders tend to be male and abused patients tend to be female may be a key explanatory factor in helping clinicians to understand the sometimes bizarre ways in which the mental health profession has often attempted to deny or discount this form of abuse, to work against the legitimate interests of patients who have been abused, and to enable perpetrators to continue or resume access to vulnerable patients (who are, as a rule, unaware that they are beginning therapy with a therapist who has previously chosen to place a patient at risk for serious and lasting harm by sexually abusing her). The profession's response to this form of abuse is a second important aspect of the context.

Taking into account such contextual forces, clinicians seeking to help patients who have been sexually involved with a previous therapist will be best prepared to help rather than harm if they maintain constant and informed awareness of the following: each patient's uniqueness, the research and clinical literature in this area, common (but not inevitable) responses that patients may have to the sexual abuse, common (but not inevitable) responses that subsequent treating therapists may have to work in this area, the need to take an adequate history, the potential (but avoidable) pitfalls associated with using standardized tests in this area, the need to let each patient move at her own pace and freely make her own decisions, and the options that the patient has for filing formal complaints, should she choose to do so.

PART TWO

Therapist Preparation and Responsibilities

7

Active Therapist Preparation

A s the preceding chapters in this book document, the forms of abuse inflicted on women and the subsequent emotional sequelae are numerous and diverse. One form of abuse—incest, for example—may produce substantially different consequences in different victims because of such factors as age, stage of development, relationship to the perpetrator, types of abuse experienced, prior abuse history, and available support system. The psychological symptoms that a 3-year-old girl would experience as a result of incest will probably differ significantly from those a 16-year-old would experience. Even when such factors as age are kept constant, victims of abuse still can differ significantly in their responses to victimization. Each client is unique and has an unmeasurable "hardiness" factor that adds to her strength. Therapeutic interventions must respect this individuality.

This diversity makes it difficult for mental health professionals to be adequately prepared to recognize, assess, and respond in a helpful manner to all clients who have suffered abuse. Nevertheless, there are certain steps that can be taken within the context of the professionals' individual backgrounds, clinical settings, and community resources to ensure that they are as prepared as possible. It is perhaps most important for therapists to have a complete knowledge of the data available concerning the different forms of abuse against women and to have dealt with their own issues concerning violence.

This chapter can be used as a checklist of sorts for therapists who are working with abused women. Licensing and office security concerns are reviewed, followed by a series of questions therapists can consider to determine whether anything in their own personal beliefs or histories will hamper therapy. Finally, several community resources are discussed from which the client can seek additional help.

VARIETIES OF ABUSE

Whenever working with female clients, it is important to keep in mind the varieties of abuse patterns that exist and to be alert to the possibility that any client may have suffered—or may in fact currently be suffering—from abuse, whether or not abuse is identified as their presenting complaint. Victims of abuse are often extremely reluctant to disclose that they have been victimized, for many different reasons including the fact that their trust in other people has been damaged by their abuse experience. Most abuse victims are better at hiding their experiences regarding the abuse than therapists are in recognizing them. For some clients, such as racial and ethnic minorities and lesbian women, other forms of societal oppression are so painful that they do not give the same priority to identifying whatever part of their victimization actually came from the abuse. Other clients may experience so many insidious forms of abuse that they do not recognize certain acts as abusive. This is particularly true for abuse victims who are raised in an atmosphere of constant violence, as in multiabusive families, and those residing in war-torn countries and countries whose populations are subjected to state-sponsored violence. Furthermore, the standard forms, checklists, or structured interviews used by hospitals, clinics, and other organizations for obtaining a client's history may lack the types of questions that could elicit such information, although most medical agencies that are accredited by the Joint Commission on Accrediting Hospitals Organization should have trained their staffs to request this information. Koss and Harvey

(1991) suggested that by asking about numerous other private matters, but omitting questions about victimization, common data-gathering procedures may tacitly communicate to the client that the topic of abuse is unimportant or taboo.

The therapist needs to remain alert to the possibility that any client may have a history of abuse that has had an impact on her, regardless of her sociocultural background. This means the therapist must have an open mind regarding the types of abuse that could have been experienced, must be aware of subtle indications of abuse, and must ask appropriate questions, even if the client does not appear to present with the stereotyped response patterns or comes from a "well-established" or "good" family in which such abuse is not expected.

LICENSE OR AUTHORIZATION

Each state differs in its basic licensing requirements for people who are providing clinical and related services. It is crucial that those seeking to help victims of abuse obtain the appropriate license or authorization to provide services and gain the necessary knowledge and training. In many states, specially trained rape crisis counselors and battered women shelter advocates are able to provide some services within the auspices of their respective centers. If they are also licensed social workers, counselors, psychiatric nurses, marriage and family therapists, psychologists, psychiatrists, or other licensed professionals, then they may also be able to provide therapy for victims of violence who require such additional treatment. Otherwise, these specialized centers should refer victims, as appropriate, to mental health professionals who are both highly skilled and experienced in abuse issues.

The importance of proper credentials goes beyond simply complying with state laws and regulations. Often the major psychological difficulties being experienced by an abuse victim are not revealed until a trust relationship is established. If other problems are dealt with first and a trust relationship is established, it may be harmful to the client to have to transfer her to another therapist when more serious problems begin to surface. Also, victims of abuse often become involved with the court system. Their involvement may be related to criminal charges against the perpetrator of the abuse, or protective orders attempting to ensure the safety of the victim. The victim might initiate a civil action to recover her damages, or take part in an administrative hearing in which a professional's license may be revoked. In the course of such legal actions, the therapist who provides assessment and therapeutic services to the victim may be called as a percipient witness (one who has knowledge of the facts of the case) or an expert witness (one who has special knowledge that might help the judge or jury to better understand the issues before the court). If the therapist is found to be practicing without a legally mandated license or other authorization, the therapist may be discredited and both the court and client would then be deprived of important testimony. In some cases, the victim can be denied compensation if the court finds that she is not receiving proper treatment, because this would make it impossible for the court to determine how much of the damage was due to the abuse trauma and how much was due to the possibly inappropriate therapy. In such a situation, the client can be revictimized even if the therapist is competent and providing good services.

Confidentiality

Victims of abuse are often exceptionally sensitive to issues of privacy. Many are reluctant to disclose the fact of their abuse—let alone the details—to anyone. Telling the therapist may be a monumental step, one taken only reluctantly and often in fear and shame. Victims often assume that whatever they tell the therapist is completely confidential. However, states differ in the degree to which they accord confidentiality and privilege to those who provide services to abuse victims. Privilege is the client's right to have the therapist keep the information learned about her confidential. Only a client can waive her privilege and permit the therapist to share information with parties whom the client selects. In some jurisdictions, confidentiality and privilege are accorded only to clients of licensed psychologists and psychiatrists, whereas in others, some measure of confidentiality or privilege may be granted to certain other caregivers such as social workers, rape counselors, or alcohol counselors. It is clearly the clinician's responsibility to determine (perhaps through consultation with a qualified attorney or the state or local professional association) which laws and regulations are applicable in his or her geographic area and how to comply with them, and to help inform clients by giving them information relevant to their decision regarding whether or not to seek services.

A rape victim, for example, might choose to obtain services in a setting in which what she discloses is legally privileged and confidential. She is generally dependent on the individual interviewer to tell her whether and under what conditions what she says is legally protected. In a growing number of states, such as Colorado and Washington, the therapist is required by law to give the client a written disclosure statement that provides information about the therapist's education, training, and theoretical approach to treatment as well as specifics about what can and cannot be legally protected information (see sample disclosure form in Appendix E). The abuse victim is generally in no position to do extensive legal research to determine which privacy, confidentiality, and privilege laws are applicable or whether a given individual has the appropriate license or other authorization. Thus, psychologists and other mental health professionals may need to assume that responsibility on behalf of the victim. Rape shield laws that are applied in most states for criminal trials may protect women from being revictimized by the legal system. Rape shield laws ensure that the rape victim's past is shielded from inquiry in a public court because her sexual history is considered irrelevant to whether or not she was sexually assaulted. These rape shield laws also apply in some civil cases, but in others, such as personal injury lawsuits in which the victim makes her mental health an issue or in administrative hearings, the rules may be different.

Records

It is important for the therapist to know the laws on confidentiality of records, particularly if a lawsuit might be filed on behalf of a client. It probably is wise to expect that the therapy notes may be used at some later date, so they should be carefully maintained, with precise documenting of all reported incidents of abuse, treatment plans, and evaluation of progress toward goals. (See chapter 9 on forensic issues for further discussion of this topic.) Often therapists are issued a subpoena to appear or a subpoena duces tecum that requires a court appearance and the submission of the records. The subpoena is simply an order signed by an attorney; it does not have the force of a judge's order, nor does it automatically waive the client's privilege, even if the client has signed a release form. It is usually the therapist's responsibility to check on informed consent with the client or client's attorney prior to responding to a subpoena. It is important to respond to the subpoena by acknowledging it, but, in order to avoid violating confidentiality, do not turn over records without an order from the judge. Sometimes the client's attorney can file a motion to quash the subpoena with the court; in some cases the therapist must hire her or his own attorney, especially if the therapist's interests are different from the client's interests. These arguments can often be settled between attorneys without going to court.

For example, in Colorado a client can request that the court perform a balancing test, sometimes called a Bond hearing, so that the client's privilege is not completely waived. The notes and records are usually turned over to the judge who reads them to decide what is important enough for the other side to know even if it risks damaging the efficacy of the woman's current and potential treatment. It is not unusual for a judge to refuse to turn over any notes or work products if the therapist testifies that doing so is likely to cause irreparable harm. However, it is much more likely that the judge will, while reading the file, cross out anything that seems too personal or not relevant to the immediate issues. The nonexcised materials may be shown to the client first, in order to give her the opportunity to appeal the decision, or the materials may simply be handed over to the opposing counsel. Judges have wide latitude in making such decisions, so it is important for therapists to be knowledgeable enough to protect the victim. Sometimes therapists may work under the supervision of another professional whose status provides privilege. In any case, it must be assumed that the abused woman's therapy records could become part of a legal action; thus, extreme care is warranted in documenting the assessment and interventions, even erring on the side of caution.

A THERAPIST'S SELF-EXAMINATION

Attitudes and Beliefs

In preparing to work with abuse victims, it is extremely useful for the therapist to conduct an inventory of his or her own personal attitudes and beliefs regarding victimization. To what extent, for example, does the therapist believe that what is customarily termed *abuse* may be justified as legitimate and warranted behavior? Does repeated striking of the back and buttocks with a metal paddle, including the "accidental" breaking of bones on a couple of occasions, constitute abuse in any and all circumstances? Is it ever justifiable (i.e., is it ever nonabusive) as a system of consistent discipline? Is it justifiable if the intent is to help rather than harm? Is it justifiable if done within the context of a family relationship (e.g., father–daughter, husband–wife)? Is it justifiable if the person being struck views it as helpful? Is it justifiable if it produces beneficial results (e.g., helping a child do homework assignments and chores around the house)? Is it justifiable if it seems to be the only way to reach an otherwise unresponsive child (e.g., one who seems withdrawn and obsessed—to the virtual exclusion of all else—with religious beliefs and practices)? What if the child is substance abusing or violating all the house rules? What if the child is oppositional and doing everything to get the parent angry?

Another important issue is the degree to which a therapist may view the victim of abuse as the cause of, or as responsible for, the abuse. What if the scenario is one in which a good-looking and seductive woman client wears short skirts and necklines that are very revealing to each session and asks for hugs that the therapist acquiesces in giving her. The hugs get longer and more seductive until they eventually become lovers. Such facts would seem to indicate a clear violation of the therapist's responsibility to refrain from sexual intimacies with a patient. Because it is the therapist who is licensed, who maintains the legal and clinical requirements for the conduct of the treatment, and who bears the fiduciary onus, it is the therapist's responsibility to maintain safe, legal, and appropriate boundaries (cf. Pope, Sonne, & Holroyd, 1993, for further discussion on how to handle sexual feelings that occur during therapy). What sort of details, however, might lead a therapist, however subtly, to begin viewing the patient as the one responsible for the violation? Consider each of the following presentations of one fictional scenario, each enriched by additional details, to see if any of them alter your assessment of the locus of responsibility.

A senior and extremely prominent therapist, one who has contributed much to the field and is recognized for his humanitarian values, is going through a painful divorce. He becomes despondent, considers suicide, but continues to try to meet the pressing and legitimate needs of his many patients who rely on him for help. A 41-year-old patient repeatedly tells him how attractive he is and how grateful she is. She wears extremely revealing tight lycra clothing and behaves in a skillfully seductive manner. During one session, suddenly and without the therapist's consent, she steps out of her clothes, unzips his pants (he is unable to prevent her), and performs fellatio on him. She then threatens to take her life unless he has sex with her each week. At a very low period in his life and extremely concerned for his patient's welfare, he gives in.

❏ ■ ❑

A chronic and severe borderline patient has, in the course of her 41 years, engaged in numerous sexualized relationships with authority figures. In four previous courses of treatment, each one of her therapists labeled her exceptionally "promiscuous." She has held only three jobs in her life. Each time she seduced her boss. She has been married four times; in each instance, her husband filed for divorce after discovering that she was having affairs with friends. In addition to the borderline condition, she has been found, on the basis of psychological testing and formal assessment, to be histrionic, alcoholic, a chronic liar, and occasionally mildly psychotic. She has had three abortions (each time unable to identify the man who impregnated her) and suffered from a variety of treatable venereal diseases.

❏ ■ ❑

The life history of Ms. X reveals her to be an exceptionally angry and litigious woman. She has initiated 11 separate lawsuits: 4 against medical doctors, 3 against therapists, 2 against stores ("slip and fall" cases alleging negligence of the store), 1 against a driver (whom she alleged ran a stop sign and hit her car), and 1 against an attorney who had represented her in one of the lawsuits. Her current therapist maintains that, as he reviews the situation in retrospect, she did not seem to be seeking therapeutic services in good faith and had only sought his help in order to file a lawsuit against him. As a result, he felt that they had never really formed a therapeutic alliance or professional relationship, and thus the sexual relationship did not seem to produce any harm, as it might have had it occurred in the context of a genuine therapeutic relationship.

The attitudes and beliefs that each person holds about abuse, its nature, and its causes can have a powerful impact on the ability to render adequate and appropriate services to those who have been abused. As subsequent chapters in this volume describe, victims of abuse may tend to deny, minimize, or mask the abuse; to provide numerous justifications; and to take on themselves the responsibility for both the abuse itself and the negative consequences that result. Some therapists refuse to believe the woman who is not the stereotypical "good victim"; a ladylike woman who is passive, grateful, and deferential toward others, particularly those who spend time trying to help her. Thus, women who fight back, who have big mouths, who take bigger risks than is typically thought to be necessary, who may choose not to report the abuse at all or not to report it right away, who are racial or ethnic minorities or lesbians, or who may be angry and hostile toward everyone including the therapist are not seen as good victims. Therefore, these women are less likely to be believed or to elicit sympathy than those who are closer to general expectations of a typical abuse victim. Similarly, society is still struggling with myths that embody these "deny the abuse" and "blame the victim" attitudes (Ryan, 1971). Everyone is influenced by the society in which they live; a personal inventory can help uncover some of the hidden assumptions and biases that could hurt and interfere with the ability to be helpful to women who have suffered abuse.

It is also important to realize that a therapist will not like every client. Each woman can be expected to have her own personality. Some abused women just may not be very nice people, regardless of their histories of abuse. Occasionally, some abused women develop nasty personalities in order to defend themselves against further vulnerability and abuse. The presence of a mean streak does not negate the abuse. In the assessment, the therapist must try to determine how much of the disagreeable part of the client's personality is the result of the victimization and how much was there even before the trauma.

Undertaking an honest and searching inventory of his or her own assumptions and views regarding the phenomena of abuse is an essential step for the therapist in preparing to be helpful to abuse victims. Repeating the inventory on a periodic basis, in light of personal changes, and in light of the clientele encountered in the course of the therapist's work, can help ensure that the inventory remains current.

The issue of therapists' perceptions of potential violence was measured by Pope and Tabatchnick (1993) in their national survey of the reported feelings of therapists that were evoked by clients. Interestingly, almost 8 out of 10 (79.3%) of therapists surveyed reported feeling afraid that a client would be physically attacked by a third party. It can be assumed that at least some of these clients had reported previous experiences of physical violence. Even more interesting, given that most therapists report that they are unprepared to deal with client violence, almost 9 out of 10 (89.1%) surveyed reported feeling afraid that a client would physically attack a third party, and well over half (60.7%) reported that at least one of their clients had done so. More than half of those surveyed (50.9%) felt that a client might physically attack them (and 18% reported that a client actually did attack them) and actually fantasized about it or were so fearful that they were unable to eat, sleep, or concentrate (53.3%). One quarter (27%) reported having summoned police or security personnel to protect them against a client, and slightly more than 3% actually obtained a weapon to protect themselves against a client. More than 80% reported feeling angry because a client had been verbally abusive toward them.

Obviously, therapists working with clients who are perceived as being in danger of experiencing or committing violence have strong feelings that can have an impact on the therapy. Training programs do not directly address the feelings that are evoked in therapists by working with abuse victims. As a result, therapists must find other continuing education, consultation, and supervision programs to help them work through these feelings and prevent them from interfering with proper client treatment.

Personal History

The ability to render adequate and appropriate help, of course, is not just a function of formal beliefs and attitudes. Each person has a unique personal history that influences, sometimes dramatically, the ways in which that person responds to those who have been victimized. As a useful step in preparing to provide services, the therapist should perform a careful review and exploration of the ways in which victimization has touched his or her life. The therapist should consider some of the following questions.

In what ways has the therapist been personally abused? Has the therapist experienced incest, rape, battery, or any of the other forms of abuse? Has the therapist ever perpetrated any abuse against another person? Has the therapist ever witnessed abuse against another person and been unable to protect the victim? If so, are there any aspects of the consequences of witnessing abuse or being either a victim or a victimizer (or both) that the therapist has not adequately worked through that might pose a barrier to his or her response to other victims? In some cases, abuse can be such a devastating, paralyzing, or numbing event that those who have witnessed or experienced abuse find themselves almost completely unable to respond to their own distress or to reach out to others for help. For clinicians, such unresolved distress can be a source of distorted or unhelpful responses to other victims. Rather than address their own pain and dysfunction, clinicians who have experienced abuse may find themselves using their clients to work through their own problems. Most victims can sense this, especially when the therapist is not behaving in a genuine manner toward the client. This phenomenon of attempting to use clinical work with others as a way to work through personal problems is not, of course, limited to those who have been subjected to some type of victimization or abuse; it can and does occur in virtually all areas of psychotherapy. In working with abuse victims, the issues of countertransference may be the most important factors in determining whether the client receives appropriate treatment.

How about the more subtle forms of psychological abuse? Has the therapist ever been involved with a feminist woman (or man) who used feminist views to attack him or her? Most men and women have experienced such unfortunate personal attacks on themselves and then misattributed the attack to the person's feminism rather than to rude behavior or personality problems. Sometimes even just one such distasteful experience can cause an otherwise well-educated person to reject all theories or explanations of behavior that have a feminist philosophy at their core.

In such situations, the therapist confuses the struggle for equality with abuse or misuse of power by women. Accusations are made that the clinician cannot be objective, has a cause to pursue, and is an ideologue. Most of the empirical research demonstrates that the forms of abuse against women described in this book have been in existence for as long as there are records (Martin, 1976). However, only in periods in which feminist ideology is taken seriously and equality between men and women is a goal is there any history of an attempt to eradicate violence against women (Herman, 1992; Jones, 1981; Walker, 1989b). Therefore, in the case of woman abuse, feminist issues about equality and power need to be addressed in both treatment and prevention strategies.

Rejecting feminist theory as biased or even using antifeminist ideas to attack all women because of bad experiences with one or even a few women is not an appropriate or an educated response, whatever one's personal views about the political aspects of the women's liberation movement. The correct definition of feminist philosophy is the belief that men and women are not currently equal in many spheres of society, that this inequality is a breeding ground for male expectations of entitlement, and that it is known to cause oppression and discrimination against women as well as some forms of psychological distress for both women and men. Notice that the definition does not include man-hating (although certainly a small number of feminists may personally support such a stance); instead, the focus on supporting the goal of women to share power with men links feminism with the movement to eliminate all forms of violence against women, children, and men. (See, e.g., publications from the American Psychological Association's Division 35, Psychology of Women; and the Feminist Therapy Institute for more information.)

Understanding the feminist philosophy helps the therapist to assist the female abuse victim in processing her anger toward men. Experiencing a period of generalized anger toward all men, as well as anger directed toward the particular abusive man or men, is a part of the healing process. The therapy process helps women feel anger at the injustice they have experienced and then uses that anger to build on their strengths in order to prevent future abuse. In time, most women recognize their rage and inappropriate generalizations and can identify their origins. The therapist must understand what fuels the victim's anger, and must not be afraid of it, in order to teach her how to feel and accept the anger without using it destructively. Then the woman will let it go at her own pace. This rage is often difficult to listen to and may stir old memories that still upset the therapist if he or she has not dealt with his or her own issues of anger and injustice. Male therapists often have a difficult time listening to the anger generated by behavior of other men. Female therapists often have a difficult time not identifying with the client's vulnerability. The goal of empowerment of women, which is discussed later (see chapters 10–14), can be confused with the encouragement of generalized anger against all men or man-hating. That is why it is important for therapists to deal with their own feelings of anger at personal injustices committed by men and women in their own relationships before they treat women for similar issues.

If the therapist cannot identify any particular ways in which he or she has been abused, has abused someone, or was hurt in relationships with men and women, does that inhibit in any way the therapist's ability to empathize with, and to respond effectively to, those who have experienced particular forms of victimization? Empathizing, feeling the other's pain, does not mean acting to stop it. The most common mistake made by therapists in their zeal to help an abuse victim is to try to do something too quickly. Most abuse victims need to be listened to with an empathetic ear, not provided with advice about what to do.

Has abuse touched the therapist's life through the witnessing of victimization of those whom he or she knows personally and cares about? Have the therapist's parents, siblings, children, friends, lovers, or colleagues suffered victimization? If so, does the therapist now accept whatever he or she did or did not do to help them? Often family members must come to accept that they did the best they could at the time, even if today, with new knowledge, they might do things differently. Did the therapist feel powerless or frightened by the abuse? Did the therapist blame the abused for their own victimization? Did the therapist support the abuser, understanding his or her stresses and problems? Did the therapist try not to take sides, learning that no one who witnesses or experiences violence is able to maintain a neutral stance for very long? Has the therapist adequately come to terms with the meaning and consequences of that victimization for his or her own life?

All of these personal experiences may affect the therapist's ability to help the woman take her own steps in coming to terms with the abuse she has experienced. For example, some therapists who were unable to effectively protect their mother from their father's abuse may attempt to rescue their client without permitting her to set her own timing for leaving the relationship. A therapist who failed to protect a sibling from incest could be overly harsh toward a mother of an incest victim by assuming that she had the power to see through the acts of the perpetrator.

It is not the presence or absence of specific types of victimization in one's life as much as the degree to which one has acknowledged, worked through, and come to terms with the meaning of that victimization that is important. Some therapists who have addressed their own abuse issues and reached a satisfactory resolution may find their own issues reactivated when dealing with clients who are working through similar ones. If the therapist has not yet come to terms with these phenomena, a variety of distortions can block his or her attempts to be of help to others. One extreme example might be the clinician who reacts almost phobically to the very possibility of abuse. The clinician may avoid any mention of abuse and may fail to recognize obvious communications from the client that abuse has occurred. At the other extreme is the clinician who focuses exclusively on abuse as if all other considerations are completely irrelevant; medical, financial, and other issues are ignored as if they did not exist. Such biases can distort the process of assessment and intervention.

Personal Resources

It is easy to overlook the fact that the professional work of therapy is conducted by human beings with personal lives. It is the responsibility of the therapist to ensure that he or she is receiving sufficient personal enjoyment and gratification in his or her private life so that he or she does not look to clients to meet these needs. Clients are not appropriate substitutes for friends, lovers, children, or playmates, and to attempt to use them in this way is both a deep betrayal of their trust and a form of revictimization.

Women who have been abused may approach therapy in an exceptionally vulnerable and needy state. The attention, concern, and help that they both need and wish to receive from the therapist can seem overwhelming. It is natural and understandable that clients may experience extreme dependency on their therapist, may tend to idealize the therapist beyond all recognition, and may (through transference or a variety of other processes) experience the therapist as if he or she were a parent, friend, lover, and so forth, during various phases of the treatment. The damage done by therapists who cross these boundaries and exploit the power implicit in the therapeutic relationship can be deep, pervasive, and lasting. As human beings, therapists are never at a loss for creating plausible-sounding (at least plausible to them) rationalizations to justify the misuse of power and to deny the harm that such misuse causes. It is essential that therapists adequately and honestly monitor their own personal needs and the degree to which they are fulfilling them so that they never abuse their professional roles and responsibilities.

Boundaries

All victims of abuse have experienced the severe violation of essential, legitimate boundaries. In many instances (e.g., rape, incest, and battering) these boundaries involve the safety and integrity of the victim's body. Each violation involves an abuse of power: The perpetrator misuses power to break through boundaries behind which a person should both be and feel safe and secure.

Therapists who work with victims of abuse need to pay particular attention to issues that involve boundaries between the therapist and the client. Such boundaries can carry immense symbolic and often practical significance. They are essential components that help define the therapeutic relationship and setting, and they exert a profound influence over whether the client feels secure enough to begin the healing process.

Aspects of the physical and personal boundaries between therapist and client (e.g., whether the therapist ever touches the client) have been addressed in chapter 6 and elsewhere in this volume. It is important to think through, define clearly, and monitor the effects of other factors that influence when, how, and under what conditions the therapist and client meet and conduct their work.

One factor that tends to create discomfort for many therapists is fees. Many therapists would like to think of themselves as altruistic healers eager to give of themselves to those who have been hurt. It complicates the picture to consider that therapists charge money and profit financially for this help. Nevertheless, money is a factor that frequently defines and regulates a boundary between the therapist and the client.

Each therapist needs to define clearly and communicate to the client the financial aspects of the relationship. What, exactly, is the fee for services? Is there a charge only for office appointments, or are phone consultations (with the client or with others), paperwork (e.g., filling out insurance forms), and other activities conducted on a fee-for-service basis? What happens if the client, for whatever reason, becomes unable to pay? What happens if the client falls behind in her payments? What will happen when insurance coverage is exhausted?

Therapists also need to define their availability clearly and communicate this to the client. Does the therapist accept calls from the client in the evening, during the night, on weekends, or on holidays? What happens when the therapist is unavailable, either for routine consultation or for responding to a crisis, because of either anticipated (e.g., vacations) or unanticipated (e.g., the therapist becoming ill) factors?

SECURITY ISSUES

Office Security

Steps should be taken to ensure the physical safety of clients who have suffered abuse. Some clients may be at risk for continued harm from perpetrators. The perpetrators may also threaten or attack the therapist or others who attempt to help the client. Although the risks must be assessed and addressed on an individual basis, therapists can take a general measure of how secure their office is from threats or violent attacks.

Does the route from the street or parking lot offer safe passage for a woman who is walking to and from the office? Is a security guard or other protective personnel available to escort a client (or therapist) who may be fearful of attack? Does the office door provide a peephole or other method of ascertaining who is in the waiting room?

Are charts and other documents adequately secure so that no unauthorized individuals can find out who is scheduled for appointments or obtain personal information (such as addresses) of clients? Are support staff (such as receptionists) provided with adequate and specific training so that they will not unintentionally disclose such information?

Are there clear and practical plans for responding to threats or actual attacks? Are emergency phone numbers (for police, paramedics, etc.) clearly posted and available? Are staff adequately trained regarding steps to take in case of violence?

Is there a security system that can be used when there is potential danger? Does the therapist have a panic button that goes to another office or the police? Scheduling those clients whose presence may pose a danger at times when others are around the office and informing office mates of the potential for a problem are some precautions that can be helpful.

Concerns About the Therapist's Own Safety

Given the great amount of violence described in this book, it is not foolish for therapists to wonder about their own safety when working with victims of violence. There is a chance that the abusive man will transfer his anger and its accompanying abuse to the therapist, although this is relatively rare. Nonetheless, it is best to deal with these issues before a potential crisis arises.

Although some therapists have been hurt by abusers, more often the abuser tries to threaten, frighten, and intimidate the therapist. For example, one woman told a therapist that her abuser had told her that he planned to shoot and kill the therapist. This threat was accompanied by hang-up calls. The therapist called the police who, as a result, more carefully patrolled her home and monitored her calls. In another case, the abuser shot arrows into the therapist's car, office, and home. Despite investigation, the police were unable to prove that the man was responsible for this terrifying behavior.

Therapists usually do not deal with these issues in their professional training unless they work with a known violent population such as in a prison, state mental hospital, or, occasionally, Veterans Administration hospitals. However, more therapists are becoming concerned about the potential for abused victims to become violent and for perpetrators to find and harm the therapist.

Goldberg (1991) has raised the issue of violence against therapists at several psychology meetings, suggesting that clinicians learn to speak openly about their experiences and fears. He and his copanelists found that by sharing their own experiences, they encouraged other therapists who also had had harrowing experiences to come forward. As might be expected, female therapists were more frightened than male therapists of being hurt when working with male patients. Female therapists were more affected by fears of the disruption of their own lives when working with abused women (Kaley, 1991). This fear of their own vulnerability must be dealt with before women can provide good therapy for other abused women. Otherwise, they tend to facilitate the client's denial, minimization, and fears of reexperiencing the trauma by not providing a safe enough place in which to deal with them.

COMMUNITY RESOURCES

Therapists who work with abuse victims must understand that they cannot take a neutral, hands-off stance; they must use community resources to supplement the psychological care they offer the victim. Becoming aware of community resources is an important step in preparing to respond to the victim's needs. Those clients who are currently in crisis may have an immediate need for shelter or a support group. Others who are in the process of healing from the abuse may want to volunteer in some way to help others who are in immediate crisis. The discussion of resources in this section is by no means comprehensive. It is intended solely as a suggestion of some of the possible community resources that both the therapist and client can use.

Shelters

Women who have been battered by a partner may need a safe place to stay, and the need may be urgent. Such a woman may have no money, she may be pursued by a perpetrator who is extremely dangerous, or she may be accompanied by her children who also need to be protected from the abuser. Her fear and terror may be great, yet her isolation may prevent her from seeking or using appropriate help on her own. With a little support, however, she may be better able to devise a safety plan and to seek shelter.

Many communities have a shelter specifically designed for battered women that may offer not only lodging but also some measure of security against perpetrators. Smaller communities may offer a system of safe homes coordinated by a task force on domestic violence or by another community group. Some offer a variety of services beyond shelter such as employment counseling and skill training; assistance with obtaining aid for dependent children and food stamps; and help in finding an apartment, furniture, and clothing. Others may serve as advocates for the woman in the legal system, providing emotional support and referral to knowledgeable attorneys. Such services help the battered woman and her children to survive the crisis and become independent.

Charitable and governmental agencies may offer temporary immediate shelter in which a woman, alone or with her children, can obtain lodging for a few days or weeks. In many areas, the demand for shelter far exceeds the supply. The therapist may want to become aware of the numbers of people the shelters are able to house as well as the procedures for allocating beds. Often trained therapists offer pro bono services to help shelter residents so that when their clients are in need, they may receive priorities that are also based on need. When former battered women work as volunteers in shelters, it can help their healing process.

Rural areas with large distances between populated places train volunteers to drive a woman and her children 25 miles to the next check point. There she is met by another driver and the process continues until the woman and children are in a safe home or shelter somewhere else, far away from the immediate danger. The battered women's shelter network has become skilled at helping a woman to move from one place to another with a minimum risk of being followed or found. This is sometimes called the "underground railroad" (Schechter, 1982; Walker, 1979, 1984a). The American Psychological Association offers a related pamphlet for abuse victims. A law now in effect in California (as of January 1994) requires psychologists to report battered women to the police so that the women can be placed in a central register. As one of the first states to institute such a requirement, California will be a testing ground for the law's progress and implementation and its impact, if any, on treatment.

Rape Crisis Centers

Some hospitals, medical centers, and other community-based organizations have established rape crisis centers. In most of these centers, all levels of staff who will be interacting with the victim have been trained to respond sensitively, empathetically, and professionally. Frequently, one staff member will become the guide, advocate, or ombudsperson for a victim from the moment she arrives until the course of services is complete. Often, clients who are in the process of healing from their own abuse provide invaluable support and service to others whose abuse is more immediate.

Rape crisis centers are designed to respond effectively to both the psychological and the medical needs of the victim. Even a routine medical examination may be potentially traumatic for a rape victim, and the procedures can be conducted in such a way that minimizes the trauma. Police are often present during hospital emergency room visits. As a result, the victim may be exposed to questioning even before her injuries are treated. Centers attempt to establish effective liaisons with law enforcement personnel who are trained to conduct rape investigations and to prosecute rape cases.

Suicide and Related Hotlines

Abuse victims can be expected to experience the ups and downs of severe emotional crises during the course of treatment. Possessing the phone number of a 24-hour suicide hotline or a similar specialized hotline (e.g., for victims of battering, sexual assault, or harassment) can provide women with immediate access to a resource during periods when the therapist and others may be unavailable. These telephone numbers are usually listed in the front pages of the local telephone directory or can be obtained through the police emergency phone lines.

Hospitals

Some victims of abuse may need or benefit from brief or long-term psychiatric hospitalization. It is important that the therapist be aware of appropriate hospitals and their policies toward abuse victims. Are the hospital staff members competent and sensitive to issues of victimization? Do they have special procedures to protect women from possible sexual harassment by the staff or other patients or even assault by other men or women? Will they permit the therapist to retain contact with his or her client during the period of hospitalization? Is the hospital financially accessible for the client? Does the process of hospitalization, from admission through discharge, impose minimal disruption on the outpatient therapeutic relationship? Most battered women shelters will not accept a woman who has a history of hospitalization because they may not have adequate staff to deal with more serious emotional problems. Thus, it is important to know the policies of community resources toward clients who have had psychiatric hospitalization experiences.

The newer posttraumatic stress disorder inpatient units may be particularly useful for clients exposed to early ritual abuse, although the presence of male patients on the same unit can prevent abused women from feeling safe enough to deal with the issues. Dissociative disorder units are another place in which many abuse victims find some measure of safety and treatment. However, many of these units keep male and female patients together. Those with multiple personality disorders may eventually need some hospitalization for self-protection, yet the impact of regression that is often encouraged by a hospital admission could be harmful to the client in the long run. Furthermore, many psychiatric hospitals have a bias reflecting the beliefs of the medical staff who control the hospital policies. This bias often leads the staff to focus on the biological basis of behavior, sometimes to the exclusion of the context in which it occurs. Obviously, for sexually assaulted and battered women, application of a biological philosophy to their subsequent reactions to the trauma may be quite misleading and inappropriate for the victim. Those units that are predominantly psychoanalytic sometimes attribute the problems of abused women to things that happened to them as children, often ignoring more critical events that occurred later. Some units use restraints routinely or overmedicate in order to keep women sedated. Obviously, these women will not be able to use the hospital experience to work through their problems. Thus, any attempt to hospitalize clients must be carefully analyzed.

A short time in a regular hospital, or in some place where there are a few beds set aside for psychiatric patients, may be useful. For some women, hospitalization is the first time they understand the seriousness of their situation. It is important for the therapist to have some knowledge of all the resources available and to attempt to tailor them to the client's needs.

Women's Centers

Women's centers, sometimes sponsored by the YWCA, colleges, or other organizations, can usually provide useful information about services and resources for women who have been abused. Some centers provide special services such as transportation, shelter, and support groups. Most large communities and university towns have at least one women's center in which women can find a variety of resources. If the women's center is located on campus, there may be special services offered to women in the community as well as to students. Often the centers have access to a vocational testing service for those women who are planning to return to school or find new careers.

Transportation

Some victims of abuse are poor. Some are newly or temporarily poor, having left their homes, carrying virtually nothing with them, in fear for their lives. For these women, transportation can constitute a major challenge. In areas in which municipal bus service is nonexistent or is impractical for some reason, charitable and related agencies may provide a van or similar transportation services. Battered women shelters usually have some money in their budget to pay for a taxi to get the woman and children there quickly and safely. In emergency situations the police or sheriff may give the woman a ride to the nearest service center. Some rape crisis centers or women's centers also have access to community resources for women with limited means. They may have advocates who can help women obtain transportation, food, shelter, and other services.

Law Enforcement

Law enforcement agencies may provide special services or resources for victims of abuse. For example, some states and municipalities have established victim/witness advocates who assist crime victims and witnesses. These advocates keep the victim informed about the progress of any criminal cases pending and assist her if she is to be a witness. If there is a postponement, which frequently happens, they usually notify the woman or spend some time with her if she has already appeared at the courthouse.

During the course of legal proceedings related to abuse, special procedures are followed. For example, the woman may be given a private room in which she can wait so that she does not have to worry about meeting the abuser in the courtroom halls. She may be given a guided tour of empty courtrooms so that she will not have to enter an unfamiliar setting in order to give her testimony. Advocates may call her from time to time to see how she is doing. In repeated surveys the abused woman who has contact with the criminal justice system ranks the victim/witness program as the most useful resource. District attorneys like the victim/witness advocates because they prepare reluctant and scared witnesses and help them win their cases.

Legislation passed by Congress, in 1984, called the Victim Protection Act and the Victim Compensation Act, permits local districts to obtain funds for the payment of a victim's medical bills and psychological treatment. Usually there is a maximum limit, often around $1,500, although in some cases it is much higher. Eligibility for such funds may require the victim's willingness to testify against the abuser in a criminal court. In some cases in which the perpetrator is unknown or there is a negotiated plea, the woman may still be eligible for services. The therapist must fill out appropriate forms much like those required to receive other third-party payments (e.g., from insurance companies). For a listing of victim/witness advocate program services, call your local prosecutor's office or write to the National Organization for Victim Assistance in Washington, DC. Some communities provide counseling for victims and abusers at low or no cost. For example, one program, JurisMoniter (located in Boulder, Colorado), trains therapists to administer its court-ordered stabilization and empowerment programs.

Religious Groups

Religious groups often provide food, transportation, temporary shelter, or other services needed by victims at little or no charge. Some religious leaders have received training in working with female victims of violence, particularly battered women. In large congregations there may be groups for those who were victimized. Divorce groups are also popular in some churches. Religion and spirituality, as well as a sense of connectedness with a woman's religious community, can be important adjuncts to helping her heal. Fortune (1983, 1987) has developed materials for religious leaders to use in setting up church programs that deal specifically with recovery from physical and sexual abuse as well as substance abuse.

It is important to remain aware that not all clergy will be helpful to the abused woman. Some are ignorant and even hostile to women who are not following what they define as the traditional woman's role. There are also some among the clergy who prey on the vulnerable. Hulme (1989) provides a more extended discussion of clergy who sexually exploit those who come to them for help. As he noted,

> People may find their own faith shaken when the symbol bearer of this faith whom they trust betrays that trust. So the offense is aggravated because of the unique and spiritual context of the community within which the clergy function. (Hulme, 1989, p. 183)

The offense is greater when it victimizes a vulnerable woman who has already suffered abuse and is turning to a representative of her faith for comfort, protection, and spiritual guidance.

Self-Help and Related Specialty Groups

Patterned after Alcoholics Anonymous, self-help groups address several forms of abuse. Many of the 12-step programs, such as Incest Survivors Anonymous, offer meetings in which all participants are women. Some women find that these groups provide a unique and valuable resource for healing. The absence of an authoritative or professional leader may help a woman to feel safer, to express her feelings among a group of woman, all of whom have endured an abusive experience, and to move at her own pace while among others with whom she can share personal experiences and encouragement.

On the other hand, 12-step models and the associated concept of co-dependency may prove to be countertherapeutic for some sexually and physically abused women. L. S. Brown (1990) discussed the difficulties with such codependency models in that they stereotype women and blame them for staying with partners who are substance dependent. Such a model provides little understanding of why and how women are encouraged and actually rewarded to take on the nurturing role, whereas men often divorce women who are addicted. Those women who find the 12-step and code-pendency model initially helpful in recognizing their problems eventually need more in-depth therapy to maintain lasting changes. It is often useful for a client in individual therapy to attend such a group at the same time, during at least part of her time in therapy.

Professional Support System

The resources discussed up to this point focus predominantly, although not exclusively, on services and support for the client. It is also important for clinicians to identify and make use of adequate professional resources for their own work.

None of us can be an expert in all things for all clients. Sometimes, obtaining consultation or supervision becomes essential because of the therapist's emotional reactions to a particular client or limited knowledge or expertise in a given area. It may make sense to refer or transfer a client to professionals who are available in the community and are skilled and experienced in working with that population. In virtually all cases, obtaining a second opinion and fresh perspectives can strengthen and enrich the therapist's work as well as identify potential problem areas and professional blind spots.

SUMMARY

A therapist who works with victims of sexual abuse or harassment must consider a number of things that go beyond the usual concerns of therapy. Besides licensing and authorization concerns, the therapist must realize that his or her client could be in danger of physical attacks by the abuser. Sometimes this violence spills over, endangering the safety of the therapist and other clients. The therapist must address issues of office security. Is a security guard needed? Do all the staff know the importance of keeping information about appointments and addresses confidential? These and other questions should be considered.

The success of the therapy will be dependent, in part, on the therapist's attitudes and beliefs about sexual abuse. The section titled "A Therapist's Self-Examination" provides a checklist of questions that will help therapists evaluate their readiness to work with abused women. This chapter closes with a description of community resources such as rape crisis centers, abuse hotlines, and women's centers that can provide additional support for the client.

8

Understanding How Abuse Blocks Access To Help

One of the tragic aspects of victimization is that the traumatic process itself often creates barriers to the victim who is seeking or accepting help. Awareness of the ways in which these barriers occur can enable clinicians to understand more fully the victim's experience and responses. To provide the most effective support for victims, the therapist must work to help remove those barriers. This chapter first looks at the barriers that can prevent a victim of abuse from seeking help or even realizing that she needs help. The second portion examines fears and behaviors that the clinician might encounter when the woman begins to work through the ramifications of her abuse in therapy.

Each client is unique. The reactions noted below are by no means universal, and no therapist should assume that a particular abused woman must react in these ways in order to be classified as a real victim. These reactions are common among victims, but as would be expected, there are numerous victims who do not experience any of them.

There are some commonalities that are frequently observed in abused women during the therapy process. Often these similarities are most visible when analyzing what are often called *transference* and *countertransference* issues, particularly when examined by therapists who use a predominantly psychodynamic orientation. *Transference* refers to the psychological process that occurs in the relationship between the client and the therapist because of the client's other interpersonal relationships that are reenacted during the therapy. *Countertransference* is the term used to describe the process that occurs during the therapy because of the impact of the therapy relationship on the therapist; it usually includes the therapist's own personal issues that may be raised in reaction to the client's issues. Because this book is written for practitioners who have many different theoretical orientations, I have attempted to avoid using language that connotes one particular type of orientation, and, as a result, when I discuss reactions that could be interpreted as transference and countertransference, I have made an effort not to use the language but instead to describe the phenomenon, unless use of the language is the most efficient way to make the point.

BARRIERS THAT PREVENT A WOMAN FROM SEEKING HELP

Denial

Complete or partial denial, minimization, and even total repression of the abusive event or events is a common occurrence among women who have been abused. Memory blocks as well as psychogenic amnesia all contribute to the victim's use of avoidance defenses to protect herself from the pain of the abuse. Virtually all therapists are aware of the degree to which anyone, when sufficiently overwhelmed by an event, may respond, at least temporarily, by denying that the event occurred. A dramatic example is when a mother who loses her daughter in an earthquake may, in shock and confusion, simply deny that her daughter is dead.

Denial seems to be the mind's way of staving off complete dysfunction that can be caused by an overwhelming trauma. To some degree, the denial may be a response to intense psychological pain. It can be thought of as a protective response, much like the state of shock that protects against sudden and overwhelming physical pain. Partial or complete denial may also be an attempt to prevent cognitive paralysis or depression. The experience of abuse can be a profoundly unsettling, disorienting experience. Denial often occurs when acknowledgment of a sexual assault could cause such a disruption of life that the victim blocks out the event in order to preserve her emotional stability. Some cultures, for example some Asian or African ones, encourage denial of abuse experiences in order for the woman to remain a proper and active member of the society. In one case, an Asian-American woman was so terrified of bringing shame to her whole family that she could not tell them that she had been raped, even though she knew they would have supported her. By the time of the trial, she was in complete denial that the event had occurred and, of course, could not be expected to testify. Denial also can occur when two conflicting emotions, such as love for and fear of the abuser, cannot be reconciled.

When humans are young, their world often revolves around their parents. Parents are the source of safety and security, of love and understanding, of nurturance and support. Incest violates the trust that is at the heart of the child's relationship with the world. Any attempt by the incest victim to reorganize her understanding of and relationship to her world when this violation occurs may be far beyond her cognitive–affective abilities. Rather than experience the cognitive paralysis or disintegration that threatens to occur when her world is disrupted to this extent, the child simply isolates each abusive event, psychologically wraps it in a sort of cognitive cocoon, and begins not to see it. The denial enables her life to continue, although this movement forward comes at a tremendous cost. A similar process has also been observed among boys who are incest victims.

The potentially adaptive nature of denial is that it enables the individual to continue functioning, although in a clearly limited way. It may enable an individual to survive and function until a period during which she is able to come to terms with the event. That period may come when she is in a safer setting (e.g., when the perpetrator is no longer around and no longer constitutes a threat for further abuse), when she is at a more advanced developmental stage, when the cost of the relationship becomes greater than the positive gain, when another trauma shocks her into recalling the previous one, or when the environment provides adequate support for her recovery. Breakthrough memories commonly disrupt denial (cf. Herman, 1992, and van der Kolk, 1987, for further discussion).

Denial that the abusive event occurred, however, can obviously block or delay the victim's access to help. If the victim believes that the event has not occurred or is not important, she sees no reason to seek or accept services. Access to services would subvert the process of denial; at least initially, the denial itself may seem absolutely fundamental to the victim's psychological survival. Sometimes the woman's community facilitates her denial and prevents her from seeking therapeutic assistance, in order to keep control over her. This occurs most often in religious communities in which the leaders insist on providing any counseling to members; such counseling is often administered by those who have little or no training in working with trauma and abuse victims.

One cost of denial is that the victim is deprived of immediate psychological, medical, and other interventions that might prevent or ameliorate some of the long-term complications. Just as a delay in access to emergency medical care can lead to serious, sometimes fatal complications, a delay in access to prompt, comprehensive psychological care for the harm caused by abuse can result in major complications. In some cases, explaining the reaction process during immediate crisis intervention can prevent a posttrauma stress reaction from turning into a posttraumatic stress disorder. Obviously, such preventive actions cannot be as useful for women who are still in denial.

An important theme of this book is the tendency of the general community to hold women unjustly accountable for the abuse that they have experienced. It is crucial that recognition and analysis of the process of denial not be used to shift blame onto the victim. The psychoanalytic construct of masochism or the more recent proposed psychiatric diagnosis of self-defeating personality disorder serve to obscure the dynamics of the victim's positive adaptive use of denial. Instead the victim is blamed for not recognizing and taking responsibility for the abuse, and then, for not doing more to stop repeated abuse. Therapists who attempt to persuade the victim to examine her role in the occurrence of the violence can stop the natural healing process and foster greater levels of denial, even when the client attempts to please the therapist by accepting self-blame. This is inappropriate treatment no matter what theoretical orientation is used.

Perpetrators may, for example, attempt to avoid responsibility for their acts by claiming that the victim had a responsibility to seek prompt help for the harm that was caused by the perpetrator. The denial that blocks access to help in no way represents the victim's negligence in seeking help or willful participation in her own injury. The denial is not a voluntary act of which the victim is aware; it is one of the consequences or sequelae of the abuse. Holding a victim accountable for denial is like a man hitting a woman on the head with a hammer in order to rape and rob her and then trying to hold her accountable because she lay unconscious for several hours rather than seeking prompt medical attention.

A victim of abuse, although in a state of partial or complete denial, may become a therapy patient. She may seek therapy ostensibly for other problems or may acquiesce to family demands that she get some help. During the course of treatment, the therapist, and maybe even the client, may begin to have reason to believe that some abusive event has occurred. Perhaps the victim's description of events surrounding the abusive act imply experience with some abuse (although such an implication is not clear to the victim herself). Perhaps concerned third parties have communicated with the therapist, perhaps the abuser has been accused of harming another woman, or perhaps the process of denial has begun to lose its strength and the victim is beginning to experience confusing flashbacks or nightmares about the event. Even when there is no cognitive memory of the abuse, there may be affective memories of terror and trauma that cannot be associated with any specific event but are similar to those experienced by other abuse victims. At that point, therapy specific to healing traumatic episodes becomes useful.

When a therapist has reason to believe that a patient is in denial about an abusive event, it is important that the therapist treat the client with empathy and respect. Attempts to break through the denial by the use of direct confrontation, use of the therapist's authority, or other aggressive means are likely to be unsuccessful and may actually result in additional harm. If the client and her defenses feel overpowered by the therapist's confrontations, arguments, and so on, the therapeutic situation itself may in some ways parallel the victim's experience of having been physically or psychologically overpowered by the perpetrator. Sometimes a client is willing to accept suggestions that are made by the therapist just to ensure that the therapist continues to like and respect her. The more safe and secure the client feels within the therapeutic relationship, the more she feels that the therapist understands and empathizes with her fears, and the more she feels that she can trust the therapist to help her meet any threats, the more likely she will be to move beyond the defense of denial at her own pace.

Abuse can also create a form of partial denial and minimization in which the victim recognizes and acknowledges that the event occurred but does not realize that it was improper or harmful. Sometimes the process of self-blame contributes to this incorrect attribution. Sometimes this inability to recognize that an action is improper may be caused not only by the process of denial, but also by a genuine lack of knowledge that the acts in question constitute abuse. Common societal myths about rape and battering compound this problem. The information in this book can help the nonspecialty therapist to become more knowledgeable so that the therapist does not contribute to the perpetuation of such ignorance.

Rape victims may recognize that they have been forced to engage in sexual activities against their will, but may not know, believe, or understand that certain nonconsensual sexual activity is in fact rape, a criminal act of abuse. A rape victim may believe that the forced sex is not really rape if the perpetrator is a husband, if she did not aggressively struggle and resist, or if she had at any time in the past engaged in consensual sexual intimacies with the perpetrator. Sometimes if the woman's body physiologically responded to the sexual stimulation, her mind may have shut out the memory of being forced into sex, and she may think that somehow she must have wanted the contact.

It is easy to underestimate the strength of the denial, minimization, and repression, especially for clinicians who are inexperienced in treating abused women. The first time an incest victim describes her home life, the therapist may be surprised and perhaps incredulous. The victim might talk about how much her father loved her and how he would come into her room at night, wake her up, and begin kissing and fondling her. Such accounts may be delivered in a neutral or conversational tone as if the client were speaking about walking to school or going to a movie. There may literally be no recognition that what is being described is incest or is improper in any way, even if she did not like the behavior, unless she actually engaged in intercourse with her abuser. Some clients report the positive aspects of their relationship with their father and are then ashamed to report the inappropriate sexual touching for fear that they will have to deny their love, too.

The deeper cognitive, affective, and developmental responses to the incestuous abuse may have become completely walled off from the woman's awareness. The client may be cognitively aware of the phenomenon of incest but have no ability to recognize it in her own life and experience. She may be aware that incest is improper, illegal, and abusive, but may be unaware that the events that she experienced constitute incest. She may even have helped a friend who was an incest victim to confront the problem, yet she may be unable to make the connection—on the intellectual, emotional, or other levels—that her own father's behavior was incestuous. Even when the woman has small glimpses of recognition, she may push them from her thoughts, in fear that no one would believe her anyway.

Sometimes this denial is partial in that the abuse is recognized but minimized. In cases in which the woman must continue to live or work with the abuser, her mind must find some compromise between constant terror and a calm external appearance. Battered women often minimize the extent of the blows that occur during an acute battering incident. Their ability to dissociate and block the pain from their awareness helps in the process of minimization. Incidents in which a woman first describes being hit or shoved may on further questioning turn out to mean being punched repeatedly in the head and thrown across the room. Often the woman herself appears to be surprised at how serious the abuse sounds during the more detailed description; in her mind it was as mild as the original description made it seem. Obviously, first-time descriptions must be accepted, but with the skeptical view that there may be more to be uncovered when the client is ready.

Self-Blame

Self-blame is another common sequelae of abuse. The victim holds herself accountable for the victimization: If she had not done something wrong, then the abuse would not have occurred. Obviously, this attribution helps the woman to retain the illusion that she has power and control over not being hurt again. Thus, the battered woman may believe that if she had been a more attentive wife or had learned to keep her mouth shut, she would not have provoked the man and invited the violent outburst. The exploited therapy client may believe that if she had not discussed her chronic fears about sexuality, her therapist would never have been tempted to have sex with her. The rape victim may believe that if she had only dressed a little more conservatively and had taken a different route home, she would not have put herself in harm's way. The graduate student may believe that she should not have flirted when she went to the professor's office alone to discuss her paper.

The victim's impulse to blame herself can gain impetus from a number of sources. First, the culture frequently blames victims for their victimization (Ryan, 1971). Second, perpetrators may encourage victims to assume responsibility for the abuse. The psychological abuse that often accompanies physical or sexual abuse may create cognitive confusion, particularly when the woman must continue to interact with the man in another more public way. Outright lies or distortions may lessen the probability that the victim will report the abuse or take other steps to prevent it. This confusion helps perpetrators to stave off any legal actions or other forms of redress and may help them to view themselves as guiltless.

Third, therapists and others to whom the victim turns for help, through misinformation, incompetence, thoughtlessness, countertransference, or other processes, may encourage the victim to believe that she is responsible for being victimized. For example, it is not uncommon for a therapist who has admitted to having sex with his client to claim that she consented, that it was not a "real" therapy relationship, and that the harm she now claims was caused by the second therapist's treatment.

No act or set of circumstances can justify or shift the offender's responsibility for rape, incest, battering, sexual harassment, or any of these forms of abuse. When a therapist accepts this tenet, then there will be no need to discuss what the client did or did not do in her part of the interaction. No matter what the client's behavior, there is nothing she could have done to deserve the abuse. Perhaps there are ways that she can find to change her behavior so that she is better protected from future abuse. However, such discussions are best left for the last part of therapy. Raising such issues initially could result in misinterpretation and self-blame on the part of the client. Instead, it is important to discuss how the client can keep herself safe by helping her to design a safety plan. Development of a safety plan is described in chapter 13 on short-term crisis intervention.

Shame and Guilt

Shame and guilt are common sequelae of abuse. Both add substantially to the victim's suffering. Either one can make it exceptionally difficult for the victim to seek or to accept help. Shame is the internal feeling that comes from being exposed and vulnerable, whereas guilt is an externally imposed feeling that comes from believing that something wrong was done. The victim of abuse may become so overwhelmed by shame or guilt that she cannot acknowledge or discuss the abuse with anyone. She may not believe that she deserves help, relief from suffering, or any form of healing and recovery. Others may reinforce her shame and guilt by their attitude toward her after they learn about the abuse. The boyfriend who treats the woman as if she were "spoiled goods" after a stranger rape, the parents and friends of the battered woman who hate the man that she married, the therapist who is unable to listen to the brutality without becoming frightened too, the new supervisor who asks the woman for graphic details about the sexual harassment, and the husband who cannot understand why his wife does not want to make love are all examples of how others can add to the woman's feelings of shame and guilt.

Cognitive Dysfunction

The trauma of abuse can be extremely disabling. The abuse may cause cognitive dysfunction, especially in the areas of attention and concentration, sometimes involving unbidden thoughts, intrusive images, flashbacks, and nightmares. Mental confusion may occur at times in which clear, concise thinking had been the rule. In some instances, a sort of cognitive paralysis may occur. The victim may suffer from other aspects of either acute or delayed posttraumatic stress disorder.

Most treatment approaches are highly dependent on cognitive understanding and insight into one's thought processes, affective responses, and behavior. Many women have learned how to hide their true thoughts and feelings from scrutiny, only allowing those that are consistent with those of the mainstream culture to be viewed by others. This ability to hide one's real thoughts and feelings is frequently enhanced by the impact of abuse. After all, safety from further abuse may be seen as dependent on the ability to keep the abuse secret, sometimes even from oneself. Cognitive confusion keeps the woman from knowing just how terrible things actually are. Changes in the woman's ability to think clearly are not easily observed when patterns of covering up are ingrained as survival skills. Thus, it must be expected that abuse victims will not let on about the specifics of cognitive confusion until they feel safe and understood by the therapist.

In some cases, the victim has suffered neuropyschological damage, usually from repeated head injuries. It is often difficult to sort out the effects of the posttrauma functional psychological injuries from the effects of the neurological ones. New data suggest that neuropsychological injuries may be responsible for slow, steady deterioration that makes it difficult to judge the progress of treatment. Thus, although it may appear that there is less progress than expected in therapy, cognitive dysfunction from neuropsychological injuries may be causing deterioration that interferes with the success of therapy. Newer rehabilitation methods that are specifically designed to restore cognitive functioning would be suggested in such cases.

Fear of Punishment From the Perpetrator

Perpetrators may actively and aggressively attempt to block the victim's access to any help. A battered woman may fear that if her husband finds out that she is seeing a therapist, it will provoke further attacks. The victim of sexual intimacies with a therapist may fear that the perpetrator will claim that she is borderline or psychotic and that her allegations are but a symptom of her pathology. She may be concerned that he will release her chart notes, revealing not only the extremely private and confidential information she told her therapist but also information fabricated by the therapist (e.g., the therapist may have threatened to put in her chart that she told him that she was a drug abuser, a shoplifter, an embezzler, a prostitute or may make some other assertion that would cause her further embarrassment and shame).

The rape victim may be told by her assailant that he knows where she lives and where her children are; he may tell her that even if he is immediately jailed, he will someday be free, and at that time he will return to torture, maim, or kill her and her loved ones. If the rapist has been arrested and is awaiting trial, friends or associates of the rapist may contact the rape victim and make these threats. Even if the threats are not made, the victim may still wonder—as anyone might were they in her position—whether disclosing the rape to others (e.g., seeking therapy, filing a complaint) would provoke some truly awful and possibly fatal form of vengeance. Even women who are incarcerated are not safe. In a number of cases in which the woman and man were codefendants because he persuaded her to become involved in a crime or to cover up a crime for him, the man found a way to let her know that he would cause her further harm if she did not keep quiet and protect him (Walker, 1989b).

Deep and pervasive fear of retribution, sometimes paralyzing, can be part of the damage suffered by the abuse victim. It can be a daunting barrier to any access to help. Furthermore, such fear prevents other people from helping the victim even when they have firsthand knowledge of the abuse. Office workers who were also sexually harassed by the accused man will shrink from publicly admitting it, because of fear. Other students who have been sexually harassed will fail to speak out publicly for fear that their careers and reputations will be harmed. Such barriers make it difficult to corroborate one woman's reports of abuse, but should not be the deciding factor in validating the woman's reports.

Therapists may fear retribution or violence from the abuser. This fear may be unconsciously expressed in the therapist's approach to treatment.

Therapists must be careful to monitor their own responses so that they do not begin to minimize the danger to the client in order to minimize their own fears.

BARRIERS TO EFFECTIVE THERAPY

Fear of the Therapist's Response

One exceptionally effective barrier that blocks access to help is the victim's fear of the therapist's reaction. Many victims fear that no one will believe them, that their account of the abuse will be dismissed as a fabrication, an exaggeration, or an attempt to evade the true work of psychotherapy. Victims may fear that the therapist will blame them for the abuse or that the therapist will discount the importance of the abuse or the harm that resulted from it. Such fears are not always groundless. Some therapists tend to dismiss virtually any account of abuse as a *screen memory*, a disguised wish, a secret fantasy, or a psychotic delusion. Some therapists believe that little if any harm comes from such forms of abuse as rape, incest, or battering. Some therapists do believe that victims must take responsibility for or "own" the abuse that they were subjected to before they can heal. This view is not supported by the relevant research or clinical experiences.

The victim's fear that seeking help will only subject her to further victimization constitutes a significant obstacle to her recovery.

Fear of "Opening Up"

Many victims of abuse manage to continue functioning despite the extensive harm that they have suffered. Sometimes they continue to function by keeping their reactions to the abuse under tight control. It is as if vast areas of their lives and experiences were walled off or kept under heavy cover. Anytime this strategy begins to fail, and the memories begin to emerge, the victim's ability to function is severely threatened. The cost involved and the energy required to maintain this equilibrium are enormous and often cause the victim to seek treatment. Yet, the strategy enables the abuse victim to survive and to function, and abandoning this coping method may be frightening to her.

Victims who are coping in this way may fear that if they attempt to gain access to help, they will become unable to function. Even mentioning to a therapist that the abuse occurred may open up repressed and suppressed material, causing the victim to fall apart, decompensate, and become completely dysfunctional. At this point, the therapist must reassure the victim that he or she will be available to assist her in regaining her ability to function.

This fear is not groundless, as trauma theory has demonstrated. When traumatic events are stored in victims' memories, the accompanying affect gets stored along with the cognitive memory. The material rarely has been processed, so when it is discussed the event unfolds as if it were recurring. The victim reexperiences the entire abusive incident, complete with all the feelings that she experienced and blocked out at the time. Thus, talking about the abuse makes it likely that she will have to experience the terror, confusion, pain, and fear all over again. Who would want to put themselves voluntarily through such a terrible experience? Therapists must offer safety and compassion if the victim finally decides to share this painful experience in an attempt to receive help.

When victims in the grip of such fears reach out for help from a therapist, it is vitally important that the therapist recognize, respect, and empathize with these fears. As emphasized elsewhere in this volume, it is crucial that the client be allowed and encouraged to move at her own pace. Such accommodations of the client's needs and time frame for pacing the therapy are necessary in order to allow her to process the traumatic events so that healing may begin to take place.

Pleasing and Compliant Behavior

Many repeatedly abused women learn to anticipate the emotional reactions of another person to their behavior. They have learned that pleasing the abuser is one way to reduce the amount of abuse they receive. Preventing the abuser from seeing how emotionally upset they might be (sometimes because the abuse will be worse if they show their feelings) is a coping strategy. This need to please and to follow directions may be carried over into the therapist's office. Such clients want to be liked and to please, feeling that the therapist will protect them if they show how ingratiating they can be. It is important to understand the significance of this behavior and to respond sensitively, respectfully, and helpfully. Unfortunately, some therapists subtly exploit the client's tendencies rather than helping her to understand her behavior, to recover, and to become more independent. Such therapists may enjoy the client's outwardly pleasant and helpful demeanor (and, therefore, reinforce the client's belief that any negative thoughts, feelings, or behaviors are off-limits), the way she prunes and waters the plants in the waiting room, makes coffee and washes dishes in the reception area, and is available to do small favors (e.g., giving the therapist a ride to the service station when the therapist's car is being repaired).

Both therapist and client may collude in the pretense that recovery for the client means being helpful to the therapist. The client assumes a helper role in which she seeks to identify and meet the needs of the therapist; the therapist rewards her for her efforts by being pleased. This misalliance reenacts abusive relationships that the client has experienced in the past: She will be rewarded by the loved person's attention when she does nice things for that person. Sometimes this distorted role reversal (in which the client is expected to meet the needs of the therapist) may lead to serious boundary violations including both sexual and nonsexual dual relationships.

A more subtle form of reenacting previous abusive relationships involves a client who shows virtually no independent thought, will, or intention. She constantly seeks direction and advice from the therapist and displays seemingly boundless determination to carry out whatever guidance she obtains. She is relentlessly agreeable, insisting that whatever her therapist suggests in the way of modifying her behavior, carrying out treatment-related "homework" assignments, or accomplishing goals are just what she needs, well within her power to perform, and certain to be completed by the next session. However, during the next session, she reports that she has been at least temporarily unable to follow through. The repetition of this pattern in therapy suggests that a tendency toward complete (if only temporary) compliance may have been a necessary survival skill in her prior abusive relationship but one that needs to be explored in the current therapy. For example, women who have been battered by parents or partners may have been forced into complying with the most outlandish demands when the abuser was raging or drunk. When the demands involved future behavior, women in such relationships may have discovered that the abuser often forgot what he wanted from one minute to the next. As a result, the victim learned to promise to comply with whatever someone demanded and to ignore or forget about the demand until the next time the issue is raised.

SUMMARY

There are many stumbling blocks that can make it hard for the abused woman to request help and to make the most effective use of the help she receives. She may deny or minimize the abuse. She may blame herself for the abuse or feel such guilt and shame that speaking to anyone about it is too painful. She may be psychologically incapable of seeking help, or she may be suffering from neuropsychological damage that adversely affects her ability to think and use good judgment. Finally, she may be intimidated by the threats of the abuser.

Some of the coping strategies that enabled the abused woman to survive the abuse can carry over into the relationship with her therapist. It is critical for the therapist to understand that pushing the woman too hard or too fast or holding her responsible for her own abuse can result in the abused woman turning away from treatment.

9

Forensic Issues

This chapter identifies some of the major issues to which the therapist must attend in light of the high potential for forensic involvement when treating abuse victims. The first section is a brief primer on the legal system, examining how it differs from the scientific approach to fact-finding, and the types of courts and actions with which the psychologist who is treating an abuse victim could become involved. The following two sections provide practical advice about dealing with specific legal situations and how the legal obligations of the psychologist affect day-to-day work with clients. Forensic issues specific to different types of abuse are examined in the last section.

It is important to emphasize that neither this nor any other general book can provide a comprehensive and specific diagram of each step to take in all circumstances. The perspective discussed here is that of a therapist rather than that of a court-appointed or attorney-selected forensic evaluator, although often what is advised is the same in both cases. It is usually a good idea to keep the forensic evaluation separate from the clinical psychotherapy evaluation, because forensic evaluators need to be free from any suspicion of bias and must use their findings to answer legal questions rather than develop treatment plans. Often a forensic evaluator needs to review legal documents in order to arrive at appropriate psychological opinions. The standards may vary from state to state and may be dependent on the type of case being presented.

It is important to remember that bias against women in the courts has been documented since 1983 by studies of such gender bias in 38 states in the United States (cf. Conlin, 1990; Schafran, 1990; Wikler, 1990). Although reform has been slowly occurring, it is still evident that women are not treated the same way as men throughout the various court proceedings (cf. the 1993 report of the 9th Federal Circuit Court Task Force on Gender Bias). Clients should be helped to understand that unfair treatment may not be a result of their behavior, but a result of the lack of understanding, compassion, and justice for women in the legal system. Psychologists who work with abused women must familiarize themselves with the implementation of the laws in their communities as well as with the actual laws themselves.

OVERVIEW OF THE LEGAL ARENA

There are many voluntary and involuntary ways in which abuse victims and their therapists can become involved in the system of courts and other formal review agencies. Victims of rape may be called on to testify in criminal proceedings against the rapist, therapists working with incest victims may be obligated to notify law enforcement authorities and participate in any subsequent legal proceedings, victims of therapist–client sex may be asked to testify in administrative hearings by licensing boards, battered women may seek help from the courts in finding safety from their attackers, or victims of sexual harassment and assault may file civil suits seeking to recover damages. Because of the need to contain violent behavior through external restraints, the likelihood of involvement with the legal system at some time is very high for those abused women who seek psychotherapy (cf. Walker, 1984c, 1989a, 1989b, 1991b).

Although participation in the legal system holds many unknowns for the uninitiated as well as for the sophisticated practitioner, there are two main reasons (in addition to the ethical mandate to follow the law whenever possible) to encourage such cooperation. First, the legal system is the only societal institution that has the power to contain the violent behavior of the offender. This can be accomplished in the criminal, juvenile, family, and other civil courts. Second, although the legal process may place an undue burden on the victim, and indeed may revictimize her, when the process goes well, it can be instrumental in helping her heal from the abuse. Unburdening the secret in itself can have long-term benefits for the victim, and if she wins the legal battle it may save years of psychotherapy. Winning is defined in different ways for different victims; often large sums of money or even long prison sentences for the abuser are less relevant to restoring the woman's sense of self than is the court's validation of her experience and pain.

The likelihood of involvement in such forensic processes has at least two major implications for the therapist working with victims of abuse. First, the potential involvement means that there may not be the customary privacy, confidentiality, and privilege that characterize most psychotherapist–client interactions. The secrets that the client tells the therapist may not remain secret. Despite the best efforts on the part of the therapist, the contents of the therapy sessions may become part of a public record, and the therapist's notes may even become subject to cross-examination by a skilled attorney seeking to discredit the client. Sometimes the records are not subpoenaed until many years after the therapy has been completed, which makes it imperative for therapists always to set up their records as though they might become part of a legal action. Sometimes therapists are called to be expert witnesses in court or at a deposition, either on the woman's behalf or in an attempt to discredit her.

The potential involvement with the judicial system also means that therapists working with abuse victims must assume a special responsibility to ensure that the forensic process does not needlessly undermine the therapeutic process and that the acts of the therapist do not undermine the legal rights of the patient. Walker (1990) outlined some of those differences as they occurred when working with children who said that they had been sexually abused. These differences are outlined below and also hold true for abused women. It is not essential to learn everyone's side of an abuse allegation in order to provide good therapy; the woman's own version is the best one to work with in such a situation. That is, it is the meaning that she has assigned to the abuse that affects her state of mind. In a forensic situation, however, it is crucial to understand the other perspectives in order to reach a professional opinion.

The statute of limitations in filing a civil tort action against someone for intentional or negligent infliction of harm has been changing, both through new laws created by legislatures and through case law (cf. Jorgenson & Appelbaum, 1991; Jorgenson & Randles, 1991; Jorgenson, Randles, & Strasburger, 1991, for a discussion relevant to the tolling of the statutes applying to sex between client and therapist cases). In most states it is important to prove when the client actually knew that she was harmed and was able to do something about it. The definition of psychological knowing has become important in these cases. It may be one thing to be aware of the sexual acts and another to recognize the extent of their harm and be able to seriously weigh and consider legal actions (cf. Jorgenson & Appelbaum, 1991, for further discussion of this point). Thus, the statute of limitations may be affected by the testimony of a therapist regarding when psychological knowing took place. In negligent harm cases, lawyers for the plaintiff often attempt to sue homeowners' insurance companies if the abuse took place in an insured home, whereas malpractice cases, including breach of fiduciary duties, are more likely to involve liability insurance companies. Although these differences are not as important to treating therapists as they are to forensic experts, paying attention to them may make the difference between some financial compensation being provided to a victim or none being provided. The therapist who knows the attorneys who specialize in these areas can be of additional support to clients who cannot always determine attorneys' legal competence.

Forensic psychologists and other mental health experts are usually hired to assess and evaluate the psychological impact of the facts. Their function is different from that of the therapist in that they need to collect the data in a systematic way to help decide legal issues. Sometimes there is no difficulty in agreeing on the relevant facts, but there can be disputes among the professionals about the evidence, depending on whether they are therapists or forensic experts. If there are opposing expert opinions, often they are based on different interpretations of the data. Some do not believe that any psychologist's opinions are expert enough in helping the factfinders make their decisions (cf. Faigman, 1986, and Faust & Ziskin, 1988, for the negative side, and Blau, 1984, and D. L. Shapiro, 1990, for opposing viewpoints on this issue).

In many cases, the disputes between professionals can be best understood by looking at the disparity in each professional's training in the area of expertise needed to answer the legal questions. Understanding the legal questions that need to be answered by mental health data will assist the forensic expert in choosing what methods are used. The therapist usually does not have such an option and must work with the data that have been provided in the therapy sessions. Although some colleagues suggest that it is not possible for a therapist to provide an objective opinion, in a case in which abuse has occurred the therapist or forensic evaluator, by piecing together even limited facts, should have no difficulty understanding the psychological impact and harm that were caused by the abuse.

Adversarial and Scientific Models

It is important to understand the adversarial nature of the legal system before getting involved in it. Although some psychologists have advocated for providing the court with an objective account of the scientific research on any given topic without taking sides or becoming adversarial, that approach is rarely possible or appropriate when a client is involved (cf. Loftus & Ketcham, 1991, for an example of the use of science in an adversarial approach). It is possible to be neutral and objective in performing the evaluation in order to arrive at a professional opinion and then, following the rules of evidence, to present that information on behalf of one side in the adversarial process.

The ways in which the legal and psychological systems seek truth are quite different. In the law, reason and the deductive method of inquiry are used. Each side has the opportunity to present its very best version of the facts, and the truth is said to lie somewhere between them. The finder of fact, usually the judge or jury, has the responsibility of sorting through the factual testimony and trying to find where truth lies. In psychology, the scientific method prevails with its inductive method of seeking truth. Using previous scientific knowledge, hypotheses or best guesses of the truth are formulated. Then objective, scientific inquiry helps determine whether or not these hypotheses meet the scientific tests of probability. Thus, it makes sense for the scientist to expect the middle ground or neutrality to be respected (cf. Monahan & Walker, 1986, and Walker & Monahan, 1987, for further discussion of social science and the law).

But the law treats the scientist's presentation of neutrality as though it were the best version presented and matches it against the adversary's position. The legal system expects the therapist to be an advocate for the client and misinterprets neutrality as advocating for the other side (cf. Faust & Ziskin, 1988, for a discussion of how a clinician can be discredited; Fowler & Matarazzo, 1988, for a general rebuttal; and Pope, Butcher, & Seelen, 1993, for a specific discussion of the Minnesota Multiphasic Personality Inventory that is popularly used in forensic proceedings). Thus, substituting the scientific hypothesis argument for what is expected to be the best interpretation in the adversarial system can easily be misunderstood and may more likely create a situation of miscarriage of justice. When working in the legal arena, it is critical to respect its definitions, rules, and boundaries and to not attempt to change the judicial system's method of understanding data while trying to present the information.

To make the best presentation of the data, it is most helpful to work with the attorney to understand things like his or her theory of the case, which is a combination of legal theory, rules of evidence, and the fact pattern as the attorney understands it. Some questions that might be discussed include the following: How will psychological information fit into the case? What are the rules of evidence for introducing the psychological data by the therapist? What are the informal courtroom rules and demeanor? Which rulings on motions, if any, will limit the testimony? In turn, the therapist must help the attorney to understand the psychological data so that he or she can formulate the proper questions to be posed and answered.

This consultation stage can be the most critical part of the case, yet neither lawyers nor mental health professionals often take the time to be clear about what each needs from the other. Information about the client that could be both positively or negatively interpreted must be carefully discussed so that there is no misunderstanding about the therapist's meaning. Often, attorneys are reluctant to talk too much to an expert, for fear they will be criticized for putting words in the expert's mouth. Some attorneys are not familiar enough with psychological research to know the potential interpretations of data. Here it may be useful to ask the attorney to discuss what would be the best version of psychological testimony so that the therapist can determine if such information fits with the data available. Of course, it is crucial to explain to the attorney that this information is to be used for guidelines and that the attorney should not expect that the therapist will so testify unless the data accurately fit the description. Some mental health professionals are so intimidated by the unfamiliar judicial system that they find it difficult to stand up to a persuasive attorney. It is important to remember that good trial attorneys practice being persuasive as part of their skills; they want and need to know the accurate psychological information that can be provided by the therapist or forensic expert. If that information is not useful to their case, they can and will attempt to refuse to permit such testimony to be used in court. Therefore, it is in the client's best interests for the therapist to be as honest as is possible about what can and cannot be said.

Types of Courts and Actions

Most court actions in which abuse victims and therapists become involved take place in state courts. Occasionally, federal court is involved, particularly if an action is committed on federal lands (including reservations and military installations) or in class action and sexual harassment cases that allege an abridgment of the woman's civil rights. Then, federal law and federal rules of evidence apply. The formal laws (set by the state legislature), case laws (set by court decisions), rules of evidence including privilege (set by state legislature, governing agencies, and case law), and similar procedures differ from state to state as well as from the federal standards. No single volume can encompass with specificity the legal standards and procedures for each type of judicial action in each state. Moreover, the laws are constantly in a state of evolution. New legislation is passed, and emerging case law provides new interpretations and new principles. This is especially true in criminal and civil matters in which the abused woman's credibility or state of mind is at issue.

There has been a great deal of change over the past 15 years in all areas of the law that apply to abuse victims. New definitions of rape and sexual assault, the establishment of rape shield laws, and the elimination of interspousal tort immunity have made it easier to prosecute rape cases without placing the victim on trial (cf. Chappel, Geis, & Geis, 1977; Estrich, 1987; P. Searles & Berger, 1987). Perhaps the area in which the most publicized gains have been made is in having the courts recognize the psychological effects of battered woman syndrome (Price, 1985; Walker, 1989b; Walker & Corierre, 1991). The admissability of expert witness testimony about battered woman syndrome and its impact on a woman's state of mind at the time a crime is committed has changed the definitions and practice of self-defense in criminal law (Bochnak, 1981; Browne, 1987; Ewing, 1987; Jones, 1981; Maguigan, 1991; Mahoney, 1991; Schneider, 1986; Walker, 1984c, 1989a, 1989b, 1992). Although the use of expert witness testimony is not without controversy (Faigman, 1986; Maguigan, 1991; Mahoney, 1991; Schneider, 1986; Walker, 1989b), most legal and mental health professionals understand the benefits of both professions working together to stop violence against women.

The approach toward sexual misconduct committed by therapists against their clients has also been evolving in the courts. By the late 1980s, many of the state statutes had been changed to provide more criminal penalty options in addition to the civil and administrative court remedies. Strasburger, Jorgenson, and Randles (1991) found that, as of 1990, seven states (Wisconsin, Minnesota, North Dakota, Colorado, California, Maine, and Florida) had passed such statutes and that other states (Iowa, Maryland, Massachusetts, New Mexico, and Pennsylvania) were considering them. Along with the change in the statute of limitations that was mentioned earlier, such revisions have succeeded in helping to change social policy and to compensate the victim through the court system.

WORKING WITHIN THE LEGAL SYSTEM

Participation in the forensic process can be an extremely stressful experience, especially for those who are not prepared. Therapists are often removed from their familiar environments (e.g., the privacy of the consulting room) and professional interactions when they begin to deal with the legal system. Suddenly thrust into an adversarial, sometimes quite brutal process in which the attorneys and judges are the ones familiar with the complex sets of rules, the naive therapist may easily be intimidated into violating a client's rights. Given that almost every word that is uttered in a legal procedure is written down for the public record, the pressure is great just to be certain that inappropriate remarks are not inadvertently made. Most therapists are shocked to read the first typed transcript of their testimony; they may feel that it seems as though they never learned how to speak in proper English! Out of context and without any nonverbal cues, the transcript must still suffice as legal record. Therefore, good preparation and carefully considered testimony are helpful in reducing the expected stress.

Some therapists handle this stress quite well and even thrive on it. Others put up with it as an unpleasant but necessary aspect of their professional work, and still others seek to avoid it whenever possible. Those who are thoroughly familiar with their subject matter, articulate in expressing their opinions, have a bit of the competitive spirit, thrive on the unfolding drama of the courtroom, have the stamina to withstand hours of answering inane questions, have quick reactions, and can see where pieces fit into the larger picture usually love the adversarial legal process. Those who like to think things through more carefully before responding with an opinion may find the legal arena too demanding to be fun. Being an expert is much like playing poker: One rarely wins without a good hand but knowing the timing of when to bid or play is essential.

Therapists must come to terms with their reactions to the forensic process in order to provide services to abuse victims effectively. The therapist's participation in the forensic process is controlled by those in the legal profession. Mental health experts do know more about psychology than most lawyers, but lawyers know how to deliver the subject matter within the legal system. Thus, each profession is dependent on learning from the other in order to be of benefit to the client and, ultimately, to society.

Humility is part of the structure of the legal system. The judge has great powers under his or her jurisdiction. Some judges, particularly those who are intimidated by a psychologist or do not trust psychological data, will test these powers just to be sure that the therapist understands who is the boss. It can be difficult, although it is essential, to let the judge keep control and to still do the proper job for which you have been called to court.

Minimizing Involvement With the Legal Process

The therapist can be subpoenaed to appear as a percipient witness (a person who testifies as to knowledge of fact and does not offer an opinion that is part of expert witness testimony) if his or her knowledge of a client is deemed useful and relevant to the court and if privilege has been waived or is inapplicable. In some instances, it is not revealed until sometime during therapy that the patient has suffered abuse and that some court involvement is likely. Nevertheless, steps can be taken to minimize involvement with the court if the therapist is uncomfortable with the forensic process.

For example, a prominent therapist who works with victims of therapist–patient sexual intimacy views court appearances as disruptive both to her therapeutic work with the client whose case is at issue and to her work schedule (i.e., her attempt to meet with her other clients on a regular basis). When victims of therapist–patient sexual intimacies seek her services, she informs them that she strives to avoid mixing therapeutic work with forensic work; thus, if they anticipate filing malpractice suits against the perpetrator, she believes that they can receive better services from another therapist (i.e., one whose theoretical approach, personal style, and work schedule are consistent with court appearances). Of course, this is not a foolproof procedure because many clients cannot make such a decision prior to the beginning of therapy. Sometimes a therapist may suggest that the victim undergo an independent evaluation with a known specialist in the area and then keep in periodic touch with that specialist. Then, if a legal proceeding occurs, the specialist becomes the expert, obviating the need to call on the therapist to give up confidentiality. Of course, some jurisdictions will not accept such alternatives, but many will respect the therapeutic process. Arrangements such as these, with the caveats mentioned, tend to serve clients and therapists well.

Responding to Subpoenas

In some cases, a client's attorney or an opposing attorney may subpoena the therapist to testify in an abuse-related civil case, assuming that the privacy of therapy is a relatively unimportant matter and that the therapist will certainly have helpful information to share with the court. The therapist will find it useful to discuss the issue with the client (who may not have been informed that her attorney had served the subpoena). If the therapist believes that opening up the therapeutic process to cross-examination in open court would be harmful to the progress of therapy, he or she should frankly and clearly outline these reservations to both the client and the client's attorney in order to attempt to maintain privilege. Written documents often must be "produced" to the court, so it is important to review every word that is written down and submitted to the attorney or placed in the file to see if it can pass court scrutiny. A review of therapy progress notes can guard against record-keeping difficulties that are described later. In some jurisdictions, therapists are permitted to keep personal notes that are not subject to subpoena.

Sometimes the client may want to follow up with her attorney, explaining the situation and asking that the subpoena be withdrawn or, in legalese, *quashed*. In other cases, especially when the subpoena has been issued by the opposing attorney, the therapist may, with the written informed consent of the client, contact the client's own attorney to explain why breaching the privacy of therapy might be harmful to the therapist's client. The situation, of course, becomes much more difficult if it is an opposing attorney who has filed the subpoena and if the therapist has no effective basis on which to claim privilege on behalf of the client. In some instances (e. g., when a client puts her mental and emotional state at issue before the courts when suing for psychological damage or in cases that deal with children), she effectively waives her rights to all privileged communications with therapists and other health care providers, not just those that affect the issues raised by the lawsuit. For example, the patient claims that she has suffered mental and emotional distress from a traffic accident in which another driver ran a red light and smashed into her car. She does not view her civil suit against the other driver as having any connection with her therapy for abuse, but the defendant may be granted access by the courts to all of the records of treatment and may compel her therapist to be deposed and to provide courtroom testimony. However, this loss of privilege should not be automatically assumed when a subpoena is served.

In most jurisdictions, there are legal bases for attempts to stop or at least limit the amount of information that is disclosed. Therapists should not turn over any information without first reviewing the file, determining what information is available, discussing it with the client and her attorney, and then seeking legal advice from an attorney whose job it is to look after the therapist's legal rights. It is important for the therapist to have access to an attorney who is familiar with the local rules of evidence and who is willing to fight against unwarranted and unnecessary disclosure of private details that have no legal relevance to the present case.

The Importance of Legal Consultation

Any therapist who is becoming involved with forensic aspects of practice needs adequate legal resources and consultation. The laws regarding what therapists must and must not do regarding responding to interrogatories, delivering documents, scheduling and reviewing deposition testimony, contacting the various parties and legal representatives, disclosing information regarding a patient, appearing in court, and so on, tend to be quite complex. Unless therapists are also trained as attorneys, they lack expertise in this area. Nor are clinical colleagues, also untrained as attorneys, trained to serve as guides and representatives in this domain (although those who are respected in the forensic field certainly should be used for consultation and, in some cases, supervision).

A therapist who is facing involvement with the forensic arena needs access to an attorney who is knowledgeable, skilled, and experienced in the relevant area of the practice of psychology. This cannot be stressed enough. There may be temptation to seek advice regarding, for example, whether to hand over chart notes in response to a subpoena, from any attorney, particularly one who is already known to the therapist. Thus, if a good friend is a real estate attorney or estate lawyer with whom the therapist has consulted in the past, it may be tempting to call and ask that person for advice. Attorneys who are inexperienced in the relevant areas of the law may be good sources of referrals to the most appropriate specialists, but they probably will be ill-suited to guide the therapist through the complexities of this area of the law. The National Register of Health Service Providers in Psychology has a legal consultation service that can provide its members with such legal advice. The group also publishes a special newsletter providing updated guidelines for practitioners who must deal with legal issues that arise in the normal practice of therapy.

Making assumptions about what is legally required in the forensic arena can lead to needless, tragic mistakes. A clinician may receive a subpoena demanding all chart records for a specific therapy client. The subpoena is duly filled out, signed, witnessed, and recorded. It appears to be a valid legal document that clearly states a deadline for the delivery of these records. In order to comply with the law, the therapist may promptly turn over the records to the individual specified on the subpoena. This may be a big mistake!

Depending on the circumstances and on individual state laws, the therapist may not have been legally required to turn over the records, and may have violated both the legal and ethical rights of the client by delivery of the documents. Furthermore, once the documents have been turned over to another party (particularly a party who is a legal adversary of the client), their contents have been disclosed, and it is, of course, impossible to make them confidential again. Whatever confidential information the records contained is now known to third parties. In addition, the therapist's violation of the client's legal rights may have a profound impact not only on the legal proceedings themselves and on the therapist (who may be subject to legal, ethical, or licensing sanctions and liabilities) but also on the clinical status of the client, the therapeutic alliance, and the course of therapy.

The therapist might be required by law to claim privilege on behalf of the client. The courts could then, if the attorney issuing the subpoena pursued the matter, review any competing claims and determine whether that attorney has a right to the records and whether the therapist had an obligation to deliver all of the records. Only after a hearing in which the judge makes a decision to compel their discovery will the therapist be legally required to turn records over to the court. Sometimes only partial records— usually those deemed relevant by the courts—may be required. All of these procedures must take place even if an attorney claims that the rules of evidence demand that the mental health provider produce the records.

Remember, in an adversarial situation, the attorney's job is to get the materials to do the job, and most will use intimidation to back up their demands. Forensic experts learn not to take these tactics seriously or personally. Instead, if the therapist knows his or her own boundaries and ethical framework and is able to communicate them clearly to the attorney, a good working relationship may become possible.

Practicing as a Therapist, Not an Attorney

Abuse clients may ask the therapist detailed questions about the legal system. Despite the understandable reluctance therapists might have to acknowledge to themselves or others that they are not knowledgeable and competent in all areas, it is crucial that therapists avoid attempting to serve as attorneys.

It is an important legal and ethical responsibility that a therapist practice only within his or her realm of competence and expertise. If a therapist has not undertaken adequate legal training or gained admission to the relevant state bar, then the therapist must be considered neither competent nor authorized to dispense legal opinions and advice to clients. To do so is, at minimum, a violation of ethical responsibility to practice within the bounds of competence.

The consequences that are brought about by therapists who begin practicing as attorneys vis-à-vis their clients are usually no better than those that would occur if they attempted to practice outside their specialization as medical doctors (unless, of course, they were trained as physicians in the relevant realm of practice). A therapist may, for example, assure a victim of abuse that she has a promising legal case and tell her that it would be best if she were to work through certain issues in therapy before contacting an attorney to file the case. This strategy, claims the therapist, is best because the client will be better able to understand all the aspects of the abuse, and to tell her story more effectively not only to her own attorney but also to the jury. The client, although eager to press charges, follows the therapist's recommendation. When the therapist determines that it is the optimal time to contact an attorney and file the case, the client finds out that, because of the delay, the statute of limitations has elapsed. She may now have no case at all. Or, she may have a malpractice case against the therapist.

On the other hand, a client may seek therapy and discover, well into the therapy, abuse that occurred years ago. She had not been consciously aware of this abuse. The denial that was a consequence of the abuse only yielded to psychotherapy. When the client asks her therapist about the possibility of filing a civil suit against the abuser, the therapist gives her the bad news: There is a statute of limitations in this jurisdiction that bars civil suits for damages after a 1-year period has elapsed. Unfortunately, many years have elapsed since the abuse occurred and the therapist believes that no suit is possible. It would be best, according to her therapist, if she continued to work through the issues in therapy, tried to put the past behind her, and tried to get on with the rest of her life. What both client and therapist may not be aware of is that, in that particular jurisdiction, the 1-year period for filing suit begins only when the individual becomes aware that the event was abusive or becomes psychologically able to file suit.

Most nonmedical therapists are aware that it is an important responsibility for them to refer clients who have medical needs to competent physicians. When clients have important needs for legal counsel and guidance, therapists must refer them to those who are trained and authorized to provide legal services rather than trying, incompetently, to meet those needs. It is a good idea to have a list of at least three attorneys in each area of specialization to give to clients. Civil personal injury, family law such as divorce and juvenile, and criminal cases are appropriate categories, although in some communities generalists or large law firms with several different types of attorneys available can be useful.

The Roles Psychologists Play in Legal Proceedings

There are areas in which the expertise of the psychologist is very important to providing assistance to clients, attorneys, and the court. Psychology can help answer legal questions that have to do with human behavior, motivation, perception, competence, and psychological injury. Experts in the area of abuse can help the legal community understand whether an abuse victim was coerced into signing a document, whether she committed fraud or other defined criminal acts under duress, whether she used violence in self-defense or in defense of others, whether she failed to protect her child because of the psychological impact of abuse, whether she was competent to understand a waiver of her rights, and other issues in the criminal justice system. Therapists who are not specialists in abuse still may be helpful to the court by placing the particular client's behavior into the general context that is described by the forensic expert.

Experts also can assist in the prosecution of violent men by providing the court with information about the impact of abuse on a child or an adult. Experts may protect a child from unduly influential and potentially damaging cross-examination. In some states, experts can give testimony about the pattern of abusers. Experts can also provide research data about the complexities of eyewitness testimony and difficulties with memory over time (Loftus & Ketcham, 1991; Loftus & Loftus, 1980).

In civil cases, experts can provide information to help the court answer the questions of liability and damages, both of the aspects of personal injury cases. Experts can help the court understand when the client became aware of the damaging aspects of the abuse, how it actually harmed her, and what the prognosis is for her recovery. Again, the therapist who is not necessarily an expert in violent issues still can provide helpful information concerning the individual woman's state of mind and the impact of abuse.

Experts can assist in the preparation of cost analysis by applying some of the research data on long-term effects of abuse and its expected impact on a particular woman. Experts can testify in malpractice suits about the community standard concerning the treatment of abuse cases and sexual misconduct of therapists. In such situations, both general testimony about psychological data as well as information specific to a particular client can be used.

Therapists who are experts can assist the courts in the protection of children and their mothers by giving custody evaluations that recommend treatment for abusive men. Expert testimony in juvenile proceedings can help in the development of appropriate treatment plans for children from abusive families. Having an expert from outside the court system involved, even if no testimony is used, may also help keep the attention focused on a child until the protective measures are put into place.

Therapists and experts can offer consultations to attorneys. Sometimes a written or even oral report may assist in arriving at a just settlement in a case in which testimony is not required. Some experts have learned to use psychological knowledge to help pick the best jury to decide a case. Others have formed psycholegal consultation businesses that provide a range of services to other mental health professionals and attorneys in cases in which there are needs for consultation, treatment planning, legal strategies, and so forth.

Preparing for Testimony

Knowing what information is relevant in a forensic setting becomes much like learning how to select relevant information to prepare a treatment plan. In those cases in which the testimony will deal only with general research and knowledge, the questions selected must help answer the legal questions. Usually, this type of testimony is used to educate the jury or judge by presenting data in a way that is similar to teaching a class. Here the expert augments his or her credibility by being familiar with the major research in each area. The chapters in this book should be of assistance in becoming familiar with the literature for those who have not specialized in this area. It is not unusual for attorneys on cross-examination to attempt to impeach the expert by taking material out of context. For example, the attorney may attempt to restate information that was provided on direct examination but in restating the information, the attorney changes the meaning. The therapist must listen very carefully and take her or his time in responding to avoid any misinterpretations of data. This calls for a level of precision and attention to detail that most therapists do not usually need to use when listening to a client. During treatment, it is often more important to listen to the dynamics underneath the details being discussed and then relate them to similar patterns of thinking, feeling, and acting that the client has displayed in other situations. However, in a forensic case, careful attention must be paid to both levels, and responses must be given to the question asked, not what the therapist thinks it means.

In most cases, when a client's state of mind or damages are at issue, an evaluation with appropriate assessment must be performed. Here, the differences between a forensic evaluation and one performed for treatment purposes include the need to review relevant documents in order to learn the adversary's best version of the facts as well. Use of psychological understanding of human behavior, and particularly the cognitive, affective, and behavioral responses to victimization, can be of enormous significance in most lawsuits. Learning how to use these data to support the client's position is a skill that most forensic experts must acquire before going on the witness stand. There are numerous books and articles written on the topic to help the therapist prepare (cf. Pope, Butcher, & Seelen, 1993, for a good discussion of such preparation, and Walker, 1989a, 1989b, 1990) as well as workshops that offer further training in the forensic area.

Surviving the Witness Stand

The first time that a therapist is called to give testimony in a court of law is often intimidating, particularly if the rules of evidence and procedures are not well understood. Of course, some preparation with the attorney who has called the witness is critical, whether that attorney is a state or local prosecutor, a defense attorney in criminal matters, a plaintiff attorney representing the client who is suing for damages, or a defense attorney in civil matters (usually representing an insurance company or other representative of the accused). In divorce matters in which custody of children is an issue, there is often an additional attorney appointed to represent the children's interests, usually called a *guardian ad litem*. Obviously, knowing who the players are and what they want from the therapist is important information that is needed to help frame the testimony. If the therapist is called as a hostile witness, for example, in an attempt to demonstrate that the client is not telling the truth in some area, the therapist may be treated as an extension of the client with a presumption of being hostile to the other side's interests, even though the therapist may want to be quite neutral in the presentation. In this type of situation, it is important to preserve as much of the client's confidentiality as possible so as not to spoil the therapeutic alliance. Therapists will find it helpful to discuss the information that may be elicited in testimony with the client, regardless of whether the client or the opposition requested the testimony, in order to avoid any major surprises when the client hears the therapist, while in the courtroom, give opinions on her state of mind.

The attorney who called the therapist as a witness gets to ask the questions first. Usually, this is performed by the attorney representing the woman, and this period of question and answer is called *direct examination*. The attorney should have gone over the general or specific questions to be asked so that she or he knows what responses to expect. Sometimes it is useful to help the attorney formulate questions that will elicit the information that is needed. It is during the direct examination that the therapist can give more fully developed explanations about psychology, the research, and its implications for the particular client. In a hostile examination, there may be no preparation, so it may be difficult to know where the attorney is going with the questions. In such cases, it is important to give only the information necessary to answer the question without adding any additional data. Often, depositions are taken by the opposing attorneys, and the questions are posed in a manner designed to discover what the therapist knows. These questions must also be answered in a succinct manner.

After the direct examination is completed, the opposing attorney gets to ask the questions or conduct the *cross-examination*. The purpose of this phase of testimony is to try to see if the testimony will hold up under closer scrutiny. Thus, the attorney gets to ask sometimes very detailed, picky questions to see if the therapist will change his or her response or admit to other possible interpretations of the data. Sometimes, in a hotly contested case, the questioning attorney seems to forget that it is not the therapist who is on trial. Here hostility and trick questions are used as a means of trying to manipulate the data presented by the therapist during direct testimony. Getting through a hostile cross-examination is not difficult if the therapist remembers to listen very carefully to the question being asked, to correct or refuse to answer a question if there are inaccurate facts embodied in it, and to keep calm. Getting anxious, upset, and angry with the attorney are not effective techniques; it is that attorney's job to shake the therapist's testimony if it is damaging to her or his client. Calmly restating the correct information and interpretation and presenting a confident and unflappable image will help the therapist get through these tough times.

If there is an attempt to *impeach* the therapist, in other words, an attempt to prove that the therapist has not told the truth, it is usually done by reading parts of a prepared report, reading other testimony given in a different setting (whether on this case or another one), or reading from the therapist's published or unpublished writings. In such situations, it is useful to ask to see whatever material the attorney is using for impeachment purposes and to make sure it is an accurate quotation. Often, on cross-examination, the attorney reads only a part of a sentence or paragraph, distorting the meaning of the entire quotation. It is important to point this out before answering the question and either the judge will permit the therapist to put the material back into context at that time or the opposing attorney will do so on redirect examination that follows the cross-examination.

One last survival clue for those who are new to the legal arena is to remember to be as thorough in preparation for testimony as one might be if preparing for a lecture to an introductory psychology class. Staying away from jargon and defining the terms used are helpful ways of explaining sometimes complex material to those who are not sophisticated or learned in psychology. Many people today have heard something about the different forms of abuse against women because of the wide media coverage of the issue. However, people still believe many myths that hold the victim responsible for the abuse. A good expert witness can demolish these myths and educate the jury. Be prepared to back up all statements made. The experience can be exciting, even fun, and helpful to both the client and the general public, who are represented in most courtrooms, too.

HOW LEGAL CONCERNS CAN AFFECT THERAPY

Client Awareness

Clients need to be aware of the degree to which forensic processes may affect their therapy. The client should know what could be disclosed to adversarial attorneys or become a matter of public record. This is information that a client has a right to consider while deciding whether to begin psychotherapy or what to disclose to a therapist. Clients who are unaware of these possibilities, who disclose extremely personal and sensitive material (memories, thoughts, fantasies, dreams, family secrets, etc.), and who suddenly find that their therapist is providing testimony in a public forum about this material may experience a profound sense of having been tricked or betrayed. Damaging in itself, such an experience may also prevent the client from seeking mental health services of any sort in the future.

Depending on individual state law and on the circumstances of the case, clinicians may be required or permitted to take action (e.g., file a report) that will breach confidentiality and bring the therapist and the client into a forensic or similar arena. Therapists may be required, on hearing from a woman that her husband batters her and her young children, to file a formal report with social services. Therapists may be required or authorized to breach confidentiality if they determine that their client is at risk for serious harm or is a danger to others. A therapist may be required to testify in order to have the client involuntarily hospitalized.

Therapists must remain aware of the current laws that are applicable in their geographic area and practice locale (e.g., a clinician working in a treatment facility run by the U. S. government may be subject to specific federal laws that may differ from the laws of the state), and must clearly distinguish between instances in which breaches of confidentiality are mandatory and those in which they are left to the professional judgment of the therapist. As stated previously, this information should not be withheld from clients who stand to be affected by it.

Therapists may be required to communicate relevant information concerning court actions to abused clients. In California, for example, the state umbrella agency for the various licensing boards supervised the development of a booklet (California Department of Consumer Affairs, 1990) to inform consumers about the phenomenon of therapist–patient sexual intimacy. Part of this booklet outlines steps that a client can take in order to file formal complaints (e.g., licensing, criminal, civil, and ethics) against a perpetrator. The booklet provides the addresses and phone numbers of the licensing boards, information about how to find an attorney for a malpractice suit, how to file a criminal complaint, and so on. The booklets have been distributed to all licensed therapists in California, who are legally required to provide a copy of the booklet to any client who indicates that he or she was sexually intimate with a prior therapist.

In Colorado, as in some other states, a therapist who engages in sex with a client commits a criminal act that can be punished by fines or jail. The regulatory department formulated a controversial rule requiring any other psychologist who learns of such behavior to report it to the grievance board. Many psychologists were concerned about client confidentiality, and, after consultation, the department changed the rule to require the client's permission to be obtained before a report is made. In California, as of January 1994, therapists are required to report spouse abuse to the local law enforcement agency. Therapists bear an important responsibility to remain aware of the current and emerging laws, rules, and regulations that affect confidentiality and privilege. They must be able to explain them clearly to their clients as part of the process of informed consent.

In some cases, the second treating therapist has been unwillingly dragged into a case by being blamed by the first treating therapist for any current observable damages to the client that were attributed to the first therapist in a legal action. For example, in one such sexual exploitation case, the client's damages were said to have occurred because the new therapist made a "big deal" out of the sexual behavior of the first therapist. Interestingly, the attorneys for the liability insurance company, which covered both therapists, would not pay for the defense of the second therapist because she was not a named party to the lawsuit. Putting pressure on therapists not to expose professional misconduct is a tactic used frequently by attorneys in the battle of the forensic experts.

Conflicts of Interest

The sometimes inevitable forensic aspects of work with victims of abuse can create complications for the therapist and for the therapeutic venture. Therapeutic tasks can become confused, agendas blurred, and therapists can feel themselves pulled in many directions. It is important that the therapist remain aware of the need to maintain clear tasks, roles, and boundaries.

It is the abuse victim who is the client, and the professional responsibility must be to her. The abuse victim's needs must come first. This basic principle is simple, but it can be exceptionally easy to forget in the adversarial atmosphere of the courtroom. Her attorney's primary agenda may be to prevail in a legal action, and the subtle pressures springing from the attorney's understandable desire for the therapist's participation in the legal process may become uncomfortable. Sometimes it is important to treat the attorney as a secondary client, especially during complex cases. Explaining the client's behavior as it relates to the abuse issues may be useful in resolving differences that may arise. For many abuse victims, trust is still a basic issue, and it is important to help the client and the attorney to understand each other.

Confusion can occur when a third party is paying the bills. If a victim assistance program is paying the therapy expenses for an abuse victim, the program administrators may attempt to place certain demands on the therapist that, if not attended to, may threaten the effectiveness of the therapist and therapy. An insurance policy may be held in the name of a battered woman's husband, but the woman may not be able to gain access to it without informing her husband that she has sought treatment. If informing the husband about the treatment is a problem, the therapist will have to discuss whether to contact the insurance company to find out if the client can obtain the benefits without her husband's knowledge.

In offering deposition or courtroom testimony, the therapist may experience competing claims or conflicts of interest. The therapist may be extremely reluctant to disclose any information that in any way might damage the client's clinical status, the therapy itself, or the client's case. However, when providing testimony, it is the therapist's primary responsibility to tell the truth. The therapist must discuss with the client what information may be disclosed in order to maintain the trust in the therapy relationship.

Consulting with disinterested colleagues can be enormously helpful in keeping priorities and responsibilities straight. Therapists confronting seemingly unresolvable pressures involving divided and competing loyalties may find it useful to read *Who Is the Client?* (Monahan, 1980). Therapists who believe that they are confronting a situation in which carrying out legally mandated responsibilities would result in unconscionable harm to their client may find it useful to read "When Laws and Values Conflict" (Pope & Bajt, 1988).

Records and Documentation

Documentation may play a key role in forensic actions involving abused female clients. It is crucial that secondary harm should not come to victims of abuse because the therapist has failed to provide sufficient documentation of the treatment.

The American Psychological Association has been studying ways to standardize the documentation in records, but finds that those with different theoretical orientations and styles cannot come to a common agreement easily. However, the current standard is to document each client session with a record of the time spent, who was present, and the charges. It is usually customary to have a sentence or two about the process or content of the session, although some prefer summaries at various intervals. Sometimes there are handwritten notes made of phrases or even just words said during the session to help the therapist remember the content. These notes are usually considered to be the therapist's work product, and, once such notes are made, they should not become part of the file because no one else could be expected to have the ability to decipher them.

The file should contain written notes of the assessment and history, differential diagnoses considered and made, the treatment plan (updated as needed), and some measurement of the client's progress. This material is usually considered to be the minimum necessary to meet community standards if records become part of a legal action. In abuse cases in which the therapist is a witness to injuries or hears about the abuse from the client, this information should be recorded as close to verbatim as possible and placed in the file. It may be the only way for the client to introduce such evidence in a court of law due to the hearsay rule and other rules of evidence that sometimes bar such material.

Fees

The sources of payment for work with a particular client, or participation in forensic activities, can become a pivotal focus of court cases. Under no circumstances should an apparent conflict of interest be created. Therapists who testify in court must avoid any arrangement in which it appears that the therapist is tailoring the content of the testimony in exchange for financial (or other) incentives. Standard textbooks in forensic psychology (e.g., Blau, 1984; D. L. Shapiro, 1990) contain explicit prohibitions against a forensic psychologist agreeing to participate for a contingency fee.

This is a controversial area, particularly when a woman may not have the financial resources to take a civil case to trial. In some communities, large law firms may be able to advance the fees for experts, but that usually occurs only when they believe strongly in a particular case. In smaller communities, or if the case does not seem likely to have the same odds of winning, it may be difficult to find an attorney who can advance the costs. Rarely will attorneys advance the money for therapy. Then, unless the therapist is willing to wait for fees, he or she should realize that if the client loses the case the fees may never be forthcoming, and there may not even be a lawsuit. Careful decisions must be made and carefully drawn boundaries must be set if there is to be any deviation from the standard cited above.

Provisions for Other Clients

If a therapist agrees to appear in court (or in some other quasijudicial setting) to offer testimony regarding an abused client, there are at least two major ways in which other clients may be affected. First, it may be difficult to know exactly when the testimony will be required or how long it will take to complete. Although there may be some advance notice regarding the scheduling of the case and when the attorney expects the therapist's testimony to proceed, numerous factors can interfere with this scheduling. Courtroom availability, continuances, delays while certain issues are appealed or otherwise adjudicated, an unexpectedly brief or drawn-out process of jury selection, or the failure to call (or unexpectedly long or short testimony of) witnesses who are scheduled to testify before the therapist, all of these are among the almost countless factors that can cause unavoidable changes in the therapist's schedule.

Such last-minute changes can affect other clients who have set aside time for appointments and who receive little advance notice that their session must be rescheduled. Some clients may be in crisis and may need to be seen by someone else on those days. For some clients, rescheduling is a considerable hardship. Still others may be extremely sensitive to any alteration in the schedule of therapy and may experience feelings of abandonment, depression, anger, or confusion, especially if the therapist is frequently involved in court proceedings, and this has not been discussed prior to beginning treatment.

The therapist is responsible for ensuring that the changes in scheduling of appointments and the interruptions of his or her availability to handle crises do not unduly interfere with the therapeutic process or place clients who are in crisis at risk. Careful planning and attention to the changing needs of each client are essential. Further discussion can be found in L. S. Brown and Walker (1990).

When therapists testify in court, the testimony becomes a matter of public record. In certain high visibility cases, an account of the therapist's testimony may be carried in the public media. The clients of the therapist who testifies in court may read or see (e.g., in the courtroom or via television) the therapist testify about one of his or her patients. It is easy to imagine the ways in which patients might be affected by such an occurrence. Other clients who have experienced abuse may have particularly intense reactions. Therapists who testify in such cases must give adequate thought to how their other clients may be affected and to how they might respond to questions or concerns raised by those patients. In any discussions that may occur with the other clients, the therapist must maintain appropriate confidentiality regarding his or her work with the patient about whom testimony was given. L. S. Brown and Walker (1990) discussed these issues in the context of their own practices and suggested ways to handle the inevitable questions that arise when the therapist is a popular media figure.

SPECIFIC FORENSIC ISSUES

Rape

If a rapist is caught and charged with an assault, it often takes a year or more for him to come to trial. Defense attorneys understand that the longer they postpone the trial, the more likely the rape victim will heal and forget the details of the assault. Therapists can preserve the victim's early memories by taking careful notes when she describes what happened. Because the perpetrator may perceive the situation differently than the victim does, such documentation is helpful, especially when the woman is afraid of retaliation or of testifying. Support from the therapist can remind her of the progress that she has made in her recovery. For some victims, the presence of their therapist at particularly stressful court hearings may help them to be better witnesses. Just acting as a stable figure and supplying supportive information may be the best role for the therapist to take. In any case, the therapist must be willing to discuss the stress resulting from the legal proceedings and to share optimism or pessimism whenever appropriate,

Other legal proceedings initiated by the victim may also have an impact on her treatment. Some women decide to sue their perpetrator or a third party who failed to protect them from the sexual assault. A typical scenario is one in which a woman is raped in a motel room by a stranger who entered by way of an open window with a faulty screen. The woman then decides to sue the motel. In another possible scenario, a woman visiting a company is sexually assaulted by an employee about whom the company has received several complaints of sexual harassment. The woman decides to sue the company. Other situations that illustrate the failure to take reasonable precautions to protect may also warrant the filing of a civil lawsuit claiming damages.

Many attorneys will take these civil personal injury legal actions on contingency, sometimes paying expenses in the hope that they will share the financial benefits should the victim/plaintiff win the lawsuit. To make their risks more manageable, however, attorneys may send a client to a psychologist to determine if there was indeed a sexual assault that caused serious psychological damage to the client. In other cases, clients who are seeing a therapist need to be reminded that they have the right to file such lawsuits and may want to preserve the right to sue by taking action within the specified time limits. Often these time limits are extended because of the inability of a client to take action as a result of psychological disability that was caused by the traumatic incident. However, as stated earlier, the client must check with a qualified attorney.

Rape victims who file civil lawsuits often experience serious psychological distress as a result of the defense attorneys' aggressive pursuit of information about their life affairs. Sometimes nothing seems private anymore, especially after particularly grueling depositions. The therapist should let the client know that the deposition is often the place in which she has the least amount of protection; attorneys who are harsh during that procedure would never behave that way in front of a jury should the case go to trial. Other high stress times occur when there is pressure to accept settlement offers that do not appear to be beneficial to the client or even to the attorney. Therapists must have some knowledge of these legal actions in order to assist the client. Often the therapist becomes the client's interpreter in relation to the attorney, resolving little differences that become magnified because of the situation and the lack of trust that results from the damage caused by the sexual abuse.

Battering

Most battered women will have contact with the legal system regarding whether to obtain a divorce, in response to the batterer's arrest, or for other civil or criminal matters. However, in regard to issues faced specifically by battered women, it is worth noting here that battered women frequently do not receive justice in the courts (Schafran, 1990; Walker, 1989a, 1989b). This is particularly true in divorce proceedings involving property settlements and child custody or visitation issues (discussed further in chapter 12 on integrating assessment data). More battered women are filing civil personal injury lawsuits against their abusive partners, particularly when their divorce settlements were unjust. Even if they do not receive large financial rewards, this can be a therapeutic action despite the emotional stress involved in depositions and courtroom testimony. Sometimes the women ask the court to set aside a prenuptial agreement or other contract, stating that it was signed under duress.

Criminal proceedings, such as assault charges against the abuser, can also cause intense stress from fear but tend to help the woman to remain safe, especially when there is a mandatory treatment program for the abusive man. It may be useful for the woman's therapist to provide information to the abuser's therapist, if the woman is willing to give her informed consent for the disclosure of certain information. Often batterers minimize and distort their abusive behavior to such an extent that it is difficult to believe that the two therapists are treating members of the same couple. Batterers who are willing to admit to their abusive acts can usually provide a good description of what led them to commit violence, but the battered woman is usually better at describing the details of the batterer's behavior. Therapists who accept as valid the batterer's complaints, justifying his abuse without holding the man completely responsible for his use of violence, may reinforce the cycle of violence. Criminal proceedings may be filed against the battered woman for assaulting or killing her abuser in self-defense or for committing other criminal acts out of fear of further beatings. Again, the therapist's contact with the court may be therapeutic if it assists the client in trying to receive justice and attempts to help the batterer to take responsibility for stopping his violent behavior.

In some jurisdictions, the prosecutors or judges may be upset with women who refuse to testify as witnesses against the men who have beaten them. They also rarely understand how frightened the woman becomes when the legal process proceeds without her input. Most battered women will do anything to calm down the batterer, including giving in to his demands to try to stop the criminal case against him. If the prosecutor will not drop the charges, and in many places there are new laws that no longer permit the woman to be the one to make such a decision, and insists on going to trial, the woman may begin to minimize the violence, become frightened, and stop talking to the prosecutor. She may go back to living with the man, who then moves into the third phase of the cycle of abuse, loving-contrition behavior (see chapter 3); she may succumb to his threats to harm her further if she dares to expose him. Those in the system who are charged with protecting the battered woman miss the point when they become angry and punitive toward her. Leaving the relationship does not necessarily keep her safe; in fact, the battered woman is at the greatest danger for homicide or more severe abuse at the time of separation. Men who batter are known to stalk and follow their victims, sometimes for 2 or more years after the women leave (Browne & Williams, 1989). Newer tools for the courts to use include high technology equipment such as an electronic monitoring device worn on the abuser's ankle that communicates with a device that is installed in the woman's home that, in turn, signals an alarm in a monitoring center that notifies law enforcement officials, who respond to the call by dispatching the police and then provide the court with a hard copy indicating violations of the court order. (This device is marketed by JurisMonitor, Inc., in Boulder, Colorado.)

Battered women may also end up in family or juvenile court on abuse, neglect, or failure-to-protect charges when they or the abuser are harming the child. Sometimes adolescent children get in trouble with the law, and their parents are required to go to juvenile court to demonstrate whether they have control over the child. In some cases, the therapist learns of the possible abuse of a child and must make a report to social services, which, if the report is verified, will pursue the matter in juvenile court. Juvenile court is supposed to be rehabilitative, rather than punishment oriented; however, that is not always the case. Although a battered woman may be lucky to escape within an inch of her life during severe beatings, the fact that she stays with the abuser may be seen as proof of her being an unfit mother. This alienation of the mother, without offering her help, support, and protection from the abuser, makes it difficult for the child and for the woman to get help. Sometimes intervention in the system by a professional who advocates for the mother can make a difference in obtaining services for the family.

Records must be kept as though they will not remain confidential, given the frequency with which a battered woman may be involved in court action. This means that only verifiable information should be put in a record; speculation is not appropriate, especially if it impugns the woman's claims of abuse without substantiation. A treatment plan should be formulated with the client after the initial visit and updated periodically as the need arises.

Child Abuse

Child abuse reporting law is one of the most difficult areas with which mental health professionals must comply. Although many therapists who work with adult survivors of child sexual abuse may never have to report a child abuse case, it is helpful to know the process (see Kalichman, 1993, for further information). Most state child abuse reporting laws make it mandatory for the professional to report a "reasonable suspicion" of child abuse. In most states, failure to comply with the law is grounds for action against the mental health professional; sometimes the actions take the form of criminal sanctions, and in some states failure to comply could result in loss of one's license to practice. Many state laws are vague in defining "reasonable suspicion" of child abuse, leaving it up to the individual mental health practitioner. The American Psychological Association and state psychological associations have been active in providing training and guidelines for psychologists who are struggling with the abuse reporting laws.

Psychologists who were interviewed by the American Psychological Association's Board of Directors' Ad Hoc Committee on Child Abuse Policy and Committee on Professional Standards in 1989 claimed that if they failed to report it was usually because they did not believe the child protective system would be helpful, and they perceived that making such a report would be bad for the therapeutic relationship. Sometimes reporting angers the client, who perceives it as a rejection, and the therapy relationship is spoiled. Because of the overloading and undertraining of the typical child protection worker, reporting does not always help the situation. Some psychologists who had made a report said they would do it again because of the assistance they received in dealing with providing for the safety of the child. Psychologists who had failed to report in questionable cases said that they would try to use the system in other, similar cases. Testimony presented at the American Psychological Association Ad Hoc Committee on Child Abuse Policy hearings indicated that those psychologists who were trained as child advocates were more likely to make reports, whereas those who were trained in family systems theory and individual analytic psychotherapy were less likely to do so (American Psychological Association Ad Hoc Committee on Child Abuse Policy, 1989). Many states are refusing to grant or renew the licenses of psychologists and other health professionals unless they complete a continuing education course dealing with the mandatory reporting of child abuse.

A woman who suffered incest as a child at the hands of her father often refuses to leave her children alone with him. However, does the therapist have an obligation to report suspicion of potential child abuse when it is not known if the grandfather could be molesting neighborhood children or other family members? What if the client is under such terrible stress as she processes her incest experiences that she is not always able to protect her child from possible incest perpetrators? These are questions that must be answered carefully depending on the child abuse laws of the state as well as on the community standard. Some states require mandatory reporting of past as well as current child abuse, whereas others are only interested in ongoing, not potential, abuse.

Most courts are reluctant to stop visitation between an offending father and his children. Most will limit the visitation rights to supervised visitation only on a strong recommendation from the child's therapist. Few therapists want to put themselves on the line by making a recommendation that would leave the child and mother unprotected. For many children, the continued contact with the incest father leaves them scared, vulnerable, and confused. They perceive that they must continue to protect themselves and to retain the coping skills that they learned prior to disclosure; so do their mothers, particularly those who begin to reexperience their own victimization. Conte and Berliner (1988) found that reporting to the legal system delays the healing process for many children; this is not surprising after analyzing the court's response.

There is a common trend toward filing personal injury lawsuits against the incest perpetrator when an incest victim remembers the abuse and recognizes how much harm it has caused her. Although these cases often take several years to pursue and can cause the woman great emotional distress during that time, especially as depositions and other legal proceedings occur from time to time, the woman often has a successful therapeutic outcome whether or not she is awarded damages.

Sexual Harassment and Discrimination

Many women who have experienced sexual harassment file complaints with federal or state civil courts or the U.S. Equal Employment Opportunity Commission (EEOC), the federal agency with regulatory powers. Most of the time the EEOC complaint must be filed and resolved before entering the civil court system. These lawsuits are usually brought in federal court under the 1983 Civil Rights Act (amended in 1991), although sometimes they are brought to a state court if the setting in which the harassment occurred has a city or state charter. The rules for bringing a civil rights lawsuit are complex and require attorneys with special knowledge and skills.

More attorneys are gaining such expertise because the 1991 revisions to the Civil Rights Act permit a maximum of $300,000 in compensatory and punitive damages, which is the part of a claim that earns attorneys as much as 40% of the award as their fees on contingency. Another change that occurred in 1991 involved the ability to choose a jury trial in federal court. Previously, the judge made the determination, and there were no compensatory or punitive damages; only actual damages relating to lost earnings were compensated. Former president Bush signed the new law, which he had threatened to veto because of these new provisions, after the Clarence Thomas confirmation hearings. The penalties against universities and companies often require stiff fines, punitive damages awarded to the complainant, reinstatement in her job, or all three. The cumbersome process can take years and frequently requires the woman to submit to one or more psychological examinations.

Because the defense against a woman's charges of sexual harassment is often an attack on her personality or mental health, it is necessary to sort out what part of the psychological damage that is currently observable was brought on by the experience of sexual harassment, and what part came from earlier or other current life experiences. Without an understanding of the effects of posttraumatic stress disorder (PTSD), such a determination is more difficult to make. If there is impact from other traumas in other subcategories of PTSD, which is common in multiple abuse victims, it is important to separate these as much as possible. In civil lawsuits, however, the general rule is that any magnification of past problems is the defense's responsibility. So, if a university professor or an employer knew (or should have known) that a woman had been an incest victim (or just knew she had a difficult personality), and he sexually harassed or exploited her anyway, he still can be held liable for any worsening of her past condition that was caused by his behavior as well as any part of her current condition that was caused directly by his behavior.

The therapist should be able to help the woman decide whether her attorney is working in her best interests, because most harassment victims do not trust anyone enough to make such judgments objectively. Thus, the therapist must become educated about the steps that should be taken in these cases and the adequacy and timeliness of the attorney's actions. It is not uncommon for attorneys to attempt to make decisions for clients and then to become angry with them when the clients do not want to follow their plans. Because the issue of harassment is always about power and feelings of powerlessness, some attorneys must be educated regarding the best way to gain the cooperation of the client; the attorney should help her to assume whatever role she can handle in the course of her case. The therapist may be able to assist the woman and her attorney in reaching a good working relationship in this manner. Other times, the therapist may provide the objectivity that the woman needs in order to determine whether the attorney is really working in her own best interests or whether he or she is allowing self-interest to interfere with decisions.

The American Psychological Association has entered amicus briefs, or friend of the court briefs, in several important sexual harassment and discrimination cases that have been decided by the U.S. Supreme Court. One of the most recent ones was filed against Price-Waterhouse by an employee, Ann Hopkins, who claimed that she was denied a promotion to partner status because of a pattern of sex discrimination against women. Evidence of what constitutes such discrimination and its negative impact on a woman's competence and mental health was presented by social psychologist Susan Fiske. Price-Waterhouse countered with evidence that the woman acted "unwomanly" by being loud and using sexually offensive language and that she needed to go to "a charm school." The woman countered by demonstrating that her behavior was no different than that of the male partners and by showing the large amount of business she had brought into the company, far more than most other partners, and claimed that the company was holding her to unrealistic standards that were gender-biased. The court ruled in the woman's favor, setting a new standard that places the burden of proof on the company to demonstrate that a different standard for men and women is necessary in order to conduct business. The psychological research presented in this case and in the American Psychological Association amicus brief is quite useful for other psychologists who are asked to testify as expert witnesses (information on the amicus brief for this case is available from the American Psychological Association Office of Legal Affairs, Washington, DC).

Several other federal court cases are also important to the understanding of forensic standards that are used in the courts. A 1991 decision by a Florida federal trial court, in *Robinson v. Jacksonville Shipyards,* excluded pin-ups and other offensive pictures from the workplace by finding them to be pornographic materials that contribute to a "hostile work environment." In the opinion, the court wrote, "A pre-existing atmosphere that deters women from entering or continuing in a profession or job is no less destructive to and offensive to workplace equality than a sign declaring, 'men only.'" The court also found that sexual harassment included sexually explicit remarks as well as the various types of pin-up pictures. A supervisor had told complaining women that men had a "constitutional right" to post the pictures. Again, in this case, expert witness testimony on the dangers of sexual stereotyping was found to be helpful to the court. No testimony was provided on actual psychological damages to the woman, but such testimony is now more common. The court did order the company to remedy the situation by adopting a sexual harassment policy that was written by the plaintiff's attorney, National Organization for Women Legal Defense and Education Fund and by paying the woman's legal fees. At the time that the lawsuit was filed, compensatory and punitive damages were not available as a remedy; today, one can only anticipate that with such a strongly worded decision monetary awards would also be part of the legally ordered remedies.

Another 1991 legal decision expands the definition of the reasonable person standard to include the expected psychological response of the *reasonable woman* victim of sexual harassment. Given the history of the law, a "reasonable person" usually refers to a reasonable man, rather than to men and women. In cases in which gender responses are different (most women will behave and respond differently than men in certain situations), such as in abuse cases, the "reasonable woman" standard is a more appropriate measure. In *Ellison v. Brady*, the 9th U.S. Circuit Court of Appeals in San Francisco made a ruling suggesting that the woman who was sexually harassed must be consulted when a company attempts to remedy a sexual harassment situation. In this case, the Internal Revenue Service transferred an employee who was accused of sexual harassment to a different facility for 4 months, then brought him back to the original job site where the woman still worked. Eventually, they transferred the woman to another facility at her request. Although the EEOC ruled that this was sufficient remedy for the company to have taken, the court ruled that in some cases the mere presence of an employee who has harassed a co-worker may create a hostile work environment, and therefore the only reasonable recourse is to discharge the harasser. In this decision the court used strong language to mandate preventive steps that take into account the victim's perspective, and defined the differences between men's and women's perspectives, setting the new reasonable woman standard. Still undefined is whether there can be accommodation for the "reasonable abused woman" within a different standard than the nonabused woman. Given the large number of abuse victims, it may be that the effects of prior abuse are encompassed in the court's definition of the new "reasonable woman" standard.

In 1992, the U.S. Supreme Court decided not to review an Ohio case in which Lucille Kauffman sued Allied Signal for sexual harassment. Kauffman worked as a machine operator at Allied Signal's Autolite Division plant in Fostoria, Ohio. When she returned from medical leave in 1988 after undergoing breast enlargement surgery, her supervisor, Donald R. Butts, began to touch her breasts, demanding to see them. When she complained to Allied's management, they fired Butts the next day. Kauffman still sued Allied for failing to prevent the harassment. The court ruled that Allied had a sexual harassment policy in effect at the time this occurred and that termination of Butts was within the policy, and, therefore, they did not have the duty to further ward off sexual harassment in this case. This decision should be interpreted as encouraging companies to develop and enforce such policies rather than as a setback to protection for women. Obviously, a company that adopts a policy, however clear and reasonable, without training its employees or being prepared for vigorous enforcement, may still be found liable for the damages it causes to women. In the 1993 case of *Harris v. Forklift*, the U.S. Supreme Court reiterated its previous stance that sexual harassment per se is an abridgement of women's rights and that a woman does not have to prove that the harassment directly caused her any psychological difficulties. Instead, she must prove only that the sexual harassment occurred. It is assumed, therefore, that such harassment can cause damage to a reasonable woman.

Even when women ultimately win their lawsuits, the long and difficult process of proving their claims takes its toll on their mental health and self-confidence. If they lose, they may face a legal action from the accused in addition to whatever psychological ramifications occur as a result of not being believed. Many women must change their careers, just as many rape victims must ultimately change their locations and many battered women must terminate their relationships, in order to feel safe and fully functional again. Those who receive worker's compensation or unemployment benefits while involved with the litigation often do better than those who are denied such assistance. With each step of the way there are new decisions for the woman to make, especially because the victim cannot seek compensation for damages under the civil rights law until the EEOC complaint is resolved or a *right-to-sue* letter is issued as a release. This may prolong the process, sometimes stretching it out over 10 years or more. It will be important to see if the streamlined process (which does not require an attorney's assistance) under the new Americans with Disabilities Act can be applied to other gender discrimination cases.

SUMMARY

Whether they like it or not, therapists treating abused women will probably have occasional encounters with the legal system. Therapists must understand that the courtroom uses an adversarial method for determining the truth. They should also keep abreast of developments in state, federal, and civil law. Various legal situations that may arise include responding to subpoenas, deciding how to comply with the court's demands for information while protecting the confidentiality of clients, or serving as an expert or a percipient witness.

The possibility of appearing in court also changes therapists' day-to-day dealings with their clients. Records must be timely and accurate in case they are used in court. Clients must be informed about laws that require the therapist to give certain information to legal authorities, for example, laws requiring disclosure of ongoing child abuse. Therapy schedules are sometimes disrupted because of court appearances by the therapists.

Certain forensic issues are particular to specific types of abuse. Therapists who take precise notes, carefully sorting facts from opinions, can help rape victims keep their memories fresh in order to testify against their assailants. Testimony about the psychological effects of battering on a woman could enable her to regain custody of her children or bolster any plea of self-defense. The therapist's recommendations could influence visitation rights in child sexual abuse cases. In cases of sexual discrimination or harassment, the therapist can provide information about the extent of the psychological distress that the victim has suffered.

PART THREE

Assessment, Crisis Intervention, and Survivor Therapy

10

What Is Survivor
Therapy?

S urvivor therapy is a treatment approach that is designed to help heal
victims of mostly man-made traumas. It is based on the treatment
approaches of both feminist therapy theory and trauma theory, integrating
the consistent philosophies and borrowing techniques from each. Although
recently named, the treatment approach of survivor therapy has been used
successfully for the past decade by clinicians working with women and children who are victims or survivors of men's violence. Men who have experienced violence have also been helped by this approach, although there is a
smaller clinical group on which to make such evaluations. On the basis of
an analysis of power, survivor therapy treats victims of violence by focusing
on their strengths, despite their injuries. It takes into account the gender-
based impact of trauma within the woman's sociopolitical, cultural, and
economic context, emphasizing respect and empathy for all women who
have been abused. Survivor therapy explores the coping strategies that the
victims have adopted and helps them build on them in new ways, so they
can become survivors. There is an attempt to integrate the current trauma
response into the woman's historical, psychological, sociopolitical, cultural,
physiological, biological, and situational context by dealing directly with
changes in affect, cognition, and behavior. Resolution of therapy occurs

when the victim feels reempowered, resolves many of the now unnecessary coping symptoms, becomes a survivor, and gets on with her life.

A case history of Kim, a battered woman who had an abusive childhood, is presented in the first section. Then, the roots of survivor therapy are explored and its key principles and goals are explained. Finally, the case history is used to illustrate how survivor therapy works.

KIM, A CASE HISTORY[11]

The caller spoke rapidly, breathlessly. She cried, sobbed, and sighed between her words. Dramatically, she said that she was a battered woman and that her "famous" husband Peter, with whom she had lived for 20 years, had just slapped her across her face so hard that her eardrum was injured. She had gone to see her doctor, who told her that she was a battered woman and suggested that she see a lawyer. The lawyer told Kim that she should not think about filing for a divorce until she had some therapy, preferably provided by someone who understood the effects of abuse on women. So, despite her crisis state, she made one more phone call for help. She seemed to feel that it was hopeless that anyone would even listen to her.

When asked if she was safe now, she started crying all over again but gave assurance of her temporary safety. She was in the couple's vacation home, and her husband never went there on his own. This home had become her safe haven whenever Peter's verbal, psychological, or physical abuse became too much for her. She said that she did not want to return to their home in the city for a few more days, so an appointment was scheduled for the time that she expected to return.

Kim arrived at the office late for her appointment and with an air of turmoil and chaos surrounding her. She had lots of papers in her hands, none of which she could fully explain, and began speaking in a rapid, rambling manner. An attractive, petite woman in her mid-40s, small-boned and with dark hair that partially hid her face and eyes, she displayed an intensity that fit the image of an artistic, creative woman.

As is common for many battered women, Kim spent most of the time

---

[11]All of the names and pertinent facts mentioned in this case history have been changed.

describing the mean and cruel behavior of her husband, who was a well-known figure in the couple's community. More than 15 years older than she, Peter, despite his own wealth and earnings, had lived off of Kim's earnings, which had been considerable until several years ago, when the economy crashed and her creative skills as an artist were no longer in demand. Even when she tried to change the focus of her business, she was unable to concentrate for long because of Peter's increasingly abusive behavior. Although Kim's lawyers later determined that Peter had at least $2 million in assets, $1 million to which he admitted, the less money Kim earned, the more Peter abused her. By the time she came to see Dr. Hobbes, a prominent therapist who specialized in working with victims of abuse, she was barely working at all. Peter was refusing to support her, although he bought the groceries and doled out money, one $20 bill at a time, when she begged and was "good." Later, she was able to understand that her business, which she inherited from her father at his death, was tainted by memories of her own father's abuse toward her. Kim knew that Peter had taken a lot of money from his first wife, Ellen, and her family, and refused to adequately support her or their four children, but she did not understand the similarities of their situations until, during her first year of therapy, she and Ellen became friends.

During the initial interview, it was clear that Kim had many strengths despite the obvious damage she had suffered from years of abuse. She had previously spent 9 years in psychotherapy, mostly with a local psychiatrist who treated her for high anxiety and depression. After diagnosing Kim as having borderline personality disorder, he concentrated on the "dysfunctional" relationship between herself and Peter and on her childhood with abusive parents. In fact, the therapist asked Peter to come in for a few sessions, which he did, and he admitted to some of his abusive behavior. However, the therapist, Kim, and Peter all failed to attribute the abuse to Peter's cruelty. Part of the blame for their troubled marriage was placed on Kim's hysterical flair for drama. When she fought back, which had become a necessary coping strategy for her even though she was hurt worse at such times, she won the label of provocateur, the masochist, and the one who obviously liked the "folie à deux." Many therapy hours were spent teaching Kim how to be a better wife, all to no avail.

Even a marriage therapist to whom the previous psychiatrist referred the couple said that they seemed to "deserve each other." After several sessions, the marriage therapist finally confronted Peter with his cruel behavior, which included making appointments with Kim and not showing up, leaving her stranded on planned vacations out of the country, and constantly telling her how stupid she was, even one time before they went to a reception for dignitaries. Peter decided he would no longer participate in therapy. He believed his role was to help his wife to stop being crazy, and he did not want to examine his own behavior. Without a system for change, the marital therapist had nothing more to offer Kim. It took over 1 year of escalating abusive behavior before Kim made the telephone call to the new therapist.

Indeed, the behavior Kim described of herself could be labeled as crazy and provocative if there was no understanding of the dynamics of a battering relationship. A typical fight would begin with several days or weeks of Peter saying that he would be home at a certain time for dinner and then not showing up. Kim would call to check on him, with each call becoming more frantic, until he finally agreed to come home. When he made it home, he would criticize her for the overcooked dinner, and she would shriek and yell in response.

These fights would escalate a little more each day, with Peter fueling them by subtly "pushing her anger buttons" and then stepping back and ignoring her while she ranted and raved at him and threw and broke objects. He would calmly state that he was leaving, pack a few clothes, and attempt to go to an apartment that he kept for his own personal use. Kim would chase after him, terrified of being left alone while in such a highly agitated state. He would use this as an excuse to grab her neck, choke her, and slam her against the wall or throw her down the basement stairs. Sometimes he would agree to stay at home while continuing to punish her, but more often, he would try to leave by physically hurting her so that she could not follow. Some of the most serious abuse, for which she needed medical attention, occurred when Peter would drive off with Kim hanging onto the car. Kim was often so grateful when he did not abandon her that she quickly forgave him, and then Peter would engage in intense, sexual lovemaking, which he would otherwise avoid, as a way to end the battering incident. After some particularly dangerous fights, he would give her whatever she wanted, treat her more kindly, or occasionally even bring her a nice present. But he never gave up his downtown apartment, nor would he communicate with her, for example, by letting her know where he was or what he was doing at any particular time.

Kim's aggressive behavior was not typical of most battered women who fight back, but she had reached a point at which she could not stop herself once she started getting agitated and angry. She was even willing to die to protect herself psychologically. She had made several suicide attempts before entering therapy with Dr. Hobbes, two of which consisted of serious overdoses of medication. There were other incidents that could have been dangerous. Once, when Peter left town without telling her where he was going, she called his office to find out where he was going and showed up at his hotel room where she found that he was with another woman (with whom he claimed to have a business relationship). Another time, during the second year of therapy with Dr. Hobbes, she followed him to the local athletic club, and an the attendant led her to a scene in which she found Peter and another man in a seductive position. She was never able to engage in sex with him again after this last discovery. Even though Peter denied being homosexual, Kim recalled lots of little incidents that suggested that he had been engaging in other relationships with men and women for years. Her refusal to have sex with him could be attributed to her learning to take better care of herself as well as to her anger toward him. Once the sexual bond between them was broken, Peter was less able to control her.

During therapy she recalled another incident. A short time after Peter and Kim started to date, he told her that he was going to a business meeting. She followed him and found him in another woman's house engaged in sexual intercourse. This incident laid the foundation for her distrust, although Peter gave her many other reasons with his constant lies and betrayal. It was common for her to follow him to his apartment in the middle of the night and yell at him from outside when he would not open the door to let her in. She knew he became more angry with her for this surveillance, and she often had a difficult emotional time with what she found, but said that it was more tolerable for her to know what was going on than to live with her suspicions and fears. She became a fairly adept sleuth, and she used her detective abilities to assist her attorney as well as to provide confirmation of her fears.

In her third year of treatment with Dr. Hobbes, Kim began to have breakthrough memories of sexual abuse from her father, in addition to the childhood physical and psychological abuse that she had worked on with her previous therapist. The incest memories began to surface during a brief, unsatisfactory relationship with an older man. Like many women from middle class backgrounds, Kim suffered abuse that was so well-disguised that it was difficult for her or her childhood friends to recognize it as abuse. The ability to engage in obvious self-destructive behavior is frequently seen in incest survivors who are also battered women.

Kim also described Peter's psychological abuse toward her two children, who often witnessed their fights. At the time she entered treatment, her son had just moved back home to await acceptance to graduate school. Her daughter was in her third year of college and lived about a half hour from Kim's home. These children were Kim's from a previous marriage but lived with Kim and Peter from the time they were very young. Kim used her children as support people, sometimes to the detriment of their needs, but mostly in an appropriate manner. Although her children agreed with the prevailing opinion that Kim was temperamental and crazy, they loved their mother and their allegiances were clearly with her, not with Peter. After Peter left the couple's home, her son stayed at home longer than he had planned in order to assist his mother in remaining safe during this period. He later began to demonstrate his anger toward Kim whenever she asked him for continued help or support. His mean behavior escalated during the time that he became engaged and married and did not subside until he was faced with Peter's continued abusive behavior toward Kim, even after Kim and Peter's divorce proceedings had ended.

The rest of Kim's family lived in another state, and while they offered her support via the telephone, they could not be there for her on a regular basis. However, her brother played an important role in supporting her when Peter refused to give her sufficient money with which to live. She was able to be with her family through several life cycle events that occurred during the 4 years of treatment. A more positive relationship was rebuilt with her mother when Kim was better able to understand her childhood. Kim also had several childhood friends who lived in different parts of the country with whom she continued to keep in close telephone contact and visited a few times a year. Although she became isolated from most of the friends she had where she lived during the marriage, her ability to establish and maintain her long-term friendships was an important strength that was used in survivor therapy.

Kim's work history also provided some strengths that helped her heal. When she began therapy, she believed that her career as an artist was over because Peter would no longer help her do the work. She never acknowledged or appreciated her own abilities, but had become so dependent on Peter's assistance that she believed his taunts that she could not work without his support. He, of course, created this false image as a way to retain his power and control over her. Although he was intensely involved in the details of her business, he never reciprocated by sharing any of his business interests with her, telling her that she was unable to understand them. As she reviewed her work history during therapy, her extraordinary talent became clearer to her. When asked what she thought she needed to help her get back into a career, she answered that she had always wanted to go into advertising and public relations and in fact, had started taking classes 10 years earlier, but Peter's demands and abusive behavior made her feel too stupid to continue. At the end of 4 years of therapy, 2 years of which were spent in major legal battles, she had been able to complete all the course work for her degree.

Interestingly, although her original complaint was that Kim was unable to let Peter go because of her own fears of abandonment, once she was able to stop following him, Peter's behavior became typical of a batterer who cannot relinquish his power and control over the woman. He would call Kim, promise her a nice dinner, or share some intimate moments reminding her about the good times in their life together, and Kim would be seduced. Not until she hired a detective and learned about his hidden life, consisting of intimate relationships with other women and men and hidden business deals and property, was she able to resist his ploys. At the same time she began to expose his abusive behavior publicly and discovered that he was being accused of similar secretive and destructive behavior in his work life. Because of the stress of the relationship breaking apart and the adverse publicity concerning court testimony about his abusive behavior, he decided to resign from his position, but immediately found an equally rewarding one elsewhere. Kim had learned that he had treated his first wife, Ellen, in a similar manner; both women felt vindicated by the demise of his career.

THEORETICAL ORIGINS OF SURVIVOR THERAPY

Feminist Therapy Roots

Feminist therapy theory is an open-energy therapy system that therapists involved with the women's liberation movement in North America in the early 1970s first developed by adapting some traditional therapy techniques to a feminist philosophical context (Brodsky & Hare-Mustin, 1980; Rawlings & Carter, 1977; Rosewater & Walker, 1985). An open-energy system suggests that the individual has an unending supply of psychic energy that she or he can access whenever it is necessary. Initially, early feminist therapists criticized the major traditional therapy theories, such as psychoanalysis, family systems, behaviorism, and humanism, for their inability to appreciate the impact of the oppression of women on their mental health. At the rise of the woman's movement, a high percentage of North American women's complaints were being treated with psychotropic drugs, a procedure that feminists viewed as an attempt to sedate the women's revolution. Feminist psychology rejected this traditional medical model, which was considered to be based on an authoritarian approach of the therapist, in favor of a more egalitarian model in which therapists actively share power and goal setting with clients.

Initially, feminist therapists borrowed techniques from the more traditional therapies, picking and choosing those that were consistent with the feminist philosophy and principles. Feminist therapy is a nonmedical model that supports human growth on the basis of expanded alternatives and choices rather than through adaptation to individual or cultural oppression. It has been guided by the ideas that arose from the latest women's movement that began in the late 1960s in the United States. Some of these principles are highlighted below. There are noted similarities to the principles of survivor therapy.

- the personal is political
- egalitarian relationships
- power is shared in therapy
- appropriate self-disclosure
- mutual goal setting
- bibliotherapy
- informed choices
- advocacy
- positive strengths
- economic independence
- sociocultural issues
- holistic approach to mind, body, and spiritual self
- nurture self and family relationships
- open-energy system
- positive mental health
- educational interventions
- nonpathology–nondeficit model

Feminist therapy went through a second stage of development that emphasized its own therapy techniques rather than the critiquing of other theories, and the second stage resulted in modifications made to its own developing theory. Some of the second stage occurred simultaneously with the period when feminist therapists emphasized that substantial changes were necessary in traditional therapies in order to incorporate the needs of women in treatment (L.S. Brown & Ballou, 1992; Cantor, 1990; Dutton-Douglas & Walker, 1988; Espin & Gawelek, 1992). It is suggested that feminist therapy theory provides a lens through which to view both the individual's current situation and the historical, cultural, and sociopolitical diversity from which she comes. Recognition of the persistent bias that more traditional therapists brought to their clinical work has affected and changed most other therapy systems. Attention to gender is now an issue in most commonly used therapy systems such as psychoanalysis, humanist and existential theories, social learning theory, cognitive and behavioral approaches, and family systems theory.

Many feminist therapists still identify strongly with the traditional therapy theory in which they have been trained, such as feminist psychoanalysis (Alpert, 1986; Cantor, 1990) and other psychodynamic theories (Eichenbaum & Orbach, 1982; Miller, 1976), feminist family therapy (Bograd, 1988; Hare-Mustin, 1978, 1980; Luepnitz, 1988), feminist gestalt and other humanistic therapy (Greenspan, 1983; Lerman, 1993), and behavioral therapies (Foa, 1989; Fodor, 1985, 1991; Wolpe, 1982). Others suggest that traditional therapy theory becomes so substantially modified by feminist principles that even its techniques more closely resemble a new type of feminist therapy rather than its original model (L.S. Brown & Brodsky, 1992; Walker & Dutton-Douglas, 1988).

Feminist therapy theory goes beyond attention to gender issues by creating a system that clearly separates an individual's problems from those experienced, in general, by all women. This separation is included in survivor therapy and helps women cope with the gender bias they will face (particularly in the legal system) as they try to stop the violence against them.

A third stage of development in feminist therapy is now in progress, and that stage consists of the creation of its own therapy theory that includes models of development for girls and women (Conarton & Silverman, 1988; Jordan, Kaplan, Miller, Stiver, & Surrey, 1991; Kaplan & Surrey, 1984; Kaschak, 1992; Unger & Crawford, 1992); an ethical code (Exhibit 10-1) with applications to a variety of clinical and community based situations (Lerman & Porter, 1990); its own theory of the therapy process (L.S. Brown & Ballou, 1992; L.A. Gilbert, 1980; Rosewater, 1988; Walker, 1990; Walker & Dutton-Douglas, 1988); and special populations in which feminist therapy is effective including lesbian women (L.S. Brown, 1992b), men (Cantor, 1990; Ganley, 1988), custody and visitation of children (Liss & Stahly, 1993;

Walker & Edwall, 1987), children who have been abused (Walker, 1990), elderly people (Midlarsky, 1988), those with eating disorders (Root, 1991), and those who have been traumatized from abuse.

The idea that women need to heal from a variety of traumatic experiences appears to underlie feminist therapy theory. For example, Graham, Rawlings, and Rigsby (in press) suggested that there is no way to understand any of the psychology of women without viewing all women's cognitive, affective, and behavioral actions as adaptations to the ever-present danger from men, whether or not individual women recognize or acknowledge such influence. They suggested an analogy with countries at war or under siege; women either identify with their aggressive captors or they rebel as a reaction. Graham and Rawlings (1991) used Stockholm syndrome theory, which describes the process by which women adapt to a world in which they lack real power individually and therefore learn to obtain their power from their male captors. Others, particularly family therapists (Luepnitz, 1988), do not think that men have the power to influence all of women's psychology, although they believe that patriarchal power is certainly a major influence on women's lives. The difficulty in sorting out an individual man's responsibility from patriarchal power in general provides for interesting debate among both men and women who are interested in creating equality. Interesting gender dialogues between male and female therapists have become one attempt to sort out these gender influences in psychology theory and practice (Walker & Levant, 1993).

Feminist therapy theory holds that there are situational factors for women who grow up in a male-oriented world that devalues women and that these are separate and apart from factors arising out of women's personal backgrounds. These situational factors combine and affect an individual woman's mental health. Embedded within feminist developmental theory are the ethnic, racial, and cultural conditions that women experience, as well as other oppressing situational factors such as bias against class, age, disabilities, and sexual orientation (L.S. Brown & Root, 1990). This context always forms and informs the background within which feminist therapy occurs. The techniques used in treatment may be borrowed from other therapy theories and integrated into feminist therapy or may have been

Exhibit 10-1

Ethical Guidelines For Feminist Therapists

I. CULTURAL DIVERSITIES AND OPPRESSIONS

    A. A feminist therapist increases her accessibility to and for a wide range of clients from her own and other identified groups through flexible delivery of services. When appropriate, the feminist therapist assists clients in accessing other services.

    B. A feminist therapist is aware of the meaning and impact of her own ethnic and cultural background, gender, class and sexual orientation, and actively attempts to become knowledgeable about alternatives from sources other than her clients. The therapist's goal is to uncover and respect cultural and experiential differences.

    C. A feminist therapist evaluates her ongoing interactions with her clientele for any evidence of the therapist's biases or discriminatory attitudes and practice. The feminist therapist accepts responsibility for taking appropriate action to confront and change any interfering or oppressing biases she has.

II. POWER DIFFERENTIALS

    A. A feminist therapist acknowledges the inherent power differentials between client and therapist and models effective use of personal power. In using the power differential to the benefit of the client, she does not take control of power which rightfully belongs to her client.

    B. A feminist therapist discloses information to the client which facilitates the therapeutic process. The therapist is responsible for using self-disclosure with purpose and discretion in the interests of the client.

    C. A feminist therapist negotiates and renegotiates formal and/or informal contracts with clients in an ongoing mutual process.

D. A feminist therapist educates her clients regarding their rights as consumers of therapy, including procedures for resolving differences and filing grievances.

III. OVERLAPPING RELATIONSHIPS

A. A feminist therapist recognizes the complexity and conflicting priorities inherent in multiple or overlapping relationships. The therapist accepts responsibility for monitoring such relationships to prevent potential abuse of or harm to the client.

B. A feminist therapist is actively involved in her community. As a result, she is especially sensitive about confidentiality. Recognizing that her client's concerns and general well-being are primary, she self-monitors both public and private statements and comments.

C. A feminist therapist does not engage in sexual intimacies nor any overtly or covertly sexualized behavior with a client or former client.

IV. THERAPIST ACCOUNTABILITY

A. A feminist therapist works only with those issues and clients within the realm of her competencies.

B. A feminist therapist recognizes her personal and professional needs and utilizes ongoing self-evaluation, peer support, consultation, supervision, continuing education, and/or personal therapy to evaluate, maintain, and improve her work with clients, her competencies, and her emotional well-being.

C. A feminist therapist continually reevaluates her training, theoretical background, and research to include developments in feminist knowledge. She integrates feminism into psychological theory, receives ongoing therapy training, and acknowledges the limits of her own competencies.

D. A feminist therapist engages in self-care activities in an

Exhibit 10-1 continues

Exhibit 10-1 continued

ongoing manner. She acknowledges her own vulnerabilities and seeks to care for herself outside of the therapy setting. She models the ability and willingness to self-nurture in appropriate and self-empowering ways.

V. SOCIAL CHANGE

    A. A feminist therapist actively questions other therapeutic practices in her community that appear abusive to clients or therapist and, when possible, intervenes as early as appropriate or feasible or assists clients in intervening when it is facilitative to their growth.

    B. A feminist therapist seeks multiple avenues for impacting change, including public education and advocacy within professional organizations, lobbying for legislative action, and other appropriate activities.

From Feminist Ethics in Psychotherapy, *H. Lerman & N. Porter. Copyright © by Springer Publishing Co. Inc., 1990, New York 10012. Used by permission.*

developed especially for feminist therapy. Some common feminist therapy treatment techniques, most of which have been adapted for use in survivor therapy and are described in this volume (chapters 13 and 14), are listed below.

- client control
- supportive role
- client's decision-making role
- timing of confrontation
- education versus interpretation
- build on strengths
- avoid victim-blaming
- realistic optimism
- controlling dissociation
- hypnosis
- guided imagery

- anxiety management
- fear reduction
- reestablish interpersonal relationships

Feminist therapy has been used for several disorders that are common to women who have traditionally been resistant to other types of psychotherapy. This is particularly true in cases of women who have been abused as well as those suffering from depression (Hamilton & Jensvold, 1992), some psychotic disorders such as schizophrenia (Greenwald, 1992), agoraphobia and panic disorders (Fodor, 1991), addiction problems (Koss & Harvey, 1991; Root, 1989), and eating disorders including anorexia and bulimia (Root, 1991). An interesting feminist critique of personality disorders, which is currently being debated, suggests that the resistance to treatment exhibited by those diagnosed with a personality disorder may be because the suggested treatment is inappropriate for that client (Walker, 1993). Feminist therapy, which does not label certain behaviors as a personality disorder, may be more successful with women who display such characteristics (L.S. Brown, 1992a; Herman, 1992; Root, 1992). Trauma theory underlies much of the personality disorder debate. Its proponents suggest that complex posttraumatic stress disorder (PTSD) diagnosis and treatment strategies are more effective than personality disorder theory and techniques (Herman, 1992). Feminist therapy has also been found to be useful with diverse populations that are not traditionally well-served by psychotherapy (Belle, 1984; L.S. Brown & Root, 1990).

Trauma Theory Roots

The development of a new trauma theory first came out of the study of psychological distress in Vietnam War combat veterans in the 1970s. During the field testing for the new category called *posttraumatic stress disorder*, proposed for inclusion in the third edition of the *Diagnostic and Statistical Manual of Mental Disorders (DSM–III;* American Psychiatric Association, 1980), similarities were noted in the psychological impact on victims of other man-made traumas (e.g., rape, child abuse, and incest, assault, bank robberies) and natural disasters (e.g., earthquakes, hurricanes, plane crashes, fire). Although psychological reactions to trauma, such as those listed in the combat fatigue diagnostic category in the *DSM–I*, and the traumatic neuroses category in the *DSM-II*, were noted earlier, trauma theory did not begin to develop until after PTSD began to be used as a diagnosis in the *DSM–III*. It is interesting to note that Freud, when developing psychoanalytic theory, initially postulated a theory of early sexual trauma underlying the hysterical and other neurotic responses of his patients, before changing his mind and labeling women's reports of abuse "fantasies" (Lerman, 1986; Masson, 1984).

Understanding of a posttraumatic stress response relies on the underpinnings of stress theory that can be traced back to the early 1900s when physiologist Cannon (1929) first described the emergency response that any organism can be expected to make when dealing with a threat or danger. Because the intent of this emergency response is to help the organism deal with the threat by either facing it (fight) or fleeing from it (flight) the response has been called the "fight or flight" response. The two major components of the PTSD diagnostic criteria are the high arousal (fight) or high avoidance (flight) responses appropriately made by the victim when initially faced with the trauma. These responses often continue beyond the actual presence of the threat because of intrusive memories or cognitive distortions suggesting that the person is still in danger. Sometimes the victim's hypervigilance is adaptive because it helps her respond more quickly to actual repeated danger.

Selye (1956) found the "fight or flight" reaction to be the first step in a complex series of physiological changes that occur in response to stress, which he labeled the *general adaptation syndrome* (GAS). Selye (as reported by Cotton, 1990) found three phases to the GAS:

The first phase, the *alarm reaction* (perhaps equivalent to the "fight or flight" response), is characterized by the arousal of the body's defenses. Sympathetic autonomic nervous system arousal occurs along with release of adrenaline. Pupils dilate, ciliary muscles relax vasoconstriction, and there is a slight secretion of glandular substances. Copious sweating may occur, the heart rate increases with an increased force of contraction, the bronchia of the lungs dilate, and blood vessels become mildly constricted; there is decreased peristalsis of the intestines, glucose is released into the blood-stream, the kidneys slow down, blood coagulation increases, the skeletal muscles gain strength, and the piloerector muscles get excited. These physi-ological reactions often accompany even mild fear responses and may become conditioned reactions to any perception of fear after being experi-enced under terror.

The second phase, the *stage of resistance* (in which coping and adapta-tion occur), is characterized by reversal of the changes that occur during the alarm reaction. Physiologically there is an increase in cortisol secretion, which causes heightened metabolism, decreases in swelling and inflamma-tion, and increased immunity; increased muscle strength remains. Although the body is at maximum resistance to the immediate danger, it is at risk for other stressor threats. Because this stage depletes the resources, the body's defense mechanisms will weaken unless the stress is resolved. In repeated stress, this stage is probably shortened by adaptation and coping mecha-nisms that temporarily fool the body into thinking the stress is resolved. This may be the underlying physiological mechanism for use of the condi-tioned avoidance responses such as minimization of the danger, denial, repression, and dissociation.

In the third phase, the *stage of exhaustion*, the organism goes into shock, and resistance to infection and other stressors is so minimal that in extreme cases the person can die. The psychological coping mechanisms that make up the PTSD response may be an attempt to prevent the escalation of the initial occurrence or to prevent the recurrence of this stage after it has been experienced during a major abuse situation. This may also help explain the trauma victim's persistent belief that she or he has a foreshortened future, sometimes to the point of predicting imminent death, even after the danger has been resolved.

Lazarus and Folkman (1984) provided a discussion of the various cop-ing strategies for managing stress that can help inform survivor therapy. They suggested that there are two main ways to deal with repeated or chronic stressors: either by trying to lessen the emotional distress caused by the stress or abuse (emotion-focused coping) or by changing the definition of the problem or meaning given to the abuse experience (cognitive problem-focused coping). Thus, therapists working with repeat stress or abuse survivors need to focus on both affect and cognition in order to maximize the efficacy of treatment. Survivor therapy specifically deals with both responses by initially focusing on the specific emotional and cognitive changes commonly seen in PTSD.

Cotton (1990) presented a description of the neural, neuroendocrine, cognitive, and behavioral changes that occur in people who are exposed to trauma. The model suggests that most people respond to both general as well as traumatic stress with four major reactions: changes in physiology, emotion, cognition, and behavior. Although such changes are considered normal responses to abnormal situations, if they become part of the victim's longer term psychological makeup, such as in a person with a PTSD, then psychotherapy may be indicated. The *DSM–IV* draft book suggests an additional trauma-based diagnosis that categorizes those reactions that have not persisted long enough to be labeled disorders. The research currently suggests a 4- to 6-week posttrauma period as the cutoff period for differentiating a trauma response from a disorder.

The trauma model suggests that one reason that a victim may be unable to return to prestress levels when the trauma is over is that intrusive memory distortions and cognitive confusion help to perpetuate the belief that the danger is still present. Learning theorists add to the explanation a description of conditioned responses that were successful in recognizing and coping with the trauma. When abuse is repeatedly perpetrated by someone who shows the victim loving behavior at other times, such as in battering, child abuse, therapist exploitation, and some forms of sexual abuse and harassment, the woman may have difficulty cognitively differentiating people who might cause her harm. In multiple abuse victims, even when the identity of the current abuser is clear in the victim's mind, the intrusive memories of the prior traumatic incident or incidents may keep the more generalized danger level high. Adaptation to cyclical or constant high stress can make the PTSD symptoms fluctuate with changing perceptions. The research that suggests the state-dependent nature of the retrieval of memories supports the negative impact of intrusive memories, especially if the woman is still living in an emotionally hostile world. In some cases, the trauma is reexperienced so vividly, accompanied by the terrorizing emotions, that it appears to the woman that she is being hurt all over again. Thus, she continues to repeat her initial stress response complete with fight or flight type physiological, emotional, cognitive, and behavioral responses.

KEY PRINCIPLES OF SURVIVOR THERAPY

The major principles of survivor therapy are

- safety
- empowerment
- validation
- emphasis on strengths
- education
- expanding alternatives
- restoring clarity in judgment
- understanding oppression
- making own decisions.

These principles are discussed below.

Safety and Empowerment

The two most important goals in survivor therapy are to ensure the woman's safety and to restore her sense of control over her life. Both are equally important in helping the woman heal from the trauma. Without genuine safety, the victim cannot give up coping strategies that protect her from further psychological harm. Without reestablishing her own personal power, the woman cannot be expected to regain control of her life. Empowerment does not only suggest independence, but also the movement past personal independence to *interdependence*—the state of being independent and sometimes dependent—with other people again. Thus, the woman's interpersonal relationships, including family and friendships, become an important part of therapy. However, to achieve the independence needed, individual or group therapy—not family systems therapy—is recommended initially. The therapist helps the woman to feel safe and empowered within the therapy session, and actively works with her so she can feel safe and empowered in life outside of the therapy session.

Validation

Validation of the survivor's rights as well as her thoughts, feelings, and choices is a critical element in survivor therapy. At the same time, the value of nonviolence is also communicated. Avoidance of judging the client, usually inherent in most therapy models, is broadened to include the avoidance of any comments that might be misinterpreted as victim-blaming. This is important in order to make clear the distinction between both the abuser's and society's tendency to place responsibility for the abuse onto the woman. In addition, the careful ethical choices that are made by the therapist and special attention that is paid to the power differences in the relationship provide important opportunities to model positive interpersonal relationships. A key to survivor therapy is the respect for and understanding of each woman's own unique place within her own cultural, sociopolitical, economic, and psychological framework.

Emphasis on Strengths

Survivor therapy emphasizes the strengths of the woman instead of the traditional deficit model often seen in medical-model based therapies. Clients are seen as having an open-energy system with a propensity for positive and creative self-growth. The very name, survivor therapy, indicates a respect for the strength of the coping strategies that permit victims to become survivors. Therapists actively support these strengths by identifying them and helping the client to become aware of their own adaptive abilities. Acceptance of the woman's ability to make changes herself while assigning responsibility to the abuser to make changes himself is important. Couples therapy often makes these changes contingent on each other; if he does this, then she commits to doing that. Such an approach is inimical to survivor therapy principles and goals.

Reduction of PTSD Symptoms

Often victims and survivors of abuse find themselves stuck in patterns of high arousal and high avoidance behaviors that interfere with their interpersonal relationships and prevent them from fully experiencing their lives. They often have intrusive reexperiences of the traumatic memories that cause them to believe that they are still in danger, whether or not that is the case. Legitimate fears of further abuse make it difficult to get on with life. Use of medication to assist in the management of PTSD symptoms is an acceptable part of survivor therapy, provided that the woman understands and gives fully informed consent to use of the drugs. Often abused women feel that medication is another method of controlling their minds and bodies. In these cases, it would not be consistent with the other principles and goals to use drugs as an adjunct to therapy.

Coping strategies that help women feel safe may also intrude on their ability to concentrate, to think clearly without mental confusion, and to distinguish new situations from those fraught with old fear and anger. Heightened emotional arousal and hypersensitivity to their own and others' emotions interfere with the women's ability to have relationships. Behaviors often range from defensive aggression to unassertive passivity. Lack of trust, overreactivity, suspiciousness, and fear of the pain caused by betrayal interfere with their ability to establish intimacy. Concentration on meeting other people's needs may block their ability to understand and accept their own needs. Mild to severe depression along with frequent periods of sadness and crying may keep them from rejoining the active world. They believe that they will never feel better again. Many of the techniques used in other therapy models to treat these symptoms can be adapted for use in survivor therapy, provided that the woman is able to perceive herself as a full participant with the therapist in making choices.

Education and Expanding Alternatives

To become an independent person, capable of making all kinds of life choices, a woman must have the skills to cope in the world. Reading recommended books and materials, working with self-help groups, and becoming active in the community all help to expand the survivor's choices and options. Economic self-sufficiency is also a goal that needs to be explored with most clients. Some women have access to money but do not know how to use it to their own advantage. Others need to learn how to get and keep their own money. In cases in which clients need to further their education in order to get a better job or career, encouraging them to do so is appropriate. Therapy is seen as an educational tool; other new ways to learn new skills should also be explored, while keeping in mind the client's abilities within the context of her sociopolitical, cultural, and economic background.

Understanding Oppression

An underpinning of the therapeutic approach includes the knowledge of the psychological impact of race, culture, ethnicity, gender, sexual orientation, class, educational level, able-bodiedness, and other factors in the lives of survivors. Other therapy models emphasize the negative internalization of such situational factors, whereas the principles of survivor therapy support both the positive value of multicultural acceptance and the generalized negative impact of oppression on women. These combined factors create the unique interaction between the woman's internal and external worlds that must be appreciated when providing therapy assistance for healing from trauma.

For some women a truly violence-free life may not be possible given the external circumstances within which they live. This is especially true for women who inhabit cultures in which state-sponsored violence is still the norm, for example in some Latin American states (Lykes, Brabeck, Ferns, & Radan). This also applies to those who are members of religious groups in which women are still oppressed, such as in some Muslim states in the Middle East, or even in a subgroup of society in which woman abuse is not actively opposed by those in power, such as in some cults and nonmainstream religious communities. These women may still benefit from survivor therapy, although the therapist must be careful not to encourage the women to give up those adaptive strategies on which their very survival depends.

HOW SURVIVOR THERAPY WORKS

The goals of survivor therapy are

- safety
- reempowerment
- validation
- explore options
- cognitive clarity and judgment
- make own decisions
- heal trauma effects.

These goals are discussed in general terms below as well as illustrated in relation to the case history of Kim that was presented at the beginning of this chapter.

Safety

Safety is the primary goal. As in Kim's case and others, working toward non-violence can be a slow process. In those cases it is important to let the client set her own timetable for becoming completely violence-free while helping her learn how to reach temporary safety. The crisis model (described in chapter 13), used when working with battered women who are still in contact with the abuser or adapted for use with other repeated abuse situations, can help the therapist deal with her or his own feelings, particularly fear for the client's safety, while still providing the client with the assistance she needs at that particular time.

Kim was not able to consider terminating the abusive relationship with her husband until her second year of survivor therapy, which was 10 years after she had begun seeking different types of psychotherapy for what she initially believed were her own problems. In the survivor therapy approach, however, Kim was able to learn quickly to control her own responses to the fight sequence that her husband had set up, so that she did not escalate the abuse through her own use of physical violence. She adapted these new strategies because they appealed to her new understanding of Peter's responsibility for the violence as well as because of the focus on being in control of her own emotions in her reactions to him. The new behavior that resulted did help stabilize the situation, even though it could not prevent several more acute battering incidents or the continuous escalation of Peter's psychological cruelty.

Kim was still in danger of being hurt at the time that she first entered therapy. She was living with Peter, thinking about getting a divorce, but also feeling desperate and trapped in her situation. This is the most dangerous time in a battering relationship. Like many battered women entering treatment, she wanted help to stop the violence without having to leave the relationship. After listening to her describe at least four prior battering incidents, it became clear that the violence was escalating, making it more dangerous, but probably not lethal, for her to remain in that relationship. It also became clear that she took most of the responsibility for the violence because of what she called her "crazy" behavior. This included her yelling and screaming at Peter, embarrassing them both in public places, throwing things, spying on him, and chasing after him when he would try to leave her after he started a fight.

Survivor therapy deals directly with the danger from abuse, concentrating on the details of the battering incidents so that escape plans to help the woman escape the man's violence can be formulated rather than attempts to get the client to somehow stop the man's violence. Proper definitions are given for abusive behavior and responsibility is clearly placed with the man no matter how obnoxious or provocative the woman's behavior might be. Unless in self-defense, there is no reason to physically, sexually, or seriously psychologically maltreat someone. Survivor therapists, trained in trauma theory, are also aware that denial, minimization, dissociation, and flashbacks of fragments of previous abuse incidents complicate the woman's current perception of danger.

The therapist presented several options to Kim as ways to decrease the possibility of her being hurt. First, suicidal ideation was assessed, knowing that she had several major attempts in the past. She was so frightened by the reactions of her children to her last attempt, when she was hospitalized, that she believed suicide was no longer an option; she did not want to harm her children. Her relationship with her children was discussed several times when she was so distraught that she verbalized suicidal thoughts. However, to her credit, she kept her word and never actually threatened or attempted suicide during the 4 years of therapy.

Second, as a condition of treatment, Dr. Hobbes guided her to make an effort to stop her own violent behavior. The therapist shared her own belief with Kim that Kim could control her use of violence and that she would help Kim learn how to prevent situations from escalating to the point at which Kim felt the need to react so aggressively. Dr. Hobbes reiterated that neither she nor Kim could change Peter's behavior; they could only help Kim change her response to it, which would affect what he did next. Fortunately, Dr. Hobbes' knowledge of battering relationships made her predictions accurate. This raised Dr. Hobbes's status as a reliable helper in Kim's eyes.

Dr. Hobbes asked her to go over several of the battering incidents again, this time concentrating on when the abuse escalated to the point that it made Kim so agitated and angry that she felt she could not control her reactions. She was able to see that she did have some choices about how she responded to Peter's abuse. The therapist helped her label certain behaviors abusive and others not; sometimes the two become blurred for repeat abuse victims. In the third year of survivor therapy, Kim and Dr. Hobbes were able to deal with some of the dissociative experiences Kim had when the abuse became unbearable for her. Interestingly, Kim distorted reality so that she could keep her perception of Peter, the important, smart, high status professional, rather than see him as others saw him: someone who lied to his own advantage, embarrassed others, and did not play fair. Peter's decision to resign from his previous position was based on his being caught leaking certain confidential information about his firm and on Kim's accusations in court regarding his violence (charges supported by Ellen, his former wife). It took Kim a long time to realize that her exposure of Peter contributed heavily to his downfall. His hold over her was still so great that she never really considered his resignation to be a loss of status and power for him.

Although it is usually the batterer, fearful of abandonment, who stalks and harasses the battered woman, in this case Kim appeared to be more frightened than Peter about separation. Dr. Hobbes suggested that Kim try to let Peter go when he threatened to leave, by pointing out that he might then react with typical batterer's behavior and not let her go, either. She was too frantic to take that chance until the second year of therapy, but once she did, to her surprise, he kept calling, chasing her, and trying to get back into the house. She chased after him only one more time, resulting in injuries to her that were documented by an emergency room physician, a battered woman advocate, and a police photographer. Although she continued to spend a lot of time with him during that period in the hopes that he would change so that they could reconcile, she never gave him a new set of keys to the house, forcing him to be a guest there and to live in his apartment. Because she was prepared for him to leave, she was better able to let him go most of the time, especially when he began to call her afterward. His insistence on keeping the apartment during their 20-year relationship was a constant source of fear and anger for her.

In Kim's case there were no longer any young children at home to worry about. Most therapists who work with survivors who have children (who may also be in danger themselves) must find ways to help their clients deal with the fear, anxiety, and pain that is caused by concern for the child. Often the risk of harm to the child is ignored by the courts and by child protective services, especially in cases in which visitation issues are involved. This leaves both the therapist and the client feeling powerless to protect the child. Sometimes, teaching the child survival strategies is helpful; in other cases, careful monitoring of the child's reactions following the visitation is the best that can be done (Liss & Stahly, 1993; Walker & Edwall, 1987).

It was important for the therapist to have some contact with Kim's adult children, both to help provide some additional safety when Kim felt that Peter was getting out of control at home and to provide additional checks on Kim's own self-destructive behavior. Contact with Peter's former wife, Ellen, and the hiring of a private detective after Kim filed for divorce, also provided an additional check on Kim's safety. Hiring the detective was suggested by Kim's lawyer and helped to stop Kim from making her own attempts at surveillance. Like most victims, Kim needed to know where Peter was and what he was doing in order to feel safe. Even those victims who feel safer because the abuser has been apprehended and incarcerated still fear that he will get out of prison someday. That fear haunts their recovery. Battered women and women who are sexually abused by therapists, co-workers, or family members rarely have the respite from fear that would be provided by the man's incarceration. Sometimes, the continuing legal battles concerning personal injury and other civil lawsuits help vindicate the victim. Rarely do battered women understand that the loss of personal property, including money they spend on lawyers' fees, may also be a form of protection for them from further abuse by that man.

Reempowerment

Reempowerment is the second primary goal of survivor therapy. The very nature of acts of violence against women makes such acts an abuse of power. The experience of victimization takes away the woman's sense of having the power to protect herself. Some suggest that it changes their entire worldview by forcing them to acknowledge that evil does exist (Kaley, 1991). Victims typically blame themselves for some part of the abusive experience. They believe that if they can figure out what they did wrong, then they can protect themselves better next time. Sometimes self-blame even helps allay some of the anxiety that accompanies the trauma response. Therapists must help the woman to understand that she still has control over much of her life even if she could not prevent the abuse. The responsibility for the abuse must be placed directly on the abuser, no matter what the victim has done. Although it may seem redundant and unnecessary, it is important for the therapist to tell the woman clearly that it was not her fault and that she will be all right again. The emphasis on identifying her strengths rather than focusing on her injuries helps toward the development of reempowerment and increased self-esteem.

The most important way for Kim to regain control of her life was to become economically self-sufficient again. She had spoken in therapy about how much better she felt when she was earning her own money. However, it was clear that she no longer wanted to work in her former capacity, although she still wanted to use her artistic talent. This meant that the survivor therapist needed to help her change her environment or situation. She made a plan to be admitted to graduate school within several months of beginning treatment. She observed how Peter pretended to be supportive of her schoolwork, even helping her sometimes with difficult homework, but always seemed to create an acute battering incident during finals so that she could not concentrate on completing her coursework. Once Kim recognized the pattern, she confronted Peter with his behavior and went to their vacation home to study.

Kim also found it empowering to have an understanding of the dynamics of the abuse. As the cycle of violence became more predictable to her, she was able to break her dependence on Peter. At no time was termination of the relationship a goal of therapy. In cases in which a woman has remained for many years in an abusive situation, the probability is that the dynamics of the relationship keep it in a status quo position. If the therapist were to try to get Kim to leave, Peter would have been able to use it to stop her from continuing in therapy. The goal was for her to be violence free, safe, and feeling reempowered. She began to read books on violence and asked questions about how what she was reading applied to her. By the third year of therapy, she was working with other battered women and guiding them through their own readings and journeys.

This concentration on changing external situations rather than focusing on the internal intrapsychic problems is an important part of survivor therapy. There is an understanding that trauma may keep a person in a static position for a period of time, but that does not mean that the person cannot move forward toward real goals at any other point. Empowerment also encourages the client to participate in making decisions about her own life. The therapist rarely tells the client what to do or even gives advice. Rather, the survivor therapist serves as a sounding board, a facilitator to help expand the woman's own range of choices. This expansion of alternatives and options is a feminist position that is applied in survivor therapy. Listening to what the client says and keenly observing how she functions are the best ways to help the client move toward reempowerment.

Validation

Validation of the client's story and of her feelings, including contradictory feelings such as both caring and anger toward the abuser, is an important early step in survivor therapy. Just listening respectfully to the client is one way to validate her experience. Repeating what the client has said back to her may be helpful in establishing that she is being heard. Being supportive rather than confrontational or interpretational helps the client feel validated. This differs from other therapy theories that are built on the therapist's interpretation of what the client says rather than on accepting it at face value. Most abuse victims lose the ability to understand neutrality or objectivity. They see people as either being with them or against them. In order to help the woman restore trust, the therapist must persuade her that she or he is on the woman's side. This can be done by avoiding discussions of what she might have done better or differently, accepting that she did the best she could at the time, and concentrating on what she did right to survive the incident or incidents.

Defining what constitutes abuse may be important in order to validate the victim's experience. For example, a woman who has been subjected to repeated sexual harassment may understand that unwanted sexual contact is abuse but may have trouble labeling sexual innuendos and jokes as abuse, especially if she laughed at them, even if she did so out of fear and anxiety. A woman who was sexually abused by her therapist may not want to define all of his sexual attention as abusive, but instead may want to cling to the belief that he really loved her. Some battered women feel this way also.

Although it was clear that Kim sometimes distorted what happened during incidents in which she was under high emotional distress, most of the time she was able to make sense of a situation before anyone else could recognize the cues. Early in treatment she was able to label some of Peter's behavior as abusive, but until she had the discussions with Ellen, Peter's former wife, she did not recognize the recurring sexual abuse. In this situation it was important that the therapist did not prematurely put labels on incomplete descriptions. This was also true when Kim began to have breakthrough memories of her father's sexual abuse. It was the recognition of similar feelings between her husband's and her father's behavior that provided the trigger for the surfacing of buried memories. Again, the danger of damaging the client's accurate memories with suggestions must be carefully avoided. It is probably true that memories of prior abuse are more likely to surface in a therapy situation that accepts the possibility of abuse. Incest and other forms of abuse against women may become buried memories precisely because no one wants to believe that such acts can be perpetrated by otherwise "good" men. Some believe that it is first necessary to provide a supportive context in which such state-dependent feelings and memories may emerge. The support for a woman's expression of the anger felt about violence against women in general, even when that woman has not been a victim herself, provides such a context. Thus, therapists working with survivors of one form of abuse may indeed be the ones to inadvertently help women recover memories of previous abuse that were repressed in a less supportive environment. This is an important concept to understand in the current climate of defensive backlash, with accusations being hurled against therapists regarding memories clients have retrieved in therapy.

It was helpful for Kim to be validated in her suspicions that Peter was lying to her. After their separation became more permanent, during the end of her second year of treatment, Kim hired a detective to follow Peter rather than spying on him herself. This helped her stay away from him and clarified that her need to know about his behavior was more an attempt to keep her own anxiety manageable than it was a need to actually see him. The more she learned about Peter, the more she understood that her discomfort and anxiety were provoked by his lies and deception. This was a difficult period of therapy because Kim had to recognize that she had been manipulated in past situations, although on reevaluation it seemed perfectly clear to her.

It was toward the end of the second year of therapy, after she had the lawyer prepare the papers to file for divorce but before they were served, that Kim made telephone contact with Ellen. The two of them became friends, sharing the horror of what they knew of Peter's cruel, deceptive, and abusive behavior. Initially, both were shocked to find out how similar their stories about life with Peter were, right down to his bilking both of them out of all their money. Kim reexamined her sexual relationship with Peter after Ellen described several incidents of marital rape that were similar to Kim's experiences. The sharing of abuse stories helped both women to validate their own realities; Ellen's determination to help Kim would help her meet her own need for justice, too.

Exploring Options

It is important for the therapist to explore options and alternatives with the client so that she can begin to make choices with an understanding of the consequences of her actions. This goal is facilitated by using a number of techniques that are similar to those described in the section on feminist therapy. Many survivors narrow their options in order to avoid further abuse; expanding those alternatives may produce anxiety that can be dealt with in therapy. Sometimes the new choices that are made by the client can upset the balance within their family and their community. Survivor therapy can help the client understand the potential short- and long-term consequences of their actions so that they can be prepared for the reactions they experience. Expanding alternatives often involves changing their interpersonal relationships, and therefore, it is important to consider the timing of change.

In Kim's case, she decided to give up her once-successful business and return to school. Her previous business, inherited from her father and supported by her husband, flooded her with memories of their abuse toward her. Living under the control of two very powerful men left her without the ability to believe in the sufficiency of her own power. Each step toward her own independence both excited and frightened her, but in the end she was able to complete her degree.

Restoring Clarity in Judgment

Cognitive clarity and judgment need to be restored in order for the client to return to work, feel more productive, and make decisions. The feelings elicited when the woman is in crisis can make it difficult for her to think clearly. This also protects the client: She does not have to make any decisions when the flood of feelings creates mental confusion. Kim's ability to go to school put her in direct conflict with her typical state of "creative confusion." During the process of survivor therapy, Kim began to notice when she would become mentally confused and when she could think clearly. She herself was able to point out that her anxiety was only temporarily reduced when she was in a state of mental confusion but that the anxiety was actually relieved when she felt that she was in good cognitive control.

Initially indifferent, Peter later tried to control Kim's schoolwork by helping her study. Sometimes, that even meant doing homework for her. Peter thought of himself as a "renaissance man" who knew everything about everything. Their relationship was based on his being smarter than she was in all areas. However, despite his attempts to help, he would often pick a fight during the week of exams, so that Kim could not concentrate to study, and therefore, she would receive a poor grade. Once Kim recognized this pattern, she began to do most of her work by herself and did not tell Peter when exams were to occur. Peter accurately interpreted her behavior as a withdrawal from him, and he escalated both his seductive behavior as well as his psychological abuse in order to try to win her back. When Kim was able to concentrate and allowed herself to sit and study, she did quite well academically. By the third year of survivor therapy, she was able to think clearly unless she purposely chose to ignore what she knew or became so obsessed with something that she could not achieve the cognitive clarity that she needed. Interestingly, a major obstacle to this part of the therapy was the advice given to her by her lawyer: She would receive more of a financial settlement if she was less able to support herself at the time of the divorce. Because Kim's ability to support herself was still unknown, her legal needs had to be respected. Her economic self-sufficiency is still an unknown.

Making Her Own Decisions

The abused woman must be allowed to make her own decisions, particularly about whether to stay in treatment, whether to report incidents to the police and to press charges, whether to stay married or in a relationship, whether to take medication, and even whether to talk about something in therapy. Attempting to push the woman into accepting the authoritarian decisions of the therapist (such as being forced to take medication or intimidated into doing something) may re-create the feelings she had from the original abusive experience. On the other hand, it is important to recognize that some types of decisions are easier to make together than others.

Some other therapists might have made it a goal for Kim to leave the relationship with Peter, understanding that she was in danger from further abuse. Indeed, her previous therapist had suggested that he could not help her any further (after 7 years in therapy) if she remained in the marriage. Although Kim first requested survivor therapy in a crisis after a physically abusive incident, she and Peter had been together for 20 years, and a lethality check indicated that there was no reason to suspect that the abuse would rapidly escalate to lethal levels. In fact, it was more useful not to make termination of the relationship a goal of therapy in order to prevent the therapist and Peter from becoming engaged in a power struggle for control of Kim's destiny. The goal was for Kim to become violence-free; if Peter would stop abusing Kim then the relationship might not need to end.

Healing the Trauma Effects

The actual symptoms resulting from the abuse, including the PTSD symptoms, need to be dealt with directly. Useful strategies are needed either to reduce the anxiety or fight response and increase the flight response, or to reduce depression and the levels of minimization, denial, repression, and dissociation.

Techniques borrowed from other therapy systems such as cognitive restructuring from cognitive–behavioral therapy, or reframing as it is called in systems therapy, are useful in helping to heal trauma by helping to refocus on cognition. Many of the most useful therapy techniques come from the behavioral therapies, particularly those that help the therapist and the client learn to give new meanings to situations by viewing them from the woman's own, and not society's, perspective. Changing the old messages that women have learned about the role of women are also helpful here. Assertiveness training techniques can be incorporated, with the caveats suggested by Fodor (1985). Some of the rational–emotive therapy techniques developed by Ellis and modified for women by Foa, Steketee, and Olasov (1989) are also useful in survivor therapy.

Relaxation training, especially deep-muscle relaxation, seems to help women who are highly anxious and tense to relax. Using relaxation training that is accompanied by guided imagery techniques may mitigate the fearful qualities of the intrusive memories. Gestalt techniques dealing with interpersonal relationships may be helpful for those survivors who have not been able to analyze moment-to-moment interactions in relationships other than for their potential for abuse. This is particularly useful when working with groups. The intimacy of another person understanding one's own feelings and thoughts can be strengthened by the psychodynamic techniques that use the therapy relationship as a model. Many of the psychodynamic techniques are helpful in moving from independence to interdependence, regaining the ability to trust, and becoming vulnerable enough to rely on others not to cause harm. Therapists also find psychodynamic discussions of transference and countertransference issues helpful when working with very difficult and damaged clients. These and other techniques are discussed in more detail in later chapters.

OTHER SURVIVOR THERAPY GOALS

Meeting the Needs of the Victim and Her Family

Kim needed to strengthen her relationship with her children. Both children were well on their way to being independent adults, although they still needed her for emotional support. Helping her to realize when she was relying on them to meet her needs too often, as well as helping her to recognize their legitimate needs, whether or not she could meet them at the time, was an important part of this process. Each child met the therapist individually. These meetings helped the children to understand their mother's healing process and strengthened the relationship they both wanted to continue with their mother. During the 4 years of therapy, Kim also took on a new role as mother-in-law when her son was married. Mourning the loss of her son's total commitment to her, and learning to share him with a woman who did not seem to be as concerned about Kim's well-being as she would have liked, was a difficult task in therapy. Kim made it through the wedding festivities feeling very shut out. She caused only one minor embarrassing scene, but it was still upsetting to the bride and groom.

Issues concerning boundaries were also important for Kim to work through. Like many abused women, she wanted to spend as much time with the therapist as possible without becoming dependent. Transference issues made it important to help her meet some of her needs while also setting clear boundary lines. For example, at one point after her files and keys were stolen from her car (verified by the detective she hired), she stored some materials in an empty room in the therapy office suite. She was there daily for a while until the novelty wore off and the work overwhelmed her. A contact telephone number was made available to Kim, a common practice for other clients, too. Although she would use the on-call associates when Dr. Hobbes was more difficult to reach, Kim, the sleuth, was able to find her almost everywhere, not so much because of a need to talk to her, but just to know that the therapist was safe wherever she told Kim that she was going. One time Dr. Hobbes gave Kim the name of a hotel in which she registered under her roommate's name and Kim became frantic when she could not reach the therapist. These situations led to discussions about how she generalized Peter's betrayal of trust to believing that everyone would behave that way toward her. They were used as examples occasionally during the second, third, and sometimes fourth years.

Differentiating General Oppression From Personal Circumstances

At the time that Kim sought treatment, she did not see the feminist movement as relevant to her problems and was unconcerned about whether her therapist was a feminist. She just wanted to survive the abuse and save her marriage. Because she had had numerous years of previous therapy dealing with the known physical and emotional abuse, it was unnecessary to deal immediately with the impact of events that had occurred in her childhood. Of course, the sexual abuse that was later recalled during the therapy with Dr. Hobbes was not known at the time.

In graduate school, where she was one of a select number of female students, she witnessed one of her female professors being abused. This helped her place her own situation within the context of oppression of women in general and within her own family and friendship circle. She began to recognize stereotyped sex-role behavior and abuse situations, including some incidents in which her son verbally abused her and his girlfriend. Each time a new "cognitive click" occurred, she was better able to understand her own situation in a larger context. This reduced her own self-blame and raised her self-esteem and self-confidence.

In the third year of therapy, she began to date a man who was a professor at another university. Within a short period of time she began to feel oppressed by his demands on her time, which caused her to rethink what kind of a relationship she wanted. No longer did she want to cook, clean, take care of, and give unlimited supplies of herself and her money to another person. She stopped looking for the perfect man to take care of her and began to think about becoming more independent. Unfortunately, this phase of therapy was contradicted by her legal situation, and a tension developed between her need to continue to have Peter support her and her own need for economic independence, which was threatened because she had given him money that she now needed.

In the fourth year of therapy, Kim began to work as an advocate for the battered women's task force near her home. Although still going through a messy divorce from Peter (it took 3 years to complete, and she lost most of her access to his money, her retirement money, and her previous lifestyle), she tried to be supportive to other women, and this helped her perhaps as much as it helped them. Her shock regarding the failure of the legal system to respond to her plight created a setback in her movement toward independence. She alternately viewed it as evidence of Peter's unstoppable power over her and as proof that the judge was corrupt and misogynistic.

Perhaps the most important growth for Kim was caused by her own disillusionment. She gave up her belief that a man would provide for and take care of a "good" woman. That she still clung to such a notion given her parents' abusive marriage shows the power of ideology as opposed to reality. In many ways, these changes in Kim's attitudes toward dependence on men were taking place throughout the therapy, but did not surface as a noticeable issue until the third year of therapy when she became sexually involved with another highly visible and powerful older man who reminded her of her father. During sex, she began to experience breakthrough memories of her father's earlier sexual demands on her. Her father and her new lover were considerably older than her, neither had intercourse with her (which may partially explain why she did not define Peter's forced sexual intercourse as abuse), both men lent her status through their community visibility, and both promised to take care of her but did not do it very well. The memories of incest were important to the understanding of her self-destructive behavior, which had, for the most part, stopped by the time these memories surfaced. At this point, the major issues in survivor therapy were healing from the incest and stopping the obsession with gaining control of Peter's money. Kim was developing new interpersonal relationships, although she was not interested in dating men, which is typical of incest survivors in this stage of the healing process.

Identification of Intrapsychic Factors

Kim came to her marriage with the effects of physical, emotional, and sexual abuse as a child. She has many of the diagnostic features of complex PTSD or borderline personality disorder. Her recurrent depressions and constant high levels of anxiety with impulsiveness are more typically associated with PTSD than with bipolar or other affective disorders, although these have not been totally ruled out. She is quick to react to any slight or feelings of being left out, which makes it difficult to respond to her neediness at times. She is unable to tolerate much anxiety, and this can precipitate lots of chaotic and frantic behavior as well as periods of depression. Often the chaotic behavior appears to be a way to prevent more serious depression. During the second year of therapy she was put on the antidepressant Prozac for a trial period. She tolerated it well and it helped even out her mood swings, and it gave her more energy to focus and concentrate on her schoolwork. She is still unable to concentrate on her own financial management, which makes her prone to spending too much money on meeting her needs, having anxiety attacks about how to pay for what she purchased, being taken advantage of financially, and then manipulating everyone around her to bail her out.

Kim often needs to be the center of attention in order to feel certain that her needs will be met. Sometimes this means that she turns the conversation to talk about herself with little sensitivity to others who are present. However, when she takes the time to plan out her contacts with friends better, she can be less demanding and more open to their needs. Her flair for drama and willingness to go all the way to get something are two qualities that others like about Kim, and they are attracted by her vivacious personality.

Once Kim began to deal directly with the buried incest memories, her sexual behavior with men changed. She was no longer interested in dating or in having sex, which she began to realize was a substitution for genuine loving interactions. Her need for drama decreased and some of the frantic edge to her actions seemed to become softer. Interestingly, she was able to break off the relationship with the older man, who had been a friend and business colleague of Peter's, understanding that she was in a dangerous legal position should Peter learn of their relationship.

Adapting Instead of Merely Coping

Kim needed to get her life situation under some control before she was able to deal with any intrapsychic factors that were involved in perpetuating the effects of PTSD. It was important for her to understand her high levels of anxiety; they appeared to be propelled by her fear of abandonment. It was also important to teach her how to be alone without becoming intolerably fearful and upset. These were some issues that she had dealt with in her previous psychotherapy, and, therefore, she was familiar with some of the focus on emotional reactions, but not with changing the cognitive meanings of the experiences.

Although it was difficult to settle her down long enough for her to concentrate on understanding cognitive shifts, she was able to do so part of the time. Previous trials on progesterone replacement also helped reduce some of her irritability and aggression responses, and Prozac helped reduce the agitated depression, but the underlying rage needed to be dealt with in therapy.

Developing Self-Confidence

Kim was able to learn about herself in ways that she never understood before. She began to understand her ability to think through and solve problems using good judgment if she could only keep her emotional responses under control. She also learned to appreciate her ability to make friends and keep them for a long time. Away from any contact with Peter, Kim was able to look forward to and feel some self-confidence about the future. She would, however, get dragged back into self-doubt whenever she had to deal with Peter's continuous legal harassment.

Living Well Is the Best Revenge

Despite 4 years of therapy, Kim still obsesses about getting even and getting back some of her money, which now belongs to Peter. In some ways, the legal battle that took place solidified this view of revenge. Had the emphasis been on getting on with her life instead of attempting, with the encouragement of her lawyer, to get at the money Peter took from her, she might have made more progress in therapy.

On the other hand, Kim is about to finish graduate school and has some exciting ideas about what to do next. She has reestablished old friendships, made some new ones, has pretty good relationships with both of her children, and is ready to get on with her life if she can only let go of her need to "get him." Unfortunately, Peter is also unable to let her go, has demanded petty things from her, such as the bed that she sleeps in and a replacement of the exact vase that she once bought him for his birthday, as part of his marital property, and continues to file legal motions to which it costs her money to respond. As long as the courts continue to treat such legal maneuvers as credible, batterers can use the legal system as a way to continue to batter women. Survivor therapy helps clients gain the strength to deal with the legal issues while at the same time trying to get on with their own lives. Every indication is that Kim is well on her way to success.

WHY SURVIVOR THERAPY IS A NEW THERAPY SYSTEM

Survivor therapy meets the guidelines for a separate therapy system as described by Corey (1977). It has a unique philosophy from which key concepts, goals of therapy, specific principles to guide the therapeutic relationship, a set of therapy techniques, and applications to specific situations have been developed.

Survivor therapy incorporates several major systems of normal life span development that are sensitive to gender issues and use an open psychic energy system to explain progress through these stages of development. The open-energy system views the individual as possessing an unending supply of psychic energy. Freud's theory of psychoanalysis, for example, is a closed-energy system, with the libido as a finite amount of energy that gets stuck in places and requires therapy to go back, revisit those stages, and release the trapped libido for later use. Humanistic therapy theories, in contrast, believe in the open-energy system and state that people are creative and move toward positive growth naturally, using their own existential experience as a guide. Existentialism usually includes the personalized meanings that are given to the moment-by-moment experience, also incorporating spiritual messages from the present or past. The goal of therapy is to help people get unstuck (getting stuck occurs for a variety of reasons) in order that they may continue their journey to search for meaning and enjoyment in life.

In survivor therapy theory, access to the infinite psychic energy becomes blocked by the experiences of trauma and abuse. Therapy, with or without adjuncts such as spirituality, is needed in order to free the woman's ability to access her own psychic energy. Many abuse victims find new-age humanistic and psychic explorations helpful in regaining or strengthening their own spirit (Garfield, 1974). Laidlaw et al. (1990) described integration of various spiritual adjuncts with therapy, and Hendricks (1984) described a similar integration with organized religion that focus on adding equality in gender issues. The spiritual realm may be especially helpful for survivors because of the fundamental attack on one's total well-being that the abuse causes.

A major feminist developmental theory proposed by Conarton and Silverman (1988; see also Silverman & Conarton, 1993) suggests that child development is not sequential but spiral in nature. This theory proposes that there are eight stages of development and that the woman goes back and revisits each stage during significant life cycle events as well as after any trauma. These stages of development are listed below.

- bonding
- orientation toward others
- cultural adaptation

- awakening and separation
- development of the feminine
- empowerment
- spiritual development
- integration

The stages are explored further in the following chapters. Understanding the coping strategies of women in general helps to sort out the role of trauma in adaptational strategies.

Another important feminist developmental theory is based on the work of Jean Baker Miller (1976) and the Stone Center at Wellesley College in Boston (Jordan, Kaplan, Miller, Stiver, & Surrey, 1991). Essentially, these theorists have proposed a new conceptualization of development for women that is reliant on connectedness with others rather than the traditional view of autonomy. Called self-in-relation, this theory radically changes the view of individual psychotherapy that concentrates on the woman's relationship with her internal self and suggests that therapy must deal with women's interpersonal relationships. According to this theory, an important way to deal with interpersonal relationships is through empathy. Research has demonstrated that inability to feel empathy is a major outcome of early and repeated abuse (Stahly, 1983). The emphasis in survivor therapy on working with redeveloping women's friendship patterns that are disrupted during the isolation caused by the abuser draws heavily on some of the Stone Center work.

A third theory of development comes from Carol Gilligan's (1982) work on women's theories of morality and justice. Until Gilligan's research, the prevailing psychological opinion was Kolberg's theory, which placed the highest standard of morality as a single objective standard of justice. Gilligan demonstrated that for women the highest standard of morality is a justice tempered with compassion for the individual. This is important in therapy work with abuse survivors, because these women must come to some understanding of justice in order to feel reempowered. If the abuser is allowed to escape without any consequences for his abusive behavior, the woman can never fully heal. However, what constitutes justice for most women is an individual resolution. Sometimes such individual resolutions include a belief in karma; if she believes in karma, the woman does not have to worry about the timing of delivering justice to her abuser. Other women want justice in this lifetime, and they need to be the ones who help the abuser to meet his deserved fate. Survivor therapy helps women to accept a standard of revenge, vindication, or justice that is predicated on and incorporates their own ability to live well.

UNDERSTANDING THE PROCESS OF SURVIVOR THERAPY

Adult women and children who survive abuse have had their world devastated by people who violated their trust, which results in boundary violations and adaptive styles that repeat themselves in the therapy relationship. Building trust in the therapy relationship is a major task, because survivors need to learn how to trust their own judgments as well as those of others. The therapist can assist the woman in rebuilding trust by being consistent in her manner of relating to the client; by not equivocating, misrepresenting, or lying to the client; and by being a real person, not a blank slate. Survivors cannot be expected to trust someone whom they do not know, someone who answers their questions with another question, or someone who uses their questions as a way to test the client's understanding of the therapist's reality or to analyze their fantasies. The business details of the therapy relationship need to be dealt with during the initial session. A check on the client's comfort level with the introduction of each new detail helps to give the client permission to share her feelings with the therapist. Control over some aspects of the therapy situation will help the client to relax and feel more of her own power. Avoiding manipulation and exploitation is important. Therapists who feel manipulated and exploited themselves in their own work situations will have much more difficulty being genuine with an abuse victim and delivering quality services. Considering the victim's sensitivity to harm, if a toxic therapy situation arises the therapist should take total responsibility for dealing with it, realistically reassuring the client of the therapist's own awareness and sensitivity to any inappropriate attempts to control the client's own setting.

The issue of boundaries and limits is important in survivor therapy. A boundary can be described as a "psychic wall" that emotionally separates each of us from another person. Because the abused woman's boundaries were violated by the abuse of power she experienced, she developed her own adaptive strategies to cope with the trauma. The client can be expected to replay in therapy the ways that she dealt with the violations of her personal space and boundaries. Therefore, it is essential that the therapist know her or his own boundaries in order to avoid inadvertently violating the client and reopening wounds caused by the earlier abuse. If violations occur and are identified by the client or therapist, they need to be dealt with quickly and given appropriate therapeutic attention. The issue of appropriate boundaries is one that will be addressed throughout the therapy process. If the therapist comes too close and violates the client's boundaries, it is expected that the client may experience the violation as another invasion. If the therapist maintains too great a distance, the client will be unable to experience the therapist as an ally in neutralizing the impact of the abuser. Thus, it is important for the therapist to self-monitor this process.

SUMMARY

Survivor therapy has its origins in feminist theory and trauma therapy. It works to help victims become survivors by helping them to regain some control over their lives. The tenets of survivor therapy include ensuring that the woman is safe, validating her experiences, identifying and building on the strengths the woman has shown in surviving her abuse, expanding her options, and understanding both her personal oppression and the oppression of all women by society.

The case history of Kim shows how various goals of survivor therapy—developing self-confidence, learning adapting skills, restoring clarity in judgment, among others—were achieved and the obstacles that had to be overcome in order to achieve them.

The future of survivor therapy will be determined by the need to help those women who have been abused to heal in a nonthreatening and nonabusive situation. Emphasis on the positive coping strengths of victims will help restore their confidence in their own abilities to survive even if they do not like their own behavior during the period of abuse. Survivor therapy is a more positive approach than most other therapies. It does not minimize the harm that abuse has done to women and provides techniques for reversing some of the psychological damage. It is grounded in both empirical research and a psychological clinical tradition of two decades of treatment. Before the development of specific treatment techniques, many women remained silent or unheard victims. It is hoped that the strength gained from the activism that is often the by-product of surviving abuse will prevent the kinds of violence against women that are described in this book and that, as a result, the need for survivor therapy will no longer exist.

11

Planning and Conducting an Assessment

Earlier chapters in this volume have described special issues, procedures, syndromes, and complications relevant to conducting an adequate assessment of women who have suffered from particular forms of abuse. In this chapter, I identify a few additional matters that are common in order to assess the impact of most forms of woman abuse. After explaining the importance of the woman's informed consent, this chapter examines strategies for obtaining accurate mental status examinations and abuse histories. Various psychological tests and how they can be applied to abused women are then reviewed. The final sections examine the particular problems that arise in custody evaluations and provide guidelines for determining when a consultant might be useful.

It is important to remember that whether the abuse has just occurred or was experienced many years ago, most women begin to reexperience the emotional fear and pain associated with the incident when retelling their stories. The assessment must be sensitive to these emotions and provide for a therapeutic encounter that will facilitate understanding and further healing at the same time that information is gathered.

Assessment of abused women combines traditional and customary psychological procedures with special methods that have been developed specifically for those who have suffered from serious abuse. What seems to plague many such assessments is incompleteness: The clinician ignored, discounted, shut off, or distorted valuable sources of information. Often the client stopped talking about the abuse because she did not think she was

---

Exhibit 11-1

Assessment Procedures

- Obtain Informed Consent
- Mental Status Examination
- Obtaining the Victim's Own Story
  Structured Interview
  Open-Ended Question and Answer
  Adequate Time Allowed
  Nonjudgmental
  No Interpretation
  Avoid Victim-Blaming Remarks
  Avoid Suggestions
  Place Story in Life Context
- Childhood Abuse History
- Adult Abuse History
- Relationship History
- Family Relationships and Friendship Patterns
- Social Skills
- Learned Helplessness Factors
- PTSD
- Medical and Physical Health History
- Racial, Cultural, and Other Potential Oppressors
- Relevant Legal Documents
- School Records
- Psychological Test Data
- Neuropsychological Tests

---

being believed. The most reliable and useful assessments examine a full range of cognitive, affective, and behavioral processes in a revealing developmental and social context. There is no one test that proves or disproves whether someone has been traumatized by abuse. Clinicians may find it helpful to use this chapter as a reminder of the large variety of sources of information that may be useful in evaluating, whether for forensic or therapeutic purposes, a woman who has been abused. See Exhibit 11-1 for an outline of suggested assessment procedures.

INFORMED CONSENT

An initial step in conducting a psychological assessment is to accord the client fully informed consent. The woman must understand why she is being assessed, what is involved in the assessment procedures, what kinds of information the assessment can yield, and the degree to which the information can or will be made available to other people. She must understand that certain kinds of information (e.g., accounts of child abuse or threats to kill an identifiable third party) may, depending on state law, obligate or allow the clinician to file special reports or take action to protect other actual or potential victims. She must understand the degree to which courts may have the right to subpoena the records of this assessment and to try to compel the clinician to testify. If her assessment or treatment is being paid for by a third party such as private insurance or a company health plan, she must understand the type of information that may be disclosed to the coverage provider and the implications of this information becoming a part of her permanent insurance or health care records. She must understand in what ways the clinician intends to record the assessment (e.g., through written notes, audio, or video recording). Forensic considerations, discussed in chapter 9, must be understood by the client in order for the clinician to make record-keeping decisions. Any concerns that the client has regarding any of these areas must be adequately addressed. In some states, signed disclosure and consent forms must become part of the record. It is a good idea to keep such a written record in most cases.

Only when the woman adequately understands this information and its implications will she be in a position to exercise her right of informed consent. For a more detailed description of informed consent issues and procedures, see Pope and Vasquez (1991).

MENTAL STATUS EXAMINATION

A mental status examination is usually performed near the beginning of most traditional assessments. However, the formal questions used in a mental status examination may prevent the abused woman from telling her story in her own way. Therefore, a general assessment of her ability to relate to the world in a reasonable, rational way will be sufficient until much later in the interview when she is better able to let the examiner provide direction without stopping the flow of information. A sample mental status examination that is used in the state of Florida can be found in Appendix A.

Letting the Woman Tell Her Own Story

It is important to give the abuse victim the time to talk about what has happened to her so that she does not feel rushed. Of all the special techniques required in order to collect reliable and valid data from the abuse victim, the need to give the woman ample time to talk to an interested, nonjudgmental, non-advice-giving person is one of the most critical. Often, the woman cannot describe the abuse in the earliest stages of therapy. She may veer away from a direct question toward long, seemingly unrelated tangents that serve to protect her from reexperiencing the intense feelings associated with remembering the abuse. Attempts to impose a dictatorial sequence of questions or to carefully control her report usually produce an incomplete, often extremely misleading version of events. If the client is being evaluated for other reasons, it is entirely possible that she will not give any information concerning the abuse and its psychological impact, especially if the evaluator does not make specific reference to the possibility of abuse or does not leave sufficient time to explore its consequences. This is one area in which the client needs to feel that she, not the evaluator, is in control. The most reliable and valid data are collected when the client leaves the assessment feeling as though she has made herself understood to the clinician.

A nonjudgmental but supportive stance on the part of the clinician is most helpful in obtaining the most reliable and valid information. Attempts to fill in the gaps or ask leading questions will often result in the woman agreeing with the interviewer, perhaps to please the interviewer, to get him or her to like her, or to end an uncomfortable experience as quickly as possible. This frequently happens in interviews with law enforcement officials. Similarly, if the evaluator approaches the interview with an openly skeptical or even a neutral attitude, the abused woman may not even attempt to describe what really happened. As mentioned in previous chapters, one of the areas damaged by abuse is the ability to perceive neutrality or objectivity. The client may interpret neutrality or objectivity as an indication that the interviewer is "against" her, and the likelihood that her best interests will not be respected influences how she responds to the interview. Thus, a slow, open-ended question-and-answer session is often the best way to begin the assessment.

Dealing With Guilt and Shame

Many abuse victims feel guilt and shame at what they have experienced, so that any attempt to speed up the story results in the woman feeling that the therapist does not understand, does not want to hear the details (which may have important meaning and provide clues leading to other significant events), or blames her. Because most abuse victims think that they are making a bigger emotional fuss over the events than necessary and should be better able to get on with their lives, any signs of impatience from the examiner reinforce this erroneous belief. The women then shut down their process of recall, frequently censoring the information that can give important clues for the development of a good treatment plan. Often the recitation of her story helps the client make new connections that help her to understand and to heal.

Clarifying Definitions

It is important to make sure definitions and descriptions are agreed on. Sometimes the client may use vague terms and euphemisms for violence such as "then he did IT to me." Here the evaluator must find out specifically what "IT" means. Other times the client may become so involved in telling the story that she uses names of people without identifying their roles and refers to places and events without clearly specifying what actually occurred, as though she assumes that the evaluator has more background information than is the case. Gentle questioning for the rest of the details in order to make sense of the story may be necessary, although if it seems peripheral to the most important data, it can just be noted and followed up on later.

Understanding Abuse Within the Life Context

Some clinicians find it useful to suggest to the woman at the beginning of the standard clinical interview that it is important for them to understand her life up until this point and that they will need her help in figuring it all out. Placing the abuse in the context of the woman's entire life will be the most helpful way to understand its impact. It may be useful to invite her to tell her story by saying something along the lines of the following: "I want to know all about what happened to you, when the harassment started at work or the first incident you can remember when you were hit or inappropriately sexually touched, how you responded, and what happened as it continued." Such comments can set the outside limits while also giving the woman lots of latitude within them.

Helping the Woman Begin

Some women understandably have trouble beginning to tell their stories. They do not know where to start. If it seems that the client needs help, it may be useful to say something like, "It doesn't matter where we start, but we will need to cover the abuse, your relationships with other important people in your life, and what in your life changed after you were raped" or "Do you have any ideas where it would be easier for you to start?" Inviting the woman to be a partner in figuring out what happened and how she managed to cope with it all can help the woman to feel that she is in a safe and supportive environment. It is important to record the details that she describes, particularly the incidents that may surround the current referral reasons.

Content and Affect

It is common for an abuse victim to demonstrate a variety of discordant emotions or no emotion at all during the retelling of the traumatic scenes. Specialists in posttraumatic stress disorder (PTSD) such as van der Kolk (1988) and Ochberg (1988) view this variability as more likely to represent a trauma response rather than an enduring aspect of personality that predated the trauma. In some instances, the woman may have incorporated all of the immediate emotional experience into the memory of a traumatic event so that when she attempts to retell the story of the abuse, she must either reexperience a variety of intense, chaotic feelings (sometimes with such immediacy that it is as though she were actually reexperiencing the abuse itself) or must find some way to block, split off, deny, or distort her feelings. As a result, some women may recount the most horrifying events in a dehumanized, almost robotic monotone; others may adopt a casual tone as if they were describing a trip to the post office; and still others may show a variety of intense emotions (e.g., anger, helpless laughter) that are clearly discordant with the events that they are describing. Sometimes the woman is able to describe an abusive incident at one session but not at the next session. This tendency to remember and then "re-forget" abusive incidents is characteristic of abuse victims who are still trying to deal with the recognition of trauma (cf. Herman, 1992, for further discussion).

DEVELOPMENT OF CHILDHOOD AND ADULT ABUSE HISTORIES

Most clinicians are trained to collect significant information about the client's childhood and social relationships including education and job histories. However, information about any abuse that happened to the client or other family members and the client's perception of its impact on her and on her family and friends is often left out of this history. This is significant in that research demonstrates that the single most important marker for further trauma is the experiencing or witnessing of abuse in childhood. Questions about discipline, anger expressed by parents, and sibling relationships are good ways to collect additional information.

There are some data suggesting that multiple victimization occurs, in part, because violent men notice those formerly abused women who do not appear to be as much in control of their lives as those who were not abused. However, much of the empirical research shows that there do not appear to be any particular vulnerabilities in the women that cause them to be attracted to abusive men (cf. Barnett & LaViolette, 1993, for a review). Research into recovery from single trauma incidents such as rape suggests that prior mental health problems may predict both short-term response and recovery outcome (Gidycz & Koss, 1990; Ruch & Leon, 1983), which makes it important that a complete history is gathered during the assessment period.

In Walker's (1984a) research with more than 400 battered women, childhood abuse and adult abuse experiences independently influenced the development of *learned helplessness*, which is the psychological construct that was first studied in the animal laboratory and then with college students in social psychology experiments by Seligman (1975, 1990) and his colleagues. Those who develop learned helplessness learn that they cannot predict what will protect them from further abuse. This noncontingency between response and outcome causes the victim to narrow her or his alternatives, choosing those actions that will have the highest probability of a specific outcome, in this case, minimizing the impact of the abuse. Learned helplessness is an explanation for the impact on cognitive processes from long-term abuse and its implications for recovery. In this research, unlike research into single incident trauma such as rape, there was no significance in the occurrence of learned helplessness from previous trauma. Nevertheless, it is still important to assess for each kind of trauma, because multiple forms of abuse can result in different treatment strategies as well as different answers to some forensic questions.

Assessing for Learned Helplessness Factors

The specific childhood events that were found to predict the development of learned helplessness (or the loss of the ability to predict that one's actions will have a particular safe outcome) include witnessing or experiencing abuse in the childhood home, sexual abuse or molestation as a child or adolescent, and experiencing self-defined critical events that the child perceives herself as having no control over (e.g., early parent loss through separation or death, alcoholism or drug abuse in one or both parents, frequent moving from one place to another, poverty or other embarrassment with other children, or school failures). The rigidity with which sex-role stereotypes are adhered to in the woman's childhood family is also significant. Socialization experiences that do not permit girls and women to fully develop all of their capabilities will damage their ability to cope with later violence. Chronic or critical illness as a child is also a factor in the subsequent development of an inability to predict that her behavior will have a particular desired outcome. In such situations, the child feels different and less capable than other children because she lacks the ability to control her physical well-being. Sometimes the restrictions placed on a child who is coping with illness give the child a negative mind-set. This makes it hard to deal with shame and being teased. When the new stressors of trauma occur, these childhood memories are recalled. A chart listing these five factors along with seven factors that need to be measured from adult relationships can be found in Appendix B (Walker, 1984a).

The assessing clinician should gather relevant information in order to understand whether any of these factors occurred during the victim's childhood, not to suggest that the woman was vulnerable to the abuse, but to understand the impact of the abuse on the woman's coping strategies. If someone has developed learned helplessness, she has not become literally helpless, but has lost the ability to predict the outcome of her own actions. She has learned to use fewer and fewer behavioral alternatives to cope with her situation. Asking questions in as supportive a way as possible helps normalize the experience and helps the woman overcome any shame and guilt that she may feel so that she can talk about the abuse. Reempowerment and self-efficacy restore the woman to her original ability to choose from many behavioral options and turn the learned helplessness into what Seligman (1990) called *learned optimism*. Obviously, this is a cognitive–behavioral theory that places less emphasis on affect and social relationships. In order to make a complete PTSD assessment, interpersonal relationships must also be carefully assessed.

Adult Abuse History

It is also important to gather a complete history of any adult relationships that have been abusive, including the particular abuse for which the assessment is being done. Most abused people feel that they have been psychologically taken advantage of, and other relationships may also seem more toxic in retrospect. This does not mean the woman is exaggerating the prior or even subsequent relationships; rather, they are being seen through a different lens. In fact, some abuse victims who have ended the abusive relationship are so sensitive to any future attempts by men to control them by psychological or physical means that they react negatively to even minor events. Sexual harassment and abuse victims, particularly, are often surprised at the strength of their anger against all men, particularly those who attempt to take any control over their lives.

Nonjudgmental Process

It is important for the evaluator not to form or communicate judgments about either the character of the abuser or the legitimacy of the woman's anger. Even attempts to define the type of abuse too narrowly will shut down the responses of the woman. During the assessment period, the evaluator should simply acknowledge the woman's feelings and gather the data to help understand her point of view. As has been stated before, objectivity is lost when a woman has experienced the psychological effects of violence. Whether the trauma has just happened or they are relating details of an incident that occurred long ago, most abused women still feel so threatened by harm that they need to know that the clinician believes them and will protect them.

PTSD Factors

Initially, the evaluator must be sure to cover the areas necessary in order to determine if a PTSD was or is still present from the abuse. The *Diagnostic and Statistical Manual of Mental Disorders* criteria are usually used to make this determination, and an abridged version of these can be found in Appendix C. First, the abuse history is used to determine whether abuse occurred. Then, the cognitive damage is measured by the presence of intrusive memories of the abuse either while dreaming, while reminded of the abuse by some stimulus, while not trying to think about it, or while reexperiencing the abuse through flashbacks, dissociation, or other experiences. Assessment of the high arousal and high avoidance symptoms must also be made, including acute as well as long-term emotional reactions. Changes in physiological conditions, such as eating and sleeping disorders, gastrointestinal problems, cardiovascular system changes (e.g., heart palpitations), reproductive tract problems, changes in sexual feelings and behavior, and other medical conditions, should be queried. Knowledge of the symptoms listed in the earlier chapters that describe the various types of abuse will be of great assistance to the evaluator. The symptoms need to have been present for at least 1 month. (These symptoms are further described in chapter 12.)

Family Relationships and Friendship Patterns

Information about family relationships and friendships with both men and women serves as important data in an assessment, particularly for treatment planning. An understanding of the client's historical pattern of social relationships as well as of current ones is needed. The degree of support that the abused woman can reasonably count on from her family or friends will be important for a therapist to know, especially because the research suggests that such support is a key factor in recovery from trauma (Conte & Berliner, 1988; Figley, 1988; Koss & Harvey, 1991).

It is not surprising that many victims of long-term, repeated abuse (e.g., as battered women, adult survivors of incest, victims of sexual harassment at work, and women exploited by therapists) have few friends who can be of support to them. Most of these women have "used up" any friends that they had before the abusive relationship began and are isolated as a result of the PTSD. A good assessment will attempt to determine if the woman had good social skills prior to the adult trauma or if early trauma prevented her from ever developing strong interpersonal relationships. It is important to make this differentiation so that a treatment plan can include the appropriate interpersonal skills needed to get the woman more involved in healthy social relationships. In either case, the women who have experienced these kinds of abuse have had their trust betrayed by someone with whom they have also had a caring relationship. This makes it difficult for them even to know how to evaluate a social relationship.

Medical Exams and Other Record Reviews

Many therapists do not attempt to collect past records at the initiation of therapy, often waiting until later on in the treatment should such information become important in answering specific questions. However, with abuse victims it is important to know the woman's medical history from the onset in order to assist her in understanding the physical changes to her body as well as the mental ones. A woman who has a long history of hypertension, for example, will react differently to the stress of a sudden trauma than a woman who has no such history. Those with eating disorders, such as anorexia and bulimia, often have sexual abuse in their backgrounds. Incest survivors are more likely to self-mutilate, and battered women often have records with unexplained accidental injuries. Other records of the client's history are important to gather if for no other purpose than to help the woman develop the ability to judge her recovery in the context of her past history.

Exhibit 11-2

Physical Health Problems for Survivors

CHRONIC HEALTH PROBLEMS FOR SURVIVORS
A. Skeletal and Neuromuscular
    Back pain
    Facial pain
    Headache
    TMJ and bruxism
    Psychogenic seizures
    Sleep disorders
B. Gynecological and Reproductive Systems
    Chronic pelvic pain
    Chronic vaginal infections

PMS
Sexually transmitted diseases
Problem pregnancies including drugs and alcohol
Sexual dysfunction
C. Gastrointestinal Systems
Irritable bowel with diarrhea and constipation
Nausea
Distended stomach, bloating, gas problems
Poor dietary habits
Eating disorders

STRESS RELATED ILLNESSES
A. Impact on Immunological System
Chronic stress
Autonomic nervous system responsiveness
Endocrine system
Immunological system
B. Neuropsychological Functioning
Long-term impact from stress related disorders
Bruising of nerves from physical trauma
Relationship to later demyelinization
Cognitive–behavioral injuries from
    "shaken baby/adult syndrome"
C. Cardiovascular Disease
High stress/time urgency/anger model
Type A theories
D. Cancer
Relationship to immunological system
Repressed emotions model
Passive acceptance of trauma theories

ADDICTIONS IN SURVIVORS
A. Drinking Alcohol
Battered women with alcoholic partners

Exhibit 11-2 continues

Exhibit 11-2 continued
>   Alcoholic batterers
> B. Drug Abuse
>   List drugs using and amount
>   Drugs used if/when pregnant
>   Psychotropic drugs
> C. Smoking Cigarettes
>   History of smoking
>   Behavioral coping response
> D. Eating Disorders
>   Anorexia and bulimia
>   Nutrition and eating patterns

In forensic cases, it is critical to corroborate one's opinion with the material (called "discovery") provided by the attorney. Sometimes the data are collected by the woman's attorney and investigators; in other instances data are provided by the opposing attorney. In either case, it is important to see what the other side says in order to make decisions about the credibility of the woman's perceptions. Any medical and psychological reports from earlier periods in the woman's life also help delineate how much of her cognition, affect, and behavior are due to the trauma and how much come from other experiences. Of course, the subtle and not so subtle interactions among race, ethnicity, sexism, class, physical abilities, and sexual orientation all must be taken into account. Women who are abused by individual men also face daily exploitation in the world, particularly at work or when going about their daily business. Strategies to cope with this constant oppression may be disrupted by the more acute abuse situation, causing an even greater magnitude of emotional response. Research has shown that sensitivity to these factors is important in understanding the impact of abuse on individual as well as on classes of women (L.S. Brown & Ballou, 1992; L.S. Brown & Root, 1990).

Medical examinations are important in treatment planning, as well as in forensic evaluations, to assess the damage done by the violence and the woman's coping strategies. It is often possible to look at x-rays of old fractures to see if they occurred as a result of human aggression or accidental or other trauma, even if the woman did not tell the doctor about abuse. Rape may also be differentiated from consensual sex by a physical exam. Tests using certain dyes may be helpful in locating vaginal or anal tears that result from force. Information about other injuries that were treated, even if the woman lied about how they occurred, can be helpful in making a diagnosis. Sexual abuse victims often have major gynecological problems including frequent infections, sexually transmitted diseases, chronic pelvic pain, bleeding disorders, and other medical complications. Sometimes these problems can be directly linked to the abuse, although at other times the connections are more indirect. For example, children who have been incest victims often demonstrate more frequent ear and other staph infections. Although proof of penetration may not be seen in a medical examination, use of certain dyes may enhance the diagnosis. Even the presence of such an examination in an adult woman's childhood medical records may provide clues to help her regain buried incest memories.

A decrease in the effective functioning of the woman's immunological system may also be noted, although there is not yet any research that can positively and directly link stress with such malfunctioning (McGrath, Keita, Strickland, & Russo, 1990). Spielberger (1991) demonstrated that higher anxiety levels combined with a time urgency mind-set and anger are consistent with the type of aggression that is compatible with early cardiovascular disease in men. Perceptions of lack of control and inability to express one's feelings are associated with a breakdown in the immunological system, particularly in the development of some forms of cancer. It is still not known exactly how high stress affects the physiological functioning of the body, but the constant release of hormones and other biochemical substances used by the body to make a "fight or flight" response is believed to have a negative impact (Cotton, 1990). See Exhibit 11-2 for a list of physical health problems that are common among survivors of abuse.

Collateral Interviews With Third Parties

It is sometimes important to document the abuse through interviews with others who know the woman in different ways. For example, it may be useful to know how her children perceived the abuse in their home, not to get to the truth, but to get another version of what the dynamics were in that setting. It is not unusual in battering homes for the children to become polarized: Sometimes they identify with the aggressor and at other times with the victim. The presence of such dichotomies may help to confirm the extent of the abuse. It may also be important to learn how other family members perceive the victim as coping with her life after a rape. Sometimes the victim views the family as less supportive than she would like several months after the rape, whereas the family's perception is that the woman has become a tyrant in her demands and has worn them all out. In other cases, family members or close friends may provide a different or a similar view of the woman's emotional equilibrium prior to the abuse. Family pictures are sometimes helpful in piecing together preabuse functioning. It is important to remember that there may be self-interest, including discharging of their own guilt feelings for failing to protect the victim, mixed into reports by close friends and family.

Meetings with one or more family members also can give the therapist some indication as to whether family therapy would be a useful adjunct to individual or group treatment. Figley (1990) has developed a strategy for using family therapy to treat victims and their families, enhancing their recovery within a supportive environment. Other family therapists have also become interested in helping female abuse victims to heal within their family structures. Sometimes this is an appropriate mode of treatment from the outset, but in other instances it may be better to help the client deal with her own feelings about her family before starting such a treatment plan. Assessment for family strengths and dysfunctions will help the clinician make those decisions.

It is also important to understand the meaning of family in the proper cultural context. Lesbian women, for example, may not view their families as supportive of helping them to deal with abuse issues if they have not yet disclosed their lesbianism or if the family has not accepted their sexuality. Of course, with therapeutic support this may be an ideal time to prepare the client to "come out," but not without adequate preparation and support as described by others (L.S. Brown, 1992b). African-American, Asian-

American, or Hispanic women whose families may still live in another culture (whether in this country or somewhere else) will also need special attention given to cultural ethos. Sometimes the families make it difficult for these women to ask for or receive emotional support (cf. L.S. Brown & Root, 1990, for further discussion of different racial, ethnic, and cultural groups). In a complete assessment, the evaluator must examine these issues with the woman to help prepare her to make decisions about how much to share with and rely on her family.

Assessing Danger to Woman

Although most therapists assess for suicide potential and dangerousness according to their state's legal standards, it is unusual for them to consider the danger to the client, especially if the abuse is ongoing. The duty-to-warn statutes were based on cases of assailants who were known to their victims. Hart (1988) suggested that the therapist's duty to the client goes beyond the usual duty-to-warn standards and includes a duty to protect the woman and children. Others who work with battered women and children would concur. Edwards (1989) and Ferraro (1989) described coordination with police and law enforcement, McLeer and Anwar (1989) described the appropriate expectations from referrals to an emergency room, and Blackman (1986, 1989) described the difficulties involved for women who kill their abusive partner in self-defense (see also Walker, 1984c, 1989b). Walker (1989c) described the difficulties involved in working with the legal system when the abuse victim becomes a defendant in a criminal case.

Obtaining and Reviewing Previous Records and Documents

In assessing the impact of abuse on a woman, it is important to gather as many different sources of information as possible in order to corroborate the opinion. All of the following help establish the credibility of the women's reporting ability: police reports (which are rare but sometimes exist); calls to the police, rape crisis lines, and battered women shelters; emergency room or doctor's records that document injuries (even if the woman did not say how they occurred); doctor's records indicating illnesses and notations about stress; and witness reports that are obtained by investigators hired in legal cases. In one case, the battered woman never reported the abuse to the police nor did she seek medical attention even though some of her injuries might have warranted it. However, she had reported that her husband had broken her glasses several times and had pulled the telephone out of the wall, which required him to call the phone company to repair it. Records from the optometrist and telephone company were obtained that documented her stories of abuse. In another case that took place in a small rural town, 20 years, worth of medical records were intact, showing "accidental" injuries that documented the woman's stories. Often the addition of little details about nonabuse occurrences during the assault adds credibility to the victim's reports. Obviously, the evaluators are not private investigators, although they must be prepared to help play detective with the client in order to find such information.

In cases in which the abuser vehemently denies the charges, it may be useful to look through the court records (particularly if he is local) to see if there are other cases in which he is either a defendant or a plaintiff or is involved in divorce actions. Sometimes the files are sealed and can be reopened if a judge is persuaded that the information contained within them might be legally (or even therapeutically) helpful. This is especially common when there are sealed juvenile records. Court records are public records and, as such, are easily accessible. This is important to remember when preparing notes and records that might end up in a court battle.

It is not uncommon for rape, sexual assault, and harassment victims to have gynecological problems for which they seek medical attention, even if they do not tell the doctor about the abuse. These records are also helpful in documenting a case. In other cases, there are previous psychological reports that provide a baseline for the woman's preabuse functioning. Old school records with test scores may be helpful in either corroborating when incest began, as demonstrated by a change in school functioning, or as a baseline with which to compare current distress. The notes of previous therapists may be helpful in understanding the dynamics of the client's current functioning. If there have been previous hospitalizations, nursing notes often provide a good glimpse into the day-to-day functioning of the client.

It is important for psychologists who are working with attorneys on legal cases to help the attorneys to understand the difference between psychological assessments and investigations better performed by trained investigators. It is possible for the psychologist to use the interviews done by investigators to make interpretations that are helpful in understanding the state of mind of the client. Sometimes, however, the psychologist needs to interview the witness separately, because other types of information may be gathered from the psychologist's questioning. If the psychologist also becomes the investigator, the attorney may need more detail for legal evidence than is typical for the mental health professional to gather. Collaborative work with investigators and attorneys provides for the best data collection.

PSYCHOLOGICAL TESTING AND BEHAVIORAL ASSESSMENT

Minnesota Multiphasic Personality Inventory

The Minnesota Multiphasic Personality Inventory (MMPI) is probably the most frequently used standardized psychological assessment instrument. It is a long, true–false test (566 questions) that measures personality patterns in an objective manner. There are now three forms of the test, the original MMPI-1, the more recently restandardized MMPI-2, and the MMPI-A for adolescents. Although the two tests are said to be compatible, there are still some problems to be worked out in the newer version.

The professional literature describes typical PTSD profiles using the MMPI-1 among individuals suffering from combat stress (Figley, 1985), battered woman syndrome (Dutton, 1992; Dutton-Douglas & Colantuono, 1987; Rosewater, 1985a, 1987a; Walker, 1989a, 1989b) and rape trauma syndrome (Kilpatrick et al., 1989; Kilpatrick, Veronen, & Resick, 1979). Some of these patterns have also been found using the MMPI-2, as reported by Pope, Butcher, and Seelen (1993).

The battered woman syndrome tends to reveal elevations on scales 2, 4, 6, and 8, which measure depression, anger, suspiciousness, and confusion, respectively. It is not unusual to find the victim who is still in crisis to be high on distress as measured by responses to those questions infrequently endorsed in the *F* scale and defensive, and low on perceptions of self-esteem and ability to cope, but covering with socially desirable responses as measured by the *K* scale and the Ego Strength scale. In child custody battles and some personal injury cases in which the woman is terrified of falling apart emotionally, a higher than usual *K* score occurs, requiring use of the correction. Although there has been some discussion about the use of the *K* correction in forensic cases or with some populations, particularly those with limited education, Pope, Butcher, and Seelen (1993) insisted that it is never invalid to use the correction. Dutton-Douglas and Colantuono (1987) found several patterns indicating more than one type of response using standardized tests, although it is important to emphasize that many victims of various forms of abuse will not, for a wide range of reasons, fit the typical patterns.

Rape trauma syndrome profiles also have been found empirically on the MMPI-1. Kilpatrick et al. (1979) found that rape victims often have elevations on scales 1 (somatic symptoms), 3 (hysteria), and 7 (ruminating, obsessions and compulsions). A woman who has been physically and sexually abused might demonstrate elevations on all seven of these scales. Different combinations may be more accurately explained by the abuse history than by the traditional code point explanations.

Rosewater (1985a, 1985b, 1987a) emphasized the importance of interpreting profiles carefully and with sensitivity to abuse issues that are not reflected in computer-assisted scoring. Her research showed that misdiagnoses, particularly with schizophrenia and borderline personality disorders, are common without a careful analysis for abuse histories. Computer-generated interpretations may not be adequately normed and validated for various populations of abuse victims and may be seriously misleading. Regardless of whether a computer-scoring and interpretation service is used, all findings on the basis of a standardized instrument such as the MMPI must be treated as hypotheses to be evaluated in light of the individual's history and other sources of information.

Because there are two forms of the instrument, clinicians must consider carefully whether to use the original or the revised version. The original version, which obviously has a longer history of use, contains items embodying sexist wording and assumptions as well as other items that may be offensive to some test-takers. Although there are studies indicating that the MMPI is not as useful when the client is from a cultural or ethnic background that is not part of the mainstream, in fact, Rosewater's (1985a, 1985b) data indicated that the abuse profiles were more significant than the other norms.

Wechsler Adult Intelligence Scale–Revised

The Wechsler Adult Intelligence Scale–Revised (WAIS–R) provides a general assessment of cognitive ability and performance. The performance on each subtest and the scatter both within and between scales may reflect the cognitive impact of the abuse, the cognitive strategies a victim calls on to meet challenges, and her patterns of intellectual strengths and weaknesses. This test is particularly useful when the client's mental judgment is called into question. A few typical findings are noted below as examples.

It is not unusual for abuse victims to develop mental confusion that blocks the abuse from their awareness. They may have trouble understanding and following directions, perform far more poorly on many of the subtests than their previous records (such as school transcripts) would suggest, and perform especially poorly on any subtest item that in any way reminds them of the abusive experience. One woman, for example, became so distressed during the Object Assembly subtest that she could not continue. One of the puzzles comprised parts of the human body, which evoked for her the theme of dismemberment associated with her abuse. On other subtests, however, her performance was at a superior intellectual level. This demonstrates the temporary and specific but still serious impact on cognitive functioning of the emotional distress that is connected with the abuse issues.

Many abuse victims have a heightened sense of hypervigilance. They have been living in great fear and have learned to constantly scan and monitor the environment for any changes, details, or signs that might signal danger. They may tend to pay great attention to small details such as those measured by the Picture Completion subtest. On the other hand, they may completely ignore some details that have significance in relation to the emotionally charged issues. The degree of concern with their trauma-induced condition may be seen in the pattern of emotional responses to questions on subtests such as Vocabulary and Comprehension. Their knowledge of social situations may be better than their ability to carry out such interactions, which may be measured by the difference between Comprehension (knowledge) scores and Picture Arrangement (practice) scores. Idiosyncratic social functioning may be revealed if descriptions of the picture arrangement cards are elicited.

Rigidity in shifting cognitive sets can also be measured by the WAIS–R subtests, particularly those that encourage a shift in focus when one analysis is not correct. Block Design, which calls for the ability to analyze and break down the details that make up the designs and, then, to synthesize that information in rebuilding the patterns under the stress of being timed, is one subtest in which the impact of additional stress on cognitive flexibility can be demonstrated clearly. The verbal subtests of Similarities and to some extent Comprehension can also provide interesting information about cognitive rigidity and flexibility changes when the stress increases because of internal factors.

Immense stress may affect a woman's ability to attend consistently to the demands of the test. Her attention to the test may fade out and in. Lapses in attention to the test may occur while she is distracted by unbidden images, intrusive thoughts, or distressing memories. Such uneven attention may produce significant intratest scatter; easier questions are failed while more difficult ones are passed. Of course, this pattern is also indicative of neuropsychological damage, so a history of head shaking and trauma will need to be explored, too.

The WAIS–R subtest analysis is also helpful in answering the typical forensic questions that come up with abuse victims. If a woman is coerced into performing a criminal act through fear of further abuse if she resists, the impact of emotional stress on her cognitive abilities may be seen in her WAIS–R responses. Impact on ability to think about things is also important in some personal injury lawsuits in order to demonstrate the damage done to the woman by the abuse. For example, a woman who sues a professor and the university for sexual harassment may charge that the damages incurred by not finishing her dissertation were due in part to the harassment's effects on her ability to concentrate and to perform other cognitive tasks necessary to complete a dissertation.

Some women are surprised to learn that, according to the test results, they are very bright. This particularly happens with women who have not completed their schooling, but have continued learning throughout life. This knowledge may make a major difference in their self-esteem, further enhancing their recovery. It is also helpful in vocational and educational planning.

Exhibit 11-3

Psychological Tests

COGNITIVE TESTING
    Weschler Adult Intelligence Scale-Revised (WAIS–R)
    Bender Visual Motor Gestalt Test
PERSONALITY TESTING
    Minnesota Multiphasic Personality Inventory
        MMPI-1, MMPI-2, MMPI-A
    Rorschach
    Thematic Apperception Test (TAT)
    Millon Clinical Multiaxial Inventory (MCMI)
ASSESSMENT CHECKLISTS
    Symptom Checklist (SCL-90)
    State–Trait Anxiety Inventory
    Profile of Mood States
    Center for Epidemiological Studies Depression Scale (CES-D)
    Beck Depression Inventory
    Modified Fear Survey
    Impact of Events Scale
    Lazarus Coping Scales
    Locus of Control Inventory
    Attitudes Toward Women Scale
    Battered Woman Syndrome Questionnaire

One of the major benefits of using a standardized test such as the WAIS–R is to be able to compare the individual woman's thinking processes with those known for other battered women as well as for nonbattered women. This can also be done with children by using the revised and third editions of the Weschler Intelligence Scale for Children (WISC–R and WISC–III, respectively). It is important to reiterate that, like any other test, the results should only be used when integrated with other test and interview data.

Rorschach and Thematic Apperception Test (TAT)

Some women who have been in continuing abusive relationships (e.g., women who have been battered by live-in partners, repeatedly raped by their husbands, sexually intimate with their therapists, or sexually involved with father figures) may have developed extensive coping mechanisms to hide the distress and dysfunction caused by the abuse. Attempts to conceal both the abuse and its sequelae may be the result of explicit threats from the abuser, feelings of shame and self-blame, or fears that they will be criticized and ridiculed by others. Some women who have suffered a single incident of serious abuse may likewise develop ways to present a good front to those around them, perhaps as part of a process of denial. Projective instruments such as the Rorschach and the TAT may be exceptionally useful in identifying deeper levels of perceptual biases, the ways the woman organizes what she perceives, thought process (and in some cases, thought disorder), and unconscious themes. These tests are particularly useful with bright, "socially acceptable" women who have learned to look good on the outside and may be out of touch with their deeper feelings.

Other Psychological Assessment Instruments

Few behavioral assessment checklists assess either directly for abuse history or indirectly for effects of abuse. Some assessment for PTSD through use of anxiety and depression measures have been reported. The most popular scales used specifically to measure anxiety include the following: the Derogatis (1977) Symptom Checklist–Revised (SCL-90-R), and some of the briefer versions updated and published by Johns Hopkins University that measure anxiety, depression, obsessive–compulsive behavior, interpersonal sensitivity, and somatization; Spielberger's State–Trait Anxiety Inventory (Spielberger, Gorsuch, & Luschene, 1970); and the Profile of Mood States (POMS), which contains bipolar dimensions of anxious–composed, elated–depressed, agreeable–hostile, energetic–tired, clearheaded–confused, and confident–unsure. The scales most often used for measuring depression specifically are the Radloff (1977) Center for Epidemiology Studies Depression Scale (CES-D), and the Beck Depression Inventory (Beck, 1976). The measurement of fear is done using the Kilpatrick et al. (1979) modification of the Modified Fear Survey (MFS), originally developed by Wolpe (1982). This scale can be administered every 6 months and the results compared with the Kilpatrick sample to help measure the healing process, particularly of rape victims.

The Impact of Events Scale, used by Horowitz, Wilner, and Alvarez (1979), measures the impact of events as disparate as rape, bereavement, robbery, and other stressful events to help assess PTSD, particularly intrusive thoughts and isolation. Modifications of the Lazarus Coping Scales have been done to include items specific to rape victims (Burt & Katz, 1988). Locus of control, or the woman's perception of power, can be measured through the Levenson (1972) Locus of Control Inventory, although other such inventories can also be used.

Specific rape symptom inventories are described by Koss and Harvey (1991). Dutton (1992) provided sample copies of a number of assessment inventories used in the Nova University Battered Women's Psychology Clinic. Walker (1984a) described the Battered Woman Syndrome Questionnaire (BWSQ) that is used to collect information about battered women.[12] There are also several checklists available to assess PTSD symptoms directly, but these generally refer to postcombat stress rather than the types of abuse discussed in this book and, as such, are not usually very helpful for understanding women who have been abused. The Millon Clinical Multiaxial Inventory (MCMI) has not been standardized using an abuse victim population and therefore gives false positives on personality disorder

---

[12]The BWSQ is not available without training in its administration because of its long and complicated administration and interpretation (it takes 6 to 10 hours to use).

dimensions that abuse impact may sometimes mimic. It is not recommended as an assessment instrument for this population because it causes too much confusion. However, in forensic situations, in which the issue of personality disorders becomes more important, the MCMI may be helpful if it rules out such disorders. See Exhibit 11-3 for a list of psychological tests that may be used to evaluate abuse survivors.

Neuropsychological Assessment

When a psychological assessment is conducted, there must be some adequate basis for screening for overt and subtle neuropsychological deficits and disorders. The anxiety, stress, and other sequelae of abuse can often mask neuropsychological impairment; an assessment that omits an adequate neuropsychological screening component may be seriously incomplete or misleading. The field of neuropsychology is advancing rapidly, and it is crucial that the assessment of possible neuropsychological disorders be conducted or supervised by someone who has the most current knowledge. Repeated abuse and head trauma may cause subtle but no less critical deficits. A referral to a neuropsychologist, who has access to the latest revised Halstead-Reitan norms that account for more subtle and long-term injuries, may be appropriate, given the results of the neuropsychological screening or a history of abuse to the head.

Some forms of neuropsychological impairment seem closely associated with physical and sexual abuse. Some battered women, for example, may have an adult version of shaken baby syndrome from the violent shaking that occurs during an attack. Punching the head repeatedly, bouncing a woman down a stairway, throwing her against a wall, and flinging her to the floor are all aspects of battering that can cause subtle or more obvious damage to a woman's brain. One woman described how her husband, in a rage, held her by the heels and swung her around until her head banged into the door.

Some abused women experience a form of neuropsychological damage similar to the boxer's punch-drunk syndrome. In some cases, individual blows may show no immediate effects. The woman may be stunned, but will recover her senses fairly rapidly, and the deterioration does not become apparent for many years. The cumulative damage caused by such assaults, however, can be severe and permanent.

It is not unusual for fluid pressure to build up in the brain or severe head injuries to result from blows by objects or by the man's fists. Emergency room records reporting concussions as well as serious neurological trauma, some even requiring surgery, need to be reviewed and careful documentation of the acute and residual damage needs to be performed, especially when damages are being measured. Therapy may also have to address rehabilitation programs so that the client may relearn the use of functions that have been damaged.

The Halstead-Reitan or Luria Nebraska batteries can assess visual-motor or language deficiencies and suggest rehabilitation strategies to overcome the damage. For an abused woman who is terrified that she is going crazy when she notices she is unable to function in the same way as before the abuse, just providing this information may help to establish trust and provide relief with the knowledge that there is a physical cause for some of her problems.

That the neuropsychological damage may be cumulative, delayed, subtle, and sometimes concealed by a woman who has learned strategies to hide her impairment underscores the importance of securing all available records of prior medical treatment as well as taking a good inventory of prior and current neuropsychological functioning.

CUSTODY EVALUATIONS

When collecting data in custody evaluations it is important to assess the impact that the abuse has on the ability of the individuals to parent their children individually and jointly. This is rarely done in current custody evaluations (cf. Deed, 1991a; Liss & Stahly, 1993). Although the issue of child custody evaluations is too large to be given proper attention here, it is important to outline some of the major concerns, because many evaluators have little training in violence issues (Stahly, 1990). Most of the literature deals with allegations of sexual abuse of children and with battered women whose custody is challenged. However, the accusations and issues raised in a custody evaluation are not that different for other abused women who find themselves in a battle for custody of their children. The psychological issues noted in such an evaluation raise concerns about the abused woman's parenting ability. Thus, special methods must be adopted in order to perform an assessment that separates the temporary effects from trauma that are exacerbated by the custody evaluation and those that may interfere in the mother's ability to parent her children. When there is evidence of trauma, either recent or past, the mother may need the therapist's help to get through the evaluation. She may show the psychological symptoms of increased suspiciousness and anger because she is unsure that her children will be well cared for and she feels that she lacks control over her own and her children's lives.

Walker and Edwall (1987) suggested that when physical or psychological battering in the relationship is suspected or alleged, each adult should be interviewed separately first, and questions about abuse should be asked individually. If there are known incidents of spouse abuse, the father and mother should not be placed together in the evaluation because the man can intimidate the woman in subtle ways that may prevent detection by the evaluator. The ease of intimidation of women who are victims of other types of abuse is similar to that seen in battered women, particularly when most women face a custody challenge and evaluation as if it were the most critical judgment anyone will ever make about them. Women have been socialized to believe that their self-esteem is based on their ability to perform as both a wife and a mother. Accusations leveled by a husband that a woman is neither can precipitate a reexperiencing of old traumas, which may cause her to perform below her actual capabilities in such an examination. See Exhibit 11-4 for Walker and Edwall's suggested custody evaluation procedures.

Deed (1991b) cautioned therapists that many families of divorce are not suffering from the dynamics of disappointed love, but from assaults that have not yet ceased. She suggested that noncustodial parents who have access to greater economic resources may be using the courts as another way to batter and intimidate the other parent. A careful evaluation consists of (a) evaluating safety for all those concerned beginning with current circumstances, (b) examining family relationships over at least three generations, (c) obtaining information about the clients' relationship style, (d) examining decision-making ability, (e) evaluating relationship to authority figures, (f) evaluating patterns of same- and opposite-sex friends and lovers (if available), (g) learning the styles of discipline, and (h) learning the methods of expressing feelings. Deed mentioned several common errors that are made by evaluators, including believing in the "it takes two to tango" philosophy of domestic violence, which subtly or overtly blames the woman. Leaving the relationship places the woman's ability to control and protect her children in jeopardy. This is one of the major reasons cited by battered women who leave shelters to return to the abuser (Stahly, 1990). Even years later, the power dynamics from an abusive relationship may still be in place, making it difficult for the mother to hold her own. Many women give in to the abusive man's demands (even years later) to obtain a feeling of psychological safety and to escape from his further influence. Deed (1991b) reminded therapists and evaluators that they may attempt to contain their own fears of possible violence directed against themselves by placating the abuser. She further cautioned not to strongly advocate for one side or the other as the best way to prevent kidnappings or homicides.

Walker and Edwall (1987) suggested specific procedures to try to equalize the situation and help assess the woman's true performance with her children. Interviews between the father and children need to be structured to measure the power and control issues in their interactions as well as the man's nurturing abilities. The mother needs to be observed to see how her ability to protect her children has been affected by the father's controlling behavior. If she is terrified that the father will continue to hurt her and the children, then the evaluators must find some ways to assure her that the children will be safe or, if that is not possible, evaluators must monitor some visitation with the father in order to avoid later difficulties. Failure to address these serious and often valid fears of the mother may invalidate the results of the entire evaluation.

Exhibit 11-4

Custody Evaluation Procedures

A. Interview Format

    1. Interview as many members of the family as is possible. Insist on offering to meet with those who are unwilling to participate. Even telephone interviews can give some information.

    2. Interview individuals at separate times so there is no possible intimidation in the waiting room or fear of being overheard.

    3. Keep family members together only if you determine that you can keep it safe and that the joint interview will yield important information. Sometimes you can get information about the woman's anxiety levels and how she changes when the man is around, which is important to document. This is also true for children.

    4. Videotape joint interviews if they do take place. This helps keep the man on his best behavior. Replays often reveal the little signals that intimidation is still taking place.

    5. Follow this typical interview schedule:

        a. Interview the mother

        b. Interview the father

        c. Interview the child or children alone and together

        d. Interview the child and the mother

        e. Interview the child and the father

        f. Interview the child and both parents together (optional)

        g. Interview both parents together (optional)

    6. Know which parent has had physical custody of the children immediately prior to the interview. Offer additional parent interactional interviews if either parent does not feel the interview reflects their relationship.

    7. Interview significant others in the children's life. Usually this

is done by telephone with grandparents, friends, other relatives, teachers, babysitters, former therapists, clergy, employers and co-workers, doctors. Interpret the information understanding that abuse may be hidden and sometimes others have self-interest including guilt feelings that affect their information.

B. Questions to ask

   1. Is battering being alleged in this relationship? (Ask a variety of questions to go beyond initial denials. Generally, questions about how each parent responds to anger reveal possible abusive situations.) If so, obtain battering history:

      a. How aware is each parent of how much violence the child has heard, seen, or knows about?

      b. How does each parent view the impact on children?

      c. How much does each parent depend on the child for emotional support?

      d. How does it affect her ability to parent?

      e. How does it affect his ability to parent?

      f. How does it impact on use of resources?

      g. How does it impact on ability to form support networks in community to help with parenting?

      h. How dangerous is it for the woman to be in charge of visitation exchange?

      i. How much risk is there that the mother will continue to be battered?

      j. How much risk is there that the child will be physically and/or psychologically battered?

      k. How much risk is there that the child will be sexually abused?

      l. How much risk is there for emotional incest?

   2. What is the current mental health of each parent and child?

      a. What does the current mental status and clinical

Exhibit 11-4 continues

Exhibit 11-4 continued

   interview show?

   b. What is each parent's mental health history?

   c. Cognitive and personality tests can be used if time is limited and a standardized sample of behavior is wanted. But tests are not always necessary or accurate, so the results must be interpreted carefully.

   d. How do these factors interact with parenting skills required? (This is the critical question, which often goes unanswered even when a full battery of tests is administered and a long, detailed social history is obtained.)

3. What are the woman's and man's current parenting skills?

   a. In what behavioral and cognitive areas do they show agreement and disagreement with each other?

   b. On what values do they agree and disagree?

   c. How do they present areas of disagreement to the child? (Joint and individual structured and unstructured tasks can be used to answer this set of questions. Observations of solving a task can be particularly significant, especially if designed to demonstrate if controlling behavior is revealed. Also, look for typical battering patterns, such as the woman's reacting with defensive strategies to the man's behavior, i.e., compliance with or hostility to his control or hostility.)

   d. What is their knowledge of developmental expectations for children?

   e. How do they handle discipline?

   f. How do they promote the child's intellectual growth?

   g. How do they promote the child's emotional growth?

4. What is the family history for the woman and the man and how does it contribute to parenting skills?

   a. What factors in each parent's family of origin contribute to positive or negative parenting ability? Was there abuse witnessed or experienced in either home that places either at high risk? Be sure to check for sexual molestation or abuse in both parents' backgrounds.

b. What are each parent's values about sex-role-stereotyped standards? Rigidity is often associated with battering behavior.

c. Who, if anyone, has had primary responsibility for parenting the child until the separation? This includes caretaking, decision making, nurturing, and scheduling responsibilities.

d. Have there been shifts in parental responsibility over time? Describe.

5. What is the developmental functioning for the child?

a. Is it age appropriate?

b. Cognitive area? (Individual intelligence tests can be used, especially if school performance is below expected level. Disparity in verbal ability in different situations can be a clue.)

c. Affective area? (Structured and unstructured measurement can be compared with observations of how the child expresses feelings with each parent).

d. Behavioral area? Does child demonstrate age-appropriate behavior? Does it change with each parent? With peers?

6. How do custody and visitation affect growth patterns?

a. Are there differences in each parent's ability to provide parenting skills required at the different development ages of the children? (It is common for batterers to be nurturing when children are young and more controlling as they age.)

b. Does the child have special needs? If so, how does each parent view them and cope with them? (Reviewing

Exhibit 11-4 continues

Exhibit 11-4 continued

videotapes of interviews often helps to demonstrate the child's needs.)

7. What kind of information does the court need for its action?

   a. Ethics of protecting raw data and conflict with legislation requiring that material to be available (often translated as required).

From Walker and Edwall, 1987, pp. 147–149.

The research and clinical information about children who witness abuse in their homes document ways to differentiate the behavior that is caused by witnessing abuse and the behavior that is due to other causes (R.L. Burgess & Youngblade, 1988; Emery, Kraft, Joyce, & Shaw, 1984; Garbarino, Guttman, & Seeley, 1987; Helfer & Kempe, 1974; Hughes & Barad, 1983; Hughes & Hampton, 1984; McCord, 1988; Patterson, 1982; Porter & O'Leary, 1980; Rosenbaum & O'Leary, 1981; Terr, 1981, 1984, 1990; Wolfe, 1985; Wolfe, Jaffee, Wilson, & Zak, 1988). The courts (Cahn, 1991; Pagelow, 1993) and the legislatures (Larson, 1991) have had a difficult time paying attention to such data. The abuser, as well as the family members, when appropriate, can be treated so that the coercive and abusive behaviors cease (Patterson, 1982; Reid, Taplin, & Lorber, 1981; Sonkin & Durphy, 1982) and children are protected.

It is important to assess the potential of the abuser to also harm the children even if there are no reports that he has previously done so. Often children will not talk about the abuse until the father is out of the home. Sometimes the mother has served as a buffer between the children and father so that he was not alone with them for long periods of time before the separation. The abuse may not begin or may not be serious enough to be noticed until then. In any case, there are two major areas of difficulty: the father's use of the children to continue to abuse the woman, and the father's direct abuse of the children. In either case, the children and their mother must be protected. Their fears should not be discounted and must be an important component in reaching the final custody and visitation plan.

A good assessment that explains the abuse dynamics to the court and predicts how different custody and visitation arrangements may affect the potential for continued abuse can be helpful. Obviously, the usual joint custody arrangements can only keep the woman feeling endangered and helpless to protect her children from continued abuse. It is unrealistic to expect two parents who are involved in an abusive relationship to be able to coparent their children after the divorce. It is also unrealistic to expect a traumatized woman to be able to coparent with someone who she perceives as intimidating and potentially harmful. It is also important to be aware of the recent studies of the difficulties that children have with joint custody when parents continue to relate to each other with high levels of conflict. These findings suggest that children respond better to one parent figure who can be consistent and place the needs of the child before himself or herself.

One of the issues that may need to be examined is the new parental alienation syndrome that is being used to combat allegations of abuse when children do not want to spend time with one parent, usually their fathers (Gardner, 1987; Ricketson, 1991). In such cases, the other parent, usually the mother, is accused of disliking the father and alienating the children from him. Gardner (1987) has labeled the syndrome, which he admitted is leveled 90% of the time at the mothers, and constructed a checklist to measure the syndrome (Sexual Abuse Legitimacy Scale), but there is no research to validate either the construct or the checklist. Although most professionals agree that there are no empirical data to support his ideas (cf. Ricketson, 1991), the idea that women can cause children to turn against perfectly wonderful fathers is supported by popular media images of the vengeful woman who keeps her children from their father, and this syndrome finds popularity in the courts today. Although the possibility of abuse, either of themselves or of their mother, is often raised as another possible reason why the children want to avoid being with the father, the courts seem less willing to accept that explanation. Numerous cases are documented by gender bias committees, which attempt to assess bias against women in the courts today, in many states (see, e.g., reports available from supreme courts of Colorado, Florida, New Jersey, and New York).

As a punishment to both the mother and the children for making accusations of abuse and disliking the father so much, it is often recommended that the children be placed the father's custody as a way to get the children to develop a relationship with the father without interference from the mother (Ricketson, 1991). This is obviously a tragic error, placing the children in danger as well as robbing them of their power and control over their own lives. For a long time, Gardner (1987) has disbelieved the research findings that children are truthful when revealing that they have been sexually abused. It is clear that his remedies do not take into account the need to protect these children should the sexual abuse not be as rare as his personal observations led him to conclude (cf. Courtois, 1988; Doris, 1991; Goodman & Helgeson, 1988; Russell, 1988; Walker, 1988). Johnston (1991) now has some empirical data on children who are forced into the sole or joint custody of a parent with whom they do not want to live, children forced into visitations despite their fear of the father, and children suffering through a major conflict between their parents. It can be anticipated from what is known about the impact of abuse that these children will be at higher risk for mental health disorders including PTSD. It is unusual for a child to dislike a father so much and to be so afraid of being with him unless the father is doing something to make the child fear him (such as making critical comments, yelling, and demeaning the mother in front of the child), withholding affection, or withdrawing from the child. It is important to understand the abuse dynamics in the family and to document them to the court so that such terrible mistakes do not continue to occur.

CONSULTATIONS AND SUPERVISION

Treatment Planning Consultation

It is not uncommon for the mental health professional to need a consultation with someone who has expertise in the area of woman abuse, when making an assessment. Sometimes, abuse information does not emerge until therapy is well under way. In such cases, an independent assessment may help revise treatment goals or confirm that the therapist is proceeding appropriately. Sometimes, an incest victim needs to work with a female therapist who is trained in working around these issues with adult survivors but still wants to work with her other therapist about other issues. A battered woman, a sexual harassment victim, or an abuse victim may also need extra support regarding the abuse components of their difficulties. This can be accomplished through consultation with the therapist who continues to provide all of the services or referral to the specialist for part of the work. In cases in which the woman is quite demanding and emotionally exhausting to work with, referral might seem like a good option. Sharing the client at these high stress times can be beneficial.

Independent Therapist and Evaluator

It is often advisable to have a separate therapist and evaluator when legal issues are involved, if only to avoid the appearance of bias in court. Here the therapist and evaluator can serve as consultants to each other. If legal issues arise in the middle of therapy, such as divorce, civil, or criminal cases, consultation with another specialist may be helpful in collecting additional data. Consultations may also be necessary if a highly emotionally charged custody battle occurs or a child abuse report to social services becomes necessary, situations that bring more professionals into the case. Because these cases do become highly emotional, consultation can be important for the therapist at times to keep her or his own emotional equilibrium.

Other Professional Consultation

Often the psychologist needs a consultation from another professional who can provide legal, medical, neuropsychological, or other professional advice. It is important to have contacts within the community with such professionals so that when such a referral is needed the client can be assured of carefully coordinated treatment, particularly when the woman is emotionally fragile and untrusting of professionals. These personal contacts also help the mental health professional to understand the colleague's findings and make it easier to explain them to the client.

Consultation or Supervision?

Use of a consultant or even a supervisor (who takes responsibility for the case management) is sometimes necessary when the therapist's or evaluator's own emotions about abuse begin to surface. It is important for the evaluator to question himself or herself about abuse issues, particularly if there are disagreements between other professionals and the evaluator. Monitoring countertransference issues may be too difficult for the therapist or evaluator to do alone. Use of a consultant is appropriate when the clinician feels comfortable enough to maintain control and responsibility of the case. If the violence is escalating, the client is deteriorating, crises seem to be increasing, or the therapist or evaluator does not want to be as involved as the client has requested (verbally or by actions), it may be appropriate to obtain some supervision of the case, so that another professional assumes responsibility. Obviously, this decision has to be carefully considered, because of the client's fear of betrayal and any legal implications. If supervision does become necessary, the client needs to be informed and introduced to the supervisor. It is usually a good idea to choose a supervisor who is somewhat familiar with the issues associated with women who have been abused.

SUMMARY

A common failing in assessing abused women is not obtaining all the information needed. Because many women are ashamed to speak about their abuse, therapists must have the patience to allow the women enough time to tell their stories. Therapists can help the woman by clarifying definitions and being nonjudgmental. Records from other sources, interviews with family members, and psychological testing can complete the picture. When collecting information for custody evaluations, the therapist should assess how abuse has affected the ability of the couple to care for their children. At times, bringing in consultants who have expertise in the field of woman abuse can help in making an accurate assessment.

12

Making Sense of
Assessment Findings

O nce the clinician has obtained as much relevant assessment data as possible, the challenge is to organize and summarize those data in a way that helps him or her to understand the woman's life in context. This chapter highlights some diagnostic themes that are helpful in understanding physically, sexually, and psychologically abused women. There has been much literature documenting the inherent weaknesses and drawbacks of all of the currently used diagnostic categories. They may stigmatize and stereotype the woman, especially if she is from an ethnic, racial, or cultural minority group, and create self-fulfilling prophecies, such as pessimism about her ability to change. The categories may carry unfair, damaging connotations, or may invite others to respond to the woman as though she is the diagnostic label rather than a unique human being. Moreover, for abuse victims, these categories often add to the victimization process by applying labels that appear to blame the victim for her own abuse (cf. Caplan, 1991).

So, why use them? Diagnostic categories can provide potential strengths for the clinician. If a clinician believes, and has data to support that a woman suffers from a particular syndrome, helpful interventions (as well as ineffective or even damaging ones) are easily identified. The diagnosis becomes a shorthand for describing how the syndrome is likely to unfold; what sorts of cognitive, behavioral, or emotional symptoms to expect; and what the associated risks and prognosis may be. Unfortunately, as the recent criticisms of the revised third edition of the *Diagnostic and Statistical Manual of Mental Disorders (DSM–III–R)* have demonstrated, the role of abuse in any of the recognized diagnostic categories, except posttraumatic stress disorder (PTSD), has not been carefully studied (Herman, 1992). Similarly, the impact of discrimination (against women, racial and ethnic minorities, cultural and ethnic groups, lesbians and gay males, etc.) in this area has remained relatively unexamined (cf. Brown, 1992a, 1992b).

However well-established, every diagnosis is to some extent a hypothesis. It represents an informed, professional judgment that likely touches—if only by implication, and with varying degrees of confidence and validity—on etiology, prognosis, and promising interventions. Making sense out of assessment data and attempting to use one of the standard diagnostic categories is a challenge for the clinician who is working with abused women. The best that can be done at this time is to use the criteria to differentiate between diagnostic themes.

Diagnostic themes must be based not only on complete, reliable, and valid data (as described in chapter 11), but also on understanding the full array of diagnostic possibilities from which there is to choose. This chapter is a reminder of a few diagnostic possibilities that, because of how frequently they occur among abused women, are often useful to secure her safety and promote her recovery. The first half of the chapter looks at various disorders that the assessor might find in an abused woman. The second half of the chapter examines possible behaviors and conditions that victims might present.

Because women who have been abused come from all demographic groups, some will have been suffering from other mental illnesses even before the abuse occurred; others will experience the effects of the abuse within the context of another, perhaps simultaneously developing but unrelated, mental disorder. If medical or brain dysfunction is also involved, it, too, will have an impact on the effects of the abuse. The length of time between the abuse experience and the assessment will also have to be considered in making a diagnosis.

DISORDERS SUFFERED BY ABUSE VICTIMS

PTSD

The diagnosis of PTSD provides the best description of the psychological symptoms observed in most abused women who present themselves for therapy. Of course, not all women develop a psychological disorder, as a result of abuse, that reaches the level of a formal diagnosis. For example, some victims have a typical trauma reaction following the event or events and then begin to heal. However, many women are so seriously harmed by the abuse experiences that it profoundly changes their lives. Many abuse victims begin to heal but then get stuck, often seeking therapy for other reasons long after the abusive incidents have occurred. It is difficult for many abuse victims to present themselves for either assessment or therapy because of their fears that they will be diagnosed as crazy. The many symptoms of PTSD often make them worry about the deterioration of their mental health each time they recall the abuse. This occurs even when the trauma symptoms last for less than the 1 month that is required to designate them a disorder. The upcoming *DSM–IV* has proposed a separate category that recognizes the less permanent but still distressing reaction syndrome.

The PTSD diagnosis with its descriptions of changes in cognitive abilities, including selective memory deficits and high avoidance symptoms, must be explored before making any other differential diagnosis. It is appropriate to check the client's symptoms against the criteria for PTSD and its various subcategories such as rape trauma syndrome, battered woman syndrome, child sexual abuse accommodation syndrome, battered child syndrome, and sexual exploitation and harassment syndromes.

Research into the incidence and prevalence of PTSD in victims suggests a high frequency of occurrence. The most extensive research examining the relationship of sexual and physical abuse to PTSD focuses on rape (Foa,

Steketee, & Rothblum, 1989; Kilpatrick et al., 1989; Rothblum, Foa, & Hoge, 1988). Kilpatrick and colleagues (1989) found that the lifetime prevalence of PTSD in a large community sample of rape victims was 57%. Criteria for PTSD were still found in 17% of the sample who were, on average, 17 years postrape. Rothblum et al. (1988) found that, in a prospective study of rape victims referred to a hospital, 97% met the criteria for PTSD at initial assessment and about 50% still met the criteria 2 months later.

Clinical reports of the use of PTSD for battered women (Walker, 1991a), child abuse survivors (Courtois, 1988; Herman, 1992; Summit, 1983; Walker, 1991a), victims of therapist–patient sex abuse (Pope & Bouhoutsos, 1986; Vinson, 1984), and sexually harassed women (Paludi, 1990) support its use with these populations as well as with rape victims. Kilpatrick (1992) and the Task Force on PTSD for the *DSM–IV* found that the PTSD symptoms accounted for the symptoms of all but 3% of those abuse victims studied in their field trials. Although there has been some controversy surrounding the use of the syndromes, most of the clinical literature agrees that such syndromes exist. Some researchers, such as Finkelhor (1990), question the adequacy of the PTSD and rape trauma syndrome diagnoses for child sexual abuse victims, suggesting that such diagnoses do not account for the large number of symptoms reported retrospectively by these children and adult women. Gelles and Strauss (1988), also sociologists and researchers, have questioned the existence of battered woman syndrome, for similar reasons (Gelles & Loeske, 1993). Others, particularly some feminist activists, have been concerned about the implications of mental disorder in battered women and therefore reject the use of PTSD and battered woman syndrome as an unnecessary medicalization of the women's normal reactions to a very traumatic situation (Blackman, 1989; Mahoney, 1991; Schechter, 1982).

Interestingly, the use of these syndromes in legal proceedings has been well-established and, as in the mental health treatment areas, there is little controversy about whether these syndromes are a subcategory of PTSD (cf. Herman, 1992; Kilpatrick, 1992; Simons, 1987). The legal debate centers around incidence and prevalence, especially for a particular woman who places it at issue during a custody determination, a civil tort action for personal injury, or a determination of state of mind in a criminal case in which self-defense or duress is claimed.

Although there are varying systems for assessing PTSD, the use of the current *DSM–III–R* system to make a diagnosis of PTSD calls for meeting five criteria (see Appendix C). The first and fifth criteria are threshold categories. The first criterion specifies that the traumatic event (or events) is at a high enough level that it would cause a serious psychological trauma in any normal person. This means that the woman's previous conditions, if any, did not have to be present to cause her the psychological harm if the symptom pattern indicates the high anxiety and high depression symptoms simultaneously with cognitive disturbances. Most trauma specialists use the Axis IV Psychosocial Stressor Rating Scale as an adjunct to rating the strength of the stressor or trauma. This scale, also in the *DSM–III–R*, ranges from 0 to 6, with 6 indicating the highest level of trauma (see Appendix D). Ongoing physical or sexual abuse is rated at a level 5, and, if kidnapping or being held as a hostage in one's own home occurs, it is rated as a level 6. Most trauma specialists agree that any event listed on level 5 or 6 would automatically meet the definition threshold for the first criterion. The fifth criterion requires the symptoms to be present for more than 1 month.

The second criterion, and the first symptom group, reflects cognitive disturbances. Only the intrusive memories are carefully delineated. There are four ways in which the disturbance can be experienced: (a) intrusive memories without a clear stimulus; (b) nightmares or dreams of the abuse; (c) reexperiencing the abuse through flashbacks, dissociation, illusions that it is really happening again, or delusions and hallucinations (even those brought on by a psychotic or alcohol-induced state); and (d) intrusive memories elicited by a stimulus that is a reminder of the abuse. Only one of these needs to be present as adequate evidence that there are intrusive memories from the abuse.

Obviously, the material in this book suggests that this category is inadequately detailed to capture fully the range, variety, and quality of cognitive disturbances that are associated with PTSD from abuse. Most abused women have elements of all four memory disturbances. Those who have been sexually assaulted may not dream for the first 6 to 8 weeks after the incident, unable to handle the replayed terror that might occur in that state. Later on, dreams often deal with the themes of anger at men specifically and the injustice of the situation in general as well as of mastery or reempowerment. For a repeat abuse victim who has a prior or continuing relationship with the abuser, the terror and danger may be magnified in her mind when each new incident brings forth memories (sometimes only memory fragments) of the prior abuse. Sometimes this process can be quite confusing to the abused woman. In such instances, abused women may dream of being chased, often by unknown or unrecognizable assailants, and are frightened that they will be captured and harmed. Sudden shifts between harmless and harmful events are also played out in dreams that can cause the women to relive the emotions even when the content is not well-understood.

Some abuse victims do not realize initially the harm they are suffering, particularly if they have been fooled into thinking that the abusive relationship is consensual. The emotional impact of each successive traumatic incident becomes magnified as the memories are replayed repeatedly. Sometimes, the women get stuck in this process. Anger and obsessiveness may seem prominent (at least temporarily). These women are always ready to fight back in some way; sometimes when the abuser is aware and sometimes when they can catch him by surprise. Sometimes the obsessions cause them to chase after the man, only to be hurt when he rejects them. If they stop chasing for a short period, they often find that he then becomes obsessed with possessing them. Stalking and tracking are commonly seen in both men and women involved in battering relationships. Despite the other pathologies that appear to be present in these women, PTSD is often the most appropriate primary diagnosis because it provides the best description of the abused woman's symptoms.

The second diagnostic criterion is high avoidance of thoughts, feelings, and actions that elicit the emotions and memories of the traumatic incidents. The abused woman tries to protect herself from chaos, confusion, and danger by trying to avoid thinking about or feeling emotions that are provoked by what happened to her. She avoids placing herself in situations that are associated with the trauma. It is as though all of her cognitive, affective, and behavioral efforts were focused on either removing herself from or avoiding an environment in which she could be abused again. For battered women, those who have been sexually harassed and exploited by therapists and others in authority positions, the goal is to reduce the potential for harm and to limit the pain. Removing themselves from the environment or breaking contact completely is not usually seen as a safe option. Coping strategies that focus on the positive aspects of the relationship with the abuser are not measured by the current diagnostic criteria, but, as in the other categories, the issue is not so much meeting the criteria specified in the *DSM–III–R* as it is recognizing the full range of details that could be helpful.

The last set of criteria reflect high arousal or anxiety. Panic disorders and anxiety disorders often justify a secondary diagnosis if they are not adequately accounted for in the PTSD diagnostic criteria. Coping strategies that keep the person from being in a chronic state of hyperarousal need to be carefully assessed.

Although the *DSM* system does not provide as much detail as would be useful for the abuse victim who is suffering from PTSD, it still provides a legitimate framework for making sense of relevant assessment data. In most cases, it is useful to provide an additional, more specific PTSD diagnosis reflecting the appropriate category, such as rape trauma syndrome (A. W. Burgess & Holmstrom, 1974; Foa, Steketee, & Olasov, 1989), battered woman syndrome (Walker, 1991a), child abuse accommodation syndrome (Briere, 1989; Courtois, 1988; Lindberg & Distad, 1985; Summit, 1983; Walker, 1991a), and therapist–patient sex syndrome (Pope, 1985, 1988), as discussed in the previous chapters in this book.

Although some research that looks at particular details of the traumatic event (such as severity of violence experienced) and the subsequent development of PTSD symptomatology did not find a strong association between presence or extent of violence per se and victim reactions (Sales, Baum, & Shore, 1984), consistent associations have emerged in other research, particularly in regard to rape (Cohen & Roth, 1987; Gidycz & Koss, 1990). Life threats, physical injury, and rape were found to contribute significantly to the prediction of the severity of PTSD (Kilpatrick et al., 1989). Koss and

Harvey (1991) suggested that it is not the characteristics of the event alone that determine the reaction, but the event as it is perceived by the victim. Thus, cognitive–affective processes may play a significant, almost pivotal role in the experience of and response to trauma. For example, many rape victims are often more likely to be paralyzed by fear, whereas some long-term battering victims tend to minimize their fears through emotional numbing, mental confusion, and other cognitive–affective distortions. Other battered women, however, develop serious anxiety disorders and phobias as a result of the constant fear.

Dissociative States and Disorders

Although there are those who believe that dissociation is a natural state of mind that many women use in a variety of situations, there has been research that clearly identifies dissociation as a coping strategy for abused women. Many abuse victims learn how to enter dissociative states in order to protect themselves from feeling the impact of the abuse. In a study of women inpatients, Chu and Dill (1990) found that a majority of those who had a history of abuse showed dissociative symptoms that tended to have been overlooked in the routine intake examinations (increasing the risk of misdiagnosis). Sexual abuse and physical abuse each were associated with higher levels of dissociative experiences, but there was also an interaction of these two main effects: The group tending to have the highest levels of dissociative experience included women who had a history of both sexual and physical abuse. Courtois (1988, 1990, 1991) cited studies that reveal that adult survivors of incest typically divide their personalities into parts that are disconnected from one another. The younger the child is when the abuse occurred, the greater will be the memory loss and the likelihood of dissociative disorders (Braun, 1986, 1988a, 1988b; Putnam, 1989a, 1989b; Ross, 1989; Steele, 1989; Watkins, 1980).

In a dissociative state, the victim has learned to separate her conscious mind from her body, blocking the pain of the abuse as it is occurring. This is not done on a conscious level but may be precipitated without thinking about it, especially when the victim is experiencing fear and stress. Many child abuse victims describe dissociative experiences, often detailing ways that they "made their mind go away" so that they did not have to deal with what was happening to their bodies. Out-of-body experiences (stepping outside of themselves and watching what was happening to them), as well as dissociative behavior (going through the motions without conscious aware-ness, thinking, or feeling) are consistently described by those who have been abused as adults or as children.

The more threatening the experience to the woman's psychological as well as physical well-being, the more likely she will go into a dissociative state in order to get through the experience. Sometimes she will return to the dissociative state during the retelling of a particularly life-threatening abuse incident. The confirmation that she is in such a state may be a change in voice pattern, tense, use of first-person pronouns, and eye movements that appear as if she is relating something that she is watching on a movie screen. In extremely dangerous situations, she may believe that she is cur-rently experiencing the incident and can give a blow-by-blow description of what is unfolding along with the emotions that she experienced at the time. In homicide cases in which the woman cannot remember all the details of the killing, dissociation has often taken place. Once in the dissociative state, the woman usually reacts without conscious awareness. van der Kolk (1994) explained the physiology of the way trauma memories are stored in subcor-tical areas of the brain and often expressed as visual images and physical sen-sations that are symptoms of PTSD.

This state can sometimes be brought out through hypnosis, although this method should be used quite sparingly because most abuse victims are not mentally prepared to deal with the intensity of feelings that can be evoked all at once. Those who are involved in criminal and civil cases may be placed in legal jeopardy, so rules around admitting hypnotically induced testimony must be checked with an attorney. Walker (1989b) hypothesized that many of the interruptions and tangents that take place during the retelling of traumatic incidents are a way to avoid feeling the pain or disso-ciating. Those women who have learned to use dissociation as a way to min-imize their pain may involuntarily go into such a state at their earliest perception of danger. This is a form of self-hypnosis and can be brought under more voluntary control by teaching actual self-hypnotic techniques.

Memory gaps that occur during a dissociative state are usually due to partial amnesia that occurs because the conscious mind cannot cope with the trauma. Psychobiological research suggests that these memories become accessible once the victim's physiological and psychological responses are treated. Some abuse victims develop more serious amnesia, such as loss of identity. Depersonalization symptoms are often diagnosed under the PTSD criteria of feeling different from and estranged from other people and numbing of feelings. However, in more extreme cases, the separate diagnosis is warranted.

Another form of dissociation is the multiple personality disorder (MPD) that is found in severe multiple abuse cases. The advances in diagnosis of MPD have brought much attention to both the disorder itself and the abuse that usually underlies its origin. It is unusual to diagnose a person who has a MPD during the first round of assessment; it often takes time for the other personalities to reveal themselves, and, as a result, the MPD diagnosis is often made after some time in therapy. However, those women with a severe and early abuse history who have unaccountable time lapses, cannot remember childhood experiences, find strange clothing or other things mixed in with their belongings, report that strangers greet them as though they know them, find bruises and cuts on their body without recollection of how they got there, and report other strange or even bizarre occurrences need to be watched for MPD (Braun, 1986; Courtois, 1988; Kluft, 1985; Putnam, 1989a, 1989b; Ross, 1989; Steele, 1989).

In examining their own findings in the context of previous research, Chu and Dill (1990) emphasized the need for clinicians to inquire routinely about dissociative symptoms and, when they are present, to consider the possibility that abuse has occurred. Of course, it is important to remember that dissociative processes are often defenses against remembering the unspeakable. Abuse victims both want to remember and want to forget what has happened to them. However, except when they are frightened for their lives, many victims are aware of the times that they dissociate and can provide reliable and valid self-reports provided that they are given the opportunity to describe their experiences in detail.

Anxiety Disorders

It is not uncommon to have other anxiety symptoms present that go beyond those expected in a PTSD. For example, agoraphobia, or fear of going outside, may be an additional diagnosis for some abuse victims who are phobic about leaving their house. Sometimes this or other phobic responses can be traced to the actual or reexperienced abuse, but in other cases its origins are not known. Cognitive therapy for phobias has been found to be effective, probably because it deals directly with the faulty fearful beliefs that may have been a result of the original trauma and subsequent intrusive abuse memories (Foa & Kozak, 1986).

Panic Attacks and Other Anxiety Disorders

Panic attacks and other anxiety disorders are commonly experienced initially after a rape or other violent episodes. If they persist, then the additional diagnosis is made and a specific treatment program to deal directly with those symptoms is prepared. Severe panic attacks may be managed by medication, although some victims refuse to take psychotropic drugs for fear of losing what little control they feel they have left. It is important to allow the woman to make the final decision, although she must be fully informed about all the options. A psychiatric consultation is important here in creating an appropriate treatment plan. Finding the appropriate psychiatrist who can work along with another treating therapist and the client in an egalitarian manner (i. e., without needing to be the professional in charge), who knows about woman abuse issues, and who is willing to discuss and prescribe medication if necessary, can be difficult, particularly in small towns and rural areas. In these cases, telephone consultation with a psychiatrist from a larger community along with a family practice doctor is the best alternative.

Some abuse victims seem to have greater degrees of anxiety than others. Often those who were traumatized in childhood repeat the same feelings of anxiety, and sometimes panic, if the abuse is repeated as an adult. It is important to measure the level of anxiety, fear, phobic responses, and panic attacks, possibly using the Subjective Units of Discomfort Scale (Wolpe & Lang, 1964). Once documented, its increase or decrease can be more reliably measured.

Obsessive–Compulsive Disorder

Obsessive–compulsive disorder (OCD) may be a way of blocking the abuse memories in some women who engage in obsessive thinking and compulsive behavior. Although recent psychological theories suggest that OCD has biochemical origins (Rapoport, 1989), it is also possible that links with abuse exacerbate the condition or even potentiate it in those who did not experience symptoms prior to abuse. Combined with somatization symptoms, OCD is very reminiscent of the conversion reactions noted by Freud (1896/1959a, 1898/1959b) in his patients who eventually revealed incest experiences.

Newer theories about men who batter and rape women have found that they are obsessional in their desire to hurt the women rather than merely being out of control of their own behavior. This obsession-driven violence can be more difficult to stop because of the man's determination to possess the woman.

Depression and Affective Disorders

Some depression is considered part of the avoidance symptoms noted in the criteria for PTSD. However, if the abuse victims' depressive symptomatology becomes a paramount issue for treatment, a separate diagnosis may be necessary. Depression is the most prevalent disorder diagnosed in women, with abuse issues a primary underlying feature, according to new research on women and depression (McGrath et al., 1990). The new antidepressant medications, particularly Prozac, Wellbutrin, and Zoloft, reportedly have an impact on reducing PTSD symptoms, which may confuse the diagnostic picture. Chronic PTSD is sometimes mistaken for bipolar or manic–depressive disorder because of the alternating high arousal and high avoidance symptoms. Abuse victims are sometimes placed on Lithium. Positive response to the Lithium is said to be diagnostic for the disorder. However, clinicians must evaluate carefully whether the woman is reporting an improvement that, in reality, she is not experiencing in order to please the doctors or to leave the hospital. When improvement does occur, it may be due to factors other than the medication (e.g., the woman is no longer living with the abuser and, thus, is in a safer, less chaotic, more supportive environment).

Personality Disorders

The *DSM–III–R* diagnostic system includes a category for diagnosing long-standing and pervasive developmental disorders that affect one's entire psychological functioning. These disorders of personality are said to have their roots in early childhood and manifest themselves as full-fledged disorders by the late teens or early twenties (Millon, 1981, 1991). Because they encompass the entire personality structure and are not just symptoms, it is said that personality disorders are difficult if not impossible to correct. There are few effective treatments for personality disorders, which often prevent the client from functioning well. Most personality disorder classifications are riddled with gender bias (Walker, 1994). Moreover, those with little experience in treating and diagnosing abused women can confuse the intractable symptoms of personality disorders with the symptoms of PTSD that persist because the person still feels under threat (Herman, 1992).

The personality disorders that are most likely to be used to label battered women and repeat trauma victims are *hysterical, borderline,* and *dependent personality* disorders. Those women who seem passive and unable to make their own decisions are considered dependent, those who seem to be screaming for attention are seen as hysterical (a label that also invalidates the trauma that they have experienced), and those who have stormy and demanding relationships with others (including demanding more from the therapist than what the therapist wants to give, even if those limits are detrimental to the client's needs) are diagnosed as borderline. Passive–aggressive is the diagnosis that is made if the woman agrees to do something and then comes back the next week having sabotaged it or neglecting it, with or without a good excuse.

Sometimes these diagnoses do represent the behavior that is observed in the client, but more often it is the reaction provoked in the therapist that wins the client the label. It is not until the woman is out of the abusive situation and the symptoms spontaneously begin to clear up that the diagnostic error is recognized. Obviously, the intransigence of a personality disorder would predict against any such spontaneous changes. Unfortunately, treatment strategies are quite different for personality disorders such as borderline, and, as a result, an abused woman diagnosed with a personality disorder and given a treatment plan that follows contemporary literature, will be at risk for further deterioration including the inability to protect herself from abuse.

Those women who do fight back in some way and who do not behave in a passive manner may be diagnosed with passive–aggressive or antisocial personality disorder. Although the diagnostic criteria are the same for men as they are for women, it appears that women need to exhibit less aggressive behavior in order to receive these diagnoses (L. S. Brown & Ballou, 1992). It is not unusual to see such a diagnosis applied to a woman who kills her abuser in self-defense and who has no other history of violent or aggressive behavior. Coping strategies such as manipulation may be seen as passive aggression particularly when the therapist perceives himself or herself as the one being manipulated. Obviously the clinician must carefully self-monitor to avoid these errors caused by gender bias and the high emotions of countertransference (Kirk & Einbinder, 1994; Kirk & Kutchins, 1992).

Masochism, or the new self-defeating personality disorder category, was proposed in 1985 as an addition to this section of the *DSM* system. Despite arguments backed up by research data that masochism as a psychological construct cannot be differentiated in abuse victims, normally socialized women, or those who engage in the self-defeating behavior specified in the criteria (cf. Rosewater, 1987b; Walker, 1987a, 1994), the category was added in the appendix with an admonition not to use it if abuse is known to have occurred. The American Psychological Association's Council of Representatives issued warnings to psychologists not to use that diagnostic category (or several others in the appendix including late luteal dysphoric disorder, which supposedly measures premenstrual syndrome, or sadistic personality disorder) because of the lack of empirical data to support it.

The debate about whether early and persistent profound abuse does cause characterological changes in the victim is one that has not yet been resolved. Empirical data on battered women, for example, does not show any characterological commonalities (Walker & Browne, 1985), whereas some clinical and anecdotal data with incest victims do suggest such changes in personality structure (L. S. Brown & Ballou, 1992; Courtois, 1988; Herman, 1992). Some of the difficulty is in the empirical construction of character or personality disorders. Data used to signify their presence are confused with coping strategies that protect from further assaults on one's psyche (Walker, 1994).

The appearance of features such as unstable interpersonal relationships, intense anger, labile emotions, and decompensation under stress (i.e., features often associated with borderline diagnosis) may encourage clinicians to focus on the possibility of a personality disorder as primary and to view the abuse as either a subsequent occurrence that is best understood in the context of a personality disorder (e.g., that the client was seductive and elicited or set the stage for the abuse) or as a false allegation made either in good faith (as a fantasy representing wish fulfillment) or in bad faith (as a lie representing the woman's rage or hostility). Although psychologists and other mental health professionals prefer not to use the label "liar," because of differences in interpretation of data already collected, sorting through the many opinions for any one case can be a challenge, particularly when there is a lot of money or someone's freedom resting on the outcome.

There does seem to be a possible link between a history of abuse and symptoms that may be consistent with borderline disorder or features (Herman, 1992). But various investigators emphasize that this does not imply that the borderline aspects are primary (e.g., developed prior to the abuse). Empirical research illustrating the inconsistent application of the *DSM–III–R* diagnosis of borderline personality disorder to women who have histories of physical and sexual abuse exemplifies some of the major problems that exist in relying on formal diagnostic categories that are applied without adequate data. For example, a study of 55 patients found that those suffering from borderline symptoms were significantly more likely to have suffered physical or sexual abuse or to have witnessed domestic violence. The researchers concluded the following:

> Conceptualizing borderline personality disorder as a complicated
> posttraumatic syndrome has direct implications for the treatment of

patients. Clinical literature on the treatment of posttraumatic syndromes has shown the importance of recovery and integration of traumatic memories with their associated affects and the necessity of validation of the patient's traumatic experiences. The integration of the trauma is a precondition for development of improved affect tolerance, impulse control, and defensive organization; the validation of the trauma is a precondition for restoration of an integrated self-identity and the capacity for appropriate relationships with others. Posttraumatic states are often undiagnosed in cases in which secrecy or stigma prevents recognition of the traumatic origins of the disorder; such patients may show remarkable improvement when the connection between symptom and trauma is recognized. Whether some of the negative therapeutic reactions so frequently observed in borderline patients might be avoided by early and appropriate recognition of the relationship between the patient's current symptoms and traumatic experiences in childhood remains to be determined. (Herman, Perry, & van der Kolk, 1989, p. 494)

Similarly, Chu and Dill (1990) emphasized the ways in which failing to recognize a history of abuse can prevent clinicians from providing adequate treatment:

If the difficulties experienced by patients with histories of abuse are directly related to the abuse experiences, it seems clear that definitive treatment cannot occur without acknowledgement of these experiences.... [E]ven the acknowledgement of the reality of the abuse can profoundly shift the attitudes of both patient and professional. In almost all instances, the victims of abuse continue to feel guilty, damaged, and defective.... Clinicians treating such patients, if unaware of the existence of the traumatic etiologies of the current disturbance, may collude with the patient in these beliefs about themselves. (p. 891)

Ogata and her colleagues' (1990) finding that individuals with borderline personality disorder were much more likely than a control group of depressed individuals to have a history of childhood abuse strengthened their conclusion about possible misunderstandings of the dynamics between a personality disorder and its potential causes:

> Clinicians who pharmacologically treat borderline patients' symptoms of anxiety and depression should exercise caution in their implicit and explicit statements about etiology, since they may unintentionally collude with the family's denial of the occurrence and impact of abuse. Similarly, psychodynamic clinicians should not dismiss the patient's recollections of sexual abuse as merely Oedipal wishes or fantasy. (p. 1012)

The research supports the notion that the abuse tends to precede those diagnostic categories with which it is most closely associated. Gathering data from a sample of 1,157 women aged 18–64 in a North Carolina catchment area, Winfield, George, Swartz, and Blazer (1990) found that sexual assault was most strongly associated with five disorders: PTSD, panic disorder, OCD, alcohol abuse or dependence, and drug abuse or dependence. With the sole exception of panic disorder, the onset of these disorders tended to occur after the sexual assault. Even for disorders that were less strongly related to abuse, such as generalized anxiety disorder and recurrent depression, the onset for an overwhelming majority of the disorders occurred only after the woman had been molested.

The whole debate on personality disorders that surrounds the *DSM–III–R* and *DSM–IV* puts their reliability and validity at issue. Researchers such as Kutchins and Kirk (1986) reviewed the empirical data used to support the various personality disorder categories and found that even the *DSM* Task Force's own reliability standards were so flawed as to make the categories meaningless from an empiricist's standards. Because the *DSM* system is supposed to be empirically sound, this type of evidence supports the position of trauma specialists that using a personality disorder category that can be confused with an abuse victim's coping symptoms is simply too unreliable and invalid to be of assistance in either thinking diagnostically or developing helpful treatment strategies.

Eating Disorders

Research has demonstrated that abuse can contribute to eating disorders. Both anorexia and bulimia are common in those who have suffered incest and other forms of sex abuse (Courtois, 1988; Root, 1991). Obviously women's socialized responses to their body image play an important part in why eating disorders occur. The client's lack of awareness of how self-destructive such behavior can be is consistent with the PTSD symptoms from abuse. Root (1991) described the etiology and treatment issues raised when eating disorders are another expression of PTSD. Obviously, because the symptoms are not accounted for in the *DSM–III–R* PTSD criteria, separate diagnoses must be given. However, the provision of treatment without placing the eating disorders within the context of the woman's entire life, including the abuse, can occur when the abuse components are downplayed and other dynamics are given center stage.

ALCOHOL AND DRUG ABUSE

In some research, a history of abuse (particularly sexual abuse) is the strongest factor predicting alcoholism or drug addiction among women (Kilpatrick & Best, 1990). It is important to provide adequate treatment for the abused woman, including drug and alcohol counseling, with the understanding that once the PTSD symptoms diminish and the woman is away from the drug lifestyle, she may not have the biochemical disturbance popularly believed to be at fault. In fact, in Walker's (1984a) and Eberle's (1982) research with battered women, it was found that those women who identified themselves as having a problem with alcohol tended to be those who were currently living with their abuser. Once they left the relationship their alcohol consumption decreased, even without treatment. This is not as frequently observed in poor, urban women who have few job skills and limited education. For them, the availability of drugs and alcohol helps numb their emotional responses to the obstacles in their lives.

It is not unusual for young children who are exposed to physical and sexual abuse, neglect, poverty, and an alcoholic parent to begin using alcohol and drugs, even during preteen years, to block out the pain. In some ways, this provides a chemically induced state of numbness or freedom from immediate, intense fear and suffering that serves a similar function to some of the dissociative states. Because such forms of self-treatment through self-medication can be so effective in blocking the PTSD symptoms, as well as other feelings, it is difficult to get these women to give them up. Even worse, no women's drug treatment programs (or even men's programs) provide specific therapy for abuse issues. Teenage runaways who use alcohol and drugs, live on the street, and sell their bodies often feel more in control of their chaotic existence than they did in their own homes. Women of color who live in violent urban areas often use alcohol and drugs to mitigate the effects of abuse. Crack cocaine is a particularly deadly drug that, like amphetamine and synthetic methamphetamine, can cause greater levels of violence, sometimes leading to death. Recent research into pregnant mothers who use drugs and alcohol during their pregnancies indicates that close to 90% of them are current or past abuse victims (Walker, 1991b). The legal cases of fetal endangerment that are being prosecuted often involve young, urban women of color who are being battered by their male partners and were abused as children (Paltrow, 1990, 1991; Paltrow & Shende, 1990). Many of the men are also substance abusing, which also endangers the fetus (Sonderegger, 1991a, 1991b), but do not face any legal consequences for their behavior. The women are frequently sent to jail to await the birth of the babies who are immediately taken from them and placed in foster care. Given the literature that suggests that these babies need to learn how to bond with caretakers, it might be a better policy to advocate for help for these mothers and to try to keep mother and child together so that bonding can occur (Paltrow, 1991; Sonderegger, 1991a, 1991b; Walker, 1991b).

DENTAL EXPERIENCES

There has been some research on the occurrence of dental problems in those women who have a history of sexual abuse (Hays & Stanley, 1993). Research indicates that the incidence of temporal mandibular joint disorder, gingivitis, bruxism, and tooth extractions is positively correlated with a history of sexual abuse. Also significant is the association of distress symptoms in sexual abuse victims while at the dentist. These distress symptoms include excessive fear, extreme anxiety, dissociation, flashbacks, gagging and nausea, and shame (Hays & Stanley, 1993). As might be expected, discomfort with the dental chair experience, being alone with the dentist, being immobilized and unable to talk or swallow, and having things inserted into one's mouth were all significantly correlated with sexual abuse history. Procedures that are accompanied by dissociation may bring about more difficulty in healing than those in which the woman is encouraged to remain present and in touch with what is actually taking place.

LONG-TERM PSYCHOTIC TRENDS

It is known that some women (and men) who have chronic schizophrenia or serious forms of affective disorders are also victims of abuse. It is not always known whether these victims develop psychotic symptoms as a way of not having to deal with the trauma, whether the trauma potentiates or actually causes psychosis in some victims, or whether some schizophrenic victims are chosen as targets because of their vulnerability caused by their mental condition. It is probable that all of these possibilities exist in different women. Incest victims who are terrified of revealing their secret because of a fear of further harm sometimes become psychotic and need to be chronically hospitalized and medicated. Others live marginal existences as part of the chronically mentally ill and homeless populations. Poverty, lack of access to good medical and mental health care, inadequate support systems, and other forms of discrimination all contribute along with abuse to the psychosis in these women.

Other women are hospitalized with hysterical or catatonic features that appear to be extreme forms of mental illness but may actually be the manifestation of their attempts to control their fears of their own anger and rage as a result of long-term abuse. There is a trend toward PTSD diagnostic units within private hospitals, although group treatment for incest survivors is also gaining popularity in state hospitals. Hansen (1990) developed a successful comprehensive treatment program for chronic patients at a

Minnesota state hospital. Many of these women had never received treatment for their incest experiences before.

Rosewater (1985a, 1985b) gave examples of misdiagnoses using MMPI results that did not take into account the abuse experience as the cause of the reported symptoms. Reviews of hospital records indicate the lack of importance that was placed on the abuse experiences of these women, if they were known to have occurred. Treatment plans that help seal over the breakthrough emotions only temporarily help the abused woman who will likely experience another breakthrough if exposed to a subsequent trauma or if time further erodes the coping strategies. Many of these women are not psychotic, but appear to have adopted psychotic symptoms in a desperate attempt to cope with the impact of abuse.

Other women tell of terrible abuse that occurred during their hospitalization. One woman who was restrained during some psychotic episodes related how a staff attendant who was assigned to watch her during these periods actually sexually fondled and abused her while she was unable to do anything. Until she could sort out her psychotic images from the actual abuse that was occurring, she was unable to report this behavior. No one wanted to believe her even when she did talk about it. Fortunately for her, a male psychiatrist listened to several other patients' stories that were similar enough to hers for him to begin an investigation that supported all of those women's accounts of sexual abuse during psychotic episodes. Some adult women describe how, as children, they were removed from abusive homes by child protective services only to be placed in group or foster homes in which they were again abused, compounding the damage from the original abuse.

LEARNING DISABILITIES

Many abused children and adults also have learning disabilities. In these cases, it is not known how much of the learning disability was caused by the interference of the childhood abuse with learning and normal development. In any case, adults with learning disabilities and abuse issues often overblame themselves for their problems and have more difficulty than is usual in sorting out the different issues. Helping the adult to become a joyful learner is one possible outcome of treatment. Educational programs to help the woman become more self-sufficient will provide some further movement toward the reempowerment goal.

ORGANIC FACTORS

Neuropsychological test results that are positive will specify those functions, particularly in the cognitive area, that have been damaged by structural, not functional, difficulties. These damages can be expected to interact with the emotional damages and need to be specifically addressed in treatment as well as in legal actions. Special rehabilitation programs may be advised in addition to psychotherapy. The areas that have been damaged may have an influence on the type of treatment approaches that are selected. For example, damage to the cerebral centers that control abstract reasoning suggests a more behavioral, less insight-oriented therapy. Identification and recognition of feelings and limitations that are placed on their expression might be a more important place to begin in a therapy plan for someone who has lost some of those functions.

It may be important to inform the client or her attorney of the presence of neurological damage in order to help make decisions regarding disability claims, civil tort actions, or maintenance needs in divorce actions. Such damage may also have an effect on the educational level attainable by the client or on her career options. If neurological problems are combined with physical symptoms such as severe headaches and neck and back problems, the client needs to decide whether she wants access to a chronic pain program, too.

PHYSICAL HEALTH

Chronic health problems often occur simultaneously with mental health problems, and the interrelationship between damage to the body and the mind is often a complex one involving the immunological response system of the body. It is important to assess these factors using the *DSM–III* Axis III guidelines.[13]

SUICIDAL AND HOMICIDAL RISK

Every abuse victim should be screened for lethality potential including suicidal and homicidal risk. The line between suicide and homicide sometimes can become blurred in abuse cases. At the point of termination of the relationship, battered women are at a higher risk of being killed by their partner, which may cause them to commit homicide in self-defense. Some women want control over whether or not they die and therefore decide to commit suicide as a response to their abuser's threats to kill them, especially when they do not believe that they have long to live, anyway. The presence of and access to weapons should be checked, and steps should be taken to encourage their disposal unless this would place the woman in more danger. If the woman's anger seems to be escalating, and she states a plan to kill either the abuser or someone else, warnings may be in order, provided that such warnings are required by the state laws. In one case, the woman threatened to take a gun to court and shoot the judge and her former husband if he was awarded possession of the home she owned from a previous marriage. After ensuring that this was a serious threat, warnings were issued to the attorneys involved, the ex-husband, and the judge. The woman was screened for possession of a weapon before the court hearing.

Although every threat of suicide and accompanying ideation should be taken seriously, those women who have made previous attempts are most vulnerable to future attempts to take their own lives. This risk is higher when the woman has a history of self-destructive behavior such as cutting herself or abusing alcohol and drugs. Women who have been sexually abused by those in a position of authority, such as another therapist, may be feeling so much pain that they are high suicide risks during crisis periods. This is also

---

[13]See Exhibit 11-2, in the previous chapter, which indicates the common chronic health problems and lists some of the stress-related illnesses that are often seen in survivors.

true for incest victims when they begin to regain memories of the abuse Hospitalization should be considered when the risk for suicide or homicide seems high. Some women mutilate themselves rather than undergoing a harsh and quick death by suicide.

RISK OF FURTHER ABUSE

In any assessment, the risk of further abuse must be determined. This includes abuse from the original abuser as well as dangerous actions that the client may be taking that put her at risk for new abuse. Any treatment plan must be screened for its ability to maintain the woman's protection and safety. For example, in some visitation arrangements courts often require the woman to seek therapy in order to learn how to negotiate with the abusive man. A therapist should not attempt to persuade such a woman to let down her protective stance and risk danger when she is with the man, without the assurance that he will no longer use violence (a difficult assurance to get from anyone other than a therapist who worked with him in a special therapy program for abusers). Obviously, receipt of such an assurance is unlikely if the abuser is still unable to deal effectively with his own power and control needs.

Any treatment plan must include ways to assist the woman in identifying real threats using her own hypervigilance. In any case, it is better to validate her concerns and to help her develop safety precautions than to dismiss her concerns as unfounded without sufficient information. It is also important to respect the woman's fears that something may place her in more danger. Supporting her recognition of danger rather than continued denial of it is appropriate unless there is no chance of further harm. For example, if a rape victim must travel past the place where the attack happened, it may be unreasonable for her to expect that she will be hurt again. However, it might be a reasonable fear if it is a routinely dangerous place. Thus, it is the therapist's job to help the woman assess the reality of her fears and to help her build protections to keep herself as safe as possible.

ASSESSMENT AND DIAGNOSIS
AS A CONTINUING PROCESS

Although a diagnosis and treatment plan may be formulated after a short period of assessment, it must constantly be updated as the dynamics of the violence and its impact on the woman become more clear. Each step of the process needs to be shared with the woman, giving her the opportunity to contribute her thoughts about the evaluator's hypotheses, adding, deleting, and offering new insights along the way. Sharing the power rather than maintaining an authoritarian role is an important way to assist the woman in regaining her own power. It also teaches her that her own interpretations are valid and important, and the therapist should respect the client's objections, if she has any, to some conclusions. Generally, the abused woman will be so relieved not to be considered incompetent by the "expert" that it rapidly increases her trust in the therapeutic relationship.

SUMMARY

Although diagnostic categories have shortcomings when applied to abused women, they can still help to determine treatment plans. Some of the disorders that abuse victims suffer include PTSD, dissociative disorders, anxiety disorders, depression and affective disorders, personality disorders, and eating disorders. Therapists should also look for substance abuse, learning disabilities, and any indication that the victim is predisposed to violence against herself.

13

Short-Term Crisis Intervention

Although the goals of survivor therapy are generally long-range, sometimes it is necessary to pay attention to short-term crisis intervention,
which may call for more direction and action on the part of the therapist.
This chapter deals with the problems that present themselves immediately
after sexual abuse (i.e., rape, battering, incest, sexual harassment, and sexual
abuse by therapists) occurs, is remembered, or is reported. The data suggest
that the acute crisis period lasts for 6 weeks to 2 months after an abusive
incident occurs (unless there is a recurring cycle of abuse that establishes its
own pattern). Helping the client feel more secure in a world that suddenly
seems unfamiliar is the primary goal.

Often a client's emotional reactions become worse before they start to
get better. Reassuring the woman that things will get better and helping her
to understand what is happening to her will help stabilize her emotional
behavior. Therapists who are available for extra phone or office visits can
help provide reassurance, especially when the woman understands that,
shortly, she will not be needing these extra services. Some women may want
to read about other abuse victims' experiences; others may want to keep
busy so that they forget about the trauma for a few moments; others want

to share the experience with women who are going through the same crisis; and still others keep themselves and those around them miserable as they experience and reexperience every painful moment. Interestingly, the latter group may heal the fastest because they have the strength to deal with the trauma immediately and completely.

THE CRISIS STAGE FOR ABUSE VICTIMS

Rape Victims

For some women who have been raped, the first person they contact may be the therapist. The woman may call from the scene of the rape or may show up unannounced at the therapist's office. She may be quite rational and coherent, holding herself together until she reaches safety, or she may be confused, panicked, or almost completely unresponsive. She may be in shock or experiencing what could be characterized as a brief reactive psychosis. Although most psychotherapists will not see many clients in this situation, those who work for clinics and hospitals are more likely to have the experience, especially as funding decreases for the rape crisis centers who had been sending trained volunteers into the local hospitals.

Safety

If, by some chance, the client is calling from the scene of the rape, ask if the rapist is still nearby or if she is in any sort of immediate danger. Ask if you need to call the police immediately. Contacting the police promptly may not only serve to ensure the victim's safety; the sooner the police are contacted, the more likely they are to find and arrest the perpetrator.

Sometimes a woman fears contact with the police for a variety of reasons; such reasons may be extremely private and may seem irrational or invalid. Nevertheless, her fear and caution should be respected. Forced contact with the police for a rape victim who is not ready for such contact may be antitherapeutic. This is especially true if she is unable or unwilling to identify the rapist.

The therapist must be sure to explain all of the relevant options to the client, including the possible consequences of actions that are taken or not taken. This will help enable the client to make an independent, informed choice about how to proceed. If she is resistant to calling the police immediately, it may be a good idea to remind her not to shower or douche in order to preserve whatever evidence there might be and to help keep her options open should she change her mind later on. Only when the therapist has reason to believe that the woman is in further danger should she or he take a more active role and call the police independently.

Identifying an Emergency Care Center

If the therapist has actively prepared to address such a crisis (see chapter 7), he or she will be familiar with the centers in the community that provide appropriate, specialized medical and related emergency services to rape victims. A therapist who is prepared in this way can then help the victim to identify and gain access to the best center available in terms of type and range of services, proximity, and so forth. If the therapist is not familiar with the community resources and has no other quick way to find out about options, a call to the police (without mentioning names) or to a local rape crisis center that is listed in the telephone directory should provide some quick information. The therapist might prefer to make the call independently, with the client present, or to give the number to the client, depending on the situation.

Neither therapist nor client can assume that a general emergency room or comprehensive community health center will be in a position to provide optimal services. Although federally funded community mental health centers (CMHCs) were intended, according to Public Law 94-163, to provide comprehensive services, a study conducted by Forman and Wadsworth (1983) found that only 75% provided rape-related services and that these services tended to be less comprehensive than the other services that were provided by the centers. A subsequent study by the same investigators (Forman & Wadsworth, 1985) found that "the services provided by these CMHCs appeared to be inadequate" (p. 402), with less that 0.5% of the average budget being allocated to rape-related services.

Centers specializing in rape, however, can provide emergency care whether they are part of a general hospital emergency complex or are freestanding medical centers. Typical approaches, along with rape protocols, are described by Klingbeil and Boyd (1984) and Yale-New Haven Hospital Emergency Service (1983). Personnel are trained not only to conduct medical screening and intervention relevant to rape but to respond competently and sensitively to the psychological needs of the victim and to the forensic aspects of any subsequent rape prosecution.

Balancing Therapeutic and Forensic Concerns

The potential forensic issues in cases of sexual assault must be addressed with great sensitivity by the therapist. Neither therapists nor victims of an adult rape are required to notify the police or to press charges against a perpetrator. The primary concern should be responding to the victims's psychological and medical needs, as well as to her need for safety. Any needs or desires of the police, the therapist, or others to see the perpetrator apprehended and prosecuted must not be allowed to interfere with the client's needs to survive and recover from the assault or with her right to make choices about how she wishes to proceed. These admonitions are more often relevant to those sexual assaults in which the perpetrator is known to the client rather than rapists who are strangers.

However, if not unwanted by or detrimental to the victim, providing information about forensic issues may be useful. For example, assurances that going promptly to an emergency medical care center to receive services in no way obligates her to file charges or to make a formal report may help a client to make an informed decision and may enable her, if she is otherwise reluctant to seek medical care, to obtain it. (Make sure to correctly represent the hospital's policy; some do have a policy of calling law enforcement while the woman is still in the emergency room.) Once the police are involved, it may be possible for the woman to receive victim compensation funds that will pay for some subsequent therapy.

Victims may also find it useful and empowering to know that delaying showering, bathing, douching, or similar cleansing methods until a medical examination is conducted can be an important aspect of gathering and preserving evidence for any subsequent prosecution. Similarly, law enforcement authorities and state attorneys may find it useful to preserve (unwashed) the clothes that the client was wearing at the time of the attack; they may contain blood, hair, or other identifying items related to the perpetrator. Modern technology also makes it possible to perform DNA tests helping to link a suspect to a rape. Gaining this knowledge promptly may prevent the client from destroying or washing her clothes immediately.

If forensic matters are pursued, it is especially important to ensure that payment issues and issues regarding informed consent are clearly understood and agreed to by the victim. Some medical examinations and other procedures may have virtually no value for the medical care of the victim; their sole value is in identifying and prosecuting the rapist. The victim has the same rights to informed consent and informed refusal that she would in regard to other medical procedures. She should clearly understand whether she will be billed for procedures related primarily or solely to forensic concerns (see, e.g., Largen, 1986).

In many states' attorneys offices there are victim/witness programs that administer funds from the federal Victim Compensation Act, which authorizes distribution of money to help the victim of a crime seek medical or psychological treatment. Most victims are not eligible for this money unless they report the crime to the police and cooperate with the prosecution of the offender. Many states are passing laws that limit a rape victim's access to abortion should she become pregnant if she fails to report the rape within a specified time period; therefore, failure to report may have long-term adverse consequences.

A therapist's records may be subject to a subpoena, or the therapist may be asked to testify regarding the psychological damage to the victim that was caused by the rape. (See chapter 9 for more information on how to deal with legal challenges to records and expert witness testimony.)

Continuity of Care

Whether the victim has phoned or has found her way to the therapist's office, it is important that the therapist ensure adequate continuity of care. If an ambulance has been summoned, the therapist should have some way of checking to make sure that it did in fact arrive and that the victim was taken to an appropriate medical facility. The client should not feel that she is being pushed into a medical care facility and abandoned by her therapist. The therapist can discuss with the woman what her needs are in terms of regularly scheduled or additional office appointments, supplementary phone sessions, and so on. Some women find it reassuring to know that the therapist is staying in contact with hospital personnel. Obviously, any information that is shared by the therapist and the hospital staff should be with the knowledge and consent of the rape victim. The therapist and the hospital workers must ensure that any potential conflicts or turf issues are addressed in such a way that does not add to the distress of the rape victim.

In some situations, the therapist may choose to make a hospital visit. Such visits may provide significant support to the client and enhance the subsequent therapy relationship. Often the therapist serves as a sort of translator, helping the client to understand and integrate the information that is provided to her by other service providers. The results of laboratory tests (which may be phrased in unfamiliar technical terms), descriptions of follow-up tests, formal descriptions of contusions, hemorrhages, and so on, may be simultaneously baffling, frightening, and overwhelming. This can be critical when informed decisions must be made. Again, the delicate balance between being a translator and an advisor must be maintained. It is easy to want to overprotect a victim who is struggling to regain her equilibrium, but do not do it! Such benevolent kindness robs the victim of learning to use her own strengths to become a survivor.

Many women turn to a close friend or relative or to police immediately after they have been raped. Often, they are guided to the emergency room of a local hospital in which a special examination called the *rape kit* is performed in addition to other medical care that the victim might need. This examination collects forensic evidence in the manner needed by the court. In many communities, rape crisis center volunteers or trained social workers are called so that the woman can receive immediate crisis counseling to help her process the traumatic event with a minimum of psychological sequelae. The counseling consists of listening to the woman, clarifying her feelings or accepting the numb reaction if that is how she is defending herself psychologically, and providing her with what is often called a *cognitive grid* or a way to cognitively understand what has just happened to her. She is usually told what common symptoms to expect and helped to understand that the reactions she experiences are considered normal. This helps many victims get through the immediate aftermath without long-lasting problems. Burt and Katz (1988), among others, have found that the rape victim's long-term negative feelings, including loss of self-esteem, can be mitigated if she can be taught how to deal with the flood of feelings that she may experience initially.

This first stage of the acute rape reaction often lasts for 4 to 6 weeks before there is resolution (A.W. Burgess & Holmstrom, 1974), although other clinicians, including myself, believe that 2 to 3 months is a more realistic time frame. Many symptoms usually become worse during this time. Sometimes this crisis period is delayed when the woman blocks the emotional response. During this crisis period the woman often feels as if the world has turned upside down, and she is unsure of her place in it. If she was also seriously physically assaulted, she may have bruises and injuries that cause her pain in addition to her emotional reaction. Long, uncontrollable periods of crying, often without a precipitant, can occur, a profound sadness is reported, and the woman feels as if nothing will ever feel all right again. Often, rape victims are unable to function even the minimum amount required to get through the day, although some immerse themselves in work to avoid having to deal with their erratic feelings. Many women go through agitation as well as depression with panic attacks that result in fear of further panic and anxiety. Women who have been raped by men often develop a fear of all men and frighten themselves by the depth of the anger that they feel toward men, even those who they know love them such as supportive family members. A stranger in the supermarket may cause a rape victim to panic and feel threatened as though she had seen someone who actually looked like her attacker. Husbands or partners who push too hard to persuade their wives to act "normally," including sexually, may attract the victim's anger toward themselves.

A.W. Burgess and Holmstrom (1974) reported on the typical symptoms described above that occur during this acute crisis phase. They suggested that the symptoms continue to become worse for awhile, which causes the victim to be even more frightened that she will never feel okay again. If the rapist was a stranger or acquaintance who has been arrested, the legal process may keep the crisis period alive longer than the initial 6 to 8 weeks. Each time the rape victim has to face her attacker or deal with the issue, her symptoms can be expected to intensify. Visiting the scene, retelling the story to those who want a factual account, having her wounds attended to, lying in bed with someone else who may touch her in the same place, being alone at night or during the day, and so on, all bring about memories of the experience as in posttraumatic stress disorder. A.W. Burgess and Holmstrom (1974) described two different types of rape attacks: they called one the "blitz" attack, which is the kind that often precipitates the above-described reactions because of its sudden onset and terrorizing aspects. They called the second type the "con" attack, in which the abusers "con" or slowly entice the women into situations in which they eventually become victimized.

The woman needs reassurance that even though she feels like her situation, thoughts, and emotions are getting worse, eventually she will start to feel better. Some women feel better if they have a specific time frame within which to expect to start feeling some improvement. Indeed, Kilpatrick et al. (1979) found that the major improvement was usually made within 6 to 18 months postrape. During the crisis stage the client is usually unable to dream, often waking herself up before or during a night terror. As she begins to heal, nightmares may begin, a signal that she is able to handle the bad dreams. Obviously, it may not be reassuring to tell a woman who is hysterical because she is beginning to experience nightmares after a period of poor sleep patterns that this is a sign that she is getting better. For some bright, well-educated clients who intellectualize as a defense, letting them read some of the studies that deal with healing from trauma may be reassuring. Other women need to see that the therapist calmly accepts their symptoms while still empathizing with the pain that they are experiencing.

Many communities provide follow-up supportive counseling with trained volunteers or paraprofessionals. Rape crisis counseling may take place with others in a group or with a volunteer who may also serve as the woman's advocate in court-related proceedings. It is not unusual for a police officer to serve as a crisis counselor in those law enforcement agencies that have special rape units. If the woman already has a psychotherapist, she is often referred to her or him. The rape crisis counselor may call the psychologist and provide immediate information or be available to share information should the therapist initiate the call after obtaining permission from the client.

In some cases, clients may develop what A.W. Burgess and Holmstrom (1974) called "silent rape trauma syndrome" in which they do not demonstrate any obvious effects of the rape immediately afterward and "keep it together" until they reach the therapist's office, sometimes many weeks, months, or even years after the rape. The therapist must then deal with the victim's flood of emotional feelings as though the rape has just occurred. Thus, whether the emotional trauma associated with a sexual assault has just occurred or whether it is being reexperienced in the therapist's office, it is important for the clinician to understand the depth of the different responses that he or she may observe.

Reassurance and Support

When a client contacts a therapist, whether she has recently been raped or is just beginning to emotionally deal with the rape, numerous matters may need prompt attention. Perhaps the first step is to provide the client with genuine reassurance. The therapist should make sure that she knows that he or she is there to help, will be with her in this crisis, and will not abandon her.

Some clients may be able to provide spontaneously the information needed to respond to this crisis. Others may require more structured support and questioning from the therapist. But in all instances, the victim should be allowed to make decisions about what steps will be taken. The therapist should always ask the client what her needs are in facing this crisis.

Touch

If the client comes to the therapist immediately after the rape, the therapist must be exceptionally sensitive concerning whether the client wants physical contact. If the therapist attempts a reassuring hand on the shoulder, a holding of her hand, or similar sympathetic and therapeutic gestures, some rape victims may feel violated. The touch may trigger a flashback to the rape itself, perhaps to the time when the client was initially touched by the rapist. In some instances, simply moving too close to the victim may have a similar effect. Male therapists, in particular, need to be sensitive to this possibility (because the rapist was most likely a man).

On the other hand, if the therapist puts too much distance between himself or herself and the victim in an effort to provide her with a safe personal space, the client may experience this behavior as evidence that she is dirty and unworthy of human contact. To ask a client how she wishes to be treated in this regard is to communicate to her that her wants and needs are taken seriously (contrary to her recent experience of violation). Allowing and encouraging her to take back her own control and to make decisions about such matters can also be empowering to her (contrary to her recent experience of being overpowered). Care must be taken, however, to allow her to move at her own pace. It is easy for a therapist to press a victim, subtly and unintentionally, to confront an overwhelming array of important decisions immediately. Even those women who are used to taking charge and making decisions competently may have trouble stabilizing after a rape. In fact, many such women may appear to be functioning quite well while they are actually falling apart inside. They have learned how to cover up effectively. Although it may be appropriate to leave these defenses unchallenged for a while, eventually the therapist will need to address the cognitive and affective issues that may be unspoken.

Battered Women

Some battered women may still be in danger when they seek treatment. A crisis plan needs to be developed so that the therapist is able to give the client the time to make decisions about her life while also attempting to keep herself violence-free. Details of the last few battering incidents need to be known by the therapist before the plan can be developed. Most of this information can be provided by the victim, although she may have to spend time thinking about some of it. For example, it is important to teach a battered woman to recognize clues that the batterer provides as tension escalates, so that she can make preparations to leave before a second phase acute battering incident occurs in which the batterer will prevent her from leaving. Attention to special ethnic and cultural needs is crucial at this time (Crites, 1991).

A typical crisis plan starts with the recognition that when the abuse is escalating, the risk of being hurt is greater than before. Sometimes it is necessary for the woman to describe the last few abusive incidents in an attempt to remember what the batterer looked and sounded like right before the acute battering incident started. Sometimes the man's facial features change dramatically. Often the woman describes a change in his eyes, as if he becomes unreachable. Other abusers might develop a physical twitch or begin a certain verbal litany that almost always precedes the more serious violence. For others, the trigger might be taking their fourth drink. In still other batterers, it may be the beginning of their "con" talk to entice the woman into a situation that is likely to result in her further victimization. Each woman has her own way of identifying the change. Once these markers have been identified, then it is important to go back even further to the cues that precede them. (The abused woman's hypervigilance to cues of impending danger is what should be used here.) This is the point at which she must take action.

Some battered women will not leave because they are afraid that the man will hurt a pet or destroy favorite objects in their home. This is not an unreasonable or irrational fear. If there are family heirlooms or items that the woman does not want to live without, they can be removed from the home at a different time, before the escalation of violence. Storage in a friend's basement or in a storage locker is advisable. Protection of pets is more difficult, especially if there is more than one animal. Some battered women shelters have arrangements with local veterinarians to board animals. These arrangements must be made in advance. Undertaking this responsibility helps the woman to take her own fears seriously without minimizing or denying the danger that she could be facing.

If there are children, provisions must be made for them, too. Because of the legal difficulties in having children returned to the mother after they have been left with the batterer, it is advisable for the woman to take them with her when she leaves, even temporarily. Many women return to find the locks on the door changed and temporary custody of the children granted to the father who claimed abandonment by the mother. It may be important for the woman to pack and hide a suitcase of clothes for herself and for the children, perhaps in the trunk of her car or at a friend's house. Money and important papers also need to be hidden safely so that there is no need to fumble around trying to find them during an emergency.

The therapist should find out how and where typical battering incidents occur and draw up a detailed escape plan from any of the locations. Sometimes it is helpful to draw a diagram of the house (most battering incidents start and end there, usually in the kitchen or bedroom). Once the escape plan is detailed, therapist and client should verbally rehearse it together. As with a fire drill, it is important to carefully go over each step. Contingency plans should be made in case the escape route is blocked. The therapist should encourage the woman to go home and walk through the escape route when the man is not there. If the children are young, the woman must figure out the best way to grab them and remove them from the house. If they are older, a signal and a meeting place away from the abuser need to be prearranged. The idea is to help the woman leave before the abuser stops her, but sometimes the abuse escalates so rapidly there is little time or warning. See Exhibit 13-1 for a checklist to use in making a crisis plan.

Exhibit 13-1

Safety Plan Checklist for Battered Women

1. Assess four battering incidents
   First
   Typical
   Worst or one of the worst
   Last prior to this interview
2. Details
   What he said (curses, lies, stories)
   How he said it

Tone of voice

Speed

Ability to listen

Effect of drugs or alcohol

Facial features (e.g., eyes)

Body posture

3. Where does the battering usually start?

Living room

Bedroom

Kitchen

Other room

4. Floor plan of house—draw map

Doors, windows, exits

Baby or young children

Signal for older children

5. What does this women need?

Money, car keys, clothes, pets

Important papers, treasures

6. Location of a safe place

Police

Family

Friends

Shelter

7. Should she tell him?

Time out

Conditions of possible return

Cycle of violence

Stalking

Lethality

8. Rehearse exit (two times or more)

Verbal

Draw map

Demonstrate

LENORE E. A. WALKER

Sometimes a woman feels more comfortable telling the batterer that she will leave if she believes he will hurt her but that she will return when he calms down; others fear that he will prevent their escape if they discuss it beforehand and prefer to say nothing until they are too afraid to stay.

Developing such a crisis plan helps to validate the woman's experiences of abuse and her fears of impending danger. It demonstrates to her that she does have alternatives and that escape is possible, even temporarily. Whether or not she ever actually uses it, having an escape plan gives her some power. This type of plan can be modified for other victims of violence who are afraid that the abuser will come after them. Armed with knowledge of how to escape, they will be less likely to feel overcome with fear and anxiety.

Less extensive crisis plans need to be developed with clients who are in the position of being forced to listen to long verbal harangues from the abuser. Even in cases in which the victim has been able to obtain a restraining order, some men feel that they are entitled to tell her what they think or to make her listen to whatever they want to say. In such cases, the woman needs to be encouraged to remove herself from the verbal abuse. Sometimes she feels safe enough to tell the abuser that she perceives his behavior as harassing and that she will not participate; in other instances, anything the woman says only makes it worse. She can hang up the telephone, walk away from him, or try never to be alone with him, only meeting him in a public place with a lot of people around. Even this does not guarantee that he will leave her alone.

Telephone harassment is a popular way for accused abusers to retaliate. The woman should get an answering machine to screen calls and record messages and conversations. She should also date and label the tapes; this helps to establish that the harassment is occurring and reminds her that she is not making up the abuse even if the tapes are never heard in court. The therapist should listen to a few of them just to check which abusive techniques are being used, then discuss them so that the woman will not respond emotionally to those that are not dangerous. Hang-up calls are also popular with violent men. Although she may not have evidence, the abused woman often becomes certain that the calls are from the abuser who is stalking her. It is important to validate that even hang-ups terrorize a woman who has been abused. Sometimes the telephone company can place a tracer on the phone, but the man usually does not stay on the phone long enough or call regularly enough for the call to be traced. Nevertheless, it should be considered an empowering option to try to stop the calls. The new caller identification devices that can be attached to telephones in some communities are a new way for the woman to verify that the man is really using the telephone to harass and intimidate her.

Some of the men who continue to harass their victims are more than bullies; they are very dangerous and will escalate their abuse just to prove that the women belong to them and cannot get away. Others see the battle as a power struggle and will pull everyone into it. These dangerous men are in the minority; most give up like bullies do and leave to prey on their next victim. But it is impossible to identify which men will escalate their violence and which ones will go away. Therefore, it is critical for the therapist to help the woman prepare for escalation of the danger and to pay attention to her hypervigilance, which has been finely tuned to sense this man's reactions. It may be necessary to help her hide from the batterer, to involve the police or private detectives, or to get her out of town temporarily or permanently. In some cases, electronic monitoring devices can be attached to a batterer who is also a stalker, and communication devices installed in the woman's home can then notify a message center to dispatch law enforcement and record any violation of a court order that has occurred (such instruments are available through JurisMonitor, Inc., Boulder, Colorado). Battered women shelters all across the country will take a woman who needs to hide; contact with the local shelter can put the woman in touch with the national network of shelters. Unfortunately, shelters often fill up and have to turn women away.

Incest Victims

Adult women in therapy who begin to recall memories of sexual abuse that occurred when they were children may, like battered women, go into crisis periods. As the memories of abuse begin to break through, the abusive incidents are relived. These memories force the woman to deal with the incomprehensible: betrayal and harm caused by someone whom they trusted and perhaps loved. The panic reaction often set in motion includes the woman's fear that she might impulsively hurt herself or someone she loves and that she deserves to die. She may believe that she is ugly, evil, and no good. Sometimes the woman unconsciously tries to prevent the memories from breaking through by becoming cognitively confused, obsessional, or even self-destructive. It is not unusual for these women to cut themselves, engage in acting-out behavior, try to shut out their feelings through drug and alcohol binges, or become openly suicidal. Often they have physical reactions that accompany the emotional ones including nausea, vomiting, diarrhea, and uncontrollable shaking and other body movements. Dissociative reactions may also occur with a resulting loss of time and memory. The primary issue for women at this point is the terror of reexperiencing the feelings that accompany the memories, including the sense of helplessness that they felt when they were children.

The client who is experiencing the panic and terror reaction that accompanies memory recall must be properly managed so that she gets through her ordeal safely. Supportive reassurance that the therapist is available to assist the client during the painful recall of these memories is critical. This may mean scheduling additional sessions, perhaps one per day, during the week, or admitting the client to the hospital for a brief period of time. In some cases telephone availability is sufficient, but most women need to know that the therapist will help them go through the pain and survive. Walking the fine line between providing the limits of protection, while also listening to what the woman needs in order to help her go through the horror, can be exhausting. Reassuring her that she can come through the crisis safely and stronger while not invalidating her fears is also a difficult balance to find. It is helpful to enlist friends and family of the victim so that they, too, can support her during this period.

Victims of Sex With Therapists and Sexual Harassment

Women who are exploited by therapists often have a combination of incest and rape trauma crisis symptoms that need to be dealt with therapeutically. Most of these women were led into situations in which the therapist misused his or her power. The crisis situations here involve the woman's confusion and self-blame for letting herself get into the situation. When the woman's feelings of betrayal, guilt, and ambivalence about the man, who may have used seductive and loving techniques to con the woman, increase without a corrective lens being placed on them, she may become so self-destructive that she attempts suicide; she may feel that her life is over and that she will never again be able to choose a man competently. She may have an enormous feeling of shame that she was so badly tricked and used by someone. These women often go through periods of decompensation, like the other victims who were described earlier.

Sometimes, filing a civil lawsuit can be therapeutic, especially for victims of sexual harassment. Having the opportunity to prove that she was wronged can help a woman overcome the humiliation of having to expose her whole life to the defense. It is important for the therapist to help those victims who have some complications that make them appear to be "bad" victims to understand that an attorney's assessment of the probability of winning a lawsuit is not the way to judge whether they have been sexually abused, exploited, or harassed. Clients who are involved in the legal process may need additional support during certain times when the stress is quite high. This topic is discussed further in chapter 9.

SUMMARY

When sexual trauma is recent (or repressed memories of sexual abuse are first being recovered) the therapy must be concerned with getting the woman through the acute crisis period. Therapists might have to increase their availability to the client during this period. Rape victims might need information to help them make decisions about forensic and legal issues. They might also need help dealing with feelings of intense guilt and shame; they might be frightened by their generalized anger toward all men. Therapy sessions should be directed toward sorting through these emotions and helping the woman understand what happened to her.

Battered women often need help escaping from the abusive partner. Crisis intervention here can consist of making escape plans and training the woman to recognize the patterns of abuse so that she can reach safety in time. Incest victims can become confused and disoriented when memories begin to break through. Again, they must be made to understand that this is a normal stage for victims of this type of abuse and that they will get better. Women who have been victims of sexual harassment or who have had sex with their therapists also suffer from guilt and self-blame. Many of these victims experience periods of depression and anxiety. The therapist, with help from the victim's family and friends, must continue to remind the woman that, with perseverance and time, these feelings will diminish.

14

Long-Term Therapy Treatment and Strategies

This chapter focuses on the development of a treatment plan and highlights of various issues that frequently arise when a victim of violence is in therapy for a substantial period of time. There are some differences for women who come into therapy soon after the trauma compared with those who are unable to deal with the abuse issues for a long time afterward. In this chapter, differences are noted that occur because of the woman's social context, such as economic status; racial, ethnic, or cultural identification group; sexual orientation; and physical abilities. Although there are certain issues that are more common to one subgroup of abused women than to others, such as an expected crisis period that occurs when an incest victim begins to deal with buried memories, most women who have been abused have similar needs in therapy. In this chapter the general principles that are helpful in treating abused women are outlined.

Forming and revising appropriate treatment plans, negotiating goals of treatment, and monitoring progress toward goals are all discussed in this chapter. The effectiveness of various therapy approaches and treatment modalities is rated in order to help therapists and their clients pick the process that is best suited for their specific situation. The last two sections identify special areas of psychological damage as well as issues with which abuse victims need to deal and suggest appropriate therapy techniques to use during the therapy.

DEVELOPMENT OF A TREATMENT PLAN

Abused women enter psychotherapy in a variety of ways. Some are referred by police or victim or witness programs while they are still in immediate crisis, whereas others wait until they can no longer cope with the increasing symptoms, and still others will not seek help until another problem arises that pushes them over the edge. Some women seek assistance for other reasons, and the issue of abuse is not uncovered until the therapy has progressed. Whatever impels the woman to seek psychotherapeutic treatment, once she is there and recognizes that she has been abused, an assessment needs to be made regarding the extent of abuse and its impact on her, even if at first it is only a clinical interview that covers the abuse history as outlined in the previous chapter. Because of legal implications, it is important to document findings at the time at which the impact of the injuries are discovered, so that effective treatment does not prevent the woman from claiming damages within the time limit of relevant statutes. (For a more detailed discussion, see chapter 9.)

Choosing a Therapist

After the assessment is completed, the results are summarized, documented, and presented to the client for her information as well as to help her make a decision about therapy. When legal issues are involved, the client may choose to have her attorney present at this time, too. If the assessment was the first contact between the client and the therapist or evaluator and a positive rapport was established, she may wish to remain in treatment with the therapist. At this time, it is important for the therapist to assess his or her own match with the client. A review of this process, outlined in chapters 7 and 8, will help the therapist to make this decision. Although there is some controversy about the treatment efficacy of one gender over another, which is not fully supported by empirical data, particularly in working with sexual abuse victims, the clinical wisdom is that most abused women are more comfortable working with a female therapist who is sensitive to abuse issues. If the therapist decides to refer the client to a colleague, it is important to try to match the client's and therapist's styles, as discussed in earlier chapters. Cantor (1990), Dutton-Douglas and Walker (1988), and Hansen and Harway (1993) provided additional information to assist the therapist in making such decisions. Mental health clinics that do not pay attention to making careful matches often lose clients because they do not offer helpful services. If further abuse occurs, the clinic or center as well as the individual therapist may be held liable for damages experienced by the client.

Negotiating the Treatment Plan

The treatment plan is negotiated between the woman and her chosen therapist, or first discussed with the evaluator, if there are two different people involved. The client needs to be a participant in helping to set the goals, which should be written down and kept in the therapist's notes. A written record is useful for the therapist to check progress as well as to remind the client of the progress in healing. Written records also facilitate the process of periodic updating of goals. Finally, a treatment plan with written goals and notations of therapeutic strategies to reach those goals are the best liability protection for the therapist.

The first step is to outline the client's areas of strength and the areas that have been damaged, supported by the assessment data. Because treatment for abuse issues should build on the woman's strengths, these need to be presented first, both to set the climate for reempowerment by identifying the victim as a survivor and to make it less of an adversarial process for the woman. Although intellectually the woman knows that she has been damaged by the abuse, emotionally she wants the damage to be minimal so that she is liked and considered "okay" by the evaluator. Even women who have filed tort actions for damages against the abuser sometimes overemphasize their best side. To listen to a list of the damaged areas reminds the woman of the abuser's criticisms and threats that no one will believe her because she is crazy. On the other hand, she also wants to know that her emotional damage can be documented and attributed to the abuse, and if she feels that the therapist is not listening to and understanding her, she may feel that treatment will be useless. The therapist must maintain a delicate balance in these situations.

Some survivors prefer to negotiate for short periods of therapy with the option to renegotiate for more when they approach the end of the originally specified time. These women may be frightened of becoming dependent on the therapist and being betrayed again, may be unsophisticated about the process of therapy, or may need to keep some control. For these clients, 12 weeks is a good start; it does not seem long enough for the woman to feel trapped, and it still allows enough time for the therapy relationship to become established and for some issues to be on the way to resolution. Once therapy takes hold, it is rare that the woman wants to stop at 12 weeks, but it is empowering for her to make that decision with input from the therapist. Other women prefer to have the assurance from the start that their therapist has no limits on the time that is available within the boundaries of the therapeutic relationship. It is important for the woman to know that she can always seek a second opinion or discharge the therapist but that the therapist will not discharge her until she and the therapist say she is ready.

An abuse victim will sometimes test the therapist to see if she will be abandoned if the violence she describes is too scary or if she does something to make the therapist angry. If the therapist has limits on what behaviors she or he will tolerate, these need to be specified at the beginning of treatment. Discussions about the telephone call policy between therapy sessions, regularity of scheduled sessions, how to be contacted in an emergency, what constitutes an emergency, and so forth, need to take place. Disclosure forms, if required by law before therapy proceeds, must be provided at this time, too. These usually include information about confidentiality, the exceptions by law to the client's privilege, and other laws regulating the practice of psychology or other therapy disciplines. See Appendix E for a sample of Colorado's required disclosure form. Then, once therapy begins, it is usually best for the client to have a therapist who listens respectfully to her experiences, makes appropriate supportive comments, and helps the client understand the range of her options and their implications.

Identifying Long-Term Therapy Approaches

Once the goals of therapy are negotiated and any crises are stabilized, long-term therapy approaches must be considered. The major therapy approaches include psychoanalytic and object relations,. psychodynamic, existential and humanistic, cognitive–behavioral and social learning theory, family systems, and feminist therapy. A good comparison of these different approaches can be found in L.S. Brown and Ballou (1992), Cantor (1990), and Dutton-Douglas and Walker (1988). The feminist therapy approach adopts some techniques from the other theories. It has been the most successful approach in helping woman abuse victims recover, because feminist therapists have dealt directly with abuse issues through an analysis of power. This approach as well as its integration with trauma theory approaches to treatment have been discussed in chapter 10. The two therapy approaches that have the most potential to be harmful to abuse victims are psychodynamic therapy and family systems therapy if not used appropriately. Following recommendations for personality disorder diagnosis can result in inadequate and even harmful treatment for abuse victims. J.L. Boyer (1990) illustrated this problem by blaming the victim.

Psychoanalytic Therapy

Sometimes a long-term psychoanalytically oriented treatment approach can be supplemented by another therapist who deals directly with the abuse issues. In strict psychoanalysis, abuse issues are usually not directly addressed by the analyst because the goal is to change how the client reacts to the world, not to change the world itself. Because appropriate treatment for the abuse focuses less on intrapsychic issues and calls for more of an action orientation by the therapist, a modified dynamic approach or supplemental treatment is probably advisable. There is real potential to blame the victim by using strict psychoanalytic interpretations of intrapsychic behaviors that do not put the abuse in the appropriate situational context. Herman (1992) and Alpert and Paulson (1990) both provided good discussions of how to avoid these pitfalls. Miller (1976) and others at the Stone Center at Wellesley, as discussed in chapter 10, have applied their relational theoretical approach to abuse victims with success.

Family Systems Theory

Generally, family systems theory has not proven useful in treating women who are healing from abuse (Walker, 1984a). Even when family systems theory attempts to account for the inequality between men and women (which is a recent addition by some therapists, according to Bograd, 1988, and Hare-Mustin, 1980), it generally tends to allocate the responsibility for whatever happens in the family fairly equally. Husband and wife may be viewed as equal partners in a process of violence, equally responsible for whatever incidents occur. Such a view may result in the analysis of the woman's response patterns without the understanding that her behavior is specific to defending against violence and is not internal. This lets the man off the hook for his abusive behavior and continues the long tradition of blaming the victim. Although family therapy may be useful in helping the couple decide what to do about their relationship, it is not the treatment of choice for an abused woman or for the abuser. When children are at high risk for abuse, family therapy with only one therapist may precipitate more danger. Hansen and Harway (1993) attempted to apply variations of family therapy treatment to those who have been involved with some form of violence.

There are numerous reports by battered women that they are not free to discuss ongoing abuse in a family session because of threats made by the abuser before and during the session. Any "mistakes" made by the woman only win her another beating, hardly a therapeutic outcome. In several cases that I have worked on, the family therapy appeared to be a direct precipitator of escalation of violence that resulted in a homicide (see, e.g., Garnets, Herek, & Levy, 1990; Lobel, 1986; Morrow & Hawxhurst, 1989). Hansen, Harway, and Cervantes (1991) used a case that resulted in homicide to show the way that a systems approach can ignore the seriousness of abuse. The man must gain control over his own abusive behavior, including subtle sexual and psychological coercion, without the female partner's cooperation or participation.

These cautions also apply to family therapy with gay men and lesbians (Garnets et al., 1990). It is important to remember that most lesbians and gay men were raised in heterosexual families in which sex-role socialization experiences created stereotypical attitudes. They can fall into the abuser and abused victim patterns, learned from their parents, into which heterosexuals can fall, although research indicates more movement between those two roles in abusive lesbian relationships (Lobel, 1986). Power and control issues based on an analysis of sex-role socialization can help provide understanding despite the actual gender of the perpetrator and victim.

Despite the data, family therapy is a popular alternative, particularly because battered women hope that it will stop the abuse and preserve the positive parts of their relationship (which is the goal most battered women would choose if it were possible). Family therapists share that hopeful vision without the full understanding of the dynamics of family abuse. Many think if they can change the woman's behavior, the man's violence will stop. Often, all this does is stop the woman from reporting the violence. It keeps the woman feeling responsible for the man, which does not allow her to make her own decisions about her life. In those cases in which the woman and man are insistent on family therapy, perhaps after individual or group treatment is completed it would be possible to try a family approach with two therapists, each with an alliance with one individual.

Choosing the Appropriate Modality

Selecting the appropriate therapy modality is an important step that is often overlooked, particularly when the therapist only provides one such modality, whether it is individual, group, or family treatment. Although many of the suggestions in this chapter are written as though individual therapy is the therapeutic mode of choice, in fact, some women make better progress in group or even family therapy, especially when these are problems involving their children.

Group Therapy

Group therapy can be used alone or in conjunction with individual therapy for most abuse victims. Usually, specific abuse groups are recommended, although some therapists have had success with mixed abuse groups. Incest survivors commonly have their own group, sometimes facilitated by a former survivor who is not a professionally trained therapist. Other groups are led by a trained therapist either at a mental health center or a large independent group practice. Rape crisis centers and the newer state crime victim centers often have groups for recent rape victims. Some college campuses also have groups for those who have experienced date rape. It is unusual to have a specific group for those women who were raped (excluding incest) many years ago but who are just beginning to deal with the emotional impact now. Battered women support groups are often part of the services offered by the local battered women's shelter or task force. Sometimes these groups are divided into those who are either just thinking about leaving or actually getting out of the relationship and those who are dealing with more long-term issues. Some victim/witness advocate services are provided for those battered women whose partners are currently in the criminal justice system. Most advocates, however, have little training in providing therapy.

In some clinics, therapists are encouraged to form groups for female abuse survivors for the sake of efficiency. It is important to pay attention to the needs of the women; each one will be ready for a group experience at a different point in her healing process. There are materials to assist in the content and process of groups for battered women (NiCarty, 1986), rape victims (Becker, Skinner, Abel, & Cichon, 1984; Gallers & Lawrence, 1991), victims of sexual abuse by a therapist (Bates & Brodsky, 1989; Bouhoutsos & Brodsky, 1985; Pope & Bouhoutsos, 1986; Pope, Sonne, & Holroyd, 1993; Sonne, 1989), sexual harassment (Charney & Russell, 1994; Gutek, 1992), and incest survivors (Bass & Davis, 1988; Courtois, 1988; Gil, 1988; Janoff-Bulman, 1985; Janoff-Bulman & Frieze, 1983; Jehu, 1988; Meiselman, 1990).

There are also groups that mix those who have problems both with being an abuse victim and with chemical dependency (Soler & Damman, 1980). These groups can be helpful if the form of abuse experienced and the woman's substance abuse are understood separately and not confused by labeling both as addictions and getting women to believe that they are codependent. There are some large, intensive group workshops, such as marathon 24- to 72-hour sessions with the same people, in which abuse issues inadvertently get raised. These intensive sessions are rarely the appropriate place to resolve the issues with which abuse victims must deal, although the fact that the women are able to discuss them there bodes well for their successful recovery if they are encouraged to seek specialized professional assistance in the resolution of these issues.

Some groups are led by facilitators who are trained in dealing with abuse issues but have little or no training in other types of disorders. If the group seems to work for the client, then it is appropriate that she continue to attend even if she begins individual therapy. Sometimes, it is important for the therapist and group leader to communicate, but in other cases it is all right for them to remain separate. It is important to pay attention to cross-cultural issues when designing these groups (Crites, 1991; Parson, 1985) and to special issues regarding lesbians and gay men (Garnets et al., 1990), although different treatment techniques are not suggested.

Self-help groups are also popular with abuse victims who need to have many places in which they can feel safe and discuss the details of their victimization (Jones, 1994; Jones & Schechter, 1992). Codependency groups are popular and trendy. Although they probably do not do great harm, they are not helpful enough to get beyond the initial posttraumatic stress disorder (PTSD) symptoms and often continue to subtly blame the victim by labeling her an "enabler" rather than placing the responsibility for the violence, no matter what the woman's behavior, on the abuser. Missing from the typical codependency analysis is the gender bias that exists in this theory (L.S. Brown, 1990). Women seem to get the "enabler" and "codependent" labels much more frequently than do men. It is futile to assign responsibility to the woman to change her own behavior when society extracts a high price for such a change. Individual women are no more to blame for inequality in society than are individual men; perhaps women need to be supported in discouraging men's dependence on them, but this dependence is not the result of the woman's pathology.

Group therapy is a particularly good modality to be used with abuse victims either alone or along with individual treatment because of the nature of the group process. It helps break down the isolation that most repeatedly abused women have experienced, teaches women that they are not the only ones who have gone through a terrible ordeal and survived, deals directly with the shame and guilt that survivors often feel, and helps redevelop social skills. For some women, a group experience breaks down the barriers of loneliness and helps to reestablish friendships with appropriate boundaries and limits between people. Although some of these benefits can be realized from a self-help group, in general, the group members require professional guidance in order to process many of the issues that are raised.

The negatives in using group therapy include problems with confidentiality, difficulties in domination by some of the more psychologically or emotionally needy group members, repetition of issues that a particular woman has already mastered, and not enough time for a woman to gain insight into her own unique issues. Most groups are found in clinics or other agencies. Employee assistance plans and other managed care facilities have also developed groups, although they usually do not have therapists available who have been specially trained in this area. Mixing those who have not experienced abuse with victims of abuse has not proven to be effective. Women who are facing the psychological issues that are caused by the trauma of abuse need specialized attention that most groups that focus on other issues are not able to adequately provide. Sometimes, private therapists who specialize in trauma therapy have a sufficient number of clients to make a group. Many of these difficulties can be resolved by having a well-trained therapist lead the group and offer some or all of the women the option of having individual sessions in addition to the group therapy.

Mixed gender groups are not as helpful for abused women as single sex groups. This is also true for men who have been both abused and abusers. These men often focus their anger at a particular woman or on the women in the group. Women find the presence of men in a group intimidating. They often revert back to sex-role-socialized behavior and begin deferring to the men, permitting the men to dominate the conversation and to censor the expression of women's anger at the injustice of their having been victimized. Some women prefer to attend a mixed gender group after dealing with many of their issues in individual or all-women group therapy. This is usually toward the end of their recovery when women are most interested in beginning new relationships with men.

Couples or Family Therapy

Couples or family therapy is another possible mode of treatment that could be selected when an abused woman presents for therapy. Although it is sometimes indicated as the treatment of choice, it is often best to save such a treatment modality until women are closer to recovery. There are several reasons why family therapy is inappropriate as an initial treatment of choice. First, most abuse victims have been betrayed by someone whom they knew well, and they have lost trust in people. This loss of trust and its accompanying hypervigilance to cues of potential danger make it difficult for a victim to perceive the neutrality or objectivity that is needed in family or couples therapy. The women see people as either supportive of them or against them. If the family therapist pays attention to the other member or members in a session, the abused woman may misinterpret this behavior as dangerous to her survival, regardless if the other person is the abusive partner; another family member; a new partner who is struggling to make the relationship work (in the case of battered women); a partner of a sexual abuse victim who is confused by the difficulties in the relationship, especially if they have occurred after therapy began; or other family members who want to help the victim to heal.

Second, in good family systems therapy, the therapist must treat each participant in the therapy fairly in order to establish an egalitarian atmosphere. If the abuse victim heals best when she is encouraged to reclaim her power, then a family systems therapist will have difficulty in empowering her if it is contraindicated for her partner. During the normal course of trauma therapy, the woman will express anger at her partner and other family members for placing what she perceives as unreasonable demands on her, and she will need to work through that anger in a nondestructive way. It is usually best to do this without the partner or other family members with whom she is angry present, especially because some of that anger may be combined with the anger at having been abused, even if she was abused by someone else. Helping the woman sort through those complexities of feelings is extremely difficult to do in family therapy, especially if she is feeling guilty about placing a burden on her family and friends (Margolin,

1988; Margolin, John, & Gleberman, 1988; Margolin, Moran, & Miller, 1989).

Third, family systems therapy has been seriously criticized for its sexist assumptions that power is equally distributed in marital relationships (Bograd, 1988). Some say it narrowly defines family and ignores clients' different cultures and sexual orientation: White European and American patriarchial culture dominates (McGoldrick, Anderson, & Walsh, 1991). Others say it attempts to place the responsibility of the abuse equally on the female victims and their abusers, particularly responsibility for causing the abuse or staying in battering relationships (Geller & Wasserstrom, 1984; Walker, 1989a). Although, there are many family therapists who are making major efforts to combine systems theory with feminism (cf. Hansen & Harway, 1993; McGoldrick et al., 1991), there are still those who wonder if it is simply an exercise in moving the chairs around on the *Titanic* (Koss & Harvey, 1991).

Nonetheless, families are seriously affected when women are traumatized and often need assistance in dealing with the issues raised by abuse. Programs designed to provide support for victim's partners and other family members have been developed, some with the assistance of the National Organization of Victim Assistance and its state affiliates. Figley (1989) has provided treatment for families in which one member has been coping with PTSD, beginning initially with combat stress victims and their families and expanding to battered women, incest survivors, and rape victims' families. Davis (1990) has a self-help book for those who love women who were sexually abused as a child. Earl (1985) provided treatment for couples in which the woman has been raped. Kaslow and Carter (1991) attempted to design gender-sensitive family therapy from an object relations perspective with depressed women. Kelly (1983) has designed a behaviorally based treatment with families in which a child has been abused. Harris (1986) described a new model based on Walker's two-therapist couples treatment for battered women and their partners, whereas Geller and Wasserstrom (1984) attempted to adapt the family systems approach in dealing with domestic violence.

Families of abused women sometimes do need support from therapists that is separate from the treatment offered to the women themselves. For example, separate sessions with the mother of an incest victim might deal with any guilt feelings she may have about her daughter's childhood, the issues raised by the current relationship with her daughter, and her current and future relationship with her grandchildren. In some cases, family members may seek therapy when they become aware of abuse in other family members' homes, such as abuse of a sister, daughter-in-law, or grandchild. Sometimes families seek therapy after the victim is killed by the assailant. In such cases, dealing with survivor guilt plays an important part in the treatment. Therapy with families of an abused woman must concentrate on helping the family figure out ways to provide support to the possibly traumatized family member or members. In the case of battering, helping family members who do not like the abuser to maintain relationships with the woman may be an additional challenge.

Family therapy also may be of great value in helping to create support for a rape victim, incest survivor, or woman who has been otherwise sexually exploited. Family members may be seen individually by the therapist or in joint sessions. Teaching family members and the client what to expect combats their fear that the woman will never get better. Sometimes rape victims make unrealistic demands on family members who are doing their best to help. Helping family members protect their autonomy by drawing specific limits may seem harsh initially but can preserve harmony in the family over time. It is important to keep the client's trust in order to avoid adding to the sense of betrayal she felt with the abuser. Thus, any decisions regarding how the family should or should not try to meet her needs should be discussed thoroughly with the client before the therapist discusses them in a session. This can be done before a family session, or it can be done while everyone is together by asking the woman if she concurs, or by sending the others out for a few minutes while the therapist and client have a private discussion. The woman, not the family, is the therapist's primary client in this type of family therapy.

Individual Therapy

The most popular modality for psychotherapy is still the once-a-week individual session that lasts between 45 and 50 minutes. Abuse victims sometimes need more frequent sessions especially when dealing with the initial crisis or additional ones that arise during treatment. If there are a number of telephone calls between sessions for more than 1 week, then increasing the number of sessions may be warranted. Some women find that one session per week is too intense at certain points and need to reduce to two or three per month for a period of time. Holding more frequent sessions than that number can provide therapeutic support, which may be all an individual woman can deal with at the moment. As with any other long-term treatment, there will be periods of intense growth and plateaus in which integration occurs at different times during the therapy.

Individual therapy has some advantages that group or family therapy does not provide. The major advantage is that the woman has the individual attention of a trained, concerned, yet calm listener for a certain reliable period of time. This helps her sort out her concerns and helps get through the difficulties of the rest of the week when she is not in therapy. It is a safe place to discuss topics that might seem ridiculous and to scream, cry, or vent rage without feeling judged. Individual therapy helps sort out those fantasies that are part of the healing process from those in which the woman is becoming stuck in her ruminations.

It is important for the therapist to understand the healing process from a PTSD viewpoint in order to give the client the reassurance that she is making progress, even if it seems too slow at some points. One of the deepest pitfalls in treatment is the desire of both the client and the therapist to move more quickly through issues that have been dealt with before. Angry feelings often do not surface for 6 months or more into therapy, and when they do, they stay for a long time. At that time, the woman needs to be assisted in separating her feelings of anger from a need to express it by harming others. Once she is in control, the angry feelings need to be accepted as a part of the healing process and not shut off too soon. Clients who begin treatment openly recognizing their anger may also need to learn to place controls on how they express those feelings defensively.

Monitoring Progress Toward Goals

It is important to take out the written list of goals and review the progress toward meeting them at least every 2 or 3 months. This process is explained in more detail and demonstrated in the case study of "Kim" that appears in chapter 10. This gives both the therapist and client the opportunity to see in which areas progress has been made and in which areas more effort is needed. Or, if little progress is noted, the goals may have to be revised to be more realistic. If a written list was not made initially, this is an ideal time to begin one. It can be therapeutic for the client to look at the areas with which she has effectively dealt and to remember when dealing with even those areas seemed to be an impossible goal. This exercise also demonstrates the sharing of the power to control the direction of therapy.

SELECTING THERAPY TECHNIQUES

There are a number of standard therapy techniques that are useful in working with abuse victims, particularly those who have developed PTSD. Psychotherapy is a "talking" treatment and most abuse victims find it cathartic and useful to talk about the pain caused by the victimization experiences as well as other parts of their lives. Therapists who listen to the client, ask questions for clarification, give a name to what the client is experiencing, and do not challenge what the client says help the woman make the most progress. Once the relationship is well-established, it may be appropriate to offer interpretations, but until then, it is most therapeutic to help point out contradictions but not offer opinions as to their possible psychological origins. Active, direct participation in validating the woman's perceptions, feelings, and experiences, in addition to acknowledging the information being shared and checking to make sure it is appropriately understood, are all important parts of treatment. Often, simply labeling the experiences as abuse and repeating what the woman has said out loud helps to validate her thoughts and feelings in ways that they have never been validated before. Simple but powerful, this may be the best approach a therapist can take even if the client is not ready to deal with other issues at that time.

Hypnosis

Hypnosis is often used as an adjunct to verbal therapy in order to gain access to buried memories, particularly buried memories of incest and other early abuse (see Rhue, Lynn, & Kirsch, 1993, for more information; Dolan, 1991; Spiegel, 1990). Those working with clients who have multiple personality disorders find hypnosis to be a useful adjunct, particularly in the eliciting of different personalities and their integration phase of treatment. In some cases, posthypnotic suggestions can help alleviate some of the emotional pain experienced during the retelling of the abuse. It is also helpful to teach the abused client self-hypnotic techniques so that dissociative experiences can be managed better by the client. Because many abuse victims already go into dissociative states, which, like hypnosis, are another level of conscious focus, they usually are inducted into trance states quite easily. When there are legal issues pending in which hypnosis may spoil the litigation because of legal restrictions or criticism of undue influence and suggestibility, then other techniques may be chosen instead.

Relaxation Therapy

Relaxation therapy is a technique developed by Jacobson (1938) and modified by behavioral therapists who use it as a way to help reduce anxiety, phobias, fears, and a variety of other high arousal types of symptoms. Even those with mild to moderate depression may be encouraged to learn the relaxation techniques because they give a person a better feeling of control over her life. The most frequently used relaxation induction technique is deep muscle relaxation in which the client is taught to contract muscles and then release them to achieve the deeply relaxed state. Each muscle group is used, and the client is "talked" into the relaxation mode; once she has reached that state, she is able to use other procedures, such as guided imagery, systematic desensitization, and eye movement therapy (discussed later in this chapter). An additional benefit of deep muscle relaxation therapy is that it assists the abused woman in regaining her feelings and control over her own body.

Guided Imagery

Guided imagery is a technique that is similar to hypnosis but without the negative connotations. The client first learns relaxation therapy and then is taught to control the intrusive thoughts and memories by substituting them with images that are more under the control of the woman and more pleasing to her. Using guided imagery to change the ending of a particularly troublesome traumatic incident can be therapeutic in helping the client to perceive her ability to restore control over her life. For example, if a sexually assaulted client becomes upset at the thought that nothing happened to stop the perpetrator, she can imagine that she has trapped him in a large net, has tied him up, and is making him plead with her to spare his life. In the image, she has the control to let him live or die, instead of him having that power over her. Although the client knows that this is simply a made-up story, it helps her to understand that she can indeed control how she thinks even if she' cannot control her feelings. Sometimes the client develops mutilation fantasies that challenge the therapist's ability to remain calm and supportive, and, in other instances, guided imagery is used along with systematic desensitization.

Obviously, this needs to be done very carefully. Although mutilation fantasies are common, especially for women who have been forced into sex, rarely do they act out such fantasies. In the highly publicized case of Lorena Bobbitt, who lived with her sexually, physically, and psychologically abusive husband, the woman actually did cut off her husband's penis and then disposed of it in a field. Fortunately for her husband, John Wayne Bobbitt, despite her dissociative state, Lorena Bobbitt told the police what she did, and the penis was retrieved and surgically reattached. Although both husband and wife were criminally charged and brought to trial, he for rape and she for malicious wounding, neither were found guilty by their juries. Perhaps even more interesting was the fascination this case held for the media, and the differences it pointed out in the seriousness with which men and women viewed the abuse that preceded the mutilation. Women, in general, understood Lorena Bobbitt's behavior as a result of fear and emotional distress, whereas men viewed it as an act of revenge. Lorena Bobbitt denied accusations that she had threatened to "cut if off" sometime before the actual incident. Had she been in psychotherapy, however, such a statement would have been neither unexpected nor evidence of premeditation.

Systematic Desensitization

A behavioral psychology technique, systematic desensitization is used to reduce high levels of anxiety and phobic responses. First, the client is taught relaxation therapy, then a step-by-step hierarchy is prepared. This hierarchy reflects how anxious the client gets in different situations. That which she becomes anxious about is paired with something that is pleasant and nonanxiety producing so that the anxiety is neutralized. Modifications in this procedure have been made so that its conditioning effects are magnified. Flooding (Gallers & Lawrence, 1991) can be used along with systematic desensitization (Pearson, Poquette, & Wasden, 1983). Phobias are treated using systematic desensitation hierarchies. For example, if someone is agoraphobic (afraid to go out of the house), a mental hierarchy could move from imagining thinking about going outside while still lying down on the couch, to getting up, walking to the window, walking to the door, waving to people, putting on outer garments, and going outside. Fodor (1991) described this process more fully, as did Foa (1989) and Foa, Steketee, and Olasov (1989), although the latter called it *stress innoculation therapy*.

Reframing and Cognitive Restructuring

Cognitive restructuring and other forms of reframing help clients gain cognitive control and understanding of what previously seemed to be confusing information. It is particularly important for women to challenge and confront all of the "shoulds" that they have learned, particularly those in conjunction with the socialized sex-role stereotypes that they were exposed to growing up. Because many of these socialized gender patterns elicit high levels of guilt when not followed, it is critical to break down the barriers and abuse myths that the victim holds. Because cognitive restructuring must first challenge old and perhaps sexist thought patterns and beliefs before new ones can be substituted, women must learn how to analyze and synthesize every step of the way. Although holding a feminist philosophy may be to the advantage of clients and therapists who are working with abused women, it is not necessary to be a feminist in order to figure out which cognitions are old and outdated and which ones are still appropriate.

Cognitive restructuring is also useful to help clients recognize when their confusion is interfering with their judgment. Often, they will go off on tangents when discussing an emotionally upsetting issue during the therapy session. Initially, it is helpful just to stop them and ask for clarification when it is difficult to determine where their story is going. When this happens later on in treatment, which it probably will, ask the client what she is thinking and feeling when she starts to go off on a tangent. This is to help the client recognize that she may block her own awareness of painful feelings and, perhaps, memories by going off on tangents. As she begins to recognize her own thought process and gain better control of her feelings, her thought processes will become less confusing to her, and, of course, it will be reflected in the therapy.

Eye Movement Therapy and Other Therapies

F. Shapiro's (1989) eye movement therapy (EMT) is a new behavioral technique designed to be used with relaxation therapy for those clients who have experienced trauma that is later primarily remembered on an affective rather than on a cognitive level. It is said to be useful for those who cannot easily verbalize what happened to them but who know from the affect that they were subjected to frightening and abusive acts. In addition, there are those victims who know exactly what happened to them but are unable to heal using traditional techniques. Basing the treatment on the recent literature that explains that trauma is stored in the unconscious and encoded in neural pathways (van der Kolk, 1988), it is necessary to revisit these pathways by recalling the traumatic memories and then to erase the neural pathways. F. Shapiro's (1989) technique assumes that by altering the eye movement pathways using EMT, the traumatic memories that are generated by those old pathways and stored in the subcortical level of the brain will be erased and substituted by those generated by new, abuse-free patterns of behavior.

Adjuncts to verbal therapy that are designed to reach the somatic level, such as movement therapy, dance, massage therapy, and other affective and spiritual therapies, can be very useful in helping abused women get in touch with their feelings. Just naming the feelings themselves, as the women recognize and attach the cognitions to the affect they experience, can help get the cognitive, affective, and behavioral domains back in some synchronicity again.

AREAS OF PSYCHOLOGICAL DAMAGE IN ABUSED WOMEN WITH PTSD

There are eight areas specific to the psychological damage that is found in most abused women who develop some PTSD symptoms. These areas that should be addressed in therapy are (a) recurrent trauma memories, (b) need for control, (c) anger and rage, (d) dissociation, (e) sexuality and body image, (f) trust and betrayal, (g) emotional intimacy, and (h) compliance and confrontation.

Recurrent Trauma Memories

The recurrent memories of the abusive incident or incidents prevent most victims from feeling that they are safe and on their way to healing from the trauma they experienced. Generally, the unpredictability of when the memories will recur and the surprising strength of the emotion that accompanies the particular incident or fragment of an incident are the two most troublesome areas for the woman to manage. Although it is usually not possible to stop those memories from recurring, some techniques that give the woman some control and prevent them from having as great an emotional impact on the woman are available.

For example, just helping the woman to expect, cognitively, that these memories will continue to occur as part of the healing process makes them less unexpectedly intrusive. Purposely avoiding some situations that stimulate the memories, or understanding that if the situations are unavoidable some memories will probably recur, also brings them more under the woman's control. Changing the content of the memory as it begins to recur is another technique for control and is described further in the section on dissociation. For example, shrinking the size of the abuser mentally helps make the memory less frightening. Thought-stopping techniques, such as making a distracting noise, perhaps by slamming a heavy book on the table, can discharge the thoughts in one's mind and proves that the women can make the thoughts go away, even if only for a minute.

During the therapy session, the woman's memories can be quite helpful in her understanding of the most frightening aspects of the trauma. These are the areas in which she must regain control in order for the PTSD symptoms to be reduced. Even time-limited treatment can help in such cases (cf. Becker, Skinner, Abel, & Cichon, 1984, 1986). Some adjunct therapies that stimulate her creative side may also serve to protect against the frightening emotional impact of the memories. Dance therapy, art therapy, and other therapies involving the whole body are useful.

Need for Control

The abused woman helps to protect herself by controlling the world in order to avoid further abuse. The battered woman tries to keep everyone and everything in her world calm in order to avoid making the batterer upset and angry. She becomes overly involved in every activity in which her child engages, as she still tries to protect the child from unknown dangers. The rape victim drives miles out of her way in order to avoid passing the site of her abduction, thereby reducing the anxiety symptoms with which she must deal. The woman who has been sexually harassed at work may refuse to deliver documents to the department in which the abuse occurred. The incest victim may turn over her entire paycheck in order to win her family's affection. The woman who was sexually abused by her therapist may become seductive, like many incest victims, in order to gain affection through her sexuality.

All of these coping strategies are manipulative in some sense (Flannery, 1987). The victim actively engages another person in some behavior in order to protect herself from further abuse and rejection. This ever constant hypervigilance and manipulation to try to avoid further abuse takes up much time and energy, even after its effectiveness is no longer useful. However, abuse victims lose their sense of objectivity and neutrality and often cannot give up their need to control things without a great deal of anxiety. They have learned that the world is not a safe place and that only their actions will make it a little bit safer.

The use of manipulative techniques extends to the therapy relationship, which is the ideal situation in which to prove that they are no longer necessary for self-protection once the woman is safe and violence-free. Initially, the therapist can reduce the need for power struggles involving control by placing very few limits and rules for the client to which the client cannot easily adhere. As the therapy relationship progresses, it is important to point out places in which the therapist feels like she or he is being manipulated, without expecting the client to do anything to stop it. If such manipulations cause the therapist pain, then that must be dealt with directly. Eventually, the client will be able to recognize when she begins to manipulate and will be ready to try not to do so. Some areas in which she wants control will be easier to give up than others. It is important to support her useful coping strategies, while pointing out the high emotional cost of such behavior. This is an area of therapy that develops slowly, and it is a good area for the therapist to use humor with the client.

Anger and Rage

The issue of anger and rage is a big one for an abuse victim. Most victims who develop PTSD can feel themselves becoming more irritated by people and by little things, but do not often connect these feelings of impatience and irritability with anger. Some victims begin to feel their rage quickly and to express it everywhere; others are frightened by the strength of their angry feelings and bury them. Other women want to be angry but feel too much compassion for the abuser to deal with their feelings, and some deny feeling angry while behaving in passive–aggressive or hostile ways without recognizing how their behavior affects others.

When the anger has been building up for years, it sometimes comes out as rage. When it is unfocused, it becomes a defense to keep others away, like a porcupine's quills or a skunk's odor; one strike and the innocent recipient of the anger goes away for good. Obviously, this increases the abused person's isolation, sense of mistrust, and poor social relationships.

Some women's anger becomes so overwhelming that they too use violence. These women often have been abused themselves but received no assistance at all for their problems. It is important to differentiate between self-defense, preemptive strikes used to get even, and violence used as a way to deal with anger-producing situations.

This type of anger may prevent the woman from effectively parenting her children, particularly when she is so angry with their father that she uses them to help fight her battles against him. It is important to help her understand how the children perceive that anger and how they can be frightened by her. However, most abused women experience this stage temporarily while they are getting in touch with their anger. It will take several months before it is known if the woman will get stuck in this stage for a long enough time to damage her relationships with her children.

In any case, dealing with anger and all of its manifestations is important at some point in therapy. Usually, this cannot be done until the woman is no longer defensive about her anger and feels more comfortable knowing that she can feel it intensely but has the control not to express it harmfully. Sometimes, it is difficult not to condone actions that seem to right the scales of justice even when the actions are caused by anger.

Controlled anger has its usefulness. It can provide the woman with the motivation to make difficult but important changes in her life. She can be encouraged to join other women who are outraged by the broader social conditions that breed abuse against women and to channel the anger into positive action.

Dissociation

The mind–body split that abuse fosters as a coping strategy has its usefulness even after the woman is safe and living in a nonviolent situation. However, like the other coping strategies the woman may adopt in order to protect herself, she needs to have control when she uses it. When dissociation is out of control, the woman can fragment the various parts of her personality as do people with multiple personality disorders, or, she can become "spacey" and confused, not concentrating for long on anything that is important.

Gaining control over dissociation is similar to the other issues raised here. First the woman needs to become aware of when she is using dissociation; then she needs to make a conscious decision whether to make her mind go away or to stay in touch. Sometimes medication is needed to reduce the feelings of fear and anxiety that precipitate the dissociation.

One way to gain some control is to teach self-hypnotic techniques that permit the woman to go in and out of trance states by giving herself commands that she has learned. Another way is to use guided imagery to help control her mental imaging. In this method, the woman would be given suggestions about changing the endings of intrusive memories that often trigger a dissociative state. For example, if a woman keeps remembering a particular abuse scene, she can step into the memory at a particular point and change what happens next. One client started beating up her husband in her trance like state, doing all the violent things to him that she had fantasized about but never would have done. Another woman mentally undressed the abuser each time he started harassing her; still another dressed him in weird clothes in the middle of an important business deal, which made him seem more like a clown than a fearful attacker. Often these changes are made naturally during dream states. If she is in such states in the therapist's office, the client can safely engage in fighting back for a short time, using all the mutilation she desires without having to worry about any undesirable consequences.

Dissociation is simply another level of consciousness, much like a mild trance state. It makes the unbearable bearable by letting the mind go away for awhile. Descriptions of dissociative states are familiar in the literature, particularly in spiritual discussions. People pay large sums of money to learn transcendental meditation, and other techniques based on Eastern religion, in order to learn how to reach other levels of consciousness. Some even spend large sums of money on drugs that induce similar effects. So, the woman who has the ability to get away from it all for even a little while has stumbled onto a secret that she should be encouraged to tame and use when needed.

Sexuality and Body Image

This area is an important one for women, given the negative body image most women have as a result of living in societies that overvalue a woman's attractiveness and undervalue her personality and competence. Self-nurturance is often seen as selfishness or, worse yet, narcissism. However, women must learn how to love themselves and nurture their bodies in order to reclaim the control over them that was taken by the abusive man. This requires some behaviors often described by psychologists as narcissistic.

Use of the health food and nutrition trends in society today are helpful in getting a woman to respect her body again. Eating properly without worrying about body image is important. Many victims of violence either gain too much weight or lose too much weight, depending on their natural body type. They indulge themselves by munching on candy bars and other foods that do not provide nutrition but give immediate satisfaction. Binge eating and throwing up or inducing diarrhea are manifestations of this damage to body image.

Working out at a health club, running, or walking with a partner for exercise are other ways to get back in touch with one's body. Exercise is helpful in stimulating the natural endorphins to alleviate some depression, too.

Women who have been sexually violated may either be more inclined to use their sexuality to get their needs met or to become unattractive in order to avoid sex totally. It is difficult to establish nonsexual working relationships with men in the best of circumstances. So many work situations are tinged with an atmosphere of sexuality that abused women are even less likely to come up with good compromises. They are angry and uncertain that men will treat them fairly and may react with sensitivity to any hints of sexuality that are present. Given the degree of misunderstanding that occurs between men and women on gender issues, it is important to validate women's perceptions as an accurate reflection of their feelings. Some therapists believe that it is their responsibility to help women feel less angry and more kindly toward men. This usually happens during the course of treatment naturally and does not require any specific attention unless the anger about men and other issues does not seem to be resolving itself after a long period of time.

Therapy can be a good place for a woman to learn more about how her body works sexually. Descriptions of sexual acts for a woman who has been raped helps her learn that her body may respond physiologically even when her mind is shouting "rape" or is shut down completely (Becker, Skinner, Abel, & Cichon, 1986). It is almost impossible for an abused woman to discuss these sexual details with a male therapist, no matter how good their relationship. Thus, it may be necessary for a man to bring in a woman therapist for this part of the therapy.

Many women's sexual needs have been ignored; they have not been able to discover what truly gives them sexual pleasure. Self-exploration and attempts to become sexually assertive with a partner are some ways to help overcome the feeling that they have no control over sex. Use of body lotions, fancy soap, and beauty care products also help the woman learn to like her feminine side again without feeling vulnerable. Some find aroma therapy to be helpful in their healing process. Teaching the woman to nurture herself and not just others is an important part of learning about her own sensuality and sexuality. Therapists who have not yet worked out these issues for themselves will find it difficult to help a client. Some therapists may try to do too much, may be benevolent but too controlling, and may even consider crossing the boundary into sexual or sensual behavior with the client, a situation that must in all cases be rejected (Durre, 1980). Therapists can unwittingly, as well as intentionally, precipitate or facilitate dangerous sexual transferences and countertransferences. (See the chapters dealing with therapist preparation for assistance should the therapist begin experiencing feelings of a sexual or romantic nature toward the client; see also Pope, Sonne, & Holroyd, 1993).

Trust and Betrayal

Women who have been abused by men who treated them lovingly or at least kindly at other times become confused about who to trust and how to anticipate betrayal. This interferes with relationships, including the theraputic relationship. However, therapy is a good place to work on these trust issues, especially when there is a good relationship established. The therapist must specifically address the issues using information that is provided in the sessions when appropriate.

There is no reason for an abuse victim to trust anyone, particularly a psychologist whom she has never met before. Giving one's trust before it is earned is as dangerous as indiscriminately refusing to trust anyone because someone has hurt you. Thus, therapists, as well as others, need to earn the trust of the client. As the process unfolds, it is helpful to point out to the woman the trust that is shown in the therapeutic relationship so that she learns how to recognize it in other relationships.

Suspiciousness and hypervigilance seem to remain longer than any of the other PTSD symptoms, perhaps as a protection from further danger, similar to animals in a forest who have been exposed to fire and therefore recognize the smell of fire faster than those who have never had such an experience. This lack of trust is a negative factor when the woman begins a new relationship with a man. In this situation, the most useful technique is to help her to help the man understand her reactions so that he does not take them personally. This may be an area that never completely heals, and, as a result, the kind, nonviolent man may have to "pay for his brother's sins." It can only be hoped that men will find it to their advantage to stop the violence that other men commit. This issue may help them decide sooner.

Emotional Intimacy

Women who have been abused have difficulty establishing emotional intimacy in subsequent relationships, sometimes because of the trust and betrayal issues raised earlier. Those who have been multiple abuse victims with incest occurring early in their lives may never have developed appropriate social skills to foster emotional closeness or intimacy. The two areas that cause the most difficulties are in establishing friendships and romantic relationships.

It is important to find out whether the abuse victim lacks friendships when she begins treatment because of isolation and PTSD symptomatology or because of a lack of social skills. Time will help establish the answer. However, treatment can focus on encouragement to make a friend, using social skills training if it seems needed and appropriate. If no one wants to be the client's friend, then she is either picking people without sensitivity or doing something to drive them away. Use the behavior seen in the therapy hour as a way to help determine her probable social behavior.

Women who dislike other women have usually been taught to be competitive with woman for the prize: the man. They may also fear getting too close to another woman because a woman cannot protect her from other abusive men. Many abused women see another man as their best protection against the abuse, and, unfortunately, sometimes they are correct. Thus, they often make friends with men more easily than with women. Men are trained to be territorial; if another man comes into the picture, most of the time the abuser leaves the woman alone. Some do not, however, and become so obsessed with the woman's new relationship that they will resort to violence in order to stop it. In such cases, the man's threats (e.g., "If I can't have you, no one will have you") need to be taken seriously. Many men are protective toward women and are willing to enter into these friendships. But strong women are good role models for the abuse victim who needs to learn that she, too, can rely on her own strength to become a survivor. In any case, these skills need to be developed in therapy.

Relationships with the men also need some attention during therapy. The rape victim often resents her husband's unchanged sexual demands when she feels like the whole world has been changed. The man, on the other hand, wants reassurance that the woman still loves him and does not hate him as she hates the rapist. The issues involving sexually violated women being "spoiled goods" will come up and need to be addressed so that the woman does not take on the self-image of a pariah.

Compliance and Confrontation

Women who have been abused fear confrontation with those whom they want to like them. Most are compliant to the point that others can easily take advantage of them. If that happens over time, these women become hostile and suspicious, still trying to please but getting angry when their own needs are not met. Friendships that develop based on the woman giving up her own needs in order to please another often fall apart when the client realizes how she is being used, again. Helping her to understand how she gets into these unhealthy relationships will be a part of dealing with her needs for approval. These women can be excellent clients as they will do things to make the therapist's life easier; plants get watered and pruned, offices get dusted, papers get straightened. The woman does not seem to complain when the therapist is late or is on the phone. In general, this client does what she is told, that is, until she feels that her needs are not being met, and then she can get angry.

Sometimes that anger is not expressed, for fear that the therapist will reject her. It is the responsibility of the therapist to pay attention and bring up issues independently. For example, going away for 3 weeks just when the client is going to have to face her abuser at a deposition is not meeting the client's needs. However, if the therapist had the vacation planned for a while and has told the client in advance, then it is important to help the client realize that the therapist's needs must be met but are not designed to hurt her. It is important to teach the woman that getting angry when her needs are not met is acceptable, but she must also learn how to assess when the slight is deliberate and when it is not anyone's intention to hurt and disappoint her. Furthermore, she must understand that confronting the therapist will not result in a termination of therapy or any other kind of rejection, although such confrontations can have that result in the real world.

It is important to deal with these issues in the context of grieving the loss of the loved person or people. Most women who have been abused by family members or close personal friends (e.g., date rape) or trusted professionals (e.g., employers, doctors, therapists) have idealized the relationship with the abuser in some way. Children form an image of the perfect family; clients, the perfect therapist; and wives, the perfect husband. These idealized images come from the culture. Clients mix true longing for emotional intimacy with television and media images of the perfect relationship. The grieving that must be done in therapy is two-fold. The client must give up the fantasized ideal image and accept the real image of the dysfunctional person. She must give up the belief that the abuser can ever be who she wants him to be and accept that his dysfunction will harm her. An enormous sadness accompanies this grieving process, even as she goes through the anger and acceptance phases. She must relearn images of relationships, particularly with family and friends, so that she can replace the fantasies with reality. Most abused women come into treatment with lots of self-doubt. During the grieving process, this doubt becomes exaggerated as they constantly question whether they will ever realize when someone is taking advantage of them. This wariness can be used as healthy skepticism until the woman feels more confident in her own judgment; her confidence usually increases after several positive relationships with both men and women have been established.

SUMMARY

When the client is no longer in a crisis state but is still in need of therapy, several things should be settled before embarking on long-range treatment plans. As always, in survivor therapy, the client should be given the information she needs to make her own choice. Some of the questions that need to be addressed: Should the client continue with her present therapist or would someone else, perhaps someone with more experience treating abused women, be a better choice? What are the goals of the treatment plan? What type of therapy approach would be most effective, and would the client prefer to work through her problems in individual therapy, group therapy, or family therapy? How should the therapist and client monitor their progress?

Once treatment issues are agreed on, therapists should decide what type of techniques to use. This chapter examines the possible use of hypnosis, relaxation therapy, guided imagery, systematic desensitization, reframing, EMT, and other therapies. Some of the damage that therapists might expect to see in patients includes recurrent trauma memories, a need for control that leads to manipulation, dissociation, and a fear of emotional intimacy.

Mental Status Examination

   I. Appearance, behavior, and attitude

     A. General appearance (physical characteristics, peculiarities, cleanliness, etc.)

     B. Motor coordination (posture, gait tremors, activity level, facial expressions, etc.)

     C. Observable behavior

  II. Speech characteristics

     A. Quality of speech

     B. Content (blocking, circumstantiality, perseveration, flight of ideas, confabulation, etc.)

 III. Emotional state and affective reactions

     A. Quality and range

     B. Dissociations

 IV. Content of thought

     A. Special preoccupations, obsessions, compulsions, delusions, etc.

  V. Orientation and awareness

     A. Consciousness and knowledge of time, place, and person

 IV. Memory

     A. Remote memory

     B. Recent recall

     C. Recall of immediate impressions

 VII. General intelligence level

VIII. Insight

     A. Understanding of symptoms and situation

Learned Helplessness Factors

CHILDHOOD

_____ 1. Witness or experience battering in childhood home

_____ 2. Sexual molestation or abuse as a child

_____ 3. Critical factors of control

    ___ Early parent loss from separation or death

    ___ One or more parents who were alcoholic or drug abusing

    ___ Frequent moving from place to place

    ___ Poverty or other situations causing shame

    ___ School failures

    ___ Other humiliation perceived as uncontrollable

_____ 4. Rigid traditionality

_____ 5. Chronic illness

RELATIONSHIP

_____ 1. Pattern of violence (Cycle present with tension-building, acute incident, and loving-contrition phases. Battering escalated and got worse over time, reaching lethal levels of violence.)

_____ 2. Sexual abuse in relationship

_____ 3. Power and control issues (Jealousy, overpossessiveness, intrusiveness, isolation)

_____ 4. Threats to kill

_____ 5. Psychological torture

    ___ Verbal degradation   ___ Mind control

    ___ Denial of powers   ___ Threats to kill

    ___ Isolation   ___ Induced debility

    ___ Monopolizing perceptions   ___ Drugs or alcohol

    ___ Occasional indulgences

_____ 6. Violence correlates
　　　_____ Violence against others
　　　_____ Violence against children
　　　_____ Violence against pets
　　　_____ Violence against property
_____ 7. Alcohol and drug abuse

Diagnostic Criteria For Posttraumatic Stress Disorder (PTSD)

309.89 DSM–III–R

_____ A. Experiencing an event outside of the range of usual human experience that would be markedly distressing to almost anyone.
Severity of Psychosocial Stressor Scale
Adults—Level 5—Extreme
Enduring Circumstances—ongoing physical and sexual abuse
Children and Adolescents—Level 5—Extreme
Enduring Circumstances—Recurrent sexual or physical abuse

_____ B. The traumatic event is persistently reexperienced in at least one of the following ways:

___ 1. recurrent and intrusive distressing recollections of the event

___ 2. recurrent distressing dreams of the event

___ 3. sudden acting or feeling as if the traumatic event were recurring (includes a sense of reliving the experience, illusions, hallucinations, and dissociative flashback episodes, even those that occur on awakening or when intoxicated)

___ 4. intense psychological distress at exposure to events that symbolize or resemble an aspect of the traumatic event, including anniversaries of the trauma

——— C. Persistent avoidance of stimuli associated with the trauma or numbing of general responsiveness (not present before the trauma) as indicated by at least three of the following:

___ 1. efforts to avoid thoughts or feelings associated with the trauma

---

DSM–III–R criteria are adapted from _Diagnostic and Statistical Manual of Mental Disorders_ (3rd ed., rev.), American Psychiatric Association, 1987. _DSM-IV_ draft criteria are used with permission of the American Psychiatric Association.

__ 2. efforts to avoid activities or situations that arouse recollections of the trauma

__ 3. inability to recall an important aspect of the trauma (psychogenic amnesia)

__ 4. marked diminished interest in significant activities

__ 5. feeling of detachment or estrangement from others

__ 6. restricted range of affect

__ 7. sense of a foreshortened future

____ D. Persistent symptoms of increased arousal as indicated by at least two of the following:

__ 1. difficulty falling or staying asleep

__ 2. irritability or outbursts of anger

__ 3. difficulty concentrating

__ 4. hypervigilance

__ 5. exaggerated startle response

__ 6. physiologic reactivity on exposure to events that symbolize or resemble an aspect of the traumatic event

____ E. Duration of more than 1 month

309.81 *DSM–IV* DRAFT CRITERIA

A. The person has been exposed to a traumatic event in which both of the following have been present:

1. the person has experienced, witnessed, or been confronted with an event or events that involve actual or threatened death or serious injury, or a threat to the physical integrity of oneself or others

2. the person's response involved intense fear, helplessness, or horror. Note: In children, it may be expressed instead by disorganized or agitated behavior

B. The traumatic event is persistently reexperienced in at least one of the following ways:

1. recurrent and intrusive distressing recollections of the event, including images, thoughts, or perceptions. Note: In young children, repetitive play may occur in which themes or aspects of the trauma are expressed

2. recurrent distressing dreams of the event. Note: In children, there may be frightening dreams without recognizable content

3. acting or feeling as if the traumatic event were recurring (includes a sense of reliving the experience, illusions, hallucinations, and dissociative flashback episodes, including those that occur on awakening or when intoxicated). Note: in young children, trauma-specific reenactment may occur

4. intense psychological distress at exposure to internal or external cues that symbolize or resemble an aspect of the traumatic event

5. physiologic reactivity on exposure to internal or external cues that symbolize or resemble an aspect of the traumatic event

C. Persistent avoidance of stimuli associated with the trauma and numbing of general responsiveness (not present before the trauma), as indicated by at least three of the following:

1. efforts to avoid thoughts, feelings, or conversations associated with the trauma

2. efforts to avoid activities, places, or people that arouse recollections of the trauma

3. inability to recall an important aspect of the trauma

4. markedly diminished interest or participation in significant activities

5. feeling of detachment or estrangement from others

6. restricted range of affect (e.g., unable to have loving feelings)

7. sense of a foreshortened future (e.g., does not expect to have a career, marriage, children, or a normal life span)

D. Persistent symptoms of increased arousal (not present before the trauma), as indicated by at least two of the following:

1. difficulty falling or staying asleep

2. irritability or outbursts of anger

3. difficulty concentrating

4. hypervigilance

5. exaggerated startle response

E. Duration of the disturbance (symptoms in B, C, and D) is more than 1 month.

F. The disturbance causes clinically significant distress or impairment in social, occupational, or other important areas of functioning.

Specify if:

Acute: if duration of symptoms is less than 3 months

Chronic: if duration of symptoms is 3 months or more

Specify if:

With delayed onset: onset of symptoms at least 6 months after the stressor

Psychosocial Stressor Rating Scales

Severity of Psychosocial Stressors Scale: Adults

Code	Term	Examples of Stressors	
		Acute events	Enduring circumstances
1	None	No acute events that may be relevant to the disorder	No enduring circumstances that may be relevant to the disorder
2	Mild	Broke up with boyfriend or girlfriend; started or graduated from school; child left home	Family arguments; job dissatisfaction; residence in high-crime neighborhood
3	Moderate	Marriage; marital separation; loss of job; retirement; miscarriage	Marital discord; serious financial problems; trouble with boss; being a single parent
4	Severe	Divorce; birth of first child	Unemployment; poverty
5	Extreme	Death of spouse; serious physical illness diagnosed; victim of rape	Serious chronic illness in self or child; ongoing physical or sexual abuse
6	Catastrophic	Death of a child; suicide of spouse; devastating natural disaster	Captivity as hostage; concentration camp experience
0	Inadequate information, or no change in condition		

From *Diagnostic and Statistical Manual of Mental Disorders* (3rd ed., rev.), American Psychiatric Association, 1987. Used with permission.

Severity of Psychosocial Stressors Scale: Children and Adolescents

Code	Term	Examples of Stressors	
		Acute events	Enduring circumstances
1	None	No acute events that may be relevant to the disorder	No enduring circumstances that may be relevant to the disorder
2	Mild	Broke up with boyfriend or girl-friend; change of school	Overcrowded living quarters; family arguments
3	Moderate	Expelled from school; birth of sibling	Chronic disabling illness in parent; chronic parental discord
4	Severe	Divorce of parents; unwanted pregnancy; arrest	Harsh or rejecting parents; chronic life-threatening illness in parent; multiple foster home placements
5	Extreme	Sexual or physical abuse; death of a parent	Recurrent sexual or physical abuse
6	Catastrophic	Death of one or both parents	Chronic life-threatening illness
0	Inadequate information, or no change in condition		

From *Diagnostic and Statistical Manual of Mental Disorders* (3rd ed., rev.), American Psychiatric Association, 1987. Used with permission.

Colorado Disclosure Form

WELCOME!

The practice of both licensed and unlicensed persons in the field of psychology is regulated by the Colorado State Department of Regulatory Agencies. Any questions, concerns, or complaints regarding the practice of psychology may be directed to the State Grievance Board listed below.

As a client here, you have certain rights. You are entitled to receive information about my methods of therapy, the techniques used here, the duration of therapy, if known, and the fee structure. A separate fee agreement will be provided. I have earned a BA degree from CUNY, Hunter College in 1962, an MS degree from CUNY, City College in 1967, and an EdD degree in psychology from Rutgers—The State University of New Jersey in 1972. I hold a Diplomate in Clinical Psychology from the American Board of Professional Psychology in 1979 and am licensed to practice psychology in Colorado (#419). Please ask if you would like to receive any additional information.

You may seek a second opinion from another therapist or terminate therapy at any time you choose.

You should know that in a professional relationship, sexual intimacy is never appropriate, and if it occurs it should be reported to the grievance board listed below.

You should understand that generally speaking, information provided by you during therapy is legally confidential at these offices because I am a licensed psychologist. There are some exceptions by law (see Colorado statutes section 12-43-218 C.R.S. [1988] in particular) that can be discussed and will be identified should any such situation arise during therapy. Examples of such situations are suspicion of child abuse and the probability that you will harm yourself or someone else. If you are involved in a legal dispute, you may be asked to waive your confidentiality privilege. Please discuss this with us, should such a possibility arise so that we can assist you in protecting your privilege.

To report any inappropriate behavior you may contact:

Mental Health Occupations Grievance Board

1560 Broadway, Suite #1340

Denver, CO 80202

(303) 894-7766

I have been informed of my therapist's degrees, credentials, and licenses. I have also read the preceding information and understand my rights as a client.

_____   _____

Client's Signature   Date

_____   _____

Therapist's Signature   Date

References

Aburdene, P., & Nesbitt, J. (1992). *Megatrends for women.* New York: Villard.

Akamatsu, T. J. (1988). Intimate relationships with former clients: National survey of attitudes and behavior among practitioners. *Professional Psychology: Research and Practice, 19,* 454–458.

Alpert, J. L. (1986). *Psychoanalysis and women: Contemporary reappraisals.* Hillsdale, NJ: Analytic Press

Alpert, J. L., & Paulson, A. (1990). Graduate-level education and training in child sexual abuse. *Professional Psychology: Research and Practice,* 21, 366–371.

Amaro, H., Fried, L. E., Cabral, H., & Zuckerman, B. (1990). Violence during pregnancy and substance abuse. *American Journal of Public Health, 80*(5), 575–579.

American Psychiatric Association. (1980). Diagnostic and Statistical Manual of Mental Disorders (3rd ed.). Washington, DC: Author.

American Psychiatric Association. (1987). *Diagnostic and statistical manual of mental disorders* (3rd ed., rev.). Washington, DC: Author.

American Psychological Association. (1963). Ethical standards of psychologists. *American Psychologist, 18,* 56–60.

American Psychological Association. (1974). Task force on sex bias and sex role stereotyping in psychotherapeutic practice. *American Psychologist, 30,* 1169–1175.

American Psychological Association. (1978). Task force on sex bias and sex role stereotyping in psychotherapeutic practice. *American Psychologist, 33,* 1122–1123.

American Psychological Association Ad Hoc Committee on Child Abuse Policy. (1989, December 1). *Report to the APA Board of Directors.* Washington, DC: Author.

American Psychological Association Insurance Trust. (1990). *Bulletin: Sexual misconduct and professional liability claims.* Washington, DC: Author.

American Psychological Association Office of Public Affairs. (1993). *Sexual harassment: Myths and realities.* Washington, DC: Author.

Atkeson, B., Calhoun, K. S., Resick, P. A., & Ellis, E. (1982). Victims of rape: Repeated assessment of depressive symptoms. *Journal of Consulting and Clinical Psychology, 50*, 96–102.

Bailey, K. G. (1978). Psychotherapy or massage parlor technology. *Journal of Consulting and Clinical Psychology, 46*, 1502–1506.

Bajt, T. R., & Pope, K. S. (1989). Therapist–patient sexual intimacy involving children and adolescents. *American Psychologist, 44*, 455.

Barnett, O. W., & LaViolette, A. D. (1993). *It could happen to anyone: Why battered women stay.* Newbury Park, CA: Sage.

Barnhouse, R. T. (1978). Sex between therapist and patient. *Journal of the American Academy of Psychoanalysis, 6*, 533–546.

Barry, K. (1979). *Female sexual slavery.* New York: New York University Press.

Barry, K. (1991). Prostitution, sexual violence and victimization: Feminist perspectives on women's rights. In E. Viano (Ed.), V*ictims' rights and legal reforms: International perspectives. Proceedings of the Sixth International Institute on Victimology, Onati proceedings, No. 9* (pp. 37–52). Onati, Spain: Onati Institute for Sociology and Law.

Barry, K. (1992). *The Penn State report: International Meeting of Experts on Sexual Exploitation, Violence, and Prostitution.* State College, PA: UNESCO and Coalition Against Trafficking in Women.

Bart, P., & O'Brien, P. (1985). *Stopping rape: Successful survival strategies.* Elmsford, NY: Pergamon Press.

Bass, E., & Davis, L. (1988). *The courage to heal: A guide for women survivors of child sexual abuse.* New York: Harper & Row.

Bateman, A. (1989). Helping the partners of rape victims. *Sexual and Marital Therapy, 4*, 5–7.

Bates, C. M., & Brodsky, A. M. (1989). *Sex in the therapy hour: A case of professional incest.* New York: Guilford Press.

Beck, A. T. (1976). *Cognitive therapy and emotional disorders.* New York: New York University Press.

Beck, A. T. (1988). Cognitive approaches to panic disorder: Theory and therapy. In S. Rachman & J. D. Maser (Eds.), *Panic: Psychological perspectives.* Hillsdale, NJ: Erlbaum.

Beck, A. T., & Emery, G. (1985). *Anxiety disorders and phobias: A cognitive perspective.* New York: Basic Books.

Becker, J. V. (1990). Treating adolescent sex offenders. *Professional Psychology: Research and Practice, 21,* 362–365.

Becker, J. V., & Abel, G. G. (1981). Behavioral treatment of victims of sexual assault. In S. M. Turner, C. H. Calhoun, & H. E. Adams (Eds.), *Handbook of clinical behavior therapy* (pp. 347–379). New York: Wiley.

Becker, J. V., Skinner, L. J., Abel, G. G., & Cichon, J. (1984). Time-limited therapy with sexually dysfunctional sexually assaulted women. *Journal of Social Work and Human Sexuality, 3,* 97–115.

Becker, J. V., Skinner, L. J., Abel, G. G., & Cichon, J. (1986). Levels of postassault sexual functioning in rape and incest victims. *Archives of Sexual Behavior, 15,* 37–49.

Belle, D. (1984). Inequality and mental health: Low income and minority women. In L. E. A. Walker (Ed.), *Women and mental health policy* (pp. 135–150). Beverly Hills, CA: Sage.

Benowitz, M. S. (1991). *Sexual exploitation of female clients by female psychotherapists: Interviews with clients and a comparison to women exploited by male psychotherapists.* Unpublished doctoral dissertation, University of Minnesota, Minneapolis.

Bernsen, A., Tabachnick, B. G., & Pope, K. S. (in press). National survey of social workers' sexual attraction to their clients: Results, implications, and comparison to psychologists. *Ethics & Behavior.*

Blackman, J. (1986). Potential uses for expert testimony: Ideas toward the representation of battered women who kill. *Women's Rights Law Reporter, 9*(3–4), 227–238.

Blackman, J. (1989). *Intimate violence: A study of injustice.* New York: Columbia University Press.

Blau, T. H. (1984). *The psychologist as expert witness.* New York: Wiley.

Blume, S. (1989). *Secret survivor: Uncovering incest and its aftereffects in women.* New York: Wiley.

Bochnak, E. (Ed.). (1981). *Women's self-defense cases: Theory and practice.* Charlottesville, VA: Michie.

Bograd, M. (1988). Power, gender and the family: Feminist perspectives on family systems therapy. In M. A. Dutton-Douglas & L. E. A. Walker (Eds.), *Feminist psychotherapies: Integration of therapeutic and feminist systems* (pp. 118–133). Norwood, NJ: Ablex.

Bolton, F. G., Morris, L. A., & MacEachron, A. E. (1989). *Males at risk: The other side of child sexual abuse.* Newbury Park, CA: Sage.

Bond, A.. (1988). American Psychological Association Division 27 sexual harassment survey. *The Community Psychologist, 21,* 7.

Borys, D. S. (1988). *Dual relationships between therapist and client: A national survey of clinicians' attitudes and practices.* Unpublished doctoral dissertation, University of California, Los Angeles.

Borys, D. S., & Pope, K. S. (1989). Dual relationships between therapist and client: A national study of psychologists, psychiatrists, and social workers. *Professional Psychology: Research and Practice, 20,* 283–293.

Bouhoutsos, J., & Brodsky, A. M. (1985). Mediation in therapist–client sex: A model. *Psychotherapy: Theory, Research, and Practice, 22,* 189–193.

Bouhoutsos, J., Holroyd, J., Lerman, H., Forer, B., & Greenberg, M. (1983). Sexual intimacies between therapists and patients. *Professional Psychology: Research and Practice, 14,* 185–196.

Bowie, S., Silverman, D., Kalick, S., & Edbril, S. (1990). Blitz rape and confidence rape: Implications for clinical intervention. *American Journal of Psychotherapy, 44,* 180–188.

Boyer, D., & Fine, D. (1992). Sexual abuse as a factor in adolescent pregnancy and child maltreatment. *Family Planning Perspectives, 24*(1), 4–11.

Boyer, J. L. (1990). Fatal attraction: The borderline personality and psychotherapy. *Register Report* (Bulletin of the National Register for Health Service Providers in Psychology), *16*(2), 5, 7.

Braun, B. (1986). *Treatment of multiple personality disorder.* Washington, DC: American Psychiatric Press.

Braun, B. (1988a). The BASK model of dissociation. *Dissociation, 1,* 4–15.

Braun, B. (1988b). The BASK model of dissociation: II. Treatment. *Dissociation, 1,* 16–23.

Bravo, E., & Cassedy, E. (1992). *The 9to5 guide to combatting sexual harassment: Candid advice from 9to5, the national association for working women.* New York: Wiley.

Briere, J. (1989). *Therapy for adults molested as children: Beyond survival.* New York: Springer.

Briere, J. (1992). Studying delayed memories of childhood sexual abuse. *The APSAC Advisor, 5*(3), 17–18.

Briere, J., & Conte, J. (1993). Self-reported amnesia for abuse in adults molested as children. *Journal of Traumatic Stress, 6,* 21–31.

Briere, J., & Runtz, M. (1987). Post sexual abuse trauma: Data and implications for clinical practice. *Journal of Interpersonal Violence, 2,* 367–379.

Briere, J., & Zaidi, L. Y. (1989). Sexual abuse histories and sequelae in female psychiatric emergency room patients. *American Journal of Psychiatry, 146,* 1602–1606.

Brodsky, A. M. (1989). Sex between patient and therapist: Psychology's data and response. In G. O. Gabbard (Ed.), *Sexual exploitation in professional relationships* (pp. 15–25). Washington, DC: American Psychiatric Press.

Brodsky, A. M., & Hare-Mustin, R. (Eds.). (1980). *Women and psychotherapy.* New York: Guilford Press.

Broverman, I., Broverman, D. M., Clarkson, F. E., Rosencrantz, P. S., & Vogel, S. R. (1970). Sex role stereotypes and clinical judgments of mental health. *Journal of Consulting and Clinical Psychology, 34,* 1–7.

Brown, G. R., & Anderson, B. (1991). Psychiatric morbidity in adult inpatients with childhood histories of sexual and physical abuse. *American Journal of Psychiatry, 148,* 55–61.

Brown, L. S. (1984). The lesbian feminist therapist in private practice and her community. *Psychotherapy in Private Practice, 2,* 9–16.

Brown, L. S. (1988). Harmful effects of posttermination sexual and romantic relationships between therapists and their former clients. *Psychotherapy, 25,* 249–255.

Brown, L. S. (1990). What's addiction got to do with it: A feminist critique of co-dependence. *Psychology of Women Newsletter, 17,* 1–4.

Brown, L. S. (1992a). Personality disorders. In L. Brown & M. Ballou (Eds.), *Personality and psychopathology* (pp. 206–228). New York: Guilford Press.

Brown, L. S. (1992b). While waiting for the revolution: The case for a lesbian feminist psychotherapy. *Feminism & Psychology, 2,* 239–253.

Brown, L. S. (in press). *Subversive dialogues.* New York: Basic Books.

Brown, L. S., & Ballou, M. B. (Eds.). (1992). *Personality and psychopathology.* New York: Guilford Press.

Brown, L. S., & Brodsky, A. M. (1992). The future of feminist therapy. *Psychotherapy: Theory, Research, and Practice, 29,* 51–57.

Brown, L. S., & Root, M. P. P. (Eds.). (1990). *Diversity and complexity in feminist therapy.* New York: Haworth.

Brown, L. S., & Walker, L. E. A. (1990). Feminist therapy perspectives on self-disclosure. In G. Striker & M. Fisher (Eds.), *Self-disclosure in the therapeutic relationship* (pp. 135–154). New York: Plenum.

Browne, A. (1987). *When battered women kill.* New York: Free Press.

Browne, A., & Williams, K. (1989). Resource availability for women at risk and partner homicide. *Law and Society Review, 23,* 75–94.

Brownfain, J. J. (1971). The APA professional liability insurance program. *American Psychologist, 26,* 648–652.

Brownmiller, S. (1975). *Against our will: Women, men and rape.* New York: Simon & Schuster.

Burgess, A. W. (1981). Physician sexual misconduct and patients' responses. *American Journal of Psychiatry, 136,* 1335–1342.

Burgess, A. W. (Ed.). (1985). *Rape and sexual assault: A research handbook.* New York: Garland.

Burgess, A. W. (Ed.). (1988). *Rape and sexual assault* (Vol. 2). New York: Garland.

Burgess, A. W., & Holmstrom, L. L. (1974). Rape trauma syndrome. *American Journal of Psychiatry, 131,* 981–986.

Burgess, R. L., & Youngblade, L. M. (1988). Social incompetence and the intergenerational transmission of abusive parental practices. In G. T. Hotaling, D. Finkelhor, J. T. Kirkpatrick, & M. A. Straus (Eds.), *Family abuse and its consequences* (pp. 38–60). Newbury Park, CA: Sage.

Burt, M. R., & Katz, B. L. (1987). Dimensions of recovery from rape: Focus on growth outcomes. *Journal of Interpersonal Violence, 2,* 57–90.

Burt, M. R., & Katz, B. L. (1988). Coping strategies and recovery from rape. *Annals of the New York Academy of Sciences, 528,* 345–358.

Butler, S. (1978). *Conspiracy of silence: The trauma of incest.* San Francisco: Bantam Books.

Cahn, N. R. (1991). Civil images of battered women: The impact of domestic violence on child custody decisions. *Vanderbilt Law Review,44*(1), 1041–1097.

California Department of Consumer Affairs. (1990). *Professional therapy never includes sex.* (Available from Board of Psychology, 1430 Howe Avenue, Sacramento, CA 95825)

Callanan, K., & O'Connor, T. (1988). *Staff comments and recommendations regarding the report of the Senate Task Force on Psychotherapist and Patients Sexual Relations.* Sacramento, CA: Board of Behavioral Science Examiners and Psychology Examining Committee.

Cammaert, L. A. (1988). Non-offending mothers: A new conceptualization. In L. E. A. Walker (Ed.), *Handbook on sexual abuse of children* (pp. 309–325). New York: Springer.

Cannon, W. B. (1929). *Bodily changes in pain, hunger, fear and rage.* New York: Appleton-Century-Crofts.

Cantor, D. W. (Ed.). (1990). *Women as therapists: A multitheoretical casebook.* New York: Springer.

Caplan, P. (1985). *The myth of women's masochism.* New York: Dutton.

Caplan, P. (1991). How DO they decide what is normal? The bizarre, but true, tale of the DSM process. *Canadian Psychologist, 32*(2), 162–170.

Carmen, E. H., Reiker, P. P., & Mills, T. (1984). Victims of violence and psychiatric illness. *American Journal of Psychiatry, 141,* 378–383.

Chappel, D., Geis, R., & Geis, G. (Eds.). (1977). *Forcible rape: The crime, the victim and the offender.* New York: Columbia University Press.

Charney, D. A., & Russell, R. C. (1994). An overview of sexual harassment. *American Journal of Psychiatry, 151,* 10–17.

Chasnoff, I. J. (1990). The prevalence of illicit drug or alcohol use during pregnancy and discrepancies in mandating reporting in Pinellas County, Florida. *New England Journal of Medicine, 322*(4), 1201.

Chesler, P. (1972). *Women and madness.* New York: Avon.

Childhood abuse: Wider impact seen. (1991, February 18). *New York Times,* p. 9.

Chu, J. A., & Dill, D. L. (1990). Dissociative symptoms in relation to childhood physical and sexual abuse. *American Journal of Psychiatry, 147,* 887–892.

Cohen, L. J., & Roth, S. (1987) The psychological aftermath of rape: Long-term effects and individual differences in recovery. *Journal of Social and Clinical Psychology, 5,* 525–534.

Cole, E., Rothblum, E. D., & Espin, O. (Eds.). (1992). Refugee women and their mental health: Shattered societies, shattered lives. Parts I & II. *Women and Therapy, 13*(1–3), 1–308.

Committee on Women in Psychology. (1989). If sex enters into the psychotherapy relationship. *Professional Psychology: Research and Practice, 20,* 112–115.

Conarton, S., & Silverman, L. K. (1988). Feminine development through the life cycle. In M. A. Dutton-Douglas & L. E. A. Walker (Eds.), *Feminist psychotherapies: Integration of therapeutic and feminist systems* (pp. 37–67). Norwood, NJ: Ablex.

Conlin, R. B. (1990). Women, power, and the law. *Trial, 26,* 22–26.

Connel, N., & Wilson, C. (Eds.). (1974). *Rape: The first sourcebook for women.* New York: New American Library.

Conte, J. R., & Berliner, L. (1988). The impact of sexual abuse on children: Empirical findings. In L. E. A. Walker (Ed.), *Handbook of sexual abuse of children* (pp. 270–308). New York: Springer.

Corey, G. (1977). *Theory and practice of counseling and psychotherapy.* Monterey, CA: Brooks/Cole.

Cotton, D. H. G. (1990). *Stress management: An integrated approach to therapy*. New York: Brunner/Mazel.

Courtois, C. (1988). *Healing the incest wound*. New York: Norton.

Courtois, C. (1990, August). *The memory retrieval process in incest survivor therapy*. Paper presented at the 98th Annual Convention of the American Psychological Association, Boston.

Courtois, C. (1991). Theory, sequencing, and strategy in treating adult survivors. In J. Briere (Ed.), *Child sexual abuse: Clinical implications* (pp. 47–60). San Francisco: Jossey-Bass.

Courtois, C., & Sprei, J. (1988). Retrospective incest therapy with adult survivors. In L. E. A. Walker (Ed.), *Handbook on child sexual abuse: Assessment and intervention* (pp. 270–308). New York: Springer.

Crites, L. (1991). Cross-cultural counseling in wife beating cases. *RESPONSE, 13*(4), 8–12.

Crull, P. (1982). *The impact of sexual harassment on the job: A profile of the experiences of 92 women*. New York: Working Women's Institute.

Cryer, L., & Beutler, L. (1980). Group therapy: An alternative treatment approach for rape victims. *Journal of Sex and Marital Therapy, 6*, 40–46.

Dahlberg, C. C. (1970). Sexual contact between patient and therapist. *Contemporary Psychoanalysis, 5*, 107–124.

Daro, D., & Mitchell, L. (1990). *Current trends in child abuse reporting and fatalities: The results of the 1989 annual fifty-state survey*. Chicago: National Committee for the Prevention of Child Abuse.

Davidson, V. (1977). Psychiatry's problem with no name. *American Journal of Psychoanalysis, 37*, 43–50.

Davis, L. (1990). *The courage to heal workbook: For women and men survivors of child sexual abuse*. New York: Harper & Row.

Davis, L. (1991). *Allies in healing: When the person you love was sexually abused as a child*. New York: HarperCollins.

Deed, M. (1991a). Court-ordered child custody evaluations: Helping or victimizing vulnerable families. *Psychotherapy, 11*, 76–84.

Deed, M. (1991b). Treatment: Perils of treating custodially challenged mothers. *Behavior Today, 22*(44), 1–4.

Derogatis, L. (1977). *SCL-90R manual L*. Towson, MD: Clinical Psychometric Research.

Dobash, R. E., & Dobash, R. P. (1979). *Violence against wives: A case against patriarchy.* New York: Free Press.

Dolan, Y. M. (1991). *Resolving sexual abuse: Solution-focused therapy and Ericksonian hypnosis for adult survivors.* New York: Norton.

Doris, J. (Ed.). (1991). *The suggestibility of children's recollections: Implications for eye-witness testimony.* Washington, DC: American Psychological Association.

Durre, L. (1980). Comparing romantic and therapeutic relationships. In K. S. Pope (Ed.), *On love and loving: Psychological perspectives on the nature and experience of romantic love* (pp. 228–243). San Francisco: Jossey-Bass.

Dutton, M. A. (1992). *Healing the trauma of woman battering: Assessment and intervention.* New York: Springer.

Dutton-Douglas, M. A., & Colantuono, A. (1987, July). *Cluster analysis of MMPI scores among battered women.* Paper presented at the Third National Conference for Family Violence Researchers, Durham, NH.

Dutton-Douglas, M. A., & Walker, L. E. A. (Eds.). (1988). *Feminist psychotherapies: An integration of therapeutic and feminist systems.* Norwood, NJ: Ablex.

Dye, E., & Roth, S. (1990). Psychotherapists' knowledge about and attitudes toward sexual assault victim clients. *Psychology of Women Quarterly, 14,* 191–212.

Dziech, B. W., & Weiner, L. (1984). *The lecherous professor.* Boston: Beacon Press.

Earl, W. L. (1985). Rape as a variable in marital therapy: Context and treatment. *Family Therapy, 12,* 259–272.

Eberle, P. (1982). Alcohol abusers and non-users: A discriminate function analysis. *Journal of Health and Social Behavior, 23,* 260.

Edwall, G. & Hoffman, D. (1988). Correlates of incest reported by adolescent girls in treatment for substance abuse. In L. E. A. Walker (Ed.), *Handbook on sexual abuse of children.* New York: Springer.

Edwards, S. S. M. (1989). *Policing domestic violence: Women, the law and the state.* Newbury Park, CA: Sage.

Eichenbaum, L., & Orbach, S. (1982). *Understanding women: A feminist psychoanalytic approach.* New York: Basic Books.

Ellis, E. M. (1983). A review of empirical rape research: Victim reactions and response to treatment. *Clinical Psychology Review, 3,* 473–490.

Ellis, E. M., Atkeson, B. M., & Calhoun, K. S. (1982). An examination of differences between multiple- and single-incident victims of sexual assault. *Journal of Abnormal Psychology, 91,* 221–224.

Ellison v. Brady, 924 F2d 872 (9th Cir. 1988). 880 n. 15 (9th Cir. 1991)

Emery, R. E., Kraft, S., Joyce, S., & Shaw, D. (1984, August). *Children of abused women: Adjustment at four months following shelter residence.* Paper presented at the 92nd Annual Convention of the American Psychological Association, Toronto, Canada.

Equal Employment Opportunity Commission (EEOC). (1991). *Guidelines on discrimination because of sex 29* C. F. R. 1604.11.

Espin, O. M., & Gawelek, M. A. (1992). Women's diversity: Ethnicity, race, class, and gender in theories of feminist psychology. In L. S. Brown & M. Ballou (Eds.), *Personality and psychopathology* (pp. 88–107). New York: Guilford Press.

Estrich, S. (1987). *Real rape.* Cambridge, MA: Harvard University Press.

Ewing, C. P. (1987). *Battered women who kill.* Lexington, MA: Lexington Books.

Faigman, D. (1986). The battered woman syndrome and self-defense: A legal and empirical dissent. *Virginia Law Review, 72,* 619–647.

Faller, K. C. (1992). Can therapy induce false allegations of sexual abuse? *The APSAC Advisor, 5*(3), 3–6.

Faludi, S. (1991). *Backlash.* New York: Crown.

Faust, D., & Ziskin, J. (1988). The expert witness in psychology and psychiatry. *Science, 241*(7), 31–35.

Feldman-Summers, S. (1989). Sexual contact in fiduciary relationships. In G. O. Gabbard (Ed.), *Sexual exploitation in professional relationships* (pp. 193–209). Washington, DC: American Psychiatric Press.

Feldman-Summers, S., & Jones, G. (1984). Psychological impacts of sexual contact between therapists or other health care professionals and their clients. *Journal of Consulting and Clinical Psychology, 52,* 1054–1061.

Feldman-Summers, S., & Pope, K. S. (in press). The experience of "forgetting" childhood abuse: A national survey of psychologists. *Journal of Consulting and Clinical Psychology.*

Ferraro, K. (1989). Policing woman battering. *Social Problems, 36,* 61–74.

Figley, C. (1985). *Trauma and its wake: The study and treatment of posttraumatic stress disorder.* New York: Brunner/Mazel.

Figley, C. (1987). Post-traumatic family therapy. In F. Ochberg (Ed.), *Post-traumatic therapy.* New York: Brunner/Mazel.

Figley, C. (1988). A five-phase treatment of posttraumatic stress disorder in families. *Journal of Traumatic Stress, 1,* 127–141.

Figley, C. (Ed.). (1990). *Treating stress in families.* New York: Brunner/Mazel.

Finkelhor, D. (1984). *Child sexual abuse: New theory and research.* New York: Free Press.

Finkelhor, D. (1990). Early and long-term effects of child sexual abuse: An update. *Professional Psychology: Research and Practice, 21,* 325–330.

Finkelhor, D., & Browne, A. (1988). Assessing the long-term impact of child sexual abuse: A review and conceptualization. In L. E. A. Walker (Ed.), *Handbook on child sexual abuse: Assessment and intervention* (pp. 55–71). New York: Springer.

Finkelhor, D., Williams, L. M., & Burns, N. (1988). *Nursery crimes: Sexual abuse in day care.* Newbury Park, CA: Sage.

Finkelhor, D., & Yllo, K. (1985). *License to rape: Sexual abuse of wives.* New York: Holt, Rinehart & Winston.

Finkelstein, N. (1990). *Treatment issues: Women and substance abuse.* Unpublished paper prepared for National Coalition on Alcohol and Drug Dependent Women and Their Children.

Finn, J., & Nile, J. (1984). A model for consolidating victim services. *Social Casework, 65,* 368–373.

Fitzgerald, L. F., Gold, Y., Ormerod, A. J., & Weitzman, L. M. (1988). Academic harassment: Sex and denial in scholarly garb. *Psychology of Women Quarterly, 12,* 329–340.

Fitzgerald, L. F., & Ormerod, A. J. (1991). Perceptions of sexual harassment: The influence of gender and academic context. *Psychology of Women Quarterly, 15,* 281–294.

Fitzgerald, L. F., & Shullman, S. L. (1985, August). *The development and validation of an objectively scored measure of sexual harassment.* Paper presented at the 93rd Annual Convention of the American Psychological Association, Los Angeles.

Fitzgerald, L. F., Shullman, S. L., Bailey, N., Richards, M., Swecker, J., Gold, Y., Ormerod, A. J., & Weitzman, L. M. (1988). The incidence and dimensions of sexual harassment in academia and the workplace. *Journal of Vocational Behavior, 32,* 152–175.

Flannery, R. B. (1987). From victim to survivor: A stress management approach in the treatment of learned helplessness. In B. A. van der Kolk (Ed.), *Psychological trauma.* Washington, DC: American Psychiatric Press.

Foa, E. B. (1989). *Manual for stress inoculation training and prolonged exposure treatment.* Philadelphia, PA: Eastern Psychiatric Institute.

Foa, E. B., & Kozak, M. J. (1986). Emotional processing of fear: Exposure to corrective information. *Psychological Bulletin, 99,* 20–35.

Foa, E. B., Steketee, F., & Olasov, B. (1989). Behavioral/cognitive conceptualization of posttraumatic stress disorder. *Behavior Therapy, 20,* 155–176.

Fodor, I. G. (1985). Assertiveness training for the eighties: Moving beyond the personal. In L. B. Rosewater & L. E. A. Walker (Eds.), *Handbook on feminist therapy: Women's issues in psychotherapy* (pp. 91–117). New York: Springer.

Fodor, I. G. (1991). The agoraphobic syndrome: From anxiety neurosis to panic disorder. In L. S. Brown & M. B. Ballou (Eds.), *Personality and psychopathology: Feminist reappraisals* (pp. 177–205). New York: Guilford Press.

Forman, B. D. (1980). Cognitive modification of obsessive thinking in a rape victim. *Psychological Reports, 47,* 819–822.

Forman, B. D., & Wadsworth, J. C. (1983). Delivery of rape-related services in CMHCs. *Journal of Community Psychology, 11,* 236–240.

Forman, B. D., & Wadsworth, J. C. (1985). Rape-related services in federally funded community mental health centers. *Journal of Community Psychology, 13,* 402–408.

Fortune, M. M. (1983). *Sexual violence: The unmentionable sin. An ethical and pastoral perspective.* New York: Pilgrim Press.

Fortune, M. M. (1987). *Keeping the faith.* New York: Harper & Row.

Fowler, R. D., & Matarazzo, J. D. (1988). Psychologists and psychiatrists as expert witnesses: Comment. *Science, 241* (9), 1143–1144.

Frazier, P. A. (1990). Victim attributions and post-rape trauma. *Journal of Personality and Social Psychology, 59,* 298–304.

Freeman, J., & Roy, J. (1976). *Betrayal.* New York: Stein & Day.

Freud, S. (1958). Observations on the transference-love. In S. Strachey (Ed. and Trans.), *The standard edition of the complete psychological works of Sigmund Freud* (Vol. 12, pp. 157–173). London: Hogarth Press. (Original work published 1915)

Freud, S. (1959a). The aetiology of hysteria. In E. Jones (Ed.), *The collected papers of Sigmund Freud* (Vol. 1, pp. 183–219). New York: Basic Books. (Original work published 1896)

Freud, S. (1959b). Sexuality and aetiology of neurosis. In E. Jones (Ed.), *The collected papers of Sigmund Freud* (Vol. 1 , pp. 220–248). New York: Basic Books. (Original work published 1898)

Freyd, J. J. (1993, August). *Theoretical and personal perspectives on the delayed memory debate.* Paper presented at the Center for Mental Health at Foote Hospital's Continuing Education Conference, Ann Arbor, MI.

Frieze, I. H. (1986, August). *The female victim: Rape, wife battering, and incest.* Paper presented at the 94th Annual Convention of the American Psychological Association, Washington, DC.

Gabbard, G. O. (Ed.). (1989). *Sexual exploitation in professional relationships.* Washington, DC: American Psychiatric Press.

Gallers, J. (1993). *Survivor therapy workshop.* Denver, CO: Domestic Violence Institute.

Gallers, J., & Lawrence, K. J. (1991). Overcoming posttraumatic stress disorder in adolescent date rape survivors. In B. Levy (Ed.), *Dating violence: Young women in danger* (pp. 172–183). Seattle, WA: Seal Press.

Ganley, A. (1981). *Court mandated counseling for men who batter: A three day workshop for mental health professional. Participant's manual.* Washington, DC: Center for Women's Policy Studies.

Ganley, A. (1988). Feminist therapy with male clients. In M. A. Dutton-Douglas & L. E. A. Walker (Eds.), *Feminist psychotherapies: Integration of therapeutic and feminist systems* (pp. 186–205). Norwood, NJ: Ablex.

Ganzarain, R., & Buchele, B. (1986). Countertransference when incest is the problem. *International Journal of Group Psychotherapy, 36,* 549–566.

Ganzarain, R., & Buchele, B. (1988). *Fugitives of incest: A perspective from psychoanalysis and groups.* Madison, CT: International Universities Press.

Garbarino, J. K., Guttman, E., & Seeley, J. W. (1987). *The psychologically battered child: Strategies for identification, assessment, and intervention.* San Francisco: Jossey-Bass.

Gardner, R. (1987). *The parental alienation syndrome and the differentiation between fabrication and genuine child abuse.* Creskill, NJ: Creative Therapeutics.

Garfield, S. L. (1974). *Clinical psychology: The study of personality and behavior.* Chicago: Aldine.

Garnets, L., Herek, G. M., & Levy, B. (1990). Violence and victimization of lesbians and gay men. *Journal of Interpersonal Violence, 5,* 366–383.

Gartrell, N., Herman, J. L., Olarte, S., Feldstein, M., & Localio, R. (1986). Psychiatrist–patient sexual contact: Results of a national survey, I: Prevalence. *American Journal of Psychiatry, 143,* 1126–1131.

Gartrell, N., Herman, J. L., Olarte, S., Feldstein, M., & Localio, R. (1987). Reporting practices of psychiatrists who knew of sexual misconduct by colleagues. *American Journal of Orthopsychiatry, 57,* 287–295.

Gartrell, N., Herman, J. L., Olarte, S., Feldstein, M., & Localio, R. (1989). Prevalence of psychiatrist–patient sexual contact. In G. O. Gabbard (Ed.), *Sexual exploitation in professional relationships* (pp. 3–14). Washington, DC: American Psychiatric Press.

Gartrell, N. K., Milliken, N., Goodson, W. H., Thiemann, S., & Lo, B. (1992). Physician–patient sexual contact: Prevalence and problems. *Western Journal of Medicine, 157,* 139–143.

Geller, J. A., & Wasserstrom, J. (1984). Conjoint therapy for the treatment of domestic violence. In A. R. Roberts (Ed.), *Battered women and their family intervention strategies and treatment programs* (pp. 33–48). New York: Springer.

Gelles, R. J., & Loeske, D. R. (1993). *Current controversies in family violence.* Newbury Park, CA: Sage.

Gelles, R., & Strauss, M. A. (1988). *Intimate violence: The causes and consequences of violence in the American family.* New York: Simon & Schuster.

Gidycz, C. A., & Koss, M. P. (1990). A comparison of group and individual sexual assault victims. *Psychology of Women Quarterly, 14*, 325–342.

Gil, E. (1988). *Treatment of adult survivors of childhood abuse.* Walnut Creek, CA: Launch Press.

Gilbert, B., & Cunningham, J. (1986). Women's postrape sexual functioning: Review and implications for counseling. *Journal of Counseling and Development, 65*, 71–73.

Gilbert, L. A. (1980). Feminist psychotherapy. In A. M. Brodsky & R. T. Hare-Mustin (Eds.), *Women and psychotherapy* (pp. 245–266). New York: Guilford Press.

Gilbert, L. A., & Scher, M. (1989). The power of an unconscious belief. *Professional Practice of Psychology, 8*, 94–108.

Gilligan, C. (1982). *In a different voice.* Cambridge, MA: Harvard University Press.

Glaser, R. D., & Thorpe, J. S. (1986). Unethical intimacy: A survey of sexual contact and advances between psychology educators and female graduate students. *American Psychologist, 41*, 43–51.

Gold, E. (1986). Long-term effects of sexual victimization in childhood: An attributional approach. *Journal of Consulting and Clinical Psychology, 54*, 471–475.

Goldberg, F. H. (1991, August). *Violence against analysts: Gender differences, countertransference and the analytic process.* Symposium presented at the 99th Annual Convention of the American Psychological Association, San Francisco.

Gomby, D. S., & Shiono, P. H. (1991). Estimating the number of substance-exposed infants. In Center for the Future of Children, the David and Lucille Packard Foundation (Ed.), *The future of children* (pp. 17–25). Los Altos, CA: Center for the Future of Children.

Goodman, G. S., & Bottoms, B. L. (Eds.). (1993). *Understanding and improving children's testimony.* New York: Guilford Press.

Goodman, G. S., & Helgeson, V. S. (1988). Children as witnesses: What do they remember? In L. E. A. Walker (Ed.), *Handbook on child sexual abuse: Assessment and intervention* (pp. 109–136). New York: Springer.

Graham, D. L. R., & Rawlings, E. I. (1991). Bonding with abusive dating partners: Dynamics of a Stockholm syndrome. In B. Levy (Ed.), *Dating violence: Young women in danger*. Seattle: Seal.

Graham, D. L. R., Rawlings, E. I., & Rigsby, R. (in press). *Loving to survive: Why women love men who abuse them*. New York: New York University Press.

Greenspan, M. (1983). *A new approach to women and therapy*. New York: McGraw-Hill.

Greenwald, D. (1992). Psychotic disorders with emphasis on schizophrenia. In L. S. Brown & M. Ballou (Eds.), *Personality and psychopathology: Feminist reappraisals* (pp. 144–175). New York: Guilford Press.

Gross, J. (1990, September 20). 203 rape cases reopened in Oakland as the police chief admits mistakes. *New York Times*, p. A-12.

Groth, A. N. (1979). *Men who rape: The psychology of the offender*. New York: Plenum.

Gurley, G. (1986). Counseling the rape victim's loved ones. *Response to the Victimization of Women and Children, 9*, 8–9.

Gutek, B. A. (1992). Understanding sexual harassment at work. *Notre Dame Journal of Law, Ethics, and Public Policy, 6*, 335–357.

Gutek, B. A., Morasch, B., & Cohen, A. (1983). Interpreting social–sexual behavior in the work setting. *Journal of Vocational Behavior, 22*, 30–48.

Hamilton, J. A., Alagna, S. W., King, L. S., & Lloyd, C. (1987). The emotional consequences of gender-based abuse in the workplace. *Women and Therapy, 6*, 165.

Hamilton, J. A., & Jensvold, M. (1992). Personality, psychopathology, and depression in women. In L. S. Brown & M. Ballou (Eds.), *Personality and psychopathology: Feminist reappraisals* (pp. 116–143). New York: Guilford Press.

Hansen, L. (1990). *Women survivors of childhood sexual abuse: A proposed inpatient group treatment design*. Unpublished doctoral dissertation, University of Denver, School of Professional Psychology, Denver, CO.

Hansen, M., & Harway, M. (Eds.). (1993). *Battering and family therapy: A feminist perspective*. Newbury Park, CA: Sage.

Hansen, M., Harway, M., & Cervantes, N. (1991). Therapists' perceptions of severity in cases of family violence. *Violence and Victims, 6*, 225–235.

Hare-Mustin, R. T. (1974). Ethical considerations in the use of sexual contact in psychotherapy. *Psychotherapy: Theory, Research, and Practice, 11*, 308–310.

Hare-Mustin, R. T. (1978). A feminist approach to family therapy. *Family Process, 17*, 181–194.

Hare-Mustin, R. T. (1980). Family therapy may be dangerous for your health. *Professional Psychology: Research and Practice, 11*, 935–938.

Hare-Mustin, R. T. (1992). Cries and whispers: The psychotherapy of Anne Sexton. *Psychotherapy, 29*, 406–409.

Harris, J. (1986). Counseling violent couples using Walker's model. *Psychotherapy: Theory, Research, Practice, and Training, 23*, 613–621.

Hart, B. (1988). Beyond the "duty to warn": A therapist's "duty to protect" battered women and children. In K. Yllo & M. Bograd (Eds.), *Feminist perspectives on wife abuse* (pp. 234–248). Newbury Park, CA: Sage.

Hays, K. F., & Stanley, S. F. (1993, August). *The impact of childhood sexual abuse on women's dental experiences.* Paper presented at the 101st Annual Convention of the American Psychological Association, Toronto, Canada.

Helfer, E. R., & Kempe, C. H. (1974). *The battered child.* Chicago: University of Chicago Press.

Henderson, D. J. (1975). Incest. In A. M. Freedman, H. I. Kaplan, & B. J. Sadock (Eds.), *Comprehensive textbook of psychiatry* (pp. 1530–1539). Baltimore, MD: Williams & Wilkins.

Hendricks, M. C. (1984). Women, spirituality, and mental health. In L. E. A. Walker (Ed.), *Women and mental health policy* (pp. 95–115). Beverly Hills, CA: Sage.

Herman, J. L. (1981). *Father–daughter incest.* Cambridge, MA: Harvard University Press.

Herman, J. L. (1992). *Trauma and recovery.* New York: Basic Books.

Herman, J. L., Gartrell, N., Olarte, S., Feldstein, M., & Localio, R. (1987). Psychiatrist–patient sexual contact: Results of a national survey: II. Psychiatrists' attitudes. *American Journal of Psychiatry, 144*, 164–169.

Herman, J. L., Perry, J. C., & van der Kolk, B. A. (1989). Childhood trauma in borderline personality disorder. *American Journal of Psychiatry, 146,* 490–495.

Herman, J. L., & Schatzow, E. (1987). Recovery and verification of memories of childhood sexual trauma. *Psychoanalytic Psychology, 4,* 1–4.

Holmes, M. R., & St. Lawrence, J. S. (1983). Treatment of rape-induced trauma: Proposed behavioral conceptualization and review of the literature. *Clinical Psychology Review, 3,* 417–433.

Holroyd, J. (1983). Erotic contact as an instance of sex-biased therapy. In J. Murray & P. R. Abramson (Eds.), *Handbook of bias in psychotherapy* (pp. 285–308). New York: Praeger.

Holroyd, J. C., & Brodsky, A. M. (1977). Psychologists' attitudes and practices regarding erotic and nonerotic physical contact with clients. *American Psychologist, 32,* 843–849.

Horowitz, M., Wilner, N., & Alvarez, W. (1979). Impact of event scale: A measure of subjective stress. *Psychosomatic Medicine,* 41, 209–218.

Howard, J. (1984). Societal influences on attribution: Blaming some victims more than others. *Journal of Personality and Social Psychology, 47,* 494–505.

Hughes, H. M., & Barad, S. J. (1983). Psychological functioning of children in a battered women's shelter: A preliminary investigation. *American Journal of Orthopsychiatry, 53,* 525–531.

Hughes, H. M., & Hampton, K. L. (1984, August). *Relationships between the affective functioning of physically abused and nonabused children and their mothers in shelters for battered women.* Paper presented at the 92nd Annual Convention of the American Psychological Association, Toronto, Canada.

Hulme, W. E. (1989). Sexual boundary violations of clergy. In G. O. Gabbard (Ed.), *Sexual exploitation in professional relationships* (pp. 177–191). Washington, DC: American Psychiatric Press.

Hyde, J. (1994). Presidential message. *Psychology of Women, Newsletter of Division 35 of the American Psychological Association, 21,* 1.

In re Howland. (1980). Before the Psychology Examining Committee, Board of Medical Quality Assurance, State of California, No. D-2212. *Reporter's transcript,* Vol. 3.

Island, D., & Letellier, P. (1991). *Men who beat the men who love them: Battered gay men and domestic violence.* New York: Harrington Park/Haworth Press.

Jacobson, A. (1989). Physical and sexual assault histories among psychiatric outpatients. *American Journal of Psychiatry, 146,* 755–758.

Jacobson, A., & Richardson, B. (1987). Assault experiences of 100 psychiatric inpatients: Evidence of the need for routine inquiry. *American Journal of Psychiatry, 144,* 908–913.

Jacobson, E. (1938). *Progressive relaxation* (2nd ed.). Chicago: University of Chicago Press.

James, J. (1978). The prostitute as victim. In J. R. Chapman & M. Gates (Eds.), *The victimization of women: Vol. 3. Sage Yearbooks in Women's Policy Studies* (pp. 175–201). Beverly Hills, CA: Sage.

Janoff-Bulman, R. (1979). Characterological versus behavioral self-blame: Inquiries into depression and rape. *Journal of Personality and Social Psychology, 37,* 1798–1809.

Janoff-Bulman, R. (1985). The aftermath of victimization: Rebuilding shattered assumptions. In C. Figley (Ed.), *Trauma and its wake: The study and treatment of posttraumatic stress disorder*. New York: Brunner/Mazel.

Janoff-Bulman, R., & Frieze, I. H. (1983). A theoretical perspective for understanding reactions to victimization. *Journal of Social Issues, 39,* 195–221.

Janoff-Bulman, R., & Lang-Gun, L. (1988). Coping with disease, crime, and accidents: The role of self-blame attributions. In L. Y. Abramson (Ed.), *Social cognition and clinical psychology* (pp. 116–147). New York: Guilford Press.

Jehu, D. (1988). *Beyond sexual abuse: Therapy with women who were childhood victims.* New York: Wiley.

Johnston, J. (1991, August). *Visitation and custody within conflict relationships.* Symposium conducted at the 99th Annual Convention of the American Psychological Association, San Francisco.

Jones, A. (1981). *Women who kill.* New York: Fawcett.

Jones, A. (1994). *Next time, she'll be dead: Battering and how to stop it.* Boston: Beacon Press.

Jones, A., & Schechter, S. (1992). *When love goes wrong: What to do when you can't do anything right. Strategies for women with controlling partners.* New York: HarperCollins.

Jordan, J., Kaplan, A., Miller, J. B., Stiver, I., & Surrey, J. (1991). *Women's growth in connection.* New York: Guilford Press.

Jorgenson, L., & Appelbaum, P. S. (1991). For whom the statute tolls: Extending the time during which patients can sue. *Hospital and Community Psychiatry, 42*(7), 683–684.

Jorgenson, L., & Randles, R. M. (1991). Time out: The statute of limitations and fiduciary theory in psychotherapist misconduct cases. *Oklahoma Law Review, 44*(2), 181–225.

Jorgenson, L., Randles, R., & Strasburger, L. (1991). The furor over psychotherapist–patient sexual contact: New solutions to an old problem. *William and Mary Law Review, 32*(3), 645–732.

Kaley, H. (1991, August). Countertransference issues with abused women. In F. H. Goldberg (Chair), *Violence against analysts: Gender differences, countertransference, and the analytic process.* Symposium conducted at the 99th Annual Convention of the American Psychological Association, San Francisco.

Kalichman, S. G. (1993). *Mandated reporting of suspected child abuse: Ethics, law, and policy.* Washington, DC: American Psychological Association.

Kaplan, A. G., & Surrey, J. L. (1984). The relational self in women: Developmental theory and public policy. In L. E. A. Walker (Ed.), *Women and mental health policy* (pp. 79–94). Beverly Hills, CA: Sage.

Kardener, S. H. (1974). Sex and the physician–patient relationship. *American Journal of Psychiatry, 131,* 1134–1136.

Kardener, S. H., Fuller, M., & Mensch, I. N. (1973). A survey of physicians' attitudes and practices regarding erotic and nonerotic contact with patients. *American Journal of Psychiatry, 133,* 1324–1325.

Kardiner, A. (1941). *The traumatic neurosis of war.* New York: P. Hoeber.

Kaschak, E. (1992). *Engendered lives: A new psychology of women's experiences.* New York: Basic Books.

Kaslow, N. J., & Carter, A. S. (1991). Gender-sensitive object relational family therapy with depressed women. *Journal of Family Psychology, 5*(2), 116–144.

Katch, E. J. (1993, July). *Traumatic memory: Research and clinical perspectives.* Paper presented at the Colorado Psychological Association Summer Conference, Aspen, CO.

Kavoussi, R. J., & Becker, J. V. (1987). Psychiatrist–patient sexual contact. *American Journal of Psychiatry, 144,* 1249–1250.

Kelly, J. A. (1983). *Treating child abusive families.* New York: Plenum.

Kilpatrick, D. G. (1990, August). *Violence as a precursor of women's substance abuse: The rest of the drugs–violence story.* Symposium conducted at the 98th Annual Convention of the American Psychological Association Convention, Boston.

Kilpatrick, D. G. (1992, June). *Posttraumatic stress for the DSM–IV and ICD–10: The introduction of a new diagnosis. Disorder of extreme stress.* Paper presented at the world conference of the International Society for Traumatic Stress Studies, Amsterdam.

Kilpatrick, D. G., & Best, C. L. (1990, April). *Sexual assault victims: Data from a random national probability sample.* Presented at the 36th Annual Meeting of the Southeastern Psychological Association, Atlanta, GA.

Kilpatrick, D. G., Saunders, B. E., Amick-Mullen, A., Best, C. L., Veronen, L. J., & Resick, H. S. (1989). Victim and crime factors associated with the development of crime-related posttraumatic stress disorders. *Behavior Therapy, 20,* 199–214.

Kilpatrick, D. G., & Veronen, L. J. (1983). *The aftermath of rape: A three-year follow-up.* Paper presented at the 17th Annual Convention of the Association for the Advancement of Behavior Therapy, Washington, DC.

Kilpatrick, D. G., Veronen, L. J., & Resick, P. A. (1979). Assessment of the aftermath of rape: Changing patterns of fear. *Journal of Behavioral Assessment, 1*, 133–148.

King, H. E., & Webb, C. (1981). Rape crisis centers: Progress and problems. *Journal of Social Issues, 37*, 93–104.

Kirk, S. A., & Einbinder, S. D. (Eds.). (1994). *Controversial issues in mental health.* Needham Heights, MA: Allyn & Bacon.

Kirk, S. A., & Kutchins, H. (1992). *The selling of the DSM: The rhetoric of science in psychiatry.* New York: Aldine de Gruyter.

Klingbeil, K. S., & Boyd, V. D. (1984). Emergency room intervention: Detection, assessment, and treatment. In A. R. Roberts (Ed.), *Battered women and their family intervention strategies and treatment programs* (pp. 7–32). New York: Springer.

Kluft, R. (Ed.). (1985). *Childhood antecedents of multiple personality.* Washington, DC: American Psychiatric Press.

Korn, S. (1991, June 4). Stanford dean responds. *San Francisco Chronicle*, p. A-21.

Koss, M. P. (1985). The hidden rape victim: Personality, attitudinal, and situational characteristics. *Psychology of Women Quarterly, 9*, 193–212.

Koss, M. P. (1988). Hidden rape: Sexual aggression and victimization in a national sample of students of higher education. In A. W. Burgess (Ed.), *Rape and sexual assault (Vol. 2*, pp. 3–26). New York: Garland.

Koss, M. P. (1990, August). *Health hazards for victims of violence.* Invited address presented at the 98th Annual Convention of the American Psychological Association, Boston.

Koss, M. P., & Burkhart, B. R. (1989). A conceptual analysis of rape victimization: Long-term effects and implications for treatment. *Psychology of Women Quarterly, 13*, 27–40.

Koss, M. P., & Harvey, M. R. (1991). *The rape victim: Clinical and community interventions* (2nd ed.). Newbury Park, CA: Sage.

Koss, M. P., Woodruff, W. J., & Koss, P. G. (1991). Criminal victimization among primary care medical patients: Incidence, prevalence, and physician usage. *Behavioral Science and the Law, 9*, 85–96.

Kronstadt, D. (1991). Complex developmental issues of prenatal drug abuse. In Center for the Future of Children, the David and Lucille Packard Foundation (Ed.), *The future of children* (pp. 36–49). Los Altos, CA: Center for the Future of Children.

Kumpfer, K. L. (1991). Treatment programs for drug-abusing women. In Center for the Future of Children, the David and Lucille Packard Foundation (Ed.), *The future of children* (pp. 50–60). Los Altos, CA: Center for the Future of Children.

Kutchins, H., & Kirk, S. A. (1986). The reliability of the *DSM–III:* A critical review. *Social Work Research and Abstracts, 22,* 3–12.

Laidlaw, T. A., Malmo, C., et al. (1990). *Healing voices: Feminist approaches to therapy with women.* San Francisco: Jossey-Bass.

Largen, M. A. (1986). Payment for sexual assault victim medical examinations. *Response to the Victimization of Women and Children, 9,* 14–20.

Larson, C. S. (1991). Overview of state legislative and judicial responses. In Center for the Future of Children, the David and Lucille Packard Foundation (Ed.), *The future of children* (pp. 72–84). Los Altos, CA: Center for the Future of Children.

Lazarus, R. S., & Folkman, S. (1984). *Stress, appraisal and coping.* New York: Springer.

Leidig, M. W. (1981). Violence against women: A feminist–psychological analysis. In S. Cox (Ed.), *Female psychology: The emerging self* (2nd ed., pp. 190–205). New York: St. Martin's Press.

Lerman, H. (1986). *A mote in Freud's eye: From psychoanalysis to the psychology of women.* New York: Springer.

Lerman, H. (1993). *The limits of phenomenology: A feminist critique of the humanistic personality theories.* Paper presented at the National Conference on Feminist Practice and Training, Boston.

Lerman, H., & Porter, N. (Eds.). (1990). *Feminist ethics in psychotherapy.* New York: Springer.

Levenson, H. (1972, September). Distinctions within the concept of internal–external control: Development of a new scale [Summary]. *Proceedings of the 80th Annual Convention of the American Psychological Association, 7,* 261–262.

Levi, P. (1988). *The drowned and the saved.* New York: Vintage International.

Levy, B. (Ed.). (1991). *Dating violence: Young women in danger.* Seattle, WA: Seal Press.

Lindberg, F. H., & Distad, L. J. (1985). Post-traumatic stress disorders in women who experienced childhood incest. *Child Abuse and Neglect, 9,* 521–526.

Lindsey, M., McBride, R., & Platt, C. (1992). *AMEND: Philosophy and curriculum for treating batterers.* Denver, CO: Author.

Liss, M., & Stahly, G. (1993). Domestic violence and child custody. In M. Hansen & M. Harway (Eds.), *Recovering from battering: Family therapy and feminism* (pp. 175–187). Newbury Park, CA: Sage.

Lobel, K. (Ed.). (1986). *Naming the violence: Speaking out about lesbian battering.* Seattle, WA: Seal Press.

Loftus, E. (1992). The malleability of memory. *The APSAC Advisor, 5*(3), 7–9.

Loftus, E. (1993). The reality of repressed memories. *American Psychologist, 48,* 518–537.

Loftus, E., & Ketcham, K. (1991). *Witness for the defense: The accused, the eyewitness, and the expert who puts memory on trial.* New York: St. Martin's Press.

Loftus, E., & Loftus, G. (1980). On the permanence of stored information in the human brain. *American Psychologist, 35,* 409–420.

Lovelace, L., & McGrady, M. (1980). *Ordeal.* Secaucus, NJ: Citadel.

Luepnitz, D. A. (1988). *The family interpreted: Feminist theory in clinical practice.* New York: Basic Books.

Lundberg-Love, P., & Geffner, R. (1989). Date rape: Prevalence, risk factors, and a proposed model. In M. A. Priog-Good & J. E. Stets (Eds.), *Violence in dating relationships: Emerging issues* (pp. –). New York: Praeger.

Lykes, M. B., Brabeck, M. M., Ferns, T., & Radan, A. (in press). Human rights and mental health among Latin American women in situations of state-sponsored violence: Bibliographic resources. *Psychology of Women Quarterly.*

MacKinnon, C. A. (1979). *Sexual harassment of working women.* New Haven, CT: Yale University Press.

MacKinnon, C. A. (1983). Feminism, Marxism, method and the state: Towards feminist jurisprudence. *Signs: Journal of Women in Culture and Society, 8,* 635–658.

Maguigan, H. (1991). Battered women and self-defense: Myths and misconceptions in current reform proposals. *University of Pennsylvania Law Review, 140*(2), 379–486.

Mahoney, M. R. (1991). Legal images of battered women: Redefining the issue of separation. *Michigan Law Review, 90*(1), 1–94.

Maltz, W., & Holman, B. (1984). *Incest and sexuality.* Lexington, MA: Lexington Books.

Mann, C. K., & Winer, J. D. (1991). Psychotherapist's sexual contact with client. *American Jurisprudence Proof of Facts* (3rd series, Vol. 14, pp. 319–431). Rochester, NY: Lawyers Cooperative.

Margolin, G. (1988). Interpersonal and intrapersonal factors associated with marital violence. In G. Hotaling, D. Finkelhor, J. T. Kirkpatrick, & M. A. Straus (Eds.), *Family abuse and its consequences: New directions in research* (pp. 203–217). Newbury Park, CA: Sage.

Margolin, G., John, R., & Gleberman, L. (1988). Affective responses to conflictual discussions in violent and nonviolent couples. *Journal of Consulting and Clinical Psychology, 56,* 24–33.

Margolin, G., Moran, P., & Miller, M. (1989). Social approval for violations of sexual consent in marriage and dating. *Violence and Victims, 4,* 45–55.

Marmor, J. (1972). Sexual acting out in psychotherapy. *American Journal of Psychoanalysis, 32,* 327–335.

Martin, D. (1976). *Battered wives.* San Francisco: Volcano Press.

Mason v. Marriage and Family Center. (1991). 228 Cal. App. 3d; 279 Cal. Rptr. 51. Petition for review denied May 30, 1991.

Masson, J. M. (1984). *The assault on truth: Freud's supression of the seduction theory.* New York: Farrar, Straus & Giroux.

Masters, W. H., & Johnson, V. E. (1975, May). *Principles of the new sex therapy.* Paper presented at the annual meeting of the American Psychiatric Association, Anaheim, CA.

Masters, W. H., & Johnson, V. E. (1976). Principles of the new sex therapy. *American Journal of Psychiatry, 110,* 3370–3373.

Mays, V. M., & Comas-Dias, L. (1988). Feminist therapy with ethnic minority populations: A closer look at Blacks and Hispanics. In M. A. Dutton-Douglas & L. E. A. Walker (Eds.), *Feminist psychotherapies: Integration of therapeutic and feminist systems* (pp. 228–251). Norwood, NJ: Ablex.

McCollough, C. (1991). The child welfare response. In Center for the Future of Children, the David and Lucille Packard Foundation (Ed.), *The future of children* (pp. 61–71). Los Altos, CA: Center for the Future of Children.

McCord, J. (1988). Parental aggressiveness and physical punishment in long term perspective. In G. T. Hotaling, D. Finkelhor, J. T. Kirkpatrick, & M. A. Straus (Eds.), *Family abuse and its consequences* (pp. 91–98). Newbury Park, CA: Sage.

McGoldrick, M., Anderson, C., & Walsh, R. (Eds.). (1991). *Women in families: A framework for family therapy.* New York: Norton.

McGrath, E., Keita, G. P., Strickland, B., & Russo, N. F. (Eds.). (1990). *Women and depression: Research, risk factors, and treatment issues.* Washington, DC: American Psychological Association.

McGregor, J. A. (1985). Risk of STD in female victims of sexual assault. *Medical Aspects of Human Sexuality, 19,* 30–42.

McLeer, S. V., & Anwar, R. (1989). A study of battered women presenting in an emergency department. *American Journal of Public Health, 79*(1), 65–66.

McNulty, M. (1987/1988). Pregnancy police: The health policy and legal implications of punishing pregnant women for harm to their fetuses. *New York University Review of Law and Social Change, 14*(2), 277–319.

Meiselman, K. C. (1990). *Resolving the trauma of incest: Reintegration therapy with survivors.* San Francisco: Jossey-Bass.

Meyer, C., & Taylor, S. (1986). Adjustment to rape. *Journal of Personality and Social Psychology, 50,* 1226–1234.

Midlarsky, E. (1988). *Feminist therapies with the elderly.* In M. A. Dutton-Douglas & L. E. A. Walker (Eds.), *Feminist psychotherapies: Integration of therapeutic and feminist systems* (pp. 252–275). Norwood, NJ: Ablex.

Miller, J. B. (1976). *Toward a new psychology of women.* Boston: Beacon Press.

Millon, T. (1981). *Disorders of personality: DSM–III, Axis II.* New York: Wiley.

Millon, T. (1991). *Toward a new personology: An evolutionary model.* New York: Wiley.

Monahan, J. (Ed.). (1980). *Who is the client?* Washington, DC: American Psychological Association.

Monahan, J., & Walker, L. (1986). Social authority: Obtaining, evaluating, and establishing social science in law. *University of Pennsylvania Law Review, 134*(2), 477–517.

Morrow, S. L., & Hawxhurst, D. M. (1989). Lesbian partner abuse: Implications for therapists. *Journal of Counseling and Development, 68*(1), 58–62.

Moscarello, R. (1990). Psychological management of victims of sexual assault. *Canadian Journal of Psychiatry, 35,* 25–30.

NiCarty, G. (1986). *Getting free: A handbook for women in abusive relationships* (rev. ed.). Seattle, WA: Seal Press.

Noel, B., & Watterson, K. (1992). *You must be dreaming.* New York: Poseidon.

Ochberg, F. (Ed.). (1988). *Posttraumatic therapy.* New York: Brunner/Mazel.

Ogata, S. N., Silk, K. R., Goodrich, S., Lohr, N. E., Westen, D., & Hill, E. M. (1990). Childhood sexual abuse and physical abuse in adult patients with borderline personality disorder. *American Journal of Psychiatry, 147,* 1008–1013.

Orzek, A. M. (1988). The lesbian victim of sexual assault: Special considerations for the mental health professional. *Women and Therapy, 8,* 107–117.

Pagelow, M. D. (1984). *Family violence.* New York: Praeger.

Pagelow, M. D. (1993). Justice for victims of spouse abuse in divorce and child custody cases. *Violence and Victims, 8,* 69–83.

Paltrow, L. M. (1990). When becoming pregnant is a crime. *Criminal Justice Ethics,* Winter/Spring, 41–47.

Paltrow, L. M. (1991). Perspective of a reproductive rights attorney. In Center for the Future of Children, the David and Lucille Packard Foundation (Ed.), *The future of children* (pp. 85–92). Los Altos, CA: Center for the Future of Children.

Paltrow, L., & Shende, S. (1990, October). *State by state case summary of criminal prosecutions against pregnant women and appendix of public health and public interest groups opposed to these prosecutions* [Memo]. New York: American Civil Liberties Union.

Paludi, M. (Ed.). (1990). *Ivory power: Sexual harassment in the academy.* New York: State University of New York.

Pantony, K., & Caplan, P. (1991). Delusional dominating personality disorder: A modest proposal for identifying some consequences of rigid masculine socialization. *Canadian Psychologist, 32*(2), 120–133.

Parson, E. R. (1985). Ethnicity and traumatic stress: The intersecting point in psychotherapy. In C. R. Figley (Ed.), *Trauma and its wake: The study and treatment of posttraumatic stress disorder* (pp. 314–337). New York: Brunner/Mazel.

Patterson, G. (1982). *Coercive family processes.* Eugene, OR: Castaglia Press.

Pearson, M. A., Poquette, B. M., & Wasden, R. E. (1983). Stress-innoculation and the treatment of post-rape trauma. *Behavior Therapist, 6*, 58–59.

Pence, E., & Paymar, M. (1993). *Working with men who batter: The Duluth model.* New York: Springer.

Perl, M., Westin, A., & Peterson, L. (1985). The female rape survivor: Time-limited group therapy with female–male co-therapists. *Journal of Psychosomatic Obstetrics and Gynecology, 4*, 197–205.

Perr, I. N. (1989). Medicolegal aspects of professional sexual exploitation. In G. O. Gabbard (Ed.), *Sexual exploitation in professional relationships* (pp. 211–228). Washington, DC: American Psychiatric Press.

Perry, J. A. (1976). Physicians' erotic and nonerotic physical involvement with patients. *American Journal of Psychiatry, 133*, 838–840.

Perry, N. W. (1992). How children remember and why they forget. *The APSAC Advisor, 5*(3), 1–2, 13.

Pheterson, G. I. (1986). *The whore stigma: Female dishonor and male unworthiness.* Dordrecht, The Netherlands: Ministry of Social Affairs and Employment.

Plaisil, E. (1985). *Therapist.* New York: St. Martin's Press.

Pollitt, K. (1990, March 26). Fetal rights: A new assault on feminism. *The Nation*, pp. 409–419.

Pope, K. S. (1985, August). *Diagnosis and treatment of therapist–patient sex syndrome.* Paper presented at the 93rd Annual Convention of the American Psychological Association, Los Angeles.

Pope, K. S. (1986, May). *Therapist–patient sex syndrome: Research findings*. Paper presented at the annual meeting of the American Psychiatric Association, Washington, DC.

Pope, K. S. (1988). How clients are harmed by sexual contact with mental health professionals. *Journal of Counseling and Development, 67,* 222–226.

Pope, K. S. (1989a). Rehabilitation of therapists who have been sexually intimate with a patient. In G. O. Gabbard (Ed.), *Sexual exploitation in professional relationships* (pp. 129– 136). Washington, DC: American Psychiatric Press.

Pope, K. S. (1989b). Teacher–student sexual intimacy. In G. O. Gabbard (Ed.), *Sexual exploitation in professional relationships* (pp. 163–176). Washington, DC: American Psychiatric Press.

Pope, K. S. (1989c). Therapist–patient sex syndrome: A guide for attorneys and subsequent therapists to assessing damage. In G. O. Gabbard (Ed.), *Sexual exploitation in professional relationships* (pp. 39–56). Washington, DC: American Psychiatric Press.

Pope, K. S. (1990a). Therapist–patient sex as sex abuse: Six scientific, professional, and practical dilemmas in addressing victimization and rehabilitation. *Professional Psychology: Research and Practice, 21,* 227–239.

Pope, K. S. (1990b). Therapist–patient sexual involvement: A review of the research. *Clinical Psychology Review, 10,* 477–490.

Pope, K. S. (1991). Rehabilitation plans and expert testimony for therapists who have been sexually involved with a patient. *Independent Practitioner, 22,* 44–52.

Pope, K. S. (1993). Licensing disciplinary actions for psychologists who have been sexually involved with a client: Some information about offenders. *Professional Psychology: Research and Practice, 24,* 374–377.

Pope, K. S. (1994). *Sexual involvement with therapists: Patient assessment, subsequent therapy, forensics.* Washington, DC: American Psychological Association.

Pope, K. S. (in press-a). Assessing patients and therapists who have been involved in therapist–patient sexual intimacies: Evaluating harm, recovery, and rehabilitation. In J. N. Butcher (Ed.), *Practical considerations in clinical personality assessment.* New York: Oxford University Press.

Pope, K. S. (in press-b). Therapist–patient sex and PTSD. In D. J. Miller (Ed.), *Handbook of posttraumatic stress disorders.* New York: Plenum.

Pope, K. S., & Bajt, T. R. (1988). When laws and values conflict: A dilemma for psychologists. *American Psychologist, 43,* 828.

Pope, K. S., & Bouhoutsos, J. C. (1986). *Sexual intimacies between therapists and patients.* New York: Praeger.

Pope, K. S., Butcher, J., & Seelen, J. (1993). *The MMPI-1, MMPI-2, and MMPI-A in court: A practical guide for expert witnesses and attorneys.* Washington, DC: American Psychological Association.

Pope, K. S., & Feldman-Summers, S. (1992). National survey of psychologists' sexual and physical abuse history and their evaluation of training and competence in these areas. *Professional Psychology: Research and Practice, 23,* 353–361.

Pope, K. S., & Gabbard, G. O. (1989). Individual psychotherapy for victims of therapist–patient sexual intimacy. In G. O. Gabbard (Ed.), *Sexual exploitation in professional relationships* (pp. 89–100). Washington, DC: American Psychiatric Press.

Pope, K. S., & Garcia-Peltoniemi, R. E. (1991). Responding to victims of torture: Clinical issues, professional responsibilities, and useful resources. *Professional Psychology: Research and Practice, 22,* 269–276.

Pope, K. S., Keith-Spiegel, P., & Tabachnick, B. G. (1986). Sexual attraction to patients: The human therapist and the (sometimes) inhuman training system. *American Psychologist, 41,* 147–158.

Pope, K. S., Levenson, H., & Schover, L. R. (1979). Sexual intimacy in psychology training: Results and implications of a national survey. *American Psychologist, 34,* 682–689.

Pope, K. S., Sonne, J. L., & Holroyd, J. (1993). *Sexual feelings in psychotherapy: Explorations for therapists and therapists-in-training.* Washington, DC: American Psychological Association.

Pope, K. S., & Tabachnick, B. G. (1993). Therapists' anger, hate, fear, and sexual feelings: National survey of therapists responses, client characteristics, critical events, formal complaints, and training. *Professional Psychology: Research and Practice, 24,* 142–152.

Pope, K. S., Tabachnick, B. G., & Keith-Spiegel, P. (1987). Ethics of practice: The beliefs and behaviors of psychologists as therapists. *American Psychologist, 42,* 993–1006.

Pope, K. S., & Vasquez, M. J. T. (1991). *Ethics in psychotherapy and counseling: A practical guide for psychologists.* San Francisco: Jossey-Bass.

Pope, K. S., & Vetter, V. A. (1991). Prior therapist–patient sexual involvement among patients seen by psychologists. *Psychotherapy, 28,* 429–438.

Porter, B., & O'Leary, K. D. (1980). Marital discord and childhood behavior problems. *Journal of Abnormal Psychology, 8,* 287–295.

Prentky, R. A., & Quinsey, V. L. (Eds.). (1988). Human sexual aggression. *Annals of the New York Academy of Sciences, 528.*

Price, R. L. (1985). Battered woman syndrome: A defense beginning to emerge. *New York Law Journal, 194,* 104.

Price-Waterhouse v. Hopkins, 490 U. S. 228 (1989).

Pruitt, J., & Kappius, R. (1992). Routine inquiry into sexual victimization: A survey of therapists' practices. *Professional Psychology: Research and Practice, 23,* 474–479.

Putnam, F. (1989a). Pierre Janet and modern views of dissociation. *Journal of Traumatic Stress, 2*(4), 413–429.

Putnam, F. (1989b). *The treatment of multiple personality disorders.* New York: Guilford Press.

Quina, K. (1994). Editorial. *Psychology of Women Quarterly, 21*(1), 12–13.

Radloff, L. (1977). The CES-D scale: A self-report depression scale for research in the general population. *Applied Psychological Measurement, 1,* 385–401.

Rapoport, J. L. (1989). *The boy who couldn't stop washing: The experience and treatment of obsessive–compulsive disorder.* New York: Dutton.

Rawlings, E. I., & Carter, D. K. (Eds.). (1977). *Psychotherapy for women: Treatment toward equality.* Springfield, IL: Charles C Thomas.

Redlich, F. C. (1977). The ethics of sex therapy. In W. H. Masters, V. E. Johnson, & R. D. Kolodny (Eds.), *Ethical issues in sex therapy* (pp. 143–157). Boston: Little, Brown.

Reid, J. B., Taplin, P. S., & Lorber, R. (1981). A social interactional approach to the treatment of abusive families. In R. B. Stuart (Ed.), *Violent behavior: Social learning approaches to prediction, management and treatment.* New York: Brunner/Mazel.

Reiser, D. E., & Levenson, H. (1984). Abuses of the borderline diagnosis: A clinical problem with teaching opportunities. *American Journal of Psychiatry, 141,* 1528–1532.

Rhue, J. W., Lynn, S. J., & Kirsch, I. (Eds.). (1993). *Handbook of clinical hypnosis.* Washington, DC: American Psychological Association.

Ricketson, M. E. (1991). Custody cases and the theory of parental alienation syndrome. *The Colorado Lawyer, Family Law Newsletter,* 53–56.

Robinson v. Jacksonville Shipyards, Inc. 118 R. R. D. 525 (M. D. Fla. 1988)

Robinson, W. L., & Reid, P. T. (1985). Sexual intimacies in psychology revisited. *Professional Psychology: Research and Practice, 16,* 512–520.

Rodkin, L. L., Hunt, E. J., & Cowan, S. D. (1982). A men's support group for significant others of rape victims. *Journal of Marital and Family Therapy, 8,* 91–97.

Roehl, J. E., & Gray, D. (1984). The crisis of rape: A guide to counseling victims of rape. *Crisis Intervention, 13,* 67–77.

Root, M. P. P. (1989). Treatment failures: The role of sexual victimization in women's addictive behavior. *Journal of Orthopsychiatry, 59,* 542–549.

Root, M. P. P. (1991). Persistent disordered eating as a gender specific form of post-traumatic stress response to sexual assault. *Psychotherapy: Theory, Research and Practice, 28,* 96–102.

Root, M. P. P. (1992). Reconstructing the impact of trauma on personality. In L. S. Brown & M. B. Ballou (Eds.), *Personality and psychopathology: Feminist reappraisals.* New York: Guilford Press.

Rose, D. S. (1986). Worse than death: Psychodynamics of rape victims and the need for psychotherapy. *American Journal of Psychiatry, 143,* 817–824.

Rosenbaum, A., & O'Leary, K. D. (1981). Children: The unintended victims of marital violence. *American Journal of Orthopsychiatry, 51,* 692–699.

Rosencrantz, P. S., DeLorey, C., & Broverman, I. K. (1985, August). *One half a generation later: Sex role stereotypes revisited.* Paper presented at the 93rd Annual Convention of the American Psychological Association, Los Angeles.

Rosewater, L. B. (1985a). Feminist interpretations of traditional testing. In L. B. Rosewater & L. E. A. Walker (Eds.), *Handbook on feminist therapy: Psychotherapy for women* (pp. 266–273). New York: Springer.

Rosewater, L. B. (1985b). Schizophrenic, borderline or battered? In L. B. Rosewater & L. E. A. Walker (Eds.), *Handbook on feminist therapy: Psychotherapy for women* (pp. 215–225). New York: Springer.

Rosewater, L. B. (1987a). The clinical and courtroom application of battered women's personality assessments. In D. J. Sonkin (Ed.), *Domestic violence on trial* (pp. 86–94). New York: Springer.

Rosewater, L. B. (1987b). A critical analysis of the proposed self-defeating personality disorder. *Journal of Personality Disorders, 1,* 190–195.

Rosewater, L. B. (1988). Feminist therapies with women. In M. A. Dutton-Douglas & L. E. A. Walker (Eds.), *Feminist psychotherapies: Integration of therapeutic and feminist systems* (pp. 137–155). Norwood, NJ: Ablex.

Rosewater, L. B. (1993). *New roles/new rules: A guide to transforming relationships between women and men.* Pasadena, CA: Trilogy.

Rosewater, L. B., & Walker, L. E. A. (Eds.). (1985). *Handbook on feminist therapy: Psychotherapy for women.* New York: Springer.

Ross, C. (1989). *Multiple personality disorder: Diagnosis, clinical features, and treatment.* New York: Wiley.

Rothblum, E. B., Foa, E. B., & Hoge, L. A. (1988, November). *Responses following sexual and non-sexual assault.* Paper presented at the 22nd Annual Meeting of the Association for the Advancement of Behavior Therapy, New York.

Roy v. Hartogs, 381 N.Y.S. 2d 587; 85 Misc. 2d 891(1976).

Rozee, P. D., & Van Boemel, G. B. (1989). The psychological effects of war trauma and abuse on older Cambodian refugee women. *Women & Therapy, 8,* 23–50.

Ruch, L. O., & Leon, J. J. (1983). Sexual assault trauma and trauma change. *Women and Health, 8,* 5–21.

Rush, F. (1980). *The best kept secret: Sexual abuse of children.* Englewood Cliffs, NJ: Prentice Hall.

Russell, D. E. H. (1984). *Sexual exploitation.* Beverly Hills, CA: Sage.

Russell, D. E. H. (1986). *The secret trauma: Incest in the lives of girls and women.* New York: Basic Books.

Russell, D. E. H. (1988). Incidence and prevalence rates of intrafamilial and extrafamilial sexual abuse of female children. In L. E. A. Walker (Ed.), *Handbook on child sexual abuse: Assessment and intervention* (pp. 19–36). New York: Springer.

Ryan, W. (1971). *Blaming the victim.* New York: Pantheon Books.

Sales, E., Baum, M., & Shore, B. (1984). Victim readjustment following assault. *Journal of Social Issues, 37,* 5–27.

Saul, L. J. (1962). The erotic transference. *Psychoanalytic Quarterly, 31,* 54–61.

Saunders, D. (1982). Counseling the violent husband. In P. A. Keller & L. G. Ritt (Eds.), *Innovations in clinical practice: A source book* (Vol. 1). Sarasota, FL: Professional Resource Exchange.

Saunders, D. (1986). When battered women use violence: Husband abuse or self-defense? *Violence and Victims, 1,* 47–60.

Schafran, L. H. (1990). Overwhelming evidence: Reports on gender bias in the courts. *Trial, 26,* 28–35.

Schechter, S. (1982). *Women and marital violence: The visions and struggles of the battered women's movement.* Boston: South End.

Schneider, E. M. (1986). Describing and changing: Women's self-defense work and the problem of expert testimony on battering. *Women's Rights Law Reporter, 9*(3–4), 195–222.

Scroggs, J. (1976). Penalties for rape as a function of victim provocativeness, damage, and resistance. *Journal of Applied Social Psychology, 6,* 360–368.

Searles, H. F. (1959). Oedipal love in the countertransference. *International Journal of Psychoanalysis, 40,* 180–190.

Searles, P., & Berger, R. J. (1987). The current status of rape reform legislation: An examination of state statutes. *Women's Rights Law Reporter,* 25–43.

Seligman, M. P. (1975). *Helplessness: On depression, development and death.* New York: Wiley.

Seligman, M. P. (1990). *Learned optimism.* New York: Wiley.

Selye, H. (1956). *The stress of life.* New York: McGraw-Hill.

Shapiro, D. L. (1990). *Forensic psychological assessment: An integrative approach.* Needham Heights, MA: Allyn & Bacon.

Shapiro, F. (1989). Efficacy of the eye movement desensitization procedure in the treatment of traumatic memories. *Journal of Traumatic Stress, 2*(2), 199–223.

Sharfstein, S. S. (1993). Report of the secretary: Summary of actions off the Board of Trustees, May 1992–March, 1993. *American Journal of Psychiatry, 150,* 1573–1588.

Sharma, A., & Cheatham, H. E. (1986). A women's center support group for sexual assault victims. *Journal of Counseling and Development, 64,* 525–527.

Siassi, I., & Thomas, M. (1973). Physicians and the new sexual freedom. *American Journal of Psychiatry, 130,* 1256–1257.

Silverman, L. K., & Conarton, L. K. (1993). Giftedness and the development of the feminine. *Advanced Development: A Journal on Adult Giftedness, 5,* 37–58.

Simons, R. C. (1987). Self-defeating and sadistic personality disorders: Needed additions to the diagnostic nomenclature. *Journal of Personality Disorders, 1,* 161–167.

Soler, E. G., & Damman, G. (1980). Women in crisis: Drug use and abuse. *Focus on Women, 1*(4), 227–241.

Sonderegger, T. (Ed.). (1991a). *Perinatal substance abuse: Research findings and clinical implications.* Baltimore: John Hopkins University Press.

Sonderegger, T. (1991b, May). *Society's youngest victims: Drug-exposed victims.* Testimony to Congressional Committee on Children, Youth, and Families, Washington, DC.

Sonkin, D., & Durphy, M. (1982). *Learning to live without violence: A book for men.* San Francisco: Volcano Press.

Sonkin, D., Martin, D., & Walker, L. E. A. (1985). *The male batterer.* New York: Springer.

Sonne, J. L. (1987). Proscribed sex: Counseling the patient subjected to sexual intimacy by a therapist. *Medical Aspects of Human Sexuality, 16,* 18–23.

Sonne, J. L. (1989). An example of group therapy for victims of therapist–client sexual intimacy. In G. O. Gabbard (Ed.), *Sexual exploitation in professional relationships* (pp. 101–127). Washington, DC: American Psychiatric Press.

Sonne, J., Meyer, C. B., Borys, D., & Marshall, V. (1985). Clients' reactions to sexual intimacy in therapy. *American Journal of Orthopsychiatry, 55,* 183–189.

Sonne, J. L., & Pope, K. S. (1991). Treating victims of therapist–patient sexual involvement. *Psychotherapy, 28,* 174–187.

Spiegel, D. (1990). Hypnosis, dissociation and trauma. In J. L. Singer (Ed.), *Repression and dissociation: Implications for personality theory, psychopathology, and health,* Chicago: University of Chicago Press.

Spielberger, C. (1991, May). *Psychosocial and personality risk factors in heart disease and cancer.* Paper presented at the New York State Psychological Association annual meeting, Montauk, NY.

Spielberger, C., Gorsuch, R., & Luschene, R. (1970). *The State–Trait Anxiety Inventory.* Palo Alto, CA: Consulting Psychologists Press.

Sprei, J., & Goodwin, R. A. (1983). Group treatment of sexual assault survivors. *Journal for Specialists in Group Work, 8,* 39–46.

Stahly, G. (1983). *Victim derogation of the battered woman, the just world, and the observer's past history of victimization.* Unpublished doctoral dissertation, University of California, Riverside.

Stahly, G. (1990, August). *Feminist issues in child custody and visitation.* Invited address presented at the 98th Annual Convention of the American Psychological Association, Boston.

Stake, J. E., & Oliver, J. (1991). Sexual contact and touching between therapist and client: A survey of psychologists' attitudes and behavior. *Professional Psychology: Research and Practice, 22,* 297–307.

Stark, E., & Flitcraft, A. (1988). Violence among intimates: An epidemiological review. In V. N. Hasselt et al. (Eds.), *Handbook of family violence* (pp. 293–318). New York: Plenum.

Steele, K. (1989). A model for abreaction with MPD and other dissociative disorders. *Dissociation, 2,* 151–159.

Steinmetz, S. (1978). The battered husband syndrome. *Victimology, 2,* 499–509.

Steketee, G., & Foa, E. B. (1987). Rape victims: Posttraumatic stress responses and their treatment. *Journal of Anxiety Disorders, 1,* 69–86.

Steward, M. S. (1992). *Preliminary findings from University of California, Davis, child memory study: Development and testing of interview protocols for young children.* Davis: University of California Press.

Stone, A. A. (1990, March). No good deed goes unpunished. *The Psychiatric Times*, pp. 24–27.

Stone, L. G. (1980). *A study of the relationship among anxious attachment, ego functioning, and female patients' vulnerability to sexual involvement with their male psychotherapists.* Unpublished doctoral dissertation, California School of Professional Psychology, Los Angeles.

Stone, M. (1976). Boundary violations between therapist and patient. *Psychiatric Annals, 6,* 670–677.

Strasburger, L. H., Jorgenson, L., & Randles, R. (1991). Criminalization of psychotherapist–patient sex. *American Journal of Psychiatry, 148*(7), 859–863.

Strauss, M. A., & Gelles, R. J. (1988). How violent are American families? Estimates from the national family violence survey and other studies. In G. T. Hotaling, D. Finkelhor, J. T. Kirkpatrick, & M. A. Straus (Eds.), *Family abuse and its consequences* (pp. 14–36). Newbury Park, CA: Sage.

Strauss, M. A., Gelles, R. J., & Steinmetz, S. (1980). *Behind closed doors: Violence in America.* New York: Doubleday.

Summit, R. C. (1983). The child sexual abuse accommodation syndrome. *Child Abuse and Neglect, 7,* 177–193.

Summit, R. C. (1992). Misplaced attention to delayed memory. *The APSAC Advisor, 5*(3), 21–25.

Surgeon General's Workshop on Violence and Public Health. (1986). *Report of 1985 meeting at Leesburg, VA* (DHHS No. HRS-D-MC). Washington, DC: U.S. Government Printing Office.

Sutherland, S., & Schuerl, D. (1970). Patterns of response among victims of rape. *American Journal of Orthopsychiatry, 40,* 503–511.

Tamzali, W. (1992). *Preface to Penn State Report.* International meeting of experts on sexual exploitation, violence, and prostitution. State College, PA: Coalition Against Trafficking in Women.

Taylor, S. E. (1990). *Positive illusions: Creative self-deception and the healthy mind.* New York: Basic Books.

Terr, L. (1981). Forbidden games: Post-traumatic child's play. *American Academy of Child Psychiatry, 20,* 741–760.

Terr, L. (1984). Time and trauma. *Psychoanalytic Study of the Child, 39,* 633–665.

Terr, L. (1990). *Too scared to cry.* New York: Harper & Row.

Terwilliger, C. (1989, October 16). Client says she sued doctor to save herself and others. *Cedar Springs (Colorado) Gazette Telegraph*, pp. D1–D2.

Turner, S., & Colao, F. (1985). Alcoholism and sexual assault: A treatment approach for women exploring both issues. *Alcoholism Treatment Quarterly, 2*, 91–103.

Twemlow, S. W., & Gabbard, G. O. (1989). The lovesick therapist. In G. O. Gabbard (Ed.), *Sexual exploitation in professional relationships* (pp. 71–87). Washington, DC: American Psychiatric Press.

Unger, R., & Crawford, M. (1992). *Women and gender.* New York: Harper & Row.

van der Kolk, B. (1985). Inescapable shock, neurotransmitters, and addiction to trauma: Toward a psychobiology of posttraumatic stress. *Biological Psychiatry, 20,* 314–325.

van der Kolk, B. (1987). The psychological consequences of overwhelming life experiences. In B. van der Kolk (Ed.), *Psychological trauma* (pp. 1–30). Washington, DC: American Psychiatric Press.

van der Kolk, B. (1988). The trauma spectrum: The interaction of biological and social events in the genesis of the trauma response. *Journal of Traumatic Stress, 1,* 273–290.

van der Kolk, B. (1994). The body keeps score: Memory and the evolving psychobiology of posttraumatic stress. *Harvard Review of Psychiatry, 1,* 253–265.

van der Kolk, B., & Kadish, W. (1987). Amnesia, dissociation and the return of the repressed. In B. van der Kolk (Ed.), *Psychological trauma,* Washington, DC: American Psychiatrist Press.

Vinson, J. S. (1984). *Sexual contact with psychotherapists: A study of client reactions and complaint procedures.* Unpublished doctoral dissertation, California School of Professional Psychology.

Vinson, J. S. (1987). Use of complaint procedures in cases of therapist–patient sexual contact. *Professional Psychology: Research and Practice, 18,* 159–164.

Waites, E. (1993). *Trauma and survival.* New York: Norton.

Walker, E., & Young, T. D. (1986). *A killing cure.* New York: Holt, Rinehart & Winston.

Walker, L., & Monahan, J. (1987). Social frameworks: A new use of social science in law. *Virginia Law Review, 73*(3), 559–598.

Walker, L. E. A. (1978). Battered women and learned helplessness. *Victimology: An International Journal, 2,* 525–534.

Walker, L. E. A. (1979). *The battered woman.* New York: Harper & Row.

Walker, L. E. A. (1984a). *Battered woman syndrome.* New York: Springer.

Walker, L. E. A. (1984b). *Women and mental health policy.* Beverly Hills, CA: Sage.

Walker, L. E. A. (1984c). Battered women, psychology, and public policy. *American Psychologist, 29,* 1179–1182.

Walker, L. E. A. (1987). Inadequacies of the masochistic personality disorder diagnosis for women. *Journal of Personality Disorders, 1,* 183–189.

Walker, L. E. A. (Ed.). (1988). *Handbook on sexual abuse of children.* New York: Springer.

Walker, L. E. A. (1989a). Psychology and violence against women. *American Psychologist, 44,* 695–702.

Walker, L. E. A. (1989b). *Terrifying love: Why battered women kill and how society responds.* New York: Harper & Row.

Walker, L. E. A. (1989c). When the battered woman becomes the defendant. In E. Viano (Ed.), *Crime and its victims: International research and public policy. Proceedings of the Fourth International Institute on Victimology, NATO Advanced Research Workshop, Il Ciocco, Tuscany, Italy* (pp. 57–70). New York: Hemisphere.

Walker, L. E. A. (1990). Psychological assessment of sexually abused children for legal evaluation and expert witness testimony. *Professional Psychology: Research and Practice, 21*(5), 344–353.

Walker, L. E. A. (1991a). Posttraumatic stress disorder in women: Diagnosis and treatment of battered woman syndrome. *Psychotherapy, 28*(1), 21–29.

Walker, L. E. A. (1991b). Abused mothers, infants, and substance abuse: Psychological consequences of failure to protect. In *Mothers, infants, and substance abuse: Proceedings of the American Psychological Association Division 12 midwinter meeting, Scottsdale, AZ* (pp. 106–139). Washington, DC: Georgetown University Child Development Center.

Walker, L. E. A. (1992). Battered woman syndrome and self-defense. *Notre Dame Journal of Law, Ethics, and Public Policy, 6,* 321–334.

Walker, L. E. A. (1993). The battered woman syndrome is a psychological consequence. In R. J. Gelles & D. R. Loeske (Eds.), *Current controversies on family violence* (pp. 133–152). Newbury Park, CA: Sage.

Walker, L. E. A. (1994). Are personality disorders gender biased? Yes. In S. A. Kirk & S. D. Einbinder (Eds.), *Controversial issues in mental health* (pp. 21–30). Needham Heights, MA: Allyn & Bacon.

Walker, L. E. A., & Browne, A. (1985). Gender and victimization by intimates. *Journal of Personality, 53,* 179–195.

Walker, L. E. A., & Corriere, S. (1991). Domestic violence: International perspectives on social change. In E. Viano (Ed.), *Victims' rights and legal reforms: International perspectives. Proceedings of the Sixth International Institute on Victimology, Onati proceedings, No. 9* (pp. 135–150). Onati, Spain: University of Onati Institute on Sociology and the Law.

Walker, L. E. A., & Dutton-Douglas, M. A. (1988). Future directions: Development, application and training of feminist therapists. In M. A. Dutton & L. E. A. Walker (Eds.), *Feminist psychotherapies: Integration of therapeutic and feminist systems* (pp. 276–300). Norwood, NJ: Ablex.

Walker, L. E. A., & Edwall, G. E. (1987). Domestic violence and determination of custody and visitation. In D. J. Sonkin (Ed.), *Domestic violence on trial* (pp. 127–152). New York: Springer.

Walker, L. E. A., & Levant, R. (1993). Intergender dialogue. *The Independent Practitioner, 13* .

Warshaw, C. (1989). Violence against women. *Gender and Society, 3,* 506–517.

Watkins, H. (1980). The silent abreaction. *International Journal of Clinical and Experimental Hypnosis, 29,* 101–112.

Webb, S. L. (1991). *Step forward: Sexual harassment in the workplace: What you need to know!* New York: Mastermedia.

Weinberg, K. (1955). *Incest behavior.* New York: Citadel.

Whiston, S. K. (1981). Counseling sexual assault victims: A loss model. *Personnel and Guidance Journal, 59,* 363–366.

White, J. W., & Koss, M. P. (1991). Courtship violence: Incidence in a national sample of higher education students. *Violence and Victims, 6,* 247–256.

Williams, L. M. (1992). Adult memories of childhood abuse: Preliminary findings from a longitudinal study. *The APSAC Advisor, 5*(3), 19–21.

Winfield, I., George, L. K., Swartz, M., & Blazer, D. G. (1990). Sexual assault and psychiatric disorders among a community sample of women. *American Journal of Psychiatry, 147,* 335–341.

Wikler, N. (1990). Gender and justice. *Trial, 26,* 36–37.

Wolfe, D. A. (1985). Child abusive parents: An empirical review and analysis. *Psychological Bulletin, 97,* 462–482.

Wolfe, D. A., Jaffee, P., Wilson, S. K., & Zak, L. (1988). A multivariate investigation of children's adjustment to family violence. In G. T. Hotaling, D. Finkelhor, J. T. Kirkpatrick, & M. A., Straus (Eds.), *Family abuse and its consequences* (pp. 228–241). Newbury Park, CA: Sage.

Wolpe, J. (1982). *The practice of behavior therapy.* Elmsford, NY: Pergamon Press.

Wolpe, J., & Lang, P. J. (1964). A fear survey schedule for use in behavior therapy. *Behavior Research and Therapy, 2,* 27–30.

Wyatt, G. E. (1985). The sexual abuse of Afro-American and White American women in childhood. *Child Abuse and Neglect, 9,* 507–519.

Xenarios, S. (1988). Group work with rape survivors. *Social Work With Groups, 11,* 95–100.

Yale-New Haven Hospital Emergency Service. (1983). Rape crisis team treatment protocol. *Victimology, 8,* 249–269.

Zuckerman, B. (1991). Drug-exposed infants: Understanding the medical risk. In Center for the Future of Children, the David and Lucille Packard Foundation (Ed.), *The future of children* (pp. 26–35). Los Altos, CA: Center for the Future of Children.

Author Index

Subject Index

About the Author

Lenore E. A. Walker, EdD, is a licensed psychologist in independent practice with Walker & Associates in Denver, Colorado, and is executive director of the Domestic Violence Institute. An international lecturer who trains at the invitation of governments, private groups, and world health organizations, she has done research, clinical intervention, training, and expert witness testimony on the impact of abuse on survivors. She is the author of *The Battered Woman*; *The Battered Woman Syndrome*; *Women and Mental Health Policy*; *The Male Batterer*, with D. Sonkin and Del Martin; *The Handbook on Feminist Psychology*, with L. B. Rosewater; *Feminist Psychotherapies: An Integration of Feminist and Therapeutic Systems*, with M. A. Dutton-Douglas; *Handbook on Sexual Abuse of Children*; and *Terrifying Love: Why Battered Women Kill and How Society Responds*. She has received a 1994 Distinguished Contributions to Women's Health Award from the American Psychological Association.